# THE CONTRAIL CHRONICLES

## AN AMERICAN FAMILY'S JOURNEY THROUGH WAR AND PEACE

### DICK NELSON

Outskirts Press, Inc.
Denver, Colorado

The opinions expressed in this manuscript are solely the opinions of the author and do not represent the opinions or thoughts of the publisher. The author has represented and warranted full ownership and/or legal right to publish all the materials in this book.

The Contrail Chronicles
An American Family's Journey Through War and Peace
All Rights Reserved.
Copyright © 2010 Dick Nelson
V7.0

This book may not be reproduced, transmitted, or stored in whole or in part by any means, including graphic, electronic, or mechanical without the express written consent of the publisher except in the case of brief quotations embodied in critical articles and reviews.

Outskirts Press, Inc.
http://www.outskirtspress.com

ISBN: 978-1-4327-5504-1

Outskirts Press and the "OP" logo are trademarks belonging to Outskirts Press, Inc.

PRINTED IN THE UNITED STATES OF AMERICA

## TABLE OF CONTENTS

*About the Author* .................................................................................................. iii

*Foreword* ............................................................................................................... iv

**Chapter 1:** *Adventure, Sacrifice, and Letters from the Grave* ........................ 1

**Chapter 2:** *In Search of a Life* ........................................................................ 17

**Chapter 3:** *Plebe Year* .................................................................................... 31

**Chapter 4:** *Trivial Pursuits and Youngster Year* ........................................... 42

**Chapter 5:** *Second Class Year—Academic Hell* ........................................... 50

**Chapter 6:** *Top of the Heap!* .......................................................................... 56

**Chapter 7:** *Links in the Chain* ....................................................................... 69

**Chapter 8:** *The Hatchlings* ............................................................................. 73

**Chapter 9:** *A Flapping of Wings* ................................................................... 80

**Chapter 10:** *Sharpening the Claws* ............................................................... 83

**Chapter 11:** *Welcome to Hollywood* ............................................................. 91

**Chapter 12:** *Take No Prisoners* ..................................................................... 99

**Chapter 13:** *The Black Max* .......................................................................... 106

**Chapter 14:** *The Pre-game Show* .................................................................. 113

**Chapter 15:** *Game Time!* ............................................................................... 123

**Chapter 16:** *Targets of Opportunity* .............................................................. 137

**Chapter 17:** *Threading the Needle* ................................................................ 153

**Chapter 18:** *Change of the Watch* ................................................................. 165

**Chapter 19:** *Great Balls of Fire!* ...................................................................... 183

**Chapter 20:** *Voyage of the Lambs* ..................................................................... 192

**Chapter 21:** *Rules of Engagement* ..................................................................... 211

**Chapter 22:** *Mutiny on the Bounty* .................................................................... 222

**Chapter 23:** *Weekend Warriors* ......................................................................... 233

**Chapter 24:** *Back to Fightertown* ...................................................................... 240

**Chapter 25:** *American Fratricide—Why Does the Eagle Eat Her Young?* ... 259

**Chapter 26:** *Epilogue and Requiem for Warriors* ............................................. 266

## *About the Author*

Dick Nelson grew up in Sarasota, Florida, and is a 1960 graduate of Sarasota High School. After receiving three appointments to the U.S. Naval Academy at Annapolis, Maryland, he graduated in 1964 with a double major in electrical engineering and foreign languages. Certified by the Navy Department as a Spanish language translator/interpreter, Dick was one of two Midshipmen selected for a special politico-military liaison assignment with the Peruvian Navy and the American Embassy in Peru. He was offered a teaching position on the Naval Academy faculty in the Foreign Languages Department, but declined in order to pursue Navy flight training.

Following training as a Naval Aviator, he served two combat tours in Vietnam as a carrier-based fighter pilot in the F-8E Crusader, receiving the Distinguished Flying Cross, 13 Air Medals, the Navy Commendation Medal with Combat "V", the Navy Unit Citation, the Vietnamese Gallantry Cross with Star, and other decorations. He flew over 200 combat missions and accrued approximately 300 carrier landings. He married Janet Lee Theurer, an American Airlines flight attendant, in 1969.

Dick was employed by Continental Airlines as a commercial pilot after leaving active duty. He served concurrently as a labor negotiator for the Air Line Pilots Association, followed by assignments as a special technology projects manager for Continental in flight operations. He left Continental in 1984 to attend the UCLA School of Law, where he graduated in 1987.

After working as a litigation attorney for two large law firms in Los Angeles, Dick started his own specialty litigation firm in Walnut Creek, California. He is admitted to the Bars of California, Colorado and the District of Columbia. He is also admitted to six federal courts, including the U.S. Court of Appeals for the Ninth Circuit. Dick has represented both plaintiffs and defendants in many high-value cases in state and federal trial and appellate courts. He has litigated cases in such areas as employment law, environmental pollution, insurance coverage, commercial contracts, intellectual property, antitrust, and unfair competition. In representing large companies and senior executives in California, he was widely recognized for his expertise in negotiating, drafting and litigating complex commercial contracts. In addition to his litigation practice, he was both a private and court-appointed arbitrator and mediator.

Dick retired from his law practice in 2005 and worked temporarily for the U.S. Dept. of Homeland Security in Miami as a Political Asylum Officer. He moved to Punta Gorda, where he now resides with Janet, seeking new adventures on his boats *Avenger* and *Liberty*.

*The American Cemetery at Cambridge, England.*

## *Foreword*

"Contrails" are those silvery white tracks left in the sky by the engine exhaust condensation from high-altitude aircraft. They show where the airborne traveler is going, as well as where he has been. They define the track of the high-speed journey, where the air is thin and danger is always present. This was the harsh testing-ground for a father and his son, from a family of Swedish immigrants—unlikely participants in the armed conflicts which would consume the world in their respective lifetimes.

The saga of the Nelson family contains joy and sorrow, triumph and tragedy, and an ample quantity of humorous stories. It is a poignant example of how wars cut deeply into a family's heart and soul, and often destroy the bonds that normally exist. My father's death in World War II had a huge impact on my life. In a sad coincidence, my wife, Janet, also lost her dad in World War II when his vehicle struck a German mine during the Allied landings at Anzio, Italy.

The core elements of this book were originally published electronically in the excellent Internet forum, "USNA-at-Large," operated by my Naval Academy classmate, ex-submariner John Howland. This predecessor version evolved as an episodic series of my own personal Naval Academy and aviation experiences in a more summarized form, under the name of *The Kayak Chronicles.* That cryptic title was intended as a humorous tweak on the U.S. Naval Academy's nickname, "The Boat School." However, it became obvious that the original title did not capture the full scope and details of my family's story.

I gratefully acknowledge the advice, factual input, and photographic contributions by many fellow veterans and various organizations. I am especially grateful to the East Anglia Aircraft Recovery Group of the U.K., which located and excavated the exact site where my father died, and provided me with invaluable information. Leads from that information have helped me to tell a more complete and accurate story.

This expanded and revised edition now describes in more detail my family's involvement with World War II, and that war's powerful effect on my mother and me. I have tried to be painfully honest in describing the full impact of a war's toll on the participants *and* on the friends and families they leave behind. There are rarely happy endings in such stories. There are only lucky escapes, and I had plenty of those.

The reader should remember that war is about destruction, not creation; fear, as well as courage; and hatred, as well as love. It is a process of violent human extremes, and not for the squeamish.

When wars erupt and involve our nation, it is vital that we have trained warriors who will step forward and protect America's people and her interests. Too often, America quickly ignores and forgets those brave men and women and their sacrifices as soon as peace is achieved, as if they never existed.

Our citizens perceive each of America's wars differently, depending upon their individual proximity to the conflict itself, and how it affects them personally. In perfect hindsight, most wars seem easy to diagnose as caused by missteps, lapses in judgment, and hidden agendas. However, some wars truly *are* necessary to protect our nation and cannot be avoided, regardless of their imperfections.

For the immediate participants and decision-makers in armed conflict, the initiation of war *always* seems—at the time—to be necessary. Even when war is unavoidable to protect the nation, it is nearly always permeated by a number of incompetent decisions, lack of leadership courage, and cynical motives. Inevitably, those who actually fight the wars find themselves to be nameless pawns on some politician's chessboard. In his 19th century treatise *On War,* Karl von Clausewitz observed, "War is the continuation of politics by other means."

In war, people often are wounded or die for no justifiable reason. The violence of war tends to have a life of its own, once it begins. Students of military history know that the best way to *avoid* war is to prepare diligently for it, and if it occurs, defeat the enemy as quickly and ruthlessly as possible. The biggest mistake is to become mired in a prolonged war of attrition and self-imposed, debilitating restrictions on the use of force. There is no "limited," "partial," or "gentlemanly" war which will ever result in success for the side that embraces such limitations. Over two thousand years ago, Chinese general Sun Tzu wrote in the classic *The Art of War*, "No country has ever benefitted from prolonged conflict."

That is why the military doctrine derived by some of the greatest military strategists—from Generals William Tecumseh Sherman to George Patton to Norman Schwarzkopf—advocates the immediate application of overwhelming force on the enemy to force a speedy resolution of the conflict. Sherman wrote, "I want peace, and believe it can only be reached through union and war, and I will ever conduct war with a view to perfect and early success."

The wars that involved the Nelsons—World War II and Vietnam—demonstrated typical leadership errors and command failures. Sadly, wars are not won in quick, bloodless victories. Historically, the winner is usually the one who makes the least mistakes along the way, and is still standing at the end. As the French politician, Georges Clemenceau, said, "War is a series of catastrophes that results in a victory." In the case of World War II, the Allies met that test, although the cost was great. In Vietnam, the Communist North Vietnamese prevailed through a combination of their own clever tactics and the lack of American determination to win.

Commentators and historians frequently neglect a hidden aspect of war—its impact on the families of the combatants who are swept up in its whirlwind of violence. Our family's story begins with a young Swedish carpenter's classic search for a better life in America. I hope you enjoy the journey.

*Dick Nelson*

# Chapter 1: *Adventure, Sacrifice, and Letters from the Grave*

*[The "Viking Age" was an important period in history, marked by Scandinavia's dominance of northern Europe from approximately 790 A.D. until the cross-Channel Norman Conquest of Britain in 1066. The fierce Viking warriors conducted military expeditions by land and sea throughout the coastal zones of Europe, Greenland, and Iceland from what is now Sweden, Norway, Finland, and Denmark. Acting on behalf of their succession of monarchs, they established permanent settlements in many of these areas, including Britain, France, Iceland, and Greenland. They also established temporary bases in North America, approximately 500 years before the trans-Atlantic explorations of Christopher Columbus. Thus, it is not surprising that every Scandinavian carries a love for adventure and exploration in his genetic makeup. The Nilssons were no different.]*

The tall young man stood at the rail and stared silently, as his decrepit steamship entered New York Harbor and passed the brooding presence of the Statue of Liberty. Lady Liberty seemed pensive on this spring day, as if she knew what the future had in store for John Albert Nilsson. Nevertheless, John Nilsson had long dreamed of this symbolic moment, as he and hundreds of other European immigrants on the ship prepared for processing at Ellis Island to become American citizens. He was 21, and the year was 1903. Over a span of years, the Nilsson family successfully immigrated from Langsele, Sweden, to Fremont, Nebraska, to begin a new life. John spoke no English, and had neither a job nor money.

Once established in Fremont, where a growing Swedish community was located, the family quickly discovered "Nilsson" was difficult for Americans to spell. Accordingly, they changed the last name to "Nelson." The Nelsons struggled to feed their family, but shared what they had with each other and found ways to get by.

John married a local Swedish woman named Esther and had three sons and two daughters. Two of the sons would become successful businessmen. The third boy was somewhat of a dreamer and had a far-away look in his eye. He also liked to box and get into fights. His name was Wendel.

Wendel graduated from high school and traveled to Houston, where he attended a junior college. He worked for a while in the newspaper business, and then in advertising. He dreamed of flying airplanes, and stood transfixed—looking up at the sky—every time an airplane flew overhead. He dreamed of sitting in those cockpits and testing the limits of those picturesque blue skies.

The news carried ominous reports of Hitler's rise to power in Germany, and Russia's attempted takeover of neighboring Finland. Concerned about the plight of fellow Scandinavians, Wendel decided to enlist in the Finnish Air Force, and was accepted. Just before he could get into combat, the Finns signed an armistice with the Russians and released him from service. He was very disappointed.

Wendel still had an appetite for flying and fighting, and it was now 1940. The war in Europe had begun a few months before with Hitler's invasion of Poland, but the United States remained neutral. Anticipating imminent involvement by the United States, Wendel applied for pilot training with the U.S. Army Air Force. To his great disappointment, he was rejected for having "poor eyesight."

At that moment, the United Kingdom was engaged in a fight for its life. The crucial air Battle of Britain had begun, and a German invasion of Britain seemed inevitable—*if* Goering's Luftwaffe could establish air superiority over the island nation. Pilot losses in the British Royal Air force (RAF) were horrendous, with the average life expectancy of an RAF fighter pilot estimated at just *fourteen days*. The depleted squadrons of Spitfire and Hurricane fighters were all that stood between British sovereignty and Nazi domination. The RAF fighter pilots were like the modern version of the famous three hundred Spartan heroes in the 480 B.C. Battle of Thermopylae, who single-handedly held back the Persian army. Wendel desperately wanted to be one of the modern Spartans in this epic struggle to save democracy.

Just as the RAF was on the verge of exhausting its meager resources, the Luftwaffe changed its strategy and postponed the invasion of Britain indefinitely. The RAF had saved Britain, since Luftwaffe chief Goering had concluded that they would need all of the Luftwaffe resources to support the planned invasion of the Soviet Union, named Operation Barbarossa. As Prime Minister Winston Churchill said with his typical, elegant simplicity:

**Never in the field of human conflict was so much owed by so many to so few. All hearts go out to the fighter pilots, whose brilliant actions we see with our own eyes day after day . . . .**

Figuring that the beleaguered RAF would not be as picky as the USAAF, Wendel drove across the border into Canada and applied for pilot training. He was instantly accepted. After flying various training aircraft (above, Wendel on the left) and receiving his wings, he was introduced to the RAF's hot new fighter, the Supermarine Spitfire.

While returning from a trip to see his parents, Wendel met my mother, Isabell, on a Greyhound bus. Three days later, they were married in Toronto. The parents of each of the newlyweds were horrified at such a short courtship.

Isabell Poston was a young schoolteacher, the daughter of a prominent dentist from Davenport, Iowa. This was a family that was accustomed to doing things "correctly," and this quick marriage did not meet their criteria.

However, after they met Wendel, they found his personality was overwhelming and his charm irresistible. They quickly warmed to the situation and welcomed him as a son-in-law.

The Nelsons of Fremont, however, were not so flexible. They felt that Isabell had captured their precious son through devious means, and that he deserved "better." Several local Swedish girls had their eye on Wendel, who cut a dashing figure in his RAF uniform.

Wendel and his new wife moved to his next RCAF base assignment in Canada. While he was completing his training in Spitfires, Wendel decided to give his new wife a low fly-over. He spotted their residence on the base, and zoomed over the house at tree top level. Unfortunately, the base commander's wife happened to be chatting with Isabell in

their front yard as the sleek fighter roared overhead. "It's OK, honey, I won't tell a soul," she said.

A few weeks later, Wendel was ordered to England, along with other new RCAF pilots. On the long ocean voyage to England, he wrote in his diary about their fear of being torpedoed by German U-boats, which at that time

were terrorizing the North Atlantic. *This would not be a proper way for a fighter pilot to die,* he thought. He expressed great relief when they arrived in England, and was glad he had not joined the Navy.

He had become good friends with another American volunteer in the RAF, Spitfire pilot John Gillespie Magee, Jr., author of the famous poem, "High Flight." Magee died in his Spitfire in a 1941 mid-air collision shortly after he and Wendel arrived in England for combat assignments.

While still flying Spitfires with the RAF, Wendel was pictured on the cover of the RCAF's magazine *Crosswinds*. This issue introduced the classic poem for the first time:

### High Flight

*Oh! I have slipped the surly bonds of Earth*
*And danced the skies on laughter-silvered wings;*
*Sunward I've climbed, and joined the tumbling mirth*
*Of sun-split clouds — and done a hundred things*
*You have not dreamed of—wheeled and soared and swung*
*High in the sunlit silence. Hov'ring there,*
*I've chased the shouting wind along, and flung*
*My eager craft through footless halls of air....*
*Up, up the long, delirious, burning blue*
*I've topped the wind-swept heights with easy grace*
*Where never lark or even eagle flew—*
*And, while with silent lifting mind I've trod*
*The high untrespassed sanctity of space,*
*Put out my hand, and touched the face of God.*

Although the peak intensity of the 1940 Battle of Britain had passed, the Luftwaffe continued its aerial attacks on Britain. Wendel was posted to Scotland to fly Bristol Beaufighter night fighters, using new radar and navigation systems to intercept night bombing raids. He was then posted to 600 ("City of London") Squadron, where he received a commendation from the mayor of London. About this time, he learned that he had a son, whom he named Richard John Lee. Wendel added my second middle name to honor his fallen squadronmate, Lee Gagnon, standing on the right next to Wendel in this early 1942 photo. Lee was killed in action just after this photo was taken. The loss of this friend affected my father for the rest of his life. As a result, he always insisted on calling me "Dickie Lee." Wendel began to realize that a combat pilot loses many friends during wartime. He began to feel that he, too, would not make it home. The daily losses incurred by the RAF in fighting the Luftwaffe continued to deplete their pilot ranks.

*Mom and me.*

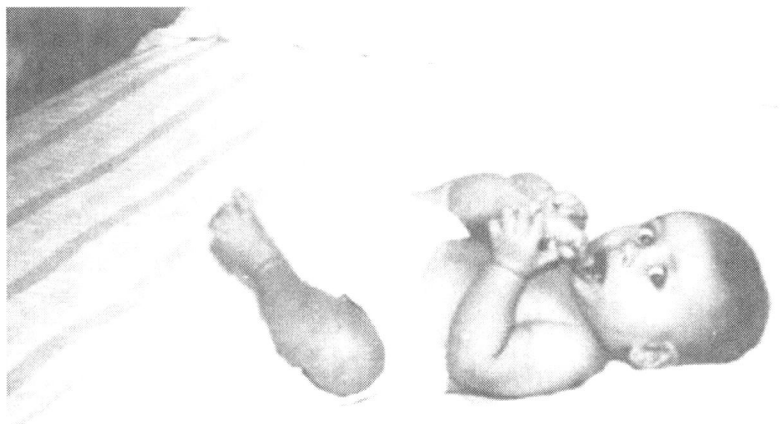

***A symbolic moment, putting my foot in my mouth for the first time. Friends and family tell me that I still perform this maneuver, and much too frequently.***

Wendel loved to write, and penned numerous, rambling letters to my mother during his overseas tours. Only three of these are still in my possession.

On March 18, 1942, shortly after I was born, he wrote this to my mother from his RAF base in England:

> My beloved wife and baby,
>
> Ah, pleasant dreams. My darling, if you only knew how much I long for a sight of you…Just to hold you in my arms again and tell you again how I love you. And to see my son! Now that I am settled down to the idea of being a father, I spend hours trying to imagine what he looks like. One thing, darling, you must tell me all about him. Is he healthy? What does he look like? You know, darling Isabell, many thoughts race through my mind about him and his future.
>
> It may be months before I see my son. He will not realize this. You, darling, will have the brunt of his training and development. I am confident that you will be and are as devoted a mother as you are my wife. I am fortunate in knowing that my wife is devoted and wonderful. I know that you are much too good for me, darling. There is a real possibility that I have left you with a burden which may be difficult for you to cope with. I sincerely hope that our boy therefore will grow up to be a cultured, well-disciplined gentleman who will always appreciate the beautiful, intelligent and devoted mother whom he has.
>
> All I can say for him is that he will never have to feel that his father deserted his mother. He may often feel that when he is growing up. Many questions will enter his groping, inquisitive mind. He shall know that his father served his country and people when their security and liberty were in danger. By that time, this struggle, which has tormented us so privately, will be just a memory, just history to him. Therefore, darling, keep these letters for him, so that some day he may realize and appreciate how much his parents loved each other and the devastating torture in our hearts caused by our separation.
>
> He will then also realize and have a full appreciation of the efforts we, the free peoples of the world, are making at the sacri-

*fice of our lives and souls to give him the freedom and equality with which we were endowed.*

*Sounds like an essay, doesn't it, honey? You know me—when I think something, I can only say it or write it to rid my heart of its weight. Unfortunately, when we are not on operations, we have too much time to think and reflect. Mostly my thoughts are of you, my darling. My parents, whom I love so sincerely, are also constantly in my thoughts. I can tell you darling, my two sisters have been wonderful to me since I've been over here, as they have all my life.*

*I received your carton of cigarettes along with one from Mother and Dad. They came a few days ago. I hadn't had any for several weeks and they were wonderful. They are really the only pleasure I have. Actually, I have very little money to buy things with so I just hang around.*

*What do you think about going to Fremont for a while with my parents? I hope that you will. I wish to thank your mother and father for their wonderful care of my dearest possession. I shall never be able to repay them for their devotion. But they shall know how much I love them for being so good to my Isabell. Well, darling, don't work too hard with the baby. Remember your husband expects not to play second fiddle. Ha! Write often and if you can, send some cigarettes—please do! Cheerio, darling, I love you so!*

*Your devoted Wen*

On a mission in southern England, his aircraft experienced engine failure, causing him to crash-land on the Knowles family estate in Yorkshire. After plowing through two stone walls, his aircraft landed in a canal. Mr. Knowles pulled him out of the sinking aircraft, unconscious. Following that unusual introduction, he and the Knowles family became close friends, and he visited them frequently while he was in England.

Next, he was posted to North Africa, flying the Hawker Hurricane "tank buster" version against Rommel's armored columns. This called for low-altitude strafing runs, using a pair of 40mm cannons. After being shot down by a German armored vehicle, he narrowly missed being captured and was wounded in the knee.

**The Hawker Hurricane fighter**

Wendel's next assignment was to the experimental high altitude defense unit in Egypt, where Spitfires were being modified to intercept German JU-86

reconnaissance aircraft at over 30,000 feet. During that time, he documented two high-altitude kills in his log book, with pilots in his flight getting two more.

These kills are even mentioned by Wikipedia, the Internet encyclopedia: "[T]he Luftwaffe ordered that some 40 older-model bombers be converted to Ju 86P-1 high-altitude bombers and Ju 86P-2 photo reconnaissance aircraft. Those operated successfully for some years over Britain, the Soviet Union and North Africa. *In August 1942, a modified Spitfire V shot one down over Egypt at some 14,500 m (49,000 ft); when two more were lost, Ju-86Ps were withdrawn from service in 1943.*" Two of these referenced kills were accomplished by my dad, who was a member of this elite RAF unit.

***Dad and four of his RAF buddies near the Sphinx and the Giza pyramids; Egypt, 1943. The pilot on the right was killed soon after this photo was taken.***

To his great dismay, the RAF decided that his hands-on knowledge of many aircraft types, combined with extensive combat experience, was too valuable to leave him at the front lines. He was ordered back to Canada to operate the RCAF aircraft test and development center.

*By his Spitfire, Flying Officer Wendel J.A. Nelson, RCAF (at right), and a squadron-mate in Egypt, 1943. During this period, Rommel's forces were defeated, setting the stage for the Allied invasion of Sicily and Italy.*

Unhappy with this non-combat assignment, Wendel transferred to the USAAF in early 1944, which was now in dire need of experienced fighter pilots for the European campaign. He was commissioned as a 1st Lt., and trained in the P-47 Thunderbolt. During that period, he enjoyed being with his family for a few months, and getting to know his two-year-old son (me). Upon completion of his training, he shipped out for England, where he joined the 360th Fighter Squadron, part of the 356th Fighter Group at Martlesham Heath air base in Suffolk, southeast England.

Shortly after he arrived, his squadron transitioned to the more advanced P-51 Mustang, the only fighter that could provide the American bombers with long-range fighter escort. However, the squadron pilots were rushed through the transition training for the Mustang, and started flying combat missions in the Mustang in November, 1944.

*Dad, me, and Mom.*

Although glad to be able to serve in the air force of his own country, Wendel experienced a degree of culture shock. In the RAF, pilots were treated like movie stars, and given the best accommodations available in the wartime environment. The USAAF treated its pilots with less deference and provided comparatively austere living conditions. Wendel was still happy that he had made the switch.

*The old Martlesham Heath air base tower and administrative building, now preserved and operated as a museum. Most of the runways have been removed to make room for residential development. A memorial containing my dad's name is on site, along with the names of other USAAF and RAF pilots who flew from Martlesham and were killed in action.*

*A 1944 view from the Martlesham Heath tower. Several P-51 Mustangs of my dad's 360th Fighter Squadron can be seen in the foreground, parked in protective revetments.*

A secondary strategy of the American bombing campaign was to bait the Luftwaffe into defending German targets, enabling the high-performance Mustangs to engage and destroy the German fighters and establish air superiority over Europe. On November 28, 1944, six months after the Normandy D-Day invasion, Wendel wrote Isabell:

*My darling wife, Isabell,*

*Hiya, dearest ones! Just a few lines to let you know that I am thinking about you two, my dearest ones.*

*As I said before, it is very difficult to write to you at home when my mail has not reached me for so long. My morale sinks way down every time I go to the mail box and find it empty. I'm anxious to learn how long you went without mail. I hope not as long as I have been. If so, it must be hell for you.*

*I don't know whether you are still in Davenport or not, so I'm continuing sending them there until I hear.*

*Oh, darling, there is so much I want to hear about you two. Every day I wonder what you are doing and how you are. My thoughts are so constantly of you and home. Just a word from you would make me so very happy. At night, I dream of you and I wake up only to find that you are not with me. Baby, my life is so incomplete.*

*Gee, Dickie Lee must be growing, even these few months. When I come home, he may not even know me. That hurts to think that, so don't let him forget his devoted Daddy. Tell me of each change he makes and his every fall, etc. And honey, you two be as happy as you can without us being together.*

*As there is such a chance that I won't come home, I do want you two to know how much I love you and how completely I belong to you. My life isn't worth much in comparison with the beautiful future my son can have. I want him and his lovely mommy to always be happy and well cared for. It always grieves me to know that record was broken, for I had a message for Dickie Lee when he grows older. Now, you'll have to tell him what his daddy wanted him to make of himself. And above all, to care for the lovely and devoted woman who is his mother and my lover. If anything should prevent me from returning, Dickie Lee will never know what a joy he has been to me. You, darling, will have to let him know. In case I should take a long trip, Stanley Lundstrom will have a letter for you to give to our son when he can understand.*

*This is a very morbid subject, but I did have to discuss it and if it should make you feel badly or sad, remember honey, I'm taking the best of care that nothing does happen, within the boundaries of war.*

*These days we are really in the scrap. Yesterday, our group got 23 Jerry fighters and we didn't lose a man. I had to sit that mission out and I could have torn my hair out. I can fly over Germany for the duration of my tour and never get a break like that. But the Hun has plenty more. However, a six-hour flight in a little Mustang is no pleasure for my big seat. But rest assured of one thing, dear. Lick 'em we will, even if it does take longer than those armchair strategists at home think. I'm really at a loss as to what to write about so I'll close for tonite. I shall close my eyes and again I'll see that vision of beauty that is you before me. And I'll know she needn't scold me for my conduct as a husband and father. I love you so, Isabell. I'm yours forever,*

*Wen*

*P.S.: Hugs and kisses for my little son*

The letter for me that he referred to was lost and we never received it. In two weeks, the Battle of the Bulge would begin, comprising Hitler's last attempt to stop the Allied advance from the West. German V-2 rockets continued to hit English cities, giving urgency to the effort against Germany. In five weeks, 1/LT Wendel J.A. Nelson would be dead.

*360th Fighter Squadron*
*APO 557, c/o Postmaster,*
*New York, NY*
*8 December 1944*

*My darling wife and sweetheart, Isabell,*

*Today was really a day to get up and cheer and celebrate. I got my first letter since my arrival here, one from you, darling, and one from my sister Wendella. If you only knew how much that letter of yours meant. It was a V-Mail, written the 28th of November. Furthermore, it was the first real assurance I had of your whereabouts. You have probably written in previous letters of your trip and Chicago, etc. If not, there are so many questions that are unanswered. For instance, has my mail been arriving* regularly? Has it ever been cut up *[by the military censors]*? What letters have you had? What is the quickest, V-Mail or Air Mail? Etc.!

It is tough to hear how your poor Dad is going down-hill. Honey, when is he going to quit? Surely by now they can afford to relax and enjoy the remainder of their days. I know that your Dad has a courage and determination that any red-blooded person would respect. And your Mom, who has so devotedly assisted him and been such an ardent friend and companion. Really, I'm only a son-in-law, but they did bring my most priceless possession into the world and for that I shall forever be interested in their welfare. For you to be there and with Dickie Lee bring cheer into their lives is wonderful. I love you more than ever for your tenderness and devotion to your parents, for you know what I think of mine or anyone's regard for their Mom and Dad. So if ever you wish and deem it wise to make your home with your parents, you have my consent, providing you first inform me of the arrangements. Even if our own personal future would probably be improved by your building a home near my people, we cannot be selfish when it comes to our dear ones' welfare. You now know my sentiments in the matter, and can judge for yourself.

I do assume that you are now in Fremont, so mail is now going there. My sister Wendella hasn't told me in her letters when the "event" will take place, so I'm naturally anxious. Give her my cheeriest and best regards for a safe delivery. Am going to write to *[your brother]* Bob now that I have his address. It may be that I can run across him in France if I ever have to land there. As of yet, I've been able to get back to England each time. However, several times I felt that the Channel looked pretty cold for a swim.

Darling, you needn't send any more fruit juice, as we now have an ample stock. But film will surely be welcome and some cake and cookies and candy. Although I'm not much of a candy eater, a Mars bar now and then would be swell. Anything you send will be appreciated, but don't go to any trouble.

We're released for the day, so I'm catching up on my correspondence. I saw Stan last night in Ipswich. We went to a movie. He had heard from his folks and they knew we were stationed near each other.

Your sweet words in your letter have sent my heart into the skies. Oh darling, I love you so dearly and so much you can only know after a life time of happiness together. That is why I have to come home, plus the pleasure and joy of living, watching the growth of my son. He must be developing at a fast rate, especially mentally. Hon, don't ever let him know that he does things outstanding, or let other people remark in front of him. I can always remember when I was a youngster when a teacher told me how bright I was, I came to believe her and consequently thought all other people stupid and boring. It still reflects on me, as you know. My son must be a broad-minded, enlightened man, but accepting God's gifts modestly and as a sacred trust, not as something to toy with, as I'm afraid I've done so often.

Dickie Lee is going to endure an era when only intelligent culture and education, plus two-fisted manliness and integrity will show above the mob. We must prepare him for this, even at the sacrifice of ourselves. It can be achieved by stern discipline and respect for knowledge and art. That is why I wanted him never to be allowed to mistreat books or any reading material. That is why I wanted to see him interested in culture such as music and art. Society can never tolerate vulgarity in manners, nor can they tolerate people who lack true courage. Even men whom I associate with daily, look askance at bad behavior in some of our buddies. Breeding is so obvious! We can do so much for our son by beginning correctly. One thing, I never want him to be a bigot!

Darling wife of mine, life can be so intolerable without you. I need you by my side. My nature rebels at our separation. I am so grateful for your beautiful love. I love you my sweet.

*Always, forever your Wen*

p.s.: Tell Dickie Lee he needn't worry about sending packages to Hitler—Daddy is taking care of that! Hugs and kisses, Dickie Lee!

*1/LT Wendel Nelson by his Mustang fighter, painted with the logo "Lord," a play on his last name. The photo was taken sometime in late 1944, just prior to his death.*

On his eleventh combat mission in the P-51, January 13, 1945, Dad was ordered to take off in a blinding snowstorm with other P-51s to fly bomber escort into Germany. He died in an unexplained crash five miles north of the field. The icy weather that day caused the death of five other fighter pilots in similar crashes in the space of just one hour. Obviously, this mission should have been canceled. Losing pilots and aircraft to adverse weather conditions did nothing to advance the war effort.

At the time, my mother and I were living with her parents in Davenport, Iowa. For many years of my childhood, I was haunted by the frightening image of some stranger knocking at the door, asking for my mother. The man handed her a Western Union telegram, which got right to the point and did not waste words. My father would never be coming home. He was dead. As a child who had lost a father, I would not be alone. My dad's U.S. Eighth Air Force went on to lose over 26,000 pilots and airmen in its European combat operations.

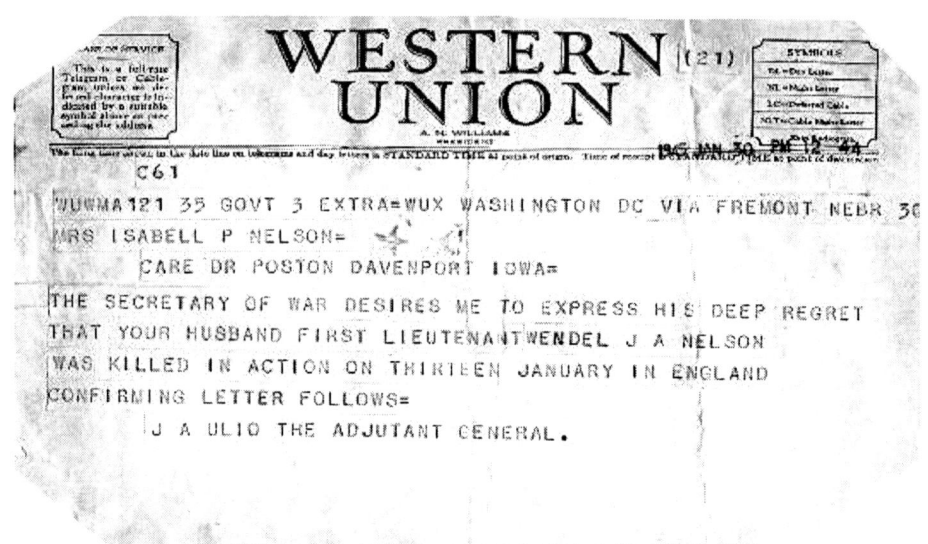

Even though I was only three, I was a smart kid and knew something had gone terribly wrong. Life for my mother and me would never be the same, and we would now travel in unexpected and unlikely directions. The journey for us would soon begin, and it would not be an easy one.

~ ~ ~

## Chapter 2: *In Search of a Life*

Although my childhood memories of those early years have now largely faded, I distinctly remembered painful details when I was younger. Even as a three-year-old child, I was affected by the family's emotional chaos in the aftermath of my father's death. My mother was a sheltered, hypersensitive woman who was not equipped to fend for herself. Although she was well educated and had worked as a schoolteacher before her marriage, she experienced a complete breakdown in what little self-confidence she ever had.

At that time, I could still remember my dad vividly—the big, smiling man in a khaki uniform—and how much fun he and I had doing things together, like going to the zoo. I remembered the time he and I were standing close to the cage of a hippopotamus, when the big monster sneezed all over us. I thought about my dad a lot, and did not understand why he would never be coming home.

The Air Force, along with various politicians, contacted my mom several times to express their condolences and fulfill their next-of-kin responsibilities. On one occasion, a big trunk arrived from England, containing my father's personal effects. She got rid of all of them, except for his old RAF flight jacket, a spare leather helmet, and a flying scarf, which she kept for me. There were two other interesting items. From a German ME-109 fighter that he had shot down in England, there was an altimeter and an aircraft attitude (gyro) indicator. My mother refused to accept these souvenirs, fearing that they could be "booby-trapped" to explode. Her paranoia had no limits.

Each time she was contacted by the Air Force, she would revisit her grief and cry for days. As a little kid, I did not know what to do to help her. In fact, I think *I* was a problem for her, because I looked so much like my father. Every time she looked at me, she was reminded of her loss. As I grew older, I began to understand this, and sometimes I felt guilty for causing her pain.

To add to her problems, an intra-family dispute erupted about where to bury my father. Initially, he had been buried in the beautiful American military cemetery in Cambridge, England. My mother wanted to leave him there, near where he fought and died. However, his Swedish parents had other ideas. They wanted his body exhumed and brought back to Fremont, where there would be a memorial service in their church, and then his reburial in a local cemetery. My mother fought this, and tried to compromise by suggesting his reburial in Arlington National Cemetery. They refused and finally got their way. She had no fight left in her. After that, she would have nothing to do with them and never saw any of them again. Family relationships were also becoming victims of the war.

We continued to stay with my maternal grandparents in urban Davenport, which was a cloistered, boring life for a little boy. At age four I developed tonsillitis, followed by pneumonia. I was hospitalized, and almost died. The doctors told my mother that I was a sickly child, and needed to live in a warm climate, not the frigid Midwest.

When I was five, we effectively became homeless vagabonds—on the road constantly, looking for warm places where I would be healthier and my mother could forget about her lost husband. We must have set mileage records on the nation's train system, as we traveled first to California (too expensive), then to Arizona (too hot), and then to Falls Church, Virginia, to stay with my aunt, uncle and cousins. My mother decided this climate was not good for me either, and we headed for Sarasota, Florida, to stay with her retired aunt and uncle.

In a few weeks, I found myself living in a huge trailer park, complete with old men playing shuffleboard. With money from my father's estate, Mom bought a small, one-bedroom trailer. For bathroom facilities, it had only a toilet, and no shower or bathtub. We had to walk about 100 yards to use a community shower. It was like camping out, which is probably why I hate camping today. We lived like that as I went through the first, second, and third grades.

The teachers in my elementary school advised my mother that I could easily perform more advanced schoolwork, and was bored with the class assignments. They recommended that I skip a grade so I would be more challenged. She refused. She felt it was more important for me to socialize with the kids my age, and I think she was correct.

Mom still refused to work, citing her parental responsibilities, which put us on a very tight budget. Then, when I was about eight, I noticed some men of her age began to ask her to go out.

One was a wealthy young man that drove a big Cadillac, which I found impressive. One day, he took us to the beach on Lido Key. As we sat around on the sand, I noticed big round scars on his shoulders. I asked him what those were (to my mother's embarrassment), and he told me that a Japanese soldier had shot him with a machine gun when he was climbing up Mount Suribachi, during the Battle of Iwo Jima. I asked him what happened to the Japanese, and he said, "I killed him." He then described in detail how he did it. I was very impressed, but Mom was horrified and refused to see the man again. She was tired of war and heroes.

Shortly after that, she got serious about a young local man that she met at a church function. Almost from our first meeting, I did not like him. As Mom and I were having dinner one evening, she told me that she was going to marry this character! My first reaction was to say, "You can't! What about my dad?" She reminded me gently that my dad was never coming home, and that we had to get on with our lives. Why she picked *this* man to marry, I will never understand.

The man she decided to marry was an uneducated "redneck"—Ted—who worked as a meter reader for the power company. Immediately, I disliked him. He could not measure up to my dad on any level. He had been drafted and then discharged as a "buck" sergeant in the Army without seeing any combat. He was crude, unmannered, and had nothing interesting to talk about. As far as I could tell, he had never accomplished anything of consequence in his entire life—except convincing my mother to marry him. Whenever he would kiss her or put his arm around her, I felt uncomfortable and disappointed in my mother's bad judgment.

The day they got married was like a funeral for me. I was left standing alone on the sidewalk outside of the church as they drove away on some bargain-basement, hillbilly honeymoon. My mother's eyes met mine through the back window of their car as they pulled away. She knew what I was thinking. *Now you are leaving me, Mom.* Ted's parents, who were nice people, took me home like an unwanted orphan to await the newlyweds' return.

When they got back, I found that I disliked Ted in his role as the new stepfather even more than before. He now had a more domineering attitude, and made it clear that *he* was in charge now. Although he pretended to like me before the wedding, he now barely gave me the time of day. I sensed his resentment—real or not—that I was around. Even worse, he decided that he did not want to be near my mother's aunt and uncle, so he had the trailer towed over to a cheap trailer park near the city limits of Sarasota. Now all *three* of us were living in the claustrophobic little trailer, with one toilet and no bathing facilities.

We had to use an outdoor shower room, where worms and bug larvae crawled routinely out of the drain from the underground septic tank. I look back on this time as the point where my life hit absolute rock bottom. Mom and I had gone from being the survivors of a proud military family to become Southern "trailer trash." There was nowhere to go but up, but I began to figure out that it was totally up to me to get out of the mess that my mother had created. It was clear that she would not be much help, because she had apparently lost her mind. I often fantasized about ways to leave home and somehow go out on my own.

When good old Ted came home from work, he would pop open a beer, take off his smelly boots, and light up a cigarette. That moment made the day for him. I sensed that he secretly wished that I were not in the picture, even though I was a "no-cost" item to him, thanks to my dad's death benefits and insurance. For him, I was a living reminder that his wife had been with another man, one with whom he could never compete.

For a couple of years, I had a parakeet as a pet, and taught him all sorts of tricks. His name was Jerry. One day, I came home from school, and found that one of the feral cats in the trailer park had managed to get into our trailer. Mom had left the door unlatched when she went to the community laundry. The cat had Jerry clamped in his mouth, with the little bird screaming in agony as he died. For the first time in my young life, I experienced rage. I grabbed at the cat as he jumped past me, running under the trailer with Jerry. I was faster than he was, and caught him under the trailer by his leg, forcing him to drop Jerry. However, I was too late. Jerry was dead. There was nothing I could do to bring him back. Now even *Jerry* had been taken from me.

It was a horrible experience for a nine-year-old. I actually scared myself in my fight with the cat, which fought back like the wild animal he was. My overriding feeling was that I had failed to protect Jerry and keep him safe. He was my responsibility, and I had lost him in a horrible death.

I buried Jerry under the trailer, placed a little cross on his grave, and prayed that God would take care of him in Heaven, and not let him hurt anymore. I closed my eyes, and said, "Dad, if you are listening, please take care of Jerry. He's a good little bird, and he doesn't eat much."

When my mother got home, I sobbed and told her what had happened. She tried to console me, but this incident seemed to epitomize the meltdown in my life, beginning with my dad's death and culminating with her marriage to Stepfather Ted. When Stepfather Ted got home and learned what had happened, his muted reaction suggested that he was secretly glad Jerry was gone.

My dislike for Stepfather Ted dominated my life. Soon, things got even worse. My mother got *pregnant.* One of the older boys in the trailer park explained in graphic terms how a woman gets pregnant, and I was shocked and disgusted. I found it hard to believe that my mother would do such gross things with someone like Stepfather Ted. I felt that my dad would have been horrified to learn of this.

My life became even more traumatic a few months later when my mother seemed to get "sick," and went to the hospital to have her baby. Stepfather Ted showed his true colors—he did not want me around. Once again, I was dumped with Ted's parents, who tried to explain it all to me in benign terms. I did not trust them—I became convinced that I was being replaced, and that they were all conspiring to get rid of me. One of the boys in the trailer park predicted that I was going to be placed in an orphanage, and I believed him. One way or the other, I really *was* a war orphan.

When Mom returned from the hospital with her squalling baby girl, I thought the world had come to an end. Now there were *four* of us living in this tiny trailer, with the added ambience of stinking baby diapers. *So <u>this</u> is how hillbillies live!* None of us really had any privacy, and this made our family relationships even more strained.

I tried to concentrate on school, because I liked the idea of knowing more than my uneducated stepfather. I made sure that I got top grades, just to stick that in his ugly face. In the off-hours, I avoided the trailer as much as possible, and explored the wildlife areas around the park.

The surrounding area contained a unique plot of land that was a microcosm of the Florida natural habitat. There was a small uplands area, called a hummock, bounded by palmetto scrub and a swampy area. This was my refuge. I knew every inch of this wild, timeless place.

Since the trailer park was on the outskirts of swampy wetlands, I became closely acquainted with the Florida wildlife. The area was richly populated by alligators, squirrels, birds, turtles, raccoons, possum, snakes, lizards, and rabbits. I learned to lie still on the ground and call quail, squirrels, and ducks within a few feet of me by mimicking their own calls and tempting them closer with nuts and seeds.

I had several encounters with alligators and poisonous snakes, including the Eastern Diamondback Rattlesnake and the Cottonmouth Moccasin, but never was bitten. I watched these formidable ambush predators carefully for hours, and learned how to approach them without making them defensive. I went to the library frequently and learned the names of all the different species of plants and animals in this  typical Florida scrub habitat, and how they used and adapted to it. This little wilderness was my escape from life in the trailer, and taught me how to blend into my surroundings. It also taught me that only the fittest and smartest survive.

One day, I decided to explore. I followed one of the rabbit trails through the palmetto scrub. Knowing the habits of my animal "friends" in the area, I walked carefully, looking for "Lucifer." This was a huge six-foot rattlesnake that loved to coil up near the path, waiting for his next rabbit meal. I never told my stepfather or mom about him, because I was afraid my stepfather would kill him. Lucifer had claimed this patch of scrub as his territory, and he was always there somewhere, *if* you could find him. I had fun looking for him, because it was like playing hide-and-seek with a very smart and dangerous adversary.

On this day, I found him in his favorite ambush place near the trail, motionless. His camouflage was perfect, as always. Most people would never have seen him. My challenge to myself was to be able to walk past Lucifer so as not to cause him to give his warning rattle, or to strike. To do this, you had to move very slowly and not cause ground vibrations with your footsteps, which he found threatening. As I eased past him, I saw him testing the air with his forked tongue. That meant he was trying to smell me, to figure out what I was. I knew his facial sensors could detect the heat of my body, and that he could see my shape. I watched to see if he tensed up, or went into a defensive strike posture and vibrated his rattles. He stayed quiet in his resting coil, and I slipped by. A passing rabbit would not be so lucky.

On another day, I was walking along the creek bank looking for small alligators. Suddenly, the bank collapsed and my leg fell through into an old alligator cave. I looked down, and found that my foot was right in the middle of a nest of deadly Cottonmouth Moccasins. One of them struck wildly at my leg, but  missed. I rolled back and checked my leg over carefully. Some of the "rednecks" told me that you often do not even feel a snakebite at first. I was lucky. You can get hurt, crashing into someone's house like that.

At Christmas, I got a bow-and-arrow set. In the nearby woods, I practiced my marksmanship constantly, until I could hit targets consistently at over 50 yards. The other boys and I had archery contests, and I usually won.

I found I was good at one of the favorite games of the local boys—"war." An old veteran gave each of us an Army helmet, and we spent many hours pretending to fight and kill each other in the wild areas around the trailer park. By that time, I had learned how to camouflage myself, and could usually sneak up on the other kids undetected, or set up an ambush in the palmetto or tall-grass areas.

*On the right, armed with two cap pistols. Our trailer is in the background.*

Two years went by, and then Stepfather Ted and my mother decided to build a modest house on the inexpensive north side of Sarasota. Just as it neared completion, I developed appendicitis, and underwent emergency surgery. Stepfather Ted accused me of deliberately getting appendicitis to get out of doing my cleanup chores on the new house. Stepfather Ted and I tacitly agreed on at least one thing—we despised each other. The dysfunctional family moved into the new house when I got out of the hospital.

At least in the new house, I had my own room and could get away from the rest of the family. I continued to focus on my school studies. I learned to speed-read and use a typewriter, and loved to write. My favorite authors then were Rudyard Kipling (*The Jungle Book*) and Edgar Rice Burroughs (the Tarzan series). The theme of an underdog hero, living among wild animals, always captured my imagination.

In those ancient days without computers, I learned to use a slide rule. I also became interested in foreign languages, codes, and ciphers. A neighbor kid and I exchanged "code books," and using flashlights, we would send each other ciphered Morse code messages from our windows. Perhaps this was the origin of text messaging.

Just to irk my stepfather, I decorated my room with photos of my dad and models of the different types of aircraft that he flew. After that, Stepfather Ted avoided this room, which I found amusing.

Although the family now lived in a small house, instead of a trailer, we lived the life of the working poor. We had basic necessities, but no luxuries—not even air conditioning. Stepfather Ted used any excess money for his hunting trips. He never did anything for my mother.

Neither Stepfather Ted nor my mother understood financial matters. Each payday, my mother would cash out his paycheck and drive around town to pay our bills with cash. She was a Depression baby, and did not believe in banks. They did not have any credit cards, loans, or even a checking account.

In those days, Sarasota was still a racially segregated society, complete with separate schools, "colored" and "white" restrooms, and even separate drinking fountains. My stepfather expected African-Americans, whom he called "Negros," to address him as "Sir" or "Mister." Apparently, he imagined himself as an Old South plantation owner or something. That always struck me as an amusing thought, because he was about as far from Southern aristocracy as you could get.

He had something negative to say about Blacks and Jews at almost every meal. He also did not like the Hispanics that were "taking over Miami." For my part, I had never met or talked to a Black or Hispanic in my entire life, but I did have some Jewish friends at school. In time, his prejudices would probably have influenced me, but something unexpected happened that made me start to think for myself.

There was a house near the railroad tracks, where a black family lived. I decided to walk down the tracks to see what the adjoining wooded area was like, when I met a young black boy about my age, carrying a football. I said, "Hey, throw me a pass!" The boy threw me a nice spiral, which I caught.

"What's your name?" I asked.

"Robert," he replied. "I live in that house."

"Well, I live over there on 25th Street."

"Yeah, the white section," he noted. I did not know what to say in response. We talked for a while, and tossed the ball back and forth.

"Well, I guess I have to go. Good to meet ya," I said.

"Sure." He walked away, looking disappointed.

When the family had dinner that night, I told my stepfather and mom about meeting this nice black kid. Stepfather Ted exploded. "Don't *ever* associate with those people!" he screamed. "They are not like you, and you can't trust them! Besides, white folks around here might think you support racial integration."

I stood my ground. "Well, I think he is a nice guy, and he can really throw that football. Maybe I should invite him over here for a touch football game with my friends sometime." I knew that would really get old Ted going. I knew how to push his buttons.

"Absolutely not! Ah don't want him hangin' around heah. You stay away from those people!" I remembered Mark Twain's *Tom Sawyer* books, and how Tom and Huck Finn treated Jim, the black kid. Treating people in that manner seemed wrong to me. I could tell that my mom did not agree with Ted, but she said nothing—she always avoided confrontation. Years later, in a delicious irony, Stepfather Ted was forced to sell that house on 25th Street, and a black family bought it.

I would learn later in life that these difficult societal issues were being resolved first by the most unlikely of institutions—our nation's military. Even before Congress and the courts tackled the issue of segregation, the Armed Services began to desegregate and eliminate racial discrimination. In war, an enemy bullet does not care what color your skin is, or how much money your parents have. *Everyone* experiences fear in combat, bleeds, and dies with the same pain. The Grim Reaper is the ultimate "equal opportunity" visitor. All applicants are welcome.

I finally convinced Stepfather Ted and my mom to let me get a dog. Someone advertised a free litter in the paper, and we got one of the puppies. He was a spunky little terrier mix, and I named him "Nipper," after the RCA mascot. Nipper and I became inseparable, and he went everywhere with me.

Nipper always became impatient when I went to school, because he could not be with me. One day, he got out of the house and actually showed up at the door of the school. He had only been there once, but remembered how to get there, or maybe he tracked me somehow.

As we walked home, I crossed busy 27th Street (now called Martin Luther King Way), but Nipper had stopped to sniff at a bush. I looked around in time to see him sprinting across the street, directly in the path of a big dump truck. It rolled right over him, crushing his abdomen and chest. His spine was also crushed, but he still dragged himself with his front legs to get to me, groaning and shivering with pain. He then died in my arms. I still get teary-eyed thinking about this. *Another* precious thing had been taken from me, and once again, I felt personally responsible. *If only I had waited and helped Nipper cross the street. . .*

By the time I entered junior high school, I had become a top performer in academics. I was obsessed with achievement. Every day that I attended school, I drove myself to put "points" on an imaginary scholastic scoreboard. Socially, I was somewhat of a loner, with only a few close friends. I was fairly athletic, but skinny, and lacked the confidence to play team sports. I also lacked physical courage and did not like taking hits. I wound up playing in the school band and orchestra instead, where I attacked music like any other academic problem, and became one of the lead instrumentalists.

In the eighth grade, my homeroom class got a new teacher, replacing a wonderful woman who was always very kind and patient with us. This old witch seemed to hate being there, and was constantly berating the students for one thing or another. This is when the rebellious side of me first surfaced. I decided to give her a little present, because I did not like her attitude.

One of my friends had brought in a big Yellow Rat Snake to his science lab. This species is non-venomous and is a very important rodent predator in the Florida ecosystem. They are quite docile and easy to handle. I agreed to "rent" the snake from him for the morning for 50 cents and promised to return it unharmed.

When the teacher arrived in class, she would always open one particular drawer and pull out a ruler, which she used to threaten those who needed discipline. Before she got there, I coiled up my rental snake, and carefully placed him in the drawer. He seemed to like it in there.

When the teacher arrived, she could sense that something was going on. This eighth grade class was entirely too quiet, which was not normal. Keeping her eyes on the class, she opened the drawer and reached in for her ruler, the symbol of her witch-like powers. She put her hand right on top of the snake, and it moved. She staggered back against the wall, screaming and hyperventilating, and slid down to the floor in a faint. *Wow!* I thought I had killed her. She nearly had a heart attack. Tomorrow's newspaper headline flashed through my mind: ***"Student charged with murder in snake incident!"***

A model student up to this point, I experienced the first in a long history of disciplinary incidents. I was called to the principal's office and my mother was asked to come to the school. I received about an hour of threats and tongue-lashing, and was almost suspended. Mom talked the principal out of that, and promised that I would be a perfect student from then on. Because of my academic record, I was allowed to return to class, with the provision that the snake had to be removed, and I had to apologize to the teacher. The big lesson I learned was that some people are afraid of snakes.

I found out I was good at touch football, in which speed and agility were paramount and tackling was not allowed. I helped score the winning touchdown in the school championship game on a defensive blocked kick, which I unfortunately blocked with my nose. My bloody nose got a lot of sympathy and attention from the girls, and I was a football hero for a day. Inspired, I then tried to play varsity (tackle), but was too light and the bigger kids flattened me on every play. I decided my football career was over, and went back to music.

As I progressed from junior high to senior high school, I continued to excel in academics, but I was definitely a "geek." I was very good in science and math. It was time to put my skills to work.

The Russians had just put a satellite in orbit, and every geek in school wanted to build rockets and be a backyard astronaut. We had launched some smaller "black powder" rockets, with mixed results and a few nasty explosions.

In chemistry class, several of my friends and I put together a secret plan to launch a bigger rocket. None of this "bottle rocket" crap for us! One of the kids used his dad's machine shop and supplied the body and fins for an eight-foot aluminum rocket. Another kid was good with electrical things, so he built a little ignition panel out of a motorcycle battery and some spare parts. When our chemistry teacher was not watching, we secretly manufactured small amounts of a powerful rocket fuel, which I think was ammonium nitrate.

One afternoon, the chemistry teacher gave us an assignment and went to a long faculty meeting. This was the break we needed. The "rocket team" gained access to the roof of the high school and set up the rocket launch gantry, which had been secretly stored in an unused closet. We placed the igniter wires inside the rocket nozzle and led the wires back behind a concrete wall, where they were attached to the launch panel.

We all hid down behind the wall and started a Cape Canaveral-style countdown. "10-9-8-7-6-5-4-3-2-1, IGNITION!" The launch switch was activated, and the big rocket lifted off the launcher in a loud roar. At about 20 feet in the air, it exploded with a huge boom. We had neglected to slow the fuel burn with spacers or a hollow core pattern, so it became more of an artillery shell than a rocket. It was a miracle that shrapnel did not hit any of us. However, down in the parking lot below, a chunk of the rocket punctured the convertible top of a teacher's car. We had to pay for repairing that.

The chemistry teacher, Miss BeVier, convinced the principal that we should not be expelled, and that we were exactly what our country needed at this time to beat the Russians—budding rocket scientists! Privately, she told us sternly, "Next time you build one of those things, boys, include me in the process. We will make a real science project out of it, so that you learn something." We really respected her. If I have had any measurable success in my life, this brilliant woman had much to do with it. She inspired many in that chemistry class to go on to significant business or professional careers.

I had become friends with some of the kids whose parents had boats. I learned about boating, fishing, and water-skiing in the beautiful waters around Sarasota Bay. I loved the water almost as much as the Florida wilderness.

Unwisely, I often snorkeled by myself out to some deep rocky areas near Lido Beach and New Pass with my spear gun and speared some good-sized fish. On one occasion, I was free diving down about 20 feet over an old house foundation. I was about to spear a big grouper when I had a sense that something big was watching *me*. A few summers before, Sarasota had three shark attacks, and one kid about my age lost his leg. All of those instincts that I had built up in my earlier years in the woods were telling me I was being tracked by something. I swam as fast as I could for the shore, frequently looking behind me for a telltale fin cutting the surface.

Just as I reached the place where a big Australian pine had fallen into the water during a storm, I looked under the log and spotted a huge shadow on the other side. Something big was just on the other side of the tree! I pulled out my dive knife, and then I heard it—a wheezing sigh, followed by some loud squeaks. I dove down and looked under the log—right into the eye of a big dolphin. It was obvious he was laughing at me, and enjoying the joke he had played. I reached out and touched his slippery skin, and he swam back to deeper water.

A month later, I decided to snorkel across New Pass at the bridge to Longboat Key. I had seen lots of big grouper, snook, snapper and sheepshead hanging out by the bridge pilings. I started from the Lido Key side, carrying my spear gun.

When I got to the area where all the big fish usually were, I noticed they were swimming rapidly away. Something was not right. Then, I heard a splash behind me and looked up. A man on the bridge had just thrown a bait bucket in the water to get my attention. "Hey, kid, get out of the water!" he yelled. "There's a goddam shark following you!"

I did not need a second invitation. I swam rapidly to the Longboat Key side, and climbed up on the shore. I saw a group of people on the bridge shouting and pointing down at the water below.

I walked up on the bridge, and asked what was going on. "Look for yourself," said a fisherman. Cruising slowly under the bridge was a big tiger shark, probably 12 feet long. I realized I had to be a little more careful.

The family of one of my close friends, John "Teddy" Fox, had a big ranch east of Sarasota. We spent many hours exploring the wooded areas of the ranch with our .22 rifles, and I became an excellent shot. While on the ranch, we observed many rare species, including Bald Eagles, Sandhill Cranes, Red-tailed Hawks, Wild Turkey, and Great Egrets. It was a wild and beautiful place.

During one of our explorations of the woods around the ranch, Teddy walked up to the base of a big oak tree and stopped in the shade. I was walking about 20 feet behind him, carrying my single-shot .22 rifle. In a flash, I saw a familiar movement and color pattern—it was a big rattlesnake going into a defensive coil. It was not as big as old Lucifer, from my trailer park days, but it was at least five feet long, and within two feet of Teddy's bare leg.

I told Teddy to freeze and not move. The big snake had not given the normal warning "buzz" with his rattles, because he was about to shed his skin and was temporarily blind. In this shedding process, a rattler will strike randomly at any perceived movement, with no warning. I carefully aimed my rifle and shot the snake in the head, killing it instantly. I did not like doing it, but it was either the snake or Teddy.

As we inspected our prize, we came up with a plan. For safety, we cut the head off and buried it. Even when a venomous snake is dead, its fangs can still kill you. We carried the headless snake back to Teddy's car and wrapped it in a burlap bag. We decided to pull a prank on Teddy's cousin, Butch, who we knew was required to feed his family's chickens in about one hour.

We got to Butch's house just in time, and placed the decapitated rattler in a sinister coil near the entry to the chicken coop. As we hid behind some trees, we saw Butch trudging down the path. As he neared the dead snake, Teddy yelled, "Hey, Butch, what's that in the bushes?"

Butch looked down, saw the unmistakable diamond pattern of a big rattler, and vaulted over the six-foot fence like an Olympic athlete. I never knew a fat kid could get that high off the ground! He also let out a blood-curdling scream, which brought his dad out of the house. "Dad, it's a rattler!" Butch bellowed.

Butch's dad quickly retrieved his 12-gauge pump shotgun. Aiming at the coiled snake, he fired off three deafening blasts. Going over to the snake, he inspected his "kill" with satisfaction.

Turning to us, he said, "This shows how good I am with this shotgun, boys. I shot his damn head off at 20 yards!" Teddy and I had a good laugh, but not for long. We got in a lot of trouble for that one.

My friends and I often wondered how it would be to serve in the military, where you had to hunt people instead of animals. We became aware that we would soon have to register for the draft. That decision was near. We often talked about which Service was the best one to join. At the time, none of us had ever heard of a place called Vietnam.

One of my uncles tried to get me interested in the Air Force Academy. However, since I loved the water, joining the Navy seemed like the natural thing to do. In my sophomore year of high school, I decided on going to the Naval Academy. I decided against trying for West Point, mostly because Stepfather Ted had been in the Army.

My family doctor told my mom that I would never pass the Academy physical unless I gained some weight and got in shape. This motivated me to start lifting weights and doing distance running with my football-playing friend, Teddy Fox. By my junior year, I had gained about 40 lbs. and could bench press 200 lbs. and do 30 chin-ups. My entire focus was on gaining admission to the Naval Academy, and nothing was going to stand in my way.

Meanwhile, I tried to obtain an appointment from my local congressman and both senators, but was politely told that they had no appointments available. I found out later that they were saving them for sons of their political friends and contributors. After doing more research, I learned that there were ways to obtain an appointment that were purely competitive, based on your grade-point average and your SAT scores, with no political influence involved. I qualified for what was then a competitive presidential appointment as a son of a deceased veteran, but only 10 slots were awarded in this program, nationwide.

I also found out that if you were in the Naval or Marine Corps Reserve, you could seek a competitive appointment under that program, and there were 160 slots available each year. These seemed like better odds. I talked to the local Navy recruiter, who told me that I could enlist after my junior year, go to boot camp during the summer, and then attend weekend "drills" once a month during my senior year. That, he said, would qualify me to apply for admission to the Academy from the Reserves.

I decided to enlist in the Navy Reserve, but my mother would not allow it. She did not want her son in the military. I began to wonder if this woman ever made sense. Fortunately, her older sister understood the problem, and fate intervened.

Mom's older sister, Virginia, was married to a high-level government executive, and we had stayed with them years before in Falls Church, near Washington. They were wonderful people, and showed me great kindness throughout my life for which I will always be grateful. They usually came down during the summer and rented a cottage on Siesta Key, giving me another escape from Stepfather Ted and his new family. Cousin Larry and I spent many hours in the water, snorkeling around the rocks and looking for big stone crabs and fish. I became a family hero when I speared a big stingray near our beach. Those were fun times, and I always hated to see the end of the summer.

Mom decided to go visit her parents back in Iowa at the end of my junior year. Aunt Virginia came down to watch over us in her absence. After Mom left on her trip, I explained to my aunt how I was having problems with the admissions process at the Naval Academy, because the local Navy recruiter could not answer my questions about using the Reserves to obtain an appointment. She said, "I'm good friends with an admiral, and I'll give him a call."

She called Rear Admiral Bill Hughes, her neighbor, and explained the problem. By coincidence, it turned out that this admiral was then in charge of the Naval Reserve, and this fell precisely within his jurisdiction. The Admiral told her that he would personally make sure that my application went smoothly, but that I had to enlist without further delay. Since I was under 18, a parent or guardian had to authorize it.

One afternoon, a shiny Navy car pulled up in the driveway, and the recruiter, a uniformed Chief Petty Officer, knocked on the door. He had enlistment papers all filled out, and asked who would be authorizing my enlistment. "*I* will," said Aunt Virginia. "I'm basically his guardian." That was not exactly true, but the recruiter did not care. The Admiral had ordered him to get it done. In an instant, I became a Seaman Recruit, United States Naval Reserve. When my mom returned, she was hysterical. "How could you do that?" she asked her sister.

"Well, I decided in a few months he would be 18, and you couldn't stop him anyway. So why not give him what he wants?" Aunt Virginia always had a sensible solution.

That summer, at the tender age of 17, I went to Navy Boot Camp at Great Lakes, Illinois. This was the first time I had been away from home by myself, and it was an important experience for me.

During senior year, I became a National Merit Scholarship semi-finalist, and received scholarships to two civilian universities, including Georgia Tech. My mother wanted me to take one of them. I refused, and applied only to the Naval Academy. This could have been a disaster if I had failed to get in. Even at this age, I had become a risk-taker.

To the surprise of many, including Stepfather Ted, I *was* accepted. I was ranked #1 of out of the Navy and Marine Corps Reserve's 160 slots, and #2 out of the presidential 10. Just before I graduated from high school, I was also awarded a senatorial alternate appointment. At high school graduation, I was #2 in our graduating class.

One of my high school friends casually asked where I was going to college, and I told him, "The Naval Academy."

His reply: "You've got to be kidding! *You?*" Obviously, I did not fit the image of a Naval Academy Midshipman.

However, I noticed that some of the girls that previously considered me a geek suddenly became friendly. Even more amusing, Stepfather Ted now pretended to claim me as "his son" to his friends and co-workers, proudly taking credit for my acceptance to the Academy. On one occasion, he even dragged me in to his office to meet his boss. Secretly, I thought to myself, *I got this in spite of you, you bastard.*

Foolishly, I began to believe the whispers of my own ego, thinking that I had reached local celebrity status. *Pride cometh before a fall.* I was about to receive the shock of my life, followed by a four-year lesson in humility among top high school students from every part of the United States. Even if you were a top performer in high school, you will only be "average" at the Naval Academy. In addition, whatever weaknesses you have—whether they are physical, mental, or moral—they *will* be exposed and corrected.

Nevertheless, the Navy was my salvation—my ticket to independence out of an unhappy life that seemed to be headed nowhere. I had no way of knowing how exciting and challenging my life would become from this point forward. I was ordered to report to the Naval Academy on July 5, 1960. I could hardly wait to get there.

My mother did not share my joy at this turn of events. She only saw history repeating itself, and the possibility of losing another member of her family in combat, in some far-away place. She had no way of knowing how closely I would follow in my dad's footsteps.

~ ~ ~

## Chapter 3: *Plebe Year*

On July 5, 1960, about 1,300 young men and I were admitted to the U.S. Naval Academy and took the oath. My mom refused to come, leaving it to my Aunt Virginia to wave goodbye to me as I was swallowed up behind the monolithic entrance of Bancroft Hall, the huge dormitory that houses the 4,400 members of the Brigade of Midshipmen. By this time, I was well accustomed to my "orphan" status. Mom's absence made no difference to me. She had left me a long time ago.

A big flag encased in Memorial Hall was one of the first things shown to our new Class of 1964. It read: "DON'T GIVE UP THE SHIP." It was obviously hand-made, and appeared to have bullet holes and possibly bloodstains on it. It was the flag flown by Commodore Oliver H. Perry in the Battle of Lake Erie during the War of 1812 against Britain. The flag, with its inspirational message, commemorates the famous order given by the dying Captain Lawrence of *USS Chesapeake* in her ill-fated battle with *HMS Shannon* near Boston.

In seeing this old tattered flag, and hearing about its history, I was truly overwhelmed with a feeling of awe. The meaning of being a Midshipman here was starting to sink in for all of us. If we made it through, we would be links in that unbroken chain of graduates, including many great Navy and Marine Corps heroes, going back to the Academy's founding in 1845. Standing before this flag, you felt enormous personal responsibility and a determination to overcome any obstacles. We would soon learn that the Naval Academy would be providing *many* obstacles, on a daily basis, for us to measure our worth as future leaders. The battle to survive had begun, and about three hundred of these carefully selected young men—one fourth of the entering class—would not make it to the end. Charles Darwin would have been proud of this selective process. This was a place where only the fittest and most committed could survive.

As an institution, the Naval Academy knew from many decades of trial-and-error how to produce the desired human product. Nothing in a Midshipman's daily life was accidental. Everything had a purpose.

We were divided into regiments, then battalions, companies, platoons, and finally squads of about a dozen. We were assigned two or three to a room, where all of our clothes were neatly folded and stowed in a locker, subject to inspection at any time. The new Fourth Classmen (there were no women in those days), or "Plebes," were directed by screaming members of the Plebe Detail to perform the various induction phases, including close haircuts, issuance of uniforms, room assignments, and immediate instruction in saluting and marching.

The "Detail" was comprised of a specially selected cadre of top-performing juniors, or Second Classmen of the Class of 1962. They were a fearsome bunch, and they were frequently "in your face" with snarling commands and belittling criticisms. If you were easily offended, you got over it quickly.

Plebe Summer (called "Beast Barracks" at West Point), which lasted until the Brigade upperclassmen returned from their summer programs, was designed to give the Plebes the indoctrination and correct mindset to survive Plebe Year, and to get everyone in top physical condition. It was also designed to weed out those who did not have "the right stuff" or could not take the pressure. We lost quite a few during this time, who decided that this environment was not right for them.

Since I had been to boot camp the summer before as an enlisted man, I found the adjustment was not that hard. This was like a "gold-plated" boot camp. I was also in good shape, having prepared for this during my last year in high school. In addition, I could swim like a fish and had no trouble with the many hours we had to spend with various swimming drills. I actually enjoyed the summer, because I had found a life that was all mine, controlled by people that I respected. My Academy classmates became my family.

While some of my Plebe classmates felt their lives had changed for the worse, the austere Academy life was actually a significant upgrade from what I had experienced as a kid at home. What I was *not* prepared for was the return of the Brigade upperclassmen in late August.

In this era, the Naval Academy was in a state of transition. The traditional naval engineering curriculum was being expanded to include a variety of other academic disciplines. The external demands of the new NASA space program, missile technology, nuclear-powered ships, and the need for enhanced geopolitical skills were having their effect. Defending the United States was becoming a more complex process. It was still a "male only" culture, and the upperclassmen viciously hazed the Plebes. The unstated objective of the Naval Academy experience is to purge each Midshipman of the usual weaknesses of pampered youth, and rebuild each person with the leadership skills to lead Sailors or Marines in combat.

Life as a Midshipman was not only highly regimented—it was also defined by strict hierarchal boundaries of behavior and traditional protocols. Each Plebe received a small book, entitled *Reef Points*. It was essential for a Plebe to memorize everything in that book, if he wanted to survive. It consisted of dozens of naval quotations, historical facts, military organizational data, and some traditional, silly items that had to be recited by Plebes when asked, such as "How's the cow?" Upperclassmen ensured that each Plebe had mastered this nasty little book.

In Bancroft Hall, Plebes were required to walk at attention, or "in a brace," in the center of the passageways (halls), square all corners, and jog around the outside of all "ladders," or stairs. All corners had to be turned "squarely." Upon an upperclassman's command "Chop, Mister!" the Plebe was required to double-time (run) to his destination.

Other rules made the Plebe's life in 1960 more like being in prison or a monastery than attending an educational institution. For example, Plebes were forbidden to date women within the Seven-mile Limit around the Academy, or even talk to a female (other than a family member) within this jurisdictional zone.

Since you were not normally permitted to go outside of the Seven-mile Limit, you were effectively denied the pleasure of female companionship until away from the Academy on leave (Christmas, Spring Break, football games, etc.). Unless you were on one of these special leaves, you could not go further than seven miles from the Academy, or you would be considered AWOL (absent without leave), subject to harsh discipline.

The only "free" time to go outside the Yard (campus) itself was after noon meal on Saturday and after mandatory religious services on Sunday. Riding in cars was strictly forbidden for Plebes. Driving a car within the Seven-mile Limit was forbidden for all classes except for the First Class, who could do so only about two months before their graduation. Drinking alcoholic beverages within the Seven-mile Limit was universally prohibited for all classes. The difference between being in prison and attending the Naval Academy as a Plebe in those days was simple—at the Naval Academy, you had to march in step and salute! This ascetic, high-pressure environment tended to weed out those who lacked perseverance and the necessary commitment to the Naval Service.

For any failure of memory or discipline, for any or for no reason at all, the First Class (seniors) or Second Class (juniors) would order a Plebe to "come around." This meant that the Plebe had to appear in the upperclassman's room during one of two normal "come-around" periods. The first one was after reveille and before morning meal formation. The second was before evening meal formation at around 1730.

The dreaded "come-around" was where most of the serious hazing took place. The upperclassmen would carefully inspect the Plebe's uniform and shoes, and then barrage him with questions:

"Who was the British admiral in command at the Battle of Jutland?"
"Who won the 1955 World Series, and by how much?"
"What were the names of the ships commanded by John Paul Jones?"
"Who said, 'You may fire when ready, Gridley?'"
"Who commanded the Japanese Army during the battle for Singapore?"
"What was the name of the B-29 that dropped the bomb on Hiroshima?"
"What is the capital of Paraguay?"

"Name three major maritime choke-points, how each one became important in a war, and why."

There were also many trick questions:

"What is the name of Bolivia's sea port?" [There is none.]

"What are the names of each of the Soviet aircraft carriers?" [At the time, the Soviets did not have any.]

"What do you do if you are sitting next to an admiral's wife during a formal dinner, and you notice that one of her breasts has popped out of the top of her dress?" Required answer: "You warm your spoon in your coffee, and then use it to slip her breast carefully back into her dress, so that she does not notice." The implied message of this humorous answer was to emphasize that an officer had to be innovative and respond calmly in an emergency, no matter how much pressure there was.

Plebes were frequently sent on "suicide" missions by upperclassmen, to pull jokes on their own classmates. Even though the helpless Plebe was nothing more than a live "guided missile" in the prank, this would result in a barrage of come-arounds and would keep that Plebe in misery for weeks. I think this was designed to teach a Plebe to complete a mission, even if casualties were inevitable. Everything had a hidden purpose.

When a Plebe made a mistake, an upperclassman would ask, "Mister, why did you do that?" The only acceptable answer was, "No Excuse, Sir." For our class ('64), a Plebe frequently was ordered do 64 push-ups to show loyalty and commitment to his class. I have often wondered how the class of '99 fared when *they* tried to comply with this tradition.

A Plebe could never answer a question with "I don't know." The correct answer, if you did not know, was "I'll find out, Sir." The Plebe then had until the next come-around (or the next meal) to learn and respond with the answer. In the days before the Internet and Google, this usually meant running to the library to do research, or asking a friendly upperclassman—if there was one. One of the upperclassmen told me, "We don't care if you don't know everything—you just need to know where to find it quickly."

In addition to their demanding academic schedule, Plebes were required to remember all of the questions they had been asked, and to which upperclassman they owed a "come-around." This was "multi-tasking" at its worst, when combined with the academics. Nevertheless, I later discovered that keeping thousands of details in your short-term memory was how you survived in real combat. All of that Plebe misery had a legitimate purpose, but it did not seem so at the time.

The imperative of completing a difficult mission was exemplified to Midshipmen by "The Message to Garcia," an essay describing an incident in the Spanish-American War. President McKinley needed to communicate with a Cuban rebel leader—Garcia—before hostilities with Spain began. He tasked Col. Andrew Rowan, U.S. Army, to take his personal message. Rowan never asked, "Where is he?" or "How do I do it?" He simply took the order and completed the difficult mission, without whining. At West Point and Annapolis, the phrase "a message to Garcia" carries a special meaning of relentless personal commitment to the mission, and is drilled into every Plebe.

"Come-arounds" were not the only threat. Each Midshipman was allotted a maximum number of demerits according to his class, which were issued as punishment for an infraction of some regulation. In those days, the Plebes could go as high as 300, with 250 for the Youngsters, 200 for the Segundos, and 150 for the Firsties. Exceeding the number was grounds for expulsion from the Naval Academy, and the fewer demerits, the better the grade in "military conduct," which even affected class standing.

All upperclassmen had authority to issue "Form 2" infractions on the Plebes, resulting in a number of "demerits," as specified by a manual. For the upperclassmen, only a member of a class ahead of them could issue infractions. The First Class were at the top of the "food chain," and only received demerits from the commissioned officers who stood OOW (Officer of the Watch) duty or who served as Company or Battalion Officers. Thus, their demerit exposure was considerably less than the lower classes. The commissioned officers also issued demerits to the other classes when infractions were found. A penalty of ten demerits was typical of a minor offense, while 40 or more indicated a serious infraction, called a "class 'A'." Demerits were given freely, especially to the Plebes. Having a dirty room, poorly shined shoes, wrinkled uniform, bad haircut, or being late to formation were typical demerit items.

For the three underclasses, demerits had to be worked off by marching around like a rifle-carrying robot for supervised hours in "Goat Court," a desolate area between the wings of Bancroft Hall. The First Class worked them off by serving room restriction on the weekends.

If that were not enough, there was also "The Honor Concept," called the Honor Code at West Point and the Air Force Academy. Lying, cheating or stealing in any form, or "tolerating those who do" was strictly forbidden, and grounds for immediate dismissal. From time to time, even some good Midshipmen had moments of ethical weakness, and suffered the harsh consequences. The rationale for this system, which even required one Midshipman to turn in another, was to instill ironclad integrity and reliability in the chain-of-command relationships of future Naval and Marine officers throughout their careers.

The hazing in those days was very physical and sometimes brutal. In one company, about half of the Plebes resigned because of the harsh treatment. On one come-around, a First Classman from another company ordered me to "asymptote." This required a simulation of that geometric curve by putting your feet on the footer of the upperclassman's bed, and your hands on the headboard rail. This had you arched precariously over the bed, so being tall was an advantage.  "If you fall, Mister, you die," he said. "And if you drop any of your filthy sweat on my pillow, I'll kill you myself." I did well for about 10 minutes, and then felt my arms and legs begin to quiver, as a drop of sweat rolled down my nose. When the drop hit his pillow, he screamed, "*Now* you've done it! Put on your raingear, get in the shower and play handball!" I got into his shower, and began bouncing a handball around for the next five minutes, while he turned on the cold water. He finally let me go, and I fortunately never bumped into this psycho again.

One of the favorite hazing games was telling a Plebe, "Come around and bring your atlas." Every Midshipman was issued a world atlas, in order to learn world geography. When you reported to the upperclassman with the atlas, he took you out in the passageway, had you bend over, and tried to break the large book on your butt. It usually took several tries, which left large black-and-blue marks on your tail. A variation on this theme occurred when an upperclassman posed a trick question to a Plebe, who made the mistake of guessing the answer. "Mister, do you bet your ass?" If the Plebe did bet and was wrong, he got a come-around and brought his atlas for a butt pounding. The point of this game was to teach the Plebes never to guess in response to a superior's question, in order to give completely accurate information. A superior must be able to rely upon the word of a subordinate at all times.

One of the standard techniques of hazing was making the Plebe "shove out." This entailed squatting down until your thighs were horizontal. Even the strongest Plebes could only last about five minutes with this position. Push-ups and long-distance runs around Bancroft's 3½ miles of corridors were routine.

Another favorite torture was the "uniform race." Midshipmen had a mind-boggling array of uniform combinations, and upperclassmen would send Plebes racing back to their rooms to change into one uniform after another, and then stand for inspection to make sure they were "rigged" correctly. To this day, I refer to any rushed process as "a uniform race." A variation on this practice was an order to put on multiple sets of sweat gear, often topped by rain gear. After about ten sets, the Plebe would look like the roly-poly Michelin Man in the tire commercials, unable to move his arms.

The entire process was designed to teach the Plebes to ignore pain and stress, and not to give up or lose focus, regardless of how much they were hurting. During a winter blizzard, a First Classman ordered me to "run the rocks." This entailed running the entire periphery of Dewey and Farragut Fields, where huge, slippery boulders formed the seawall that marked the boundary with the Severn River and Annapolis Harbor. After I completed it, he realized I was not even winded, so he sent me out again. After doing the second and third runs in a freezing rain, I was finally wiped out and collapsed. He seemed pleased.

The day began for a Plebe when the reveille bell rang at 0615, and usually earlier. There were only a few minutes to shave, shower and get into the proper uniform, and then make the entire room ready for inspection.

The worst times were at the meal tables in King Hall. There, all 4,400 Midshipmen sat down to eat together three times per day. On a typical table, assigned by company, the Plebes sat on one side of the table. Across from them were the Youngsters, or Third Class (sophomores).

The Youngsters had no real authority over the Plebes, and generally tried to help keep them out of trouble. They had fresh memories of how horrible it was to be a Plebe.

At one end of the table, fully in charge, were the First Class (seniors). They normally had a more reasonable and mature approach toward the Plebes, and seemed to emphasize professional or academic questions. At the other end sat the fiendish Second Class (juniors). By tradition, they hazed the Plebes mercilessly, often with ridiculous orders and questions.

While at the table, the Plebes were required to sit at attention, on the edge of their chairs, and bring food to their mouths in square patterns. Eating from this erect posture inevitably resulted in food dropping on your uniform, which brought instant criticism from the upperclassmen for being "a pig." Proper table manners were a priority at all times.

The instant that an upperclassman spoke to a Plebe, he had to drop his utensils on his plate, stop eating, and sit at attention. If you got an upperclassman "on your ass," you could almost starve. You could be quizzed during most of the meal, with no time to eat. There were no alternative food sources then in Bancroft Hall. You hoped you would have a few scraps left on the table to eat after the upperclassmen departed. Otherwise, the pickings were slim. As I joined a group of Plebes grabbing for the table leftovers one evening, I thought to myself, *We have become a pack of wild dogs.*

As soon as you left the table at breakfast and lunch, you were on a race to square away your room, find the right books, and rush to class across the campus, or "Yard." The Plebe courses challenged even the best students: college-level mathematics, engineering drawing, English composition and literature, calculus, chemistry, geometry, foreign language, statistics, and physical education, comprising about 22 semester hours.

Academic classes at the Naval Academy were (and still are) a distinctly different experience than a young person had at a civilian university or college. The class instruction, like everything at the Academy, is intense and demanding. The small class size (about 12-15) gives the professor ample time to focus on *you*. You *always* know that you will be called upon to discuss the assigned material, or will go to the blackboard to show how you got the answer to a homework problem. There are constant quizzes and tests, just to make sure you are "getting it." There is no way to "coast" through a class at the Naval Academy, because the pressure is always on. In every class, there is always someone smarter than you are, making *you* look stupid.

There were four academic "periods" in the morning, followed by a close personnel inspection at the spit-and-polish noon meal formation. This was another opportunity for a Plebe to get in trouble, especially at the tables in the huge mess hall.

Immediately after the last afternoon class of the day, there was a two-hour period for military drills, and/or intramural or varsity sports. *Every* Midshipman was required to play a sport—you could not simply go back to your room and study or sleep. The athletic period was followed by a Plebe come-around period and evening meal, after which study hour went until "Plebe lights out" at 2200. That gave you about 2½ hours to study and complete academic assignments. Many Plebes found it necessary to study under a blanket with a flashlight or in the shower stall, in order to keep up with the intense academics. As in a combat environment, there was never enough time to get everything done.

The best solution for this onerous existence was on the athletic field, where you could interact with the upperclassmen without the usual formalities. If you did not play a varsity sport, you had to sign up for one of the intramural sports, where the twenty-four companies and six battalions competed against each other. I quickly found out that an intramural sport at the Naval Academy is like a varsity sport elsewhere, because everyone (except me) was formerly a high school varsity athlete. For example, one of my roommates was a former High School All-American football player.

Being a loner, I found cross-country and track to be a good fit. However, I developed stress fractures in both legs, resulting in boot casts and crutches. For six weeks, this made hiking from Bancroft to classes a painful experience.

Those Plebes who participated in the "important" varsity sports like football, track, cross-country, basketball, soccer, lacrosse, baseball, wrestling, or swimming were allowed to eat separately with their teams without "bracing up," instead of enduring the hazing of the company tables. The varsity team members also got special "training meals," which were considerably better than the normal fare. These Plebes, like one of my roommates, always looked healthier than the rest of us because they were able to eat without harassment. Being a gifted athlete really paid off. Many of us supplemented our food with "care packages" from girl friends or family members.

The new Second Class (class of '62) had apparently attended training at the Marquis de Sade Institute of Plebe Abuse, because they were especially motivated to cause us pain. The new Firsties ('61) watched our hazing with quiet approval.

Luckily, I was befriended and "spooned" (put on a first-name basis) by one of the Second Class in my company, who was a member of the Drum and Bugle Corps. Learning of my extensive music background, he recruited me to join the Drum and Bugle Corps, which ate together like the varsity teams. That became my attempt to escape from the Gulag of my company's tables. This Segundo was very smart, but his "grease" (military aptitude ranking) was terrible. He spoke fluent Russian, and was an electronics nut. One day, just prior to the Air Force game in Baltimore, he asked me if I wanted to participate in a major operation against the Zoomies (Air Force Academy cadets). How could I say no?

We dressed up the Drum and Bugle Corps in fake uniforms, and papered over the bass drum with the logo "Goucher College AFROTC Drum & Bugle Corps." (Goucher was a women's college.) After playing a hideous rendition of "Up we go, into the wild blue yonder....." in front of the Zoomie stands, we peeled off the fake jackets and showed the USNA flag, playing *Anchors Aweigh*. Very cool, and relatively harmless.

The real caper was yet to come. During half time, the Zoomies brought out their trained falcons for an air show. My Second Class mentor had found out that they use high-frequency dog whistles to signal the birds and retrieve them. He and his buddies had used the electronics lab to create a high-frequency oscillator and powerful amplifier system that would duplicate, or "jam" the Zoomies' dog whistle signals. They brought this gear in trucks behind the stands, and hooked up to a powerful generator in one of the trucks. Using a converted bullhorn, complete with an added gun sight, my mentor and his pals took aim at the birds and waited.

One of the Zoomie trainers threw a string with bait out on the field and called one of the birds down from his orbit. As the bird swooped down, our "sniper" team squeezed off a burst of inaudible sound. It was apparently *very* audible to the bird, who looked like he had been hit by a Sea Sparrow missile. He did several aileron rolls, and skidded to a landing near the 50-yard line, leaving a line of feathers. He then flew off in the direction of New York, never to be seen again. The other bird got it next, and he landed on the scoreboard and refused to return to his trainers. The Zoomies never found out what happened.

Bill the Goat, the Naval Academy mascot, thus got his revenge for various Zoomie goat-napping attempts, including one in which Bill was captured and flown all the way to the Air Force Academy at Colorado Springs on an Air force cargo plane. These attempts became so frequent that Bill finally had to be kept at the Naval Academy dairy, guarded by a squad of Marines. It was rumored that Bill had a "body double" that made public appearances for him while he remained hidden from view in a secret, undisclosed location.

*Bill the Fifteenth, the Navy mascot of that era. He was especially evil-tempered, and frequently butted anyone who walked within striking distance. The handlers finally had to fit rubber balls to the tips of his horns to prevent serious injury to bystanders.*

A few months later, my Second Class mentor emerged from obscurity and became quite a celebrity. Because he was president of the Russian Club and spoke fluent Russian, he was able to arrange for the noon meal visit of the Soviet Naval Attaché from the Soviet Embassy in Washington. It was quite a dramatic scene, as he proudly escorted this Soviet admiral to his table. None of us had ever seen a real Russian before, and here he was, having lunch with us! This one  looked like a character from a James Bond movie, complete with bald head and Khrushchev-like face. I was seated at an adjacent table, braced up as usual, next to the First Class end. The Firstie next to me leaned over with a grin and said, "Nelson, see that Russian admiral over there?"

"Yes, Sir."

"OK, this is a *message to Garcia*, lad. I want you to take this bowl of mashed potatoes over there and Wild Man that Commie bastard." In the event that this quaint custom is not common knowledge, here is how it works: you would slip up behind the targeted individual, dump a bowl of food on his head, and massage it in his hair while yelling, "Wild man, wild man, Sir!" This normally resulted in several years' worth of come-arounds and vicious retribution from the upper-classman who was the victim. In this case, however, the victim would be a Russian admiral, and there would be more than just a few come-arounds involved after he received a bowl of mashed potatoes on his head.

I was well aware that this Firstie was trying to be funny, but I thought it was time he learned that orders should not be given frivolously, especially to an unpredictable Plebe like me. I replied "Aye, aye, Sir!" and bolted from the table with the mashed potatoes, heading for the Russian admiral.

"Nelson, STOP!!" he screamed, realizing that World War III was about to be triggered by his order. At the very last second, I veered away from the Russian, and did a wide victory lap around the nearby tables, to the cheers of all hands. An international incident had been narrowly averted, and I had saved the Free World from yet another nuclear crisis. It was clear that I possessed an early aptitude for Cold War foreign relations and diplomacy.

Plebe Year in those days was like Dante's Inferno, but we had a few good moments. Our football team beat Army (thanks to Joe Bellino, '61, a Heisman winner), we went to the Orange Bowl, and we marched in JFK's Inaugural Parade.

At the end of the Army-Navy game, tradition required that the Plebes from both Academies meet on the football field and exchange one cufflink. This trophy had to be worn by the Plebes as a reminder of the bond between West Point and Annapolis. Failure to make this trade would bring the wrath of upperclassmen on the wayward Plebe.

For beating Army, the Naval Academy Plebes got "carry-on" through the end of the calendar year, which was wonderful. No bracing up, and no square corners. For a while, we felt almost human again. Then the Dark Ages (from the end of

Christmas leave to Spring Break) set in, and the First Class began looking for their Hundredth Night victims, including me.

A time-honored Naval Academy milestone occurs 100 days before First Class graduation. On that evening, the roles of Plebes and Firsties are reversed. Plebes assume the powers of the First Class, and haze them unmercifully for one night. In anticipation of that event, each First Classman tries to determine which Plebe is "gunning" for him, at the beginning of the Dark Ages. The First Classmen put maximum pressure on the Plebes in order to induce a Plebe to issue a Hundredth Night "come-around." Once a Plebe has issued a "come-around," the targeted First Classman makes that Plebe's life a special misery.

When the magic evening of Hundredth Night arrived, I ran my Firstie until he almost had a heart attack. Now that I think about it, perhaps that was my objective. This guy was a vicious little twit, and I made him pay the price for making my life miserable during the preceding weeks.

When the study hour bell finally rang, there was a big cheer throughout Bancroft. The Firsties were overjoyed to have survived our hazing, and we were secretly glad that they would soon be graduating and out of our lives. At the same time, the upperclassmen shifted their focus to the next set of shoulder boards, and most of the hazing stopped.

In the tradition marking the end of Plebe Year, one of our class climbed the greased Herndon Monument, replaced a Plebe hat with an upperclassman's hat, and we were emancipated. Those of us who remained had made it through Plebe Year at the Naval Academy, an unforgettable lifetime experience.

It would be many years before I had the maturity and life experience to understand the incalculable value of that year, and how it helped me later to get through many difficult and dangerous situations. It was one of the most important years of education that I ever had, and I am grateful for it.

In a strange way, the Naval Academy provided me with a multi-faceted, paternal force that I had desperately needed, but lost when my dad was killed. I remember thinking that he would have been proud that I made it through this first test on the way to manhood.

~ ~ ~

# Chapter 4: *Trivial Pursuits and Youngster Year*

The Class of 1964 had completed the hellacious Plebe Year, and we were now Third Class, or Youngsters (sophomores). Nevertheless, we were still held captive by the smothering embrace of "Mother Bancroft," the traditional name for the Bancroft Hall dormitory.

During the summers between academic years, Midshipmen are required to participate in various programs, which give them exposure to the different units of the Navy and the Marine Corps. During my time at the Naval Academy, the new Youngsters served aboard a Navy ship in the role of enlisted men. About thirty of us were assigned to an old destroyer, and the senior enlisted Petty Officers could hardly wait to give us a taste of how it feels to be a "White Hat," or Sailor. Essentially, this was another phase of Plebe Year, which we all thought was over. We got every dirty job the old ship had to offer, and she had plenty. My wife wonders why even today, I hate the sight of a mop, a paint brush, or a paint chipper.

During the cruise, we steamed up the Hudson River, past West Point, all the way to Albany. On the way, we passed the Statue of Liberty, as my Swedish grandfather had done 58 years before. It was an interesting trip, but our next port call would be even more fun: Miami!

When we arrived in Miami, we were surprised to learn that we would be assigned as escorts to contestants in the 1961 Miss Universe Contest. Because I spoke fluent Spanish, I was assigned to Miss Spain, a breathtaking beauty from Madrid. We appeared with the contestants at the Coronation Ball, and found ourselves, at the age of 19, dancing and having dinner with some of the most beautiful women in the world.

By the next day, we were back to harsh reality and aboard our rusty old destroyer, heading back to Annapolis. After a few weeks of leave, we arrived back in Bancroft Hall. Now we were watching a new crop of Plebes get "the treatment."

Compared to Plebe Year, Youngster Year was academically more difficult. We plowed rapidly through courses like advanced calculus, probability and statistics, modern European history, physics, engineering materials, U.S. foreign policy and geography, and languages.

A few more classmates became victims of these academic monsters, which were taking their toll. I did fairly well, and maintained a high "B" average, which put me in about the top third of the class. At the Boat School, there was no "grading on the curve" and there were no "pass-fail" courses. Even the physical education course was graded. You received your "raw" score only, without statistical adjustment.

In those days, a Midshipman failed out if he received less than 2.5 (out of 4.0) in *any* course, including physical education. You got one chance to take a re-exam, and then you were *out*. There were a few cases where a Midshipman was "turned back," or allowed to repeat that year, but that was rare and only done where the Midshipman was outstanding in all other aspects.

One of our company classmates, an ex-Marine, was having trouble with calculus and physics. He failed the final exams, and was granted a "re-take." He had studied hard, but these courses were his nemesis and he knew it. He thought he had a chance on the calculus exam, but he knew the physics test would get him. Since that test was multiple-choice, his solution was to carve a letter in five sides of a hexagonal pencil. For each question, he rolled the pencil until he got a letter on the top side, and used that for his answer. He actually *passed* the physics test with this random method,  but *failed* the calculus test, where he thought he *had* accurately solved the problems. He was terminated.

One fall evening, I heard loud cheers from the south side of the Sixth Wing. I looked out from a classmate's window on that side, and realized there was a "para-mice" contest going on. Two companies had challenged each other to a duel, after secretly keeping cages of mice in their rooms. Expert technicians from each side had constructed small parachutes and harnesses, from which the four-legged jumpers dangled. At the command of a neutral referee, the mice were dropped and would land in the courtyard below, where Plebes retrieved them back to the fourth deck (floor). This was repeated until one mouse competitor was unable to jump, when the other one was then declared the winner. One of these unlucky rodents, named "Geronimo," had nearly 100 jumps and multiple victories under his belt. He was a pro, and the envy of all the para-mice jumpmasters. Geronimo was heavily favored in the mouse betting pool.

Then, after several jumps by Geronimo, I heard a shout: "Streamer! Look out below!" Geronimo's chute failed to open, and he was hurtling toward the concrete. Our eyes followed his trajectory, and saw that Marine Major John Love ('51), one of the sternest of all Company Officers, was exiting the door below. Geronimo hit the sidewalk at terminal velocity right in front of the Major's spit-shined shoes. There was a sound of windows closing as the Marine looked up for the culprits. The jumpmasters were never caught. Geronimo was buried at sea in a solemn ceremony near Triton Light, with full honors, including a Plebe Honor Guard, and one of the Drum & Bugle Corps members playing "Taps." I get choked up even today, just thinking about his bravery. Geronimo was a legend in his own time.

In the days of 24 companies (later, 36), my company—the Nineteenth—had earned a reputation as a rather motley crew of incorrigibles, and the nickname "Night Crawlers." This came from a famous caper in which the Night Crawlers used the old underground steam tunnels during June Week to make their way at night out to the parade grounds on Worden Field. Once there, they moved the company markers and prevented the last several companies from having room to line up across the field. "The Lost Battalion" stopped awkwardly behind the Brigade, with a lot of laughing. The VIPs and the Superintendent were not amused. To further demonstrate their expertise, the Night Crawlers cut the tie-downs on the A-4 Skyhawk static display that was tethered down near Dahlgren Hall, and pushed the aircraft all the way over to a new resting place in the Superintendent's residence driveway.

As the Army-Navy game approached, things became difficult for those unlucky officers that were exchanged between the Academies. We learned our Navy company exchange officer at West Point was being unmercifully harassed. It was time to settle that score.

After the end of study hour, several of the Night Crawlers met at the front of Dahlgren Hall, where the door was decorated with a pair of huge 16-inch diameter shells along either side. Like the Egyptians building the pyramids, we slowly rolled and maneuvered the heavy battleship projectiles over to a side door to Bancroft, and took the shells up in the elevator, along with one of the Yard's old cannons. One of our crew picked the lock on the door to the Army exchange officer's office, and the shells and cannon were placed appropriately inside. How he got them out of there is still a mystery.

A week later, another Special Ops team placed a donkey in his office (they could not locate a real mule), complete with bales of hay. The little burro got claustrophobic during the night, and kicked a few holes in the walls to make his point. He also seemed to dislike his ride in the elevator. As a parting gift, the angry animal left an assortment of smelly "trail markers" the next morning to greet the Army exchange officer.

During Youngster Year, I was almost terminated from the Academy. My two roommates were taking their annual physical when one of the Medical Department staff overheard them discussing my nightly respiratory problems, including loud snoring. The staffer informed the Medical Director, who concluded that I had asthma or allergies—a disqualifying condition.

Although a thorough physical exam showed no symptoms, the Academy Medical Director, a Navy Captain M.D., was convinced that I should never have been admitted to the Academy and had "falsified the entrance paperwork." I pointed out that I was running track and cross-country, so how could I have asthma? The Medical Director replied, "You guys with lung problems learn to compensate, and you probably don't need as much oxygen." *Who gave this guy his medical degree?*

With no medical evidence to support his allegation, he then sent me for a psychiatric exam, on the theory that my alleged "asthma" was caused by psychological problems from Academy stress. However, to the Director's dismay, the shrink concluded that I was a "normal Midshipman" (whatever *that* is), and referred me back to the Medical Director. Obviously, this shrink—certifying *me* as normal—was obviously incompetent.

In an episode that probably contributed to the formation of my rebellious attitude, the Director scheduled me for a "medical survey," meaning a medical discharge from the Service. I was in a state of shock. I realized that my childhood dream of graduating from the Naval Academy was destroyed. However, I quickly adjusted and was accepted to Columbia's School of International Affairs for the next semester. Through the connections of one of my uncles, I obtained a tentative slot with the U.S. Foreign Service upon my graduation from Columbia. The future was bright again. However *[Career tip!]*, you are often unaware of what is lurking just over the horizon, and your best-laid plans and calculations can become instantly obsolete.

My Aunt Virginia heard of my imminent departure, and complained to her friend and neighbor, Rear Admiral Hughes, the same admiral that helped me obtain the Academy appointment through the Naval Reserve. Without my knowledge, the Admiral called the Academy Medical Director, and bluntly ordered him *not* to discharge me. Just as I was about to depart Bancroft Hall, with my bags packed, I received a note to report to the Medical Director. When I entered his office, the Director glared at me and said, "I don't appreciate people that play politics and pull strings, Nelson." When I asked what he was talking about, he said, "You *know* what I'm talking about! You got Admiral Hughes to save your butt. OK, you have your wish—we are going to keep you for some additional observation."

"How long will that be, Sir? I have to start at Columbia in a couple of weeks."

"Oh, about *two and a half years*, I suppose. But after you graduate from here, you *will* be a civilian."

I returned to my room and unpacked in a state of emotional confusion. I was not sure, at this point, whether I was happy or disappointed. Initially, they labeled me as "NPQ," or Not Physically Qualified for commissioning. Then, my nemesis—the Director—retired, and the Medical Department lost interest in making me a civilian. Soon, they qualified me for Surface Warfare or the Marine Corps, and finally, by First Class year, I passed the aviation physical. That guaranteed my Navy Air slot. I was back on track.

One of the wonderful new privileges of being an upperclassman was being able to "drag," or date girls within the Seven-mile Limit. In our hormone-driven enthusiasm, now released from Plebe Year's restrictions, we rarely missed an opportunity to meet girls and establish "relationships." In those days, civilian residents of Annapolis found a lucrative opportunity in registering their homes with the Academy as "drag houses," and renting space to our female imports.

There were only a few hotels in Annapolis back then, and they were very expensive. Every weekend, hundreds of young women (termed "drags") needed a place to stay while in town. A typical drag house would contain as many as 8-10 women each weekend. Drag house owners were supposed to act as chaperones, to keep things under control. At the most popular houses, the owners would quietly leave for the evening.

Not too different from the fraternity house shenanigans in a civilian university, the Midshipmen found the drag houses to be a permissive atmosphere for their pent-up lust. Nevertheless, privacy was in short supply. On Saturday nights, most drag houses were completely blacked out, with their floors and furniture covered in writhing bodies. Many a future warrior had his manhood tested there first, in a perfume-intensive version of close-quarters combat. Johnnie Mathis records played endlessly and a murmuring of moans and assorted primal sounds filled the air. It is amazing how loud the sound of a zipper can be in a dark room. Occasionally, you would hear some of the louder participants in the midst of their rutting struggles, forgetting, in their passion, how close their fellow floor-dwellers were:

"Honey, please don't! We can't! Not until we're engaged!"

"Gary, what are you *doing?*"

"David, this isn't the right time of the month!"

"Bob, I can't find my bra!"
"That's not so bad—I can't find my underwear."

"Honey, it's OK—I'll use something!"
"Jack, make sure you don't put it on backwards again!"

"Please, Mary, I really love you—besides, I only have fifteen minutes to get back to Bancroft!"

"Jeff, stop! That's my armpit!"

Although I disliked the lack of privacy in the drag house environment, I managed to meet several nice young women during the year. One of them was the gorgeous young daughter of an admiral. Dating this deadly debutante prepared me well for future combat. Out of eternal respect for her image, I will refer to her as "Jennifer," which, of course, is not her real name.

Jennifer was only 18, but in terms of sophistication, she was going on 40. Her life as a Navy "junior" (the equivalent of an Army "brat") had prepared her well for conquering the men in her life. She was clever, beautiful, and a classic *femme fatale,* as the French would say. She knew how to manipulate men, including her dad. He was a hero of the World War II Submarine Service, and an Academy graduate. After he found out I was dating Jennifer, he invited me down to the Norfolk Naval Base for a weekend so he could look me over and let me know he was keeping an eye on me.

Knowing this was a "command performance," I prepared for the long weekend in Norfolk as if I were going into battle. I made sure I had clothes for every occasion, and some little gifts for Jennifer's mom. This was going to be my finest hour.

Instead of inviting me to stay at their house, the Admiral reserved a room for me in the Bachelor Officers Quarters (BOQ) inside the NATO compound, where the admirals' quarters were located. *Just like Bancroft Hall*, I thought. This arrangement kept me safely away from Jennifer. *Thanks, Admiral!*

On Friday evening, the Admiral and his wife took Jennifer and me with them during their social calls on other senior officers. I noticed that the Admiral and his wife always left the correct number of calling cards at each house in the ubiquitous silver card tray near the door. They would introduce us, have one perfunctory cocktail, and leave within 15 minutes for the next stop. *What a strange way to live!* The Admiral referred to this as "doing the rounds." It was very superficial, and did not seem like much fun. The Admiral's wife kept careful records of which officers they had called on, and who owed them a "card call." She told me that an officer's failure to comply with this protocol could show a lack of etiquette and jeopardize a future promotion.

By the Admiral's clever design, I never had any time alone with Jennifer, and wound up returning to the BOQ by 9:00 p.m. each night. On the last day, we all went out to the Admiral's vacation house and had a nice day at the beach, where I at least had a chance to stare at Jennifer in her bikini. During lunch, the Admiral asked me what my career plans were, and I told him I wanted to be a Naval Aviator. He frowned. "I lost a lot of classmates doing that," he said disapprovingly. "You should consider nuclear subs. That's where the real career opportunities are."

Realizing I had to be careful not to offend him, I said, "Thank you, Sir. I will do that. Perhaps I can talk to you in the future about how to prepare for that academically, and who I might contact to learn more about the Submarine Service." He liked that response, and I could tell I had scored points. Jennifer winked and smiled at me from across the room.

After I got back to Bancroft, I called Jennifer and asked her how she thought it went. She replied, "My dad thinks you are just a typical Youngster [sophomore]." *So much for making great impressions.*

When Jennifer visited Annapolis to see me, the Admiral required her to stay at the majestic residence of the Academy Superintendent, a friend of his, instead of the passion pit environment of the drag houses. Very smart—no wonder he was an admiral. He obviously remembered from his days at the Academy how the drag houses operated. Now I *really* had to behave myself. However, I did have the great privilege of getting to know the Superintendent and his family. They were very gracious and kind to a lowly Midshipman.

When spring break weekend came up, I headed to Arlington, Virginia, to stay with my Uncle Bob and Aunt Helen. After checking with my aunt and uncle, I invited Jennifer to stay with us for the weekend. My uncle, who was counsel for a congressional committee, was taking my aunt to a big dinner party in Washington. My two cousins were staying with friends. The setup was perfect. All I needed now for a night of unlimited passion was Jennifer's arrival, as she had promised.

When she failed to show up, I called her parents' home in Norfolk and spoke with the Admiral's wife. "Oh, Jennifer is at a beach party. I'll tell her you called." I became very angry. I thought to myself, *The little bitch stood me up! Time to have a drink!*

After my fourth rum and Coke, I decided it was time to call *all* of my old girl friends. Each time, as if by a diabolical plan, the girl's mother answered, telling me the daughter was out on a date! Finally, I called the last one, and as I was telling the woman how much I still loved her daughter, I fell off the bar stool onto the floor, breaking my glass. I remember lying there, semi-conscious, hearing a woman's distant voice. "Dick! Are you all right?" The phone was on the floor, next to my head.

"Oh, yes, I'm just fine. Tell Sandra I will be thinking about her." I got up off the floor and staggered down the stairs to my basement bedroom. I crawled onto the bed and passed out.

About an hour later, I woke up and realized I was going to be very sick. I puked directly on the floor, which was covered with a very expensive Persian rug. I ran into the bathroom, and repeated my body's violent rejection of the rum and Cokes several times. I stood in the cold shower, sobering up. After I cleaned up the bathroom, I realized the big rug was impossible to clean. There was only one solution, which was to stuff it into my aunt's washing machine. I stupidly thought, *She'll never know this happened.*

I jammed the bulky rug into the washer and turned it on. After a few revolutions, the machine's motor was destroyed, and it ground to a halt. I then threw the rug into the utility tub and scrubbed it down. It finally looked clean, but now the problem was how to dry it out. In my alcoholic haze, I remembered that my aunt had a clothesline about 50 feet outside of the basement door. I trudged out the door and over to the line, pulling the rug through the snow, and then hung it up to dry. That is when I realized I was out in the snow, cold and barefoot, and clad only in my underwear. I returned to the scene of the crime and fell asleep.

The next morning, I could barely climb the stairs, but made it to the breakfast table, where my aunt and uncle were glaring at me. My aunt spoke first: "Your uncle cut his finger when he cleaned up the glass you broke, Dickie Lee!"

"I am sorry, Uncle Bob. Is there anything I can do?"

My aunt chimed in, "Yes, I want you to look at what is hanging on my clothesline!"

I looked out the window, and saw a barf-stained Persian rug hanging over the line, frozen solid. It was a disgusting sight, and I wondered who could have done such a thing. My footprints were still visible in the snow, and that was very incriminating evidence. I decided there was not much chance of pleading insanity or mistaken identity.

"And that's not all! You broke my washing machine!"

"Uhh, well, of course I'll pay for that, Aunt Helen. I'm sorry, but Jennifer stood me up and I drank a little too much." It was a long time before I was invited back.

After the "lost weekend," Jennifer and I parted ways. By chance, I bumped into her during the next summer at the Little Creek Naval Base O'Club. She stuck her patrician nose in the air and pretended not to remember me when I said hello. She then informed me that she was engaged to a Naval officer (*God help him!*) who was assigned to a ship at the Norfolk Naval Base. At age 20, she had now made the "big time." I realized that I was probably only one of many young men with a broken heart that had fallen victim to her coquettish, manipulative ways and had competed unsuccessfully for her affection. Such experiences, while painful, are still useful, because they teach you to form better relationships in the future. It is part of growing up, and I needed to do a lot of that.

Finally, the class of '62 graduated, threw their caps in the air, and became new Navy Ensigns or Marine Second Lieutenants. Simultaneously, we moved up to become new Second Classmen. Power was finally within our grasp. First, we were off to experience the adventures of Second Class Summer.

This was one of the more interesting programs in the entire four years. In our Academy era, we split the summer between Naval Aviation and the Marines. First, they issued us Marine utilities, a helmet and a rifle, and loaded us aboard a couple of old troop transport ships. We arrived off the beaches at Little Creek, Virginia, and under the close supervision of Marine sergeants, we climbed down rope ladders into landing craft and stormed the beach, just like in a John Wayne movie. We were required to get over beach obstacles, like barbed wire, and perform unit assaults on "enemy" positions. Since no one was actually shooting at us, it was a lot of fun and our Marine instructors were impressive. We also were briefed by the Marine Recon personnel, who are highly trained special operations warriors similar to Navy SEALs.

Next, we toured the various Naval Aviation commands, and rode in several different types of aircraft. During a ride in a jet trainer, a TF-9 Cougar, my instructor allowed me to fly the aircraft in a simulated dogfight with another TF-9. That was the moment when I became really hooked on flying jets. It just felt *right,* and I knew that I would be good at it.

All too soon, that great summer and our few weeks of personal leave were over. It was back to Bancroft Hall, and many new challenges were waiting for us *and* for our country.

~ ~ ~

# Chapter 5: *Second Class Year—Academic Hell*

Upon our return to the Yard, we faced the dreaded Second Class academic year. For two years, we had listened to each Second Class group bemoaning the mental tortures of this bloated package of deadly courses. We received our class schedules, and I saw a formidable array of difficult subjects: thermodynamics, electrical science, differential equations, spherical trigonometry, navigation, terminal ballistics, U.S. government, target intercept analysis, economics, and public speaking. Traditionally, this was the academic year that caused the highest attrition rate. Nevertheless, I initially did much better than I expected. I still maintained a "B" average, but found electrical science subjects increasingly difficult. Some people easily see the world as a two-dimensional circuit diagram, but my brain increasingly perceived the world as a blurred collage of issues and abstract theories. Perhaps the lawyer in me was starting to take over.

In addition, we continued to have physical education as a graded subject. We were constantly doing swimming drills, in preparation for the demanding swimming tests of First Class Year, which included the dreaded high tower jump. If a Midshipman could not pass the rigorous swimming tests, he was placed on "the sub squad." These poor souls had to report to the swimming coach several times per week until they passed. If they still could not pass, they were terminated from the Academy. If you want to graduate from the Naval Academy, either you *can* swim, or you will *learn* to swim. There are no exceptions.

On one drill, we were required to swim for 40 minutes without touching the sides of the gigantic pool. Another classmate and I were good swimmers, and decided to play a joke on the instructor. At the middle of the pool was a wooden barrier that formed a partition and walkway. It was a hollow box structure that was supported by a steel frame. There was an air pocket inside of it, but you had to dive down to the deep pool bottom and swim up inside the structure to reach the air.

The two of us waited until the instructor was looking the other way, then dove down about 15 feet and came up inside the walkway barrier. The hardest part was trying to keep from laughing and being discovered in our hiding place. With about three minutes to go, we dove back down, cleared the barrier and swam up inside the group of exhausted swimmers, having rested for a luxurious 30 minutes. At the end of the drill, the instructor proved he was smarter than we were. "OK, you all passed. Except for you, Nelson, and your buddy over there. You two wise guys owe me another 40 minute swim, so I'll see you here on Saturday afternoon at 1400." *Another weekend ruined!* I knew that my date for the weekend was going to be very upset, but I thought she would like to watch an exciting 40-minute swim.

In October, we became aware of the Cuban Missile Crisis. The Soviets had placed ballistic missiles in Cuba, loaded with nuclear warheads. President

Kennedy issued an ultimatum to Premier Khrushchev to remove the missiles, and then "quarantined" Cuba with a naval blockade. This was purely a Navy show.

As the crisis escalated, rumors were spreading throughout the Brigade that the Second and First Classes might be graduated early, commissioned, and sent to Fleet units. We all had trouble keeping our eye on the academic ball because of this distraction. However, the crisis was resolved and the Soviet missiles were removed. Now it was back to the academic grind.

Navigation was another insidious course, and more difficult than it first appeared. There was a final exam in which you plotted the course for an imaginary ship around some difficult waters, taking star fixes, computing tides, and trying to avoid a navigation error. Any error tended to compound itself, frequently causing a failing grade.

The year before, a Second Classman inherited a sizeable part of his family's tobacco fortune. He no longer found himself motivated to make the Navy a career, and wanted out of the Academy. However, if you resigned, the Navy placed you on active duty as an enlisted man. If you failed out after your first two years, you merely had to be an enlisted rank in the inactive Naval Reserve for a few years, which was harmless enough. This was his situation, but he did not want to fail a transferable "civilian" course and damage his academic record for transferring credits to a civilian university. He decided to fail one of the professional courses and chose navigation, figuring that this course would not matter to a civilian school.

On the day of his exam, the would-be escapee committed deliberate and flagrant mistakes. He placed his hand on the chart and drew the ship's course around his fingers. He then accomplished a five-star fix that placed the ship's position on a mountaintop. For good measure, he ran the fictional ship *aground* several times. As expected, he failed the course.

When the grades were published, his Battalion Officer, LtCol Twisdale, called him in. "Mister, you failed navigation, and we know what you are trying to pull. We heard about your inheritance. Son, do you realize your Academy education is worth a million dollars?"

The failed navigator perked up, pulled a checkbook and pen from his pocket, and said, "What was that amount again, Sir?" He was permitted to leave the Academy soon afterward, and is probably enjoying the life of a multi-millionaire today. His legend is eternal.

Because of the diverse and difficult subjects included in the Naval Academy curriculum, most Midshipmen stumbled on one or more courses during their four years. My downfall was electronics. For some reason, I found the diagrams of transistor circuits to be a bewildering puzzle.

During my years at the Academy, each Midshipman was required to take the "basic" curriculum, which led to a Bachelor of Science in electrical engineering. For those who desired to major in another academic area, the Academy required them to take sufficient "overload" courses that would qualify as an *additional* major. For me, that was foreign languages. During the first two years, I had "validated," or skipped the required language courses because of my fluency in the Spanish language. I took "overload" courses instead. I became interested in learning Japanese, and had a special course arranged through the Foreign Service Institute. However, after my barely-passing grades from the electronics course were published, I was pulled out of the "overload" curriculum. Luckily, I already had enough advanced language credits to complete the double major.

In the spring, all language majors received notice of a special summer program, instead of the usual assignment to the surface fleet in a junior officer role. I had no desire to ride around on another destroyer all summer, so I signed up for the special program.

We were offered selection opportunities for a list of foreign countries that used the language of our major. I won a spot, along with one other classmate, for summer assignment to the Peruvian navy.

After the class of '63 graduated, I inherited the balance of my father's trust fund. Now in possession of great riches (about $20,000), I could not wait to spend it. My first purchase was a new Austin-Healey 3000 convertible. I drove it at supersonic speed all the way home to Sarasota and left it for my return from Peru.

Along with the other selected Midshipman, I departed for Lima, Peru. We were met at the airport by a Peruvian naval officer, who would be our supervisor for the summer. We were first assigned to the Peruvian submarine force, and stayed in relative luxury in their naval base BOQ. In Peru, military officers were part of the ruling elite and enjoyed an upscale lifestyle.

One day, the Peruvians took us out on one of their three submarines, which  were very modern diesel boats (submariners refer to their vessels as "boats" instead of "ships"), made in the U.S. They originally had four, but one sank with all hands after colliding with a large fishing net. They were quite proud of these boats, which they said were needed to neutralize the Chilean navy, one of their bitter foes in the War of the Pacific in the 1800s. I asked one of the Peruvian officers why they needed submarines, and he replied, "To sink the Chilean surface fleet."

After clearing the port of Callao, the sub initiated a dive to 300 feet. My classmate and I were not going into submarines after graduation, and we felt a little apprehensive about being in this metal tube, far below the surface.

The Captain invited us to have lunch with him, so we sat down with most of the officers in their little wardroom. The most junior officer was assigned to "have the con," or manage the ship during lunch.

Just as we were enjoying the delicious Peruvian food, the sub suddenly went into an emergency dive, causing water to spill on us from an overhead pipe. The

Captain raced for the control room to see what had happened. It turned out that the young Ensign had panicked when he learned the sub was near a fishing trawler, and decided to dive well below the level of its nets. The officers were very embarrassed, and the unfortunate Ensign received a strong reprimand. I was now sure that I *never* wanted to spend any time in a submarine!

The Peruvians then took us to their naval base at Iquitos, in the headwaters of the Amazon River. This jungle outpost had a large military and naval presence to prevent the Ecuadoreans from violating the Peruvian border. From time to time, the two neighbors exchanged gunfire. The Peruvians had denied the Ecuadoreans river access by patrolling the area with an old river gunboat, armed to the teeth.

On one side-trip, the Peruvians took us several miles up a narrow tributary of the Amazon, promising an interesting time. We came around a bend in the creek, and saw a small village. We docked and a European-looking man in his forties came down to meet us. He introduced himself in accented Spanish, and invited us to lunch in his home.

During lunch, he showed us pictures of himself with Field Marshal Erwin Rommel, driving around the North African desert. He had been Rommel's chauffer during World War II, and had escaped by boat from the defeat of the Afrika Corps in Tunisia. I thought about how strange life could be. This former Wehrmacht driver and my dad were undoubtedly in close proximity in some of the same combat areas in North Africa, just twenty years before, trying to kill each other.

The man had feared that the Allies would hang him, so he made his way to Brazil, and then all the way up the Amazon River to the outskirts of Iquitos. In those days, a fierce tribe of Indian headhunters ruled the area and had captured him. He had to make a "deal" with the chief in order to stay alive, by marrying one of the chief's daughters and agreeing to care for two of his sons. The German had also convinced the Peruvians to keep his location secret. For some reason, probably because of his close relationship with Rommel, he still feared being prosecuted as a war criminal.

Three children with blond hair played in the yard, and the two Indian brothers-in-law were snoring nearby in hammocks. The German woke them up and told them to give us a blowgun demonstration, which was quite impressive.

As we walked down to the dock to get in our boat, the German said, "Watch out for the big Jergón [also called Fer-de-lance]. He bit one of my Indians last week and the man died. He likes to hide in the boats." That got our attention, as we carefully looked around the boat for a stowaway. Having studied the world's snakes as a kid, I knew that the Fer-de-lance is one of the most aggressive and dangerous venomous snakes in South America, and its bite is often fatal or results in an amputation.

The next day, we flew back to Lima and found that we had been reassigned to stay at the Peruvian naval academy, *La Escuela Naval*. Most of the Peruvian cadets did not seem to like us, and were not very friendly. Some were openly hostile. I never figured out why.

We learned quickly about one of their unusual customs. The Peruvian cadets each hoarded their own toilet paper rolls, and brought them back to their rooms after using the head. They also stole ours, which made life rather miserable until we figured out how to lock them up.

The Peruvians had made the mistake of assigning a Peruvian navy car to us, complete with a Peruvian Chief Petty Officer driver, whom we called "Sancho," after the fictional character that traveled with Don Quixote. This car was a temptation too great to resist, as we took turns exploring Lima with the chauffeured car.

Like all naval academies, this one had a Commandant, and he found out that we had been going over the wall after hours to use the car on our social forays into Lima. We were called to the Commandant's office, and he gave us a stern reprimand for our self-indulgent ways. He then restricted us to the academy, except for authorized field trips.

The other Midshipman and I still found an opportunity to go over the wall, and met up with Sancho and the car in a side street. It was a beautiful Saturday night in Lima, as we drove down one of the main boulevards in upscale Miraflores, headed for a party. As we stopped at a red light, we experienced a scene like the one portrayed in *Ferris Bueller's Day Off.* I looked over to our left, and behind the wheel of the car in the next lane was our Peruvian escort officer! He was in civilian clothes and fortunately, was staring straight ahead. I whispered to my buddy, "Hit the deck!" and we dove to the floor of the back seat.

Sancho had a big laugh about this, saying "Cadetes, donde están? Hay problema?" ["Cadets, where are you? Is there a problem?"] Apparently, the Lieutenant never saw us, or if he did, he was cool enough to keep our secret.

Although we tried not to drink the tap water, I somehow got a bad case of "Incas' Revenge," an intestinal bug. I became so dehydrated, the Peruvian officers had me admitted to their naval hospital, one of the best in Lima. After many tests and antibiotics, I started getting better.

I became good friends with a flamboyant Peruvian cadet in the next room, who had been brought in from a soccer game a few weeks before with a broken ankle. He was a real character, and a bad influence. He gave me a supply of Playboy magazines, saying "Para tu salud, Gringo!" [For your health, American!] One of the Catholic nuns who patrolled the halls of the hospital caught me reading one, and gave me quite a tongue-lashing. She would have really freaked out if she had known that my Peruvian buddy was importing prostitutes to his room during the night hours. He told me, "I would have sent them over to your room, but the Sisters are watching you, Gringo!"

Finally, the summer was over and we headed back to Mother Bancroft. The "final lap" was ahead of us. Graduation was less than a year away, and the timing was perfect. The Vietnam War was waiting for us, along with millions of other young Americans. It never occurred to us that our President and his advisors were not competent to manage our government, let alone a war in Asia. We had been taught that our chain-of-command *always* knew what it was doing. As it turned out, our leaders were clueless and "flying by the seat of their pants." Such carelessness often ends in a crash.

~ ~ ~

## Chapter 6: *Top of the Heap!*

On my return from Peru, I drove my Austin-Healey back to Annapolis and hid it in an older lady's spare garage. Knowing how risky this was for me, she charged me an outrageous rent, partly to buy her silence. On weekends, my buddies and I would go over the wall, around the seawall fence, or through the Field House gate disguised as visiting athletes. We would head for that garage, change into our civilian disco attire, and zoom out to places like Washington or Glen Burnie. This was living on the edge, and life seemed a little more tolerable. However, getting caught would bring swift and harsh punishment in the form of a sizeable number of demerits. Perhaps that is what made it even more fun.

At the Naval Academy, life in the Brigade of Midshipmen is controlled by two layers of authority. At the top is the Superintendent, an active duty admiral. Reporting to him is the Commandant of Midshipmen—a Navy captain, who is usually on a career "fast track," presumed to be admiral material. Together with support staff and the officers and non-commissioned officers of the Executive Department, this organization is responsible for all non-academic aspects of Academy life, including the discipline system.

The academic side is primarily managed by the Academic Dean, whose credentials mirror those of civilian university deans throughout the U.S. Most of the faculty are civilians with Ph.D. degrees and military officers with at least a Master's. Most of the military instructors are assigned to the military subjects, such as weapons systems, leadership, and navigation.

The next layer of authority consists of the Brigade of Midshipmen organization, led by the current First Class. A pyramidal chain-of-command starts with the prestigious Brigade Commander position, and connects downward to the regimental, battalion and company units. Naval Academy life is highly structured and organized, down to the smallest details. Even for unorthodox characters like me, experiencing this system was of enormous value, especially when confronted by situations that would come later in life. Nevertheless, it was frequently unpleasant while you were in the middle of it.

During the first semester, I became ill with some sort of virus and was hospitalized. Academically, this was a large problem for me, because class participation is critically important at the Naval Academy.

Contrary to what we had expected, our First Class curriculum did *not* become easier. The Navy was under constant pressure to modernize and intensify the subject matter, and the changes were coming fast and furious. For example, two years before, the weapons course largely consisted of memorizing the parts of a five-inch naval gun. For us, the course now centered on missile technology and computers. We now had a daunting array of difficult courses, like advanced electrical science, fluid mechanics, weapons and systems dynamics, naval operations, naval history, meteorology, leadership and military law, advanced composition and literature, and of course, physical education, known as "physical abuse." This was still a graded course, which included subjects like swimming, tower jumping, boxing, wrestling, obstacle courses, sprint and distance running, gymnastics, and other categories.

After missing weeks of classes, I struggled to stay up with the academic courses while in the hospital. I was finally released around late September, and returned to Bancroft.

During the fall, I attended one of Navy's "away" football games, at Duke. Only a few hundred Midshipmen were allowed to attend, and I was happy to be out of Bancroft Hall for a while. It was a competitive game, but quarterback Roger Staubach ('65), led the Navy team to victory. While I was at the Academy, we had *two* Heisman Trophy winners—Bellino and Staubach. It was phenomenal that a college with only 4,400 students could be a football powerhouse, and have two Heisman winners in such a short time.

After the game, some of the Duke fans were very upset at their unexpected loss. Four rough-looking locals decided to take it out on the first Midshipman they could find, which turned out to be me. As I entered the men's room, a big man punched me in the head from behind, knocking my cap off. I recovered quickly, and realized I was confronting four large opponents by myself, and I was in serious trouble. Fortunately, I had been studying combat-oriented martial arts on my own for several years, which probably saved my life.

I slammed my elbow into my first attacker's face, and then landed a strong kick in the groin of #2, who dropped to the floor. I dodged another punch, and kicked #3 into the wall of a toilet stall, where he fell unconscious. The fourth man charged me from the side, knocking me to the floor. I knew I had to get back on my feet, and fast, because the first man was now coming at me again, and he was much bigger.

From the floor, I kicked one man backward, allowing me to roll away and get back on my feet. Another kick sent the man headfirst into a urinal, cracking his head and knocking him out. The remaining attacker threw a punch at me, and I put him in an outside wristlock. I then dislocated and broke one of his fingers, causing him to scream and lose interest in the fight. Full of adrenaline, I yelled, "The next guy who touches me is friggin' *dead*!" That got their attention, and fortunately, they believed me. The fight was over. Because of the Naval Academy, I no longer was that scared little kid who shied away from fights.

I went outside, just as a Navy limousine with the Superintendent and his wife drove by me. The Admiral's wife stared in shock at my dirty, bloodstained uniform, but they did not stop. I hoped that they did not recognize me from the "Jennifer days." For the rest of the evening, I had a bad headache and bruise from the "sucker punch" I had taken. At least I won the fight, which—ultimately—is all that counts.

In late November, President Kennedy was assassinated in Dallas. The rumors flew, especially when it became known that the shooter, Lee Harvey Oswald, had previously defected to the Soviet Union and had returned with a Russian wife. Once again, we anticipated war with the Soviets, and speculated that we might graduate early. Things took on a more serious note. Finally, the government declared Oswald to be the sole assassin.

As I staggered through academics into my final semester, I found that I had been selected for Navy Air after graduation. At that point, all I wanted was to get to Pensacola and start flying. This "short-timer" attitude was not helpful, especially to my class standing in academics.

I began to make more frequent excursions "over the wall," to destinations outside of the Seven-mile Limit. My Austin-Healey became my deliverance from the pressures of the Academy. The attitude exemplified by having this hot little car started my slide into Demerit Purgatory, from which there is no return. However, the most successful missions usually require support and teamwork. Going over the wall was no exception.

Each Plebe is assigned to a First Classman, who acts as mentor, protector, and general advisor. My Plebe was an ex-Marine and knew no fear—the perfect pawn on my chessboard. You always need someone to fall on the barbed wire for you *[Note: Career tip!]*. In exchange for me protecting him from upper-class sadists, he performed special missions for me—such as wedging an obscure basement door open for my return from nighttime debauchery in the forbidden zone outside of the Seven-mile Limit.

I acquired a small Sony TV that fit perfectly in the confidential materials locker in my desk. *[These were the olden days, when no TVs or radios were allowed in your room or even the company wardroom.]* The problem was that we needed a better antenna. Drawing upon my marginal knowledge of electronics, I solved the problem quickly.

Pigeons were a big problem around Bancroft Hall, as they liked to perch and nest on Bancroft's hundreds of ledges, and then defecate on the Midshipmen formations below. The Academy solved this by installing a giant network of low-voltage wires on the building walls that shocked the birds and kept them away. I disconnected the power to the Bancroft pigeon-shocker system near our window, and connected that huge wire network to my TV. It must have been the world's largest TV antenna. We were even receiving stations from far beyond Washington and Baltimore with total clarity. Study hour became a pleasant event, and my room became a popular meeting place for my company classmates. The little TV was our electronic connection to the outside world.

I then became weary of leaping out of bed with the reveille bell at 0615. Obviously, it was necessary to sleep in to compensate for watching late-night TV. However, if the Officer of the Watch caught you even sitting on your bed after 0615, you received an automatic 20 demerits. *Aha!* All I needed was an OOW Early Warning System. One weekend, I visited a hardware store in Annapolis and bought a doorbell, some insulated wire, and a transformer. I came back to my room on the fourth deck and placed the transformer under my rack and the doorbell behind the window blinds. I then pried up some floor tile and ran the wires to the bell and the transformer. Then, I ran a long length of wire along the pigeon ledge outside and back in to the Mate's desk, where I installed the actuator button.

Each Plebe "Mate of the Watch" was instructed that if an OOW arrived on deck, nearly always from the elevators, he was to push the button behind him before saluting. The doorbell would ring in my room, allowing time to get out of bed, hide the TV, etc. I would then pound on the adjoining wall, initiating a series of wall-to-wall signals that danger was approaching. This allowed all of my classmates to avoid being caught sleeping in. My electrical science professor would have been proud. It worked like a charm, and life improved dramatically with this extra technology.

Then the unexpected happened. We had a big storm in January, and the wire bundle blew partially over the edge of the roof. Some sharp-eyed lieutenant commander noticed it from Goat Court, and came up to investigate while I was at class. He followed the wires to my room and found the bell, the transformer, and the Mate's button. I got about 40 demerits for that one, and was placed on restriction. As additional punishment, the Company Officer (Lieutenant, later Captain Smedberg) ordered me to re-rig the system between his office and our Company Commander's room, and commented, "Nice engineering work. Too bad you got caught!"

I felt compelled to get even with The System, which was a big mistake. There are some battles from which you should retire smartly at 30 knots, making smoke and zigzagging, in order to fight another day. However, history is replete with impulsive commanders who chose the wrong battlefield and paid dearly for it. The worst self-inflicted damage for me was yet to come.

I narrowly averted the loss of my Navy Air selection during First Class Year with the nuclear power recruiting incident. The notorious Admiral Rickover felt he was not getting his share of candidates from the Naval Academy for the Submarine Force, and in typical fashion, decided to use the "sledge hammer" approach: *impressment*. Some history buffs may remember that our nation fought the War of 1812 with the Brits over this issue.

Hyman G. Rickover ('22) was hated by the Navy establishment, but loved by a succession of presidents and congressional leaders—a connection he carefully cultivated. He was passed over for Rear Admiral twice, but finally was promoted and eventually made four-star rank because of congressional pressure. He was an obsessive micro-manager, and considered a tyrant by many who worked for him. Nevertheless, our Navy's nuclear ships, with their advanced technology and perfect reactor safety record, would probably not have existed without him. In addition, he had forced monumental changes in the Naval Academy curriculum, pushing it, "kicking and screaming," into the twentieth century. It was now our turn to experience Rickover's power to get what he wanted.

All Firsties with GPAs over a certain mark were *ordered* to report to Rickover's offices to be considered for nuclear power school. Just when I thought I had Navy Air locked in, here came *another* threat to my career plans. A forbidding caravan of gray Navy buses rolled up one Saturday morning near the Field House. The nuclear power "candidates" were herded up like cattle for the slaughter, and taken to Rickover's Washington headquarters for interviews.

Each candidate was interviewed by three of Rickover's staff. One was a foreign affairs type. I scored well with him, but started thinking that maybe *failing this process was better for my career preference to start flight training in Pensacola.* I did not need to worry very long.

The next interviewer was a psychologist. He asked why I had so many demerits, and whether I had problems with life in the military and following the rules. *This could be an important response that would keep me bound for Pensacola.* I replied, "Yes, perhaps I do." He scribbled quickly on his notepad.

The next interviewer was a scientist/engineer type. He said, "Well, you seem to have had academic problems with electronics. Describe for me the components of a super-heterodyne receiver, and then how an antenna works in terms of electromagnetic theory." *Whoa! Time to punt!*

The final interview was to be with Rickover himself. Just before I was called, I entered the head, nearly knocking down a wiry little guy with white hair and bushy eye-brows in civilian clothes who was going the other way. "*Excuse me!*" he snarled. "Sorry," I replied. I wondered who the little jerk was.

Then I was briefed by a Navy captain (in civilian clothes). Rickover kept all prospective COs of nuclear ships and subs assigned to his office for about six months, so he could evaluate them on a daily basis. "I'll be sitting right behind you when you see the Admiral. Speak only when the Admiral asks you a question. If you feel my hand on your shoulder, stop talking immediately." These poor guys had to worship Satan himself in order to keep their careers on track.

"Yes, Sir." But I thought, *This is really ridiculous. What is this admiral thinking? This is no way for him to become acquainted with the candidates, build rapport, and become popular!*

We entered the room. Seated behind a messy desk was the *same* little man from my collision in the door of the head, staring down at a file—mine. Books were stacked in piles on the surrounding floor. I remember thinking it was a good thing I wanted to go Navy Air, because this was not going well.

"Sit down!" the little man growled. I did.

After a few minutes, he looked at me and said, "Nelson, why in the hell have you taken all of these foreign language courses?"

"That's my interest, Admiral."

"Well, nuclear power school is conducted in *English*, so you have wasted valuable academic opportunities. If you *are* selected, would you be interested in surface nuclear or nuclear subs?"

"Frankly, Sir, I would rather fly airplanes."

"*Get out!*" he screamed, and my captain escort dragged me from the room, with my feet barely touching the floor.

I turned to my escort and said, "Well, Sir, that seemed to go quite well." He stared at me in disbelief. I was dropped from the nuclear power list by the time I got back to Bancroft.

Rickover's bizarre behavior was not only directed at me. Many of my classmates experienced his abusive outbursts during the interview. One story, in particular, sticks in my mind.

One of my classmates was a very good-looking guy who had rowed on the crew team, giving him a Greek-god-like physique that attracted lots of female attention. Reportedly, Rickover screamed across the desk at him, "You are the ugliest son-of-a-bitch I ever saw! Go into the next office, and tell that female lieutenant that twenty virgins have declared you the ugliest man they ever saw!" After he complied, Rickover told the candidate, "OK, I'm accepting you in the nuclear power program. Now get out."

I found out that Rickover required most, if not all, of the successful candidates to sign statements promising to raise their grades by the time they graduated. For the top Midshipman in our class, having an incredible 3.99 average (as I recall), that was mathematically impossible, but he was selected anyway. Clearly, this was not the program for me.

My academic performance had deteriorated, but I still got an "A" in one subject—physical education! *Who would have thought?* In addition, I was undefeated in Brigade (intramural) cross-country. Perhaps I should have used my running ability to escape one particular young lady, who had me squarely in her sights.

Life-changing events sometimes sneak up on you. On a blind date during the winter, I met an attractive young woman from New Jersey. We had a series of romantic weekends, but I started thinking of how I was going to cut off the relationship. I did not want to carry any "baggage" into my career as a Navy pilot, because there would be plenty of opportunities in Pensacola to meet young women. Obviously, I had still not learned that women are much cleverer than men.

One evening in March, I received an "emergency" telephone call from her. In those days, you had to go down to the basement where the pay phones were located. E-mails, cell phones and Blackberries did not exist. I called and she answered. She immediately began sobbing. "Dick, I'm *pregnant!*" she said.

Before that moment, I did not know you could actually hear your own heart stop. I froze, like a deer in the headlights. *So this is what combat feels like!* My mind was racing, but I did not know what to say.

Suddenly, I heard a click and *her mother* was now on the line. "What have you two been *doing?*" she said, joining her daughter in sobbing. *If you only knew,* I thought.

"Mother, we love each other!" the expecting mother-to-be replied. It was certainly nice of her to be my spokesperson. I was still trying to get my mouth and brain coordinated, and said nothing.

If a Midshipman inadvertently became a father, that was one thing. However, if he were to *marry* the woman before graduation, he would be immediately terminated from the Academy. This policy created an annual stampede of hundreds of couples to the altar after every graduation.

Stupidly, I said, "Well, we want to get married, so we will—as soon as I graduate." It never occurred to me to suggest that she might get an abortion as the optimum solution. For four years, I had been taught to *accept* responsibility, not run from it.

"Oh, thank God!" said her mother. My pregnant fiancée and her mother instantly stopped crying. Who *knew* there was an ON/OFF switch for tears? She and her mom smoothly shifted gears and began calmly discussing arrangements for the wedding, as if they were planning for a major military campaign. At this point, I was simply along for the ride. *I wonder whether it's a boy or a girl,* I thought to myself.

Within 48 hours, a big June wedding was arranged in East Orange, New Jersey, complete with several of my classmates doing the traditional sword arch, two ministers, 200 guests, a big reception, and a honeymoon suite in a New York hotel. These women could teach our military planners a thing or two. I decided to make the best of the situation, and put on a "happy face." I proudly told my closest friends that I was engaged. They were appalled, because they were aware I had only known this girl for a few weeks. I did not mention that a baby was on the way.

The warriors of ancient times, like the Japanese samurai, had an unambiguous method of apologizing for failure, such as losing a battle. They impaled themselves on their sword in front of their leaders. The modern equivalent has evolved as a sword-less metaphor—now only a stoic acceptance of personal responsibility, even when others are at fault. I was about to get a very costly lesson about the hazards of self-expression at the Naval Academy.

Because of the quantity of demerits I had received for the OOW Early Warning System, it took weeks to work off the restriction. Finally, one blustery Saturday afternoon, I was finally able to walk out of the gate and stroll around town. I was aimlessly walking around Annapolis when I passed by a pet store window with a large aquarium in front. A sign said, "Real piranha—$15.00."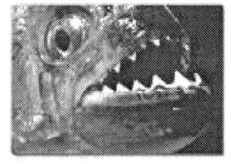

At that time, there was a huge aquarium below Memorial Hall in the Steerage (soda fountain) area. A brilliant idea struck me. This lonely piranha, which was about six inches long, sporting a full set of needle-like dentures, truly deserved to become a resident of the Naval Academy aquarium! With a little luck, he would not be discovered until after I graduated and escaped to Pensacola.

I paid my $15 and brought this nasty little critter back to Bancroft Hall in a goldfish container. I rounded up my Plebe to help with the mission, and during study hour, we commenced our Strike Op.

The Steerage area was deserted. We launched "Fang," our toothy protégé, into the lighted aquarium, and then sat quietly in the back of the Steerage to see what would happen. It took him a few minutes to stabilize his gyros, but he finally started his combat patrol up and down the big tank.

To our shock and amazement, two Midshipmen walked past on the way to the library and spotted Fang cruising through the lighted aquarium. "Wow! Look, Bill, *that's* a piranha!" Now think about it. How many guys at the Boat School would recognize a piranha, even if it bit them in a sensitive place? As I recall, the Academy has not produced many biology majors. Fang had only just completed a ten-minute reconnaissance run through the tank, and we had *already* been discovered! *[Career tip: Always expect the unexpected, and adapt quickly. No battle plan survives the first shot.]*

In a flash, a noisy crowd of Midshipmen gathered around the aquarium, which soon attracted the attention of the Officer of the Watch up in the Rotunda. Coming down the marble stairs, this lieutenant commander demanded to know what the ruckus was about. "Sir, we have a *piranha* in the aquarium!" was the answer from the crowd. This unlucky officer saw the situation as a career-ending event, and ran to call the Commandant for guidance as to whether the piranha was "authorized." The Commandant thought it was a joke, and told him, "Just take care of it." Back he came, and told his Midshipman Officer of the Watch to spear the piranha with his sword! I will always treasure this image of a Midshipman in his blue service uniform, complete with white gloves and cap, stabbing his sword at a wildly zigzagging piranha, while the crowd cheered for the fish.

The OOW finally found a large piece of screen, and inserted it to keep Fang walled off at one end of the tank. By that time, Fang had already performed several strafing runs with his sharp teeth, and had nearly wiped out the entire aquarium population. Apparently, he had worked up an appetite. Fish guts and blood clouded the tank and Fang seemed to have a wry smile on his little face, as if he knew something I did not know. Unknown to us, this aquarium was a special project of a senior officer in the Executive Department. The resident fish were very rare and <u>very</u> expensive. A feeding frenzy of a different kind was now about to focus on me and my Plebe.

I felt a strange sinking feeling, which I did not experience again until about three years later, when I saw my first North Vietnamese SAM [surface-to-air missile] heading my way, or found my name on the carrier's night flying schedule. This operation had started as a small snowball, but now had become an avalanche, and it was headed right for me. The thought occurred to me that I could not afford more demerits, so it was time to lay low and stay under the radar.

I might have escaped detection, but unfortunately, I had an overly creative Plebe who had decided to have some fun of his own.

My Plebe, Rick, saw life as a constant opportunity to excel and display his ingenuity. Without my knowledge, he decided on his own to make a call to *The Washington Post* newspaper, and let them know about "our new mascot." A few days later, a small story appeared on the front page of *The Washington Post*: "**Middies Protest, Piranha Taken.**" It stated that the Midshipmen wanted to replace the goat with a new mascot—the piranha—which the Academy administration had confiscated. The article cited Midshipmen protest signs like "Save our man-eating fish from fish-eating man."

Apparently, every general and admiral in Washington read the article, thought it was amusing, and called up the Superintendent to jerk his chain. The embarrassed Superintendent issued a hang-on-sight order for the apprehension of the piranha perpetrators. Career-minded stripers [midshipman officers] and commissioned officers alike beat the bushes and squeezed their intelligence sources for the names of the culprits. The heat was on, and I felt the pressure. Like a condemned prisoner, I would wake up at night in a cold sweat, imagining the footsteps of the death-row chaplain and guards coming to take me on that last walk.

It did not take them long. One of the senior stripers in my class saw an opportunity to gain the Supe's favor, and squealed. This is called "bilging" a classmate, and is considered despicable behavior unless the situation involves an honor offense, in which reporting is mandatory. The sniveling striper reported to the Commandant that it was someone from the infamous 19th Company. (I recently saw this man at my 45th Class Reunion, and noticed he avoided eye contact. "Bilging" a classmate is never forgotten. Perhaps he owes part of his career success to the piranha, and he knows it.)

The wheels of injustice were in motion. I was soon called down to the 19th Company Officer's office. I knew instinctively what was coming. "Nelson, after that OOW Early Warning System caper, I thought you would stay out of trouble. I just got a call from the Commandant. He told me someone in *my company* undoubtedly had pulled the piranha gig, and it wasn't hard for me to figure out who. The only other character who would do something as perverted as *this* is on emergency leave, so that leaves *you*. I'll ask you just once—*did you do this?*"

"Do I have to answer, Sir? That hardly seems fair." Lieutenant Smedberg and I both knew that the Honor Concept made it impossible to lie. My answer had to be the truth.

"Yes, immediately!" This is not how the criminal justice system is supposed to work. *What about the Fifth Amendment?* Maybe this is why I later became a lawyer.

The only other time I lost my voice like this was when I got married, and it was time to say, "I do." Finally, I mumbled, "Yes, Sir."

My Company Officer then burst into laughter. "Nelson, this was worthy of Philo McGiffen [the legendary Naval Academy prankster of the 19th Century].

But it's out of my hands, and they are going to hang you high, pal." And they did. At least I took the heat for my Plebe, who had also been snared in the Admiral's dragnet. I used the Nuremberg Defense for him ("the kid was just following orders"), and he only got a few demerits.

Next, I was ordered to report to the Executive Officer of Bancroft Hall, a humorless Navy captain. This was a guy you *never* wanted to meet, and he never brought good news. When I announced my presence in his outer office, his secretary looked at my nametag and giggled. I was ushered into what amounted to a Captain's Mast proceeding, which is discipline just below a court martial. The four-striper glared at me, and I noticed a copy of the *Washington Post* article on his desk, along with my demerit file. "Nelson, this was a totally immature civilian college prank. We can't tolerate this type of behavior around here. Why did you do it? Come on, the Commandant and I really want to know."

"Well, Captain, I was bored from several weeks of restricting, I had fifteen extra dollars, and I thought it would be a nice upgrade for the aquarium."

"You still think this is funny? I've got news for you, Mister. This thing is on the Admiral's desk now, and I'm not sure what he is going to do. Get out!"

This was doubly embarrassing, because Admiral Minter knew me from the time I was dating Jennifer, when she had stayed with the Minters. The Admiral wrote a personal letter to my mom, telling her that I would be expelled from the Academy for "the slightest additional infraction." They made me take the piranha back to the pet store, which was a very emotional moment for Fang and me. They then proceeded to nearly max me out on demerits, all the way to ten under the limit. I was placed on the Admiral's *personal* probation and restriction, where I stayed until the precise moment of graduation. I could not even see my fiancée during this time. This is not the Supe's List that you wanted to be on.

With all these distractions, my grades deteriorated. In addition to the electrical science courses, the weapons course was much more difficult than I expected. Where Midshipmen once studied weapons hardware, the course was now at the other abstract extreme, involving complex ballistic equations. I nearly failed the exam, which required us to "derive the equation that describes the trajectory of an intercontinental ballistic missile, traveling from New York to Moscow." The correct answer had to be about three pages long, and I could only come up with *one*. My prior hospital stay was coming back to haunt me.

Someone was spreading the ugly rumor that I had an illegal car out in town, and had been doing "missionary work" outside the Seven-mile Limit. One of my classmates had already bought the car from me, so I thought I was in the clear. However, fate often intervenes with a vengeance. Just when you think you are home free, the hammer falls.

The classmate who had purchased my car had not yet transferred the registration from the State of Virginia. His roommate had just acquired a new Alfa-Romeo, but did not yet have his own license plates. The roommate apparently decided to borrow the plates from the Austin-Healey so he would not attract attention while driving around Annapolis. One rainy weekend, he drove to a big party near Washington, some 60 miles away.

When returning from the party, he spun out on a rain-soaked highway and died in the crash, apparently without a legible ID. The Virginia Highway Patrol traced the plates to a "Richard Nelson, U.S. Naval Academy, Rm. 6402, Annapolis, MD 21402." They assumed I was the deceased driver, and notified the watch officer at Bancroft Hall.

For some time, the Executive Department had suspected that I had been going over the wall and was driving a car illegally. This tragic accident would indirectly prove that I, indeed, *had* been driving a car for several months. According to the Academy rules at the time, this was not legal and would put me over the top on demerits.

In the wake of the piranha episode, they had been watching me closely. The watch officers were "bed-checking" me three times per night, to make sure I was not "over the wall." On this particular night, a Mate of the Watch came into the room and shined a flashlight in my face, as usual. My roommate was away from the Academy on a special leave. "Sir, your roommate has been killed in a car accident." I woke up and asked how it happened. The young Plebe did not know. "I'm sorry, Mr. Austin," he said.

"No, I'm not Austin [my roommate]—I'm Nelson."

"Sir, I don't think that's funny. Mr. Nelson is dead." At this point, I realized something strange must have occurred. Even though it was 0300, I knew there would be an Officer of the Watch (OOW) in his Rotunda office. I got dressed and went to the watch office.

As I approached the door, I saw a lieutenant seated behind a desk. I knocked on the door frame.

"Enter," he said. Looking at my nametag, his jaw dropped. *"Nelson?"* he asked.

"Yes, Sir. I understand there has been an accident."

"Aren't you the guy we have to bed-check every night?"

"Yes, Sir."

He stared at me for a minute, trying to sort out what had just happened on his watch. "OK, what is going on? I have a report about a Midshipman who has been killed in a car accident, and the cops tell me his name is the same as *yours*. What is your connection to this?"

"Well, Sir, I recently sold my car to a classmate. I'm afraid he must have been the one in the accident. The police must have traced my old plates."

The lieutenant stared at me. "So you also had an illegal car?"

"Yes, Sir."

He thought for a minute. "Nelson, the death of a Midshipman is not only a terrible tragedy, it's a huge deal to the Supe and the Commandant, for obvious reasons. It attracts a lot of attention. Do you realize if I report the details of this mess to the Commandant, that will put you over the top on demerits?"

"Yes, Sir." It was beginning to appear that I would become a civilian after all.

"What are you going to do after graduation?"

"I'm going Navy Air, Sir." He smiled. I noticed a set of gold wings on his jacket.

"I'm going to stick my neck out here. I'm going to eliminate your name from my report, so no one will know you had a car. Since you weren't in this car, I see no reason to mention your name. But you need to contact this Virginia Highway Patrol officer and explain to him what happened with the car and plates. You might want to tell him to only contact you, to keep this below the radar."

"Yes, Sir! Thank you, Sir!"

"You aren't out of the woods yet, pal. If you are really lucky, this will blow over once they find out who was actually in that car. Now get out of here, and keep your nose clean for a few more weeks!"

"Aye, aye, Sir!" I probably owe my successful graduation to this officer, and I do not even remember his name. Perhaps I will learn who he is when he reads this book and contacts me.

It seemed like my boyish transgressions were catching up to me. I did a lot of soul-searching about my classmate's accidental death. If I had never possessed the "illegal" car, and never had sold it to a member of my class, would his roommate still be alive? Obviously, one action had nothing to do with the other, but I learned a poignant lesson about the insidious Law of Unintended Consequences. When you screw around and act irresponsibly, some innocent bystander may get hurt in the unforeseen chain of events. When you least expect it, people, places, and events may become interconnected in some strange way.

Throwing my cap in the air on graduation day now would have a double meaning for me, as it would end restriction and I could see my girl again. A week before June Week, things around Bancroft seemed a lot looser and more laid back. I had just finished evening meal, and was heading back to my room. Since I lived on the fourth deck, I decided it was time to relax and ride in the elevator. This was a privilege only held by commissioned officers, and was worth at least 20 demerits if a Midshipman, even a First Class, was caught using the elevator.

I did a quick scan, made sure there were no officers around, and pushed the button. As the doors opened, I turned to enter and—there he was! Major Love, USMC: The Darth Vader of Company Officers, the Demerit God, the Grim Reaper of Form 2s [the demerit form]. This Marine took things *very* seriously. It was rumored that he slept on the floor in his combat boots with a loaded .45 under his pillow, which consisted of an old ammo can. He would frequently prowl the passageways of Bancroft at all hours, relentlessly searching for any Midshipman who was not in proper uniform or where he was supposed to be.

Being a good Marine, the major had planned his ambush well. He was seated in the elevator behind a card table, with a stack of Form 2s and a pen. "Well, well.

I knew someone would try this. It looks like I've caught the big fish himself. Get in, Mr. Piranha!"

"Uh, good evening, Major."

"It is for me, but not for you. How many demerits do you have now, Nelson?"

"One hundred forty, Sir." *Gulp.*

"And you are only allowed one hundred fifty, right? And when I fry you for this, you will be over the top, right?"

"Yes, Sir." Thinking quickly, I was wondering if I could somehow jam the elevator between decks, and perhaps overpower the Major and keep him trapped in the elevator and out of communication for a few days until I graduated. I could have my Plebe wear a ski mask and lower MREs (dry rations) and canteens to him every day, just to be humane. Suddenly, my planning was interrupted with a jolt, as we reached the fourth deck.

"OK, get out. I'm giving you an early graduation present—a warning. But don't do this again, *do you read me?*"

"OOORAHH, loud and clear, Sir!"

Years later, I still meet people who say, "Oh, yeah—you are the piranha guy!" A dubious honor, to be sure. Not like, "Oh, you were a Rhodes Scholar," or "Didn't you catch that touchdown pass to beat Army?" or "Weren't you the Brigade Commander?" When I was checking the bulletin boards for class standing info, just prior to graduation, I wondered why I had dropped so far. It then became obvious. Under the category of "military conduct," I was ranked <u>last</u> out of our graduating class. The only thing to do at that point was either to join the French Foreign Legion or become an F-8 Crusader pilot. I chose the latter, because it looked like more fun—and it really *was*. Now *that* reminds me of a few other stories. . . . . .

~ ~ ~

# Chapter 7: *Links in the Chain*

*Four years together by the bay where Severn joins the tide,*
*And by the service called away we scatter far and wide.*
*But still when two or three shall meet and old tales be retold,*
*From low to highest in the Fleet, we'll pledge the Blue and Gold!*
   ---Naval Academy Alma Mater, second verse

One of the more significant and unique aspects of being an Academy graduate is the lifetime bond between classmates. You never forget those with whom you endured those four years, and the chances are good that you will see them again and need their help, or you will be able to help them. The Blue and Gold Chain is for life.

So it was with my classmate John Sande ('64). I first met this husky Norwegian kid when we both went out for Plebe football. Within a week, after we missed too many tackles and dropped too many passes, the coaches cut both of us. They obviously did not recognize true talent when they saw it.

John was very smart, and usually wore the little lapel stars which proclaimed the academic prowess of being on the Supe's List. But John's intelligence sometimes got him in trouble. That is how we became tied for *last* place in our Class in the "military conduct" category. We had a lot in common already, including a bad attitude during First Class Year.

Like me, John only wanted to fly airplanes, which frequently seems to correlate to various behavioral problems. There are those who manage to stay focused—stripers, destined for Flag or General rank—and others (like John and me) who are drawn to the pursuit of adventure, usually resulting in an abrupt career change.

As I would learn later, John had a shrewd business aptitude. He demonstrated this early on, when he identified an unsatisfied demand among the Midshipmen for study-hour snacks. In those days, you could not bring food into your room. It was also a violation to engage in commercial transactions with other Midshipmen. Nevertheless, John decided that the deprived Midshipmen would pay a princely sum for a hotdog (complete with mustard and relish) during study hour. The problem was (1) how to manufacture them, and (2) how to distribute them without getting caught.

John's devious mind came into play, as he bribed the "mokes" [janitors] and obtained a key to the attic storage area above the fourth deck, known as the "moke locker." He set up an assembly line of rotisseries in the moke locker, along with a refrigerator. Academy staff engineers began to notice an unexplained spike in electric power demand in Bancroft Hall.

During study hour, Plebe "runners" traversed Bancroft Hall, taking hotdog orders and delivering the merchandise. This may have been the forerunner of the nation's pizza delivery system. A designated "bag man" would collect the money from each distribution point and return it to John. As the operation grew, John realized it was necessary to emulate the CIA and "compartmentalize" the operation in order to avoid being caught. He then sold "franchises" to trusted members of the class, who started setting up duplicate manufacturing sites. John's confidential publications locker became stuffed with cash, as he assumed the role of an entrepreneurial "holding company," leaving the operational risk to others in exchange for an appropriate royalty fee.

The operation became so large that commercial delivery trucks were regularly coming through the Academy gate loaded with buns and wieners. The Jimmy Leg [civilian] gate guards assumed they were going to the Mess Hall, but the trucks would stop near one of the back wings of Bancroft Hall. Plebes would then unload the goods and take them to the moke locker. The OOW once caught a Plebe bag man with a sack of money, but John was never apprehended. When we graduated, John bought a hot new car—for cash.

Although we were in different air wings, John and I flew the same aircraft type in Vietnam (the F-8E Crusader), we each destroyed a SAM site, and later we were assigned to the same F-8 Replacement Air Group at Miramar as instructors. We then left active duty at the same time to join Continental Airlines in the same class. We also flew together in the F-8 Reserves at Miramar, and jointly owned a computer business.

John and I were laid off by Continental in the first year. John, in typical fashion, talked his way back on active duty to ride out the layoff. He then wangled an assignment as a pool lifeguard and safety assistant with the "Dilbert Dunker" survival training unit in Pensacola. This was the contraption that all pilots had to endure in order to get their wings. It roared down a track into a deep swimming pool, flipped upside-down, and you had to un-strap and swim to the surface.

When he tried to check a Navy car out of the base motor pool, he was told they were reserved for captains and above. John insisted he needed the car for "surveillance operations," and that he could not supply more information because of national security. The motor pool officer figured he was with Naval Intelligence or NCIS, and gave him the car. John conducted nightly "surveillance" of the Pensacola bars and night spots, and was waved through the base gates and saluted by respectful guards. He could always make a good situation out of a bad one.

While on active duty, he had more than his share of close calls. On one occasion, while his carrier was in the middle of the Pacific, en route to Vietnam, he was launched to intercept a Russian "Bear" aircraft. The Russians delighted in forcing the carriers to send up fighters to intercept them before they overflew the carrier. Usually, they timed it so the intercept would be at night or in bad weather, always far from any air base.

Upon returning to the ship from his intercept, he was confronted by a wildly pitching deck. When he landed and caught a wire, his tail hook broke off, but he was able to get airborne. Because the nearest "bingo" (alternate) airfield was thousands of miles away, he was forced to make a dangerous barricade arrestment.

During a chaotic Alpha Strike raid on Hanoi, John happened to be one of the last pilots to see John S. McCain ejecting from his A-4 Skyhawk and parachuting into the lake in downtown Hanoi, on his way to becoming a POW. He narrowly escaped death again on *USS Oriskany* when a fire broke out and killed over 30 pilots in their rooms. By pure chance, John was flying at the time, while his roommate died in the fire.

*Soviet TU-95 "Bear" with F-8 escort, and carrier in the background. We were required to have one fighter fly wing on the Bear, while the other pilot took a photograph. We were told this was necessary to prove the carriers were not vulnerable to air attack, and could easily intercept the "bad guys."*

**USS Oriskany** *on fire.*

John continued his career with Continental, while I became a lawyer. On one occasion, I represented John in a business lawsuit. Although we had pursued different careers, we kept in touch.

After retiring as a Continental DC-10 captain, John learned he had contracted multiple myeloma and a type of leukemia from exposure to Agent Orange. His luck finally ran out. After two years of agony, he left us in 2007. John's ashes were scattered at sea by his wife and family.

A mutual close friend, retired Continental Captain Billy Foster (also a former F-8 driver) paid his respects on behalf of all of those who knew John by doing a hazardous dive on *USS Oriskany* (now sunk off of Pensacola). Captain Foster left John's silver uniform belt buckle and a photo of an F-8 on the old ship at over a 130' depth. John and *Oriskany* are now reunited for eternity. As with all things, both have returned to the sea. John, we miss you.

*Eternal Father, Strong to save,*
*Whose arm hath bound the restless wave,*
*Who bid'st the mighty Ocean deep*
*Its own appointed limits keep;*
*O hear us when we cry to thee,*
*for those in peril on the sea.*

*---The Navy Hymn*

~ ~ ~

# Chapter 8: *The Hatchlings*

It was June of 1964, and my life had just been jump-started. More than 900 graduates of the class of 1964 listened to the usual uninspiring VIP speeches, and then threw their caps in the air, ending the four years of monastic preparation to lead in combat. By that symbolic act, we instantly became Ensigns and Second Lieutenants, and for a few brief moments, we felt very important.

The threat of demerits and after-effects of the piranha incident were gone, and I was reborn. By the end of that beautiful month, I had been released from restriction upon graduation; got married to a girl I hardly knew; and reported for flight training at Pensacola. *How good can it get?* The great adventure had begun.

On the eve of the big wedding, my bride-to-be casually advised me, "I'm so relieved! I just got my period! I'm not pregnant after all!" That was when I knew I had been duped, and I felt very stupid. That is what happens when you think with your glands instead of your brain. On the other hand, she was very good-looking, and I really did like her. Having her around would make life much more pleasant during flight training. *What the hell! I can take a joke!* We never spoke about the "mystery pregnancy" again. *Forgive and forget . . . . .*

In order to get into the training pipeline as quickly as possible, I waived my graduation leave, and got into the first flight training class available. I found myself driving happily to Pensacola with my new (and much more attractive) roommate, now Wife #1.

For the Academy trainees in Pensacola, flight ground school was relatively easy. We understood the engineering theories, and the number-intensive procedures seemed familiar. For the first time, we also began to sense the animosity toward Academy graduates felt by non-Academy officers. Making enemies in the Flight Training Command can cost you grades, which will cost you the best Fleet Air assignments. We avoided public discussions of the Academy, Army-Navy games, and other related subjects. Some even decided not to wear their Academy ring, which was like having a target painted on your chest.

During an abbreviated escape-and-evasion training course, we were taken over to the large wilderness area of Eglin AFB, east of Pensacola. After some classroom instruction, the instructors took us out in the woods and gave us an escape-and-evasion drill to complete. They told us there would be armed "enemy" soldiers searching for us, and that it was rare for anyone to reach the "safe" area without being caught. This sounded like fun.

I looked around and realized this was the same Florida palmetto scrub environment that had been my "playground" as a young boy. I knew what to do, and how to do it. I was teamed up with two students who had never been in a wild place like the Florida scrub before. They quickly realized this and made me the team leader.

The instructors gave us a 30-minute head start, and we jogged to the edge of a palmetto area, which always contains a good supply of rattlesnakes. I found the usual animal trail, which was worn like a tunnel through the palmettos. We carefully moved to the center of the dense scrub area, watching for snakes. This was like a snake-infested "mine field," but it would be difficult for people to follow us.

I spent a few minutes resting with my team, carefully attaching branches and plant materials to our clothes in order to blend in with the brush. We then proceeded on our assigned escape route.

Since the instructors had assigned this route, I knew there would be an ambush somewhere. After walking for an hour, I heard the sounds of people moving through the scrub, breaking twigs with their footsteps. We dove under a big log and heard conversations. "I think I heard them over here, Sergeant," the man said. He appeared to be moving closer to us.

At that moment, two big deer jumped over our log and ran by the men. "OK, it was just a couple of deer—let's go south." Their noise faded as they moved past us.

Next, we found ourselves at a critical road crossing. There was no way to avoid this open area, and the road had to be crossed. We watched from the woods alongside, and saw several vehicle patrols moving around. I spotted a sign in the adjacent field nearby that said, "DANGER! THIS AREA CONTAINS UNEXPLODED ORDNANCE! DO NOT ENTER!"

I told my teammates that we needed to distract the roving patrols, or we would never get across this area. While they stayed hidden, I sprinted over to the prohibited area, which had a large, sandy area between the road and the woods beyond. I was sure any ordnance would have to be hundreds of yards into the woods, so there was no danger. While the patrols were at the other end of the road, I stomped big footprints into the prohibited area, and then walked backwards, stepping precisely in the tracks. To anyone looking at the tracks, it would look like several people had walked into the ordnance area.

To make sure they would see the tracks, I broke off the sign and tossed it on the side of the road. I ran back to my teammates' hiding place and waited.

As expected, one of the patrol vehicles came by and spotted the broken sign, and then saw the footprints in the sand. They radioed for help, and started carefully searching the woods in the ordnance area. This drew the patrols off the road, and we ran across to the cover of the next wooded area without being seen.

We successfully arrived at the "finish line," to the amazement of the instructors. "Did any of you guys go into the ordnance drop area?" asked the lead instructor.

"No, but we saw a couple of the Marines going in there. Most Marines can't read signs," I said.

The instructor looked at me, and said, "Son, *I'm* a Marine, and that's not funny!" *Oops!*

Soon we were up at Saufley Field, training in the single-engine T-34 prop. This *was* fun, but required a new set of skills, which none of us really had. The big challenge was to score high enough in the curriculum, compared to your fellow students, to qualify for jets. Otherwise, you went next to Whiting Field and then were locked into either props or helicopters, somewhat of a career dead-end. Comparatively few officers have ever made admiral from the multi-engine prop or helo communities. For most of the ambitious Boat School boys, that meant jets were the only answer.

While the prop and helo squadrons were and are vital to the Navy's mission, the harsh reality was that admirals were selected disproportionately from those who had been CO of an attack carrier. Nearly all the carrier COs had been jet pilots from the fighter and attack squadrons. If you had ambitions for reaching senior rank, it was wise not to offend anyone, especially the instructor pilots and the squadron CO, or you could be placed in the prop/helo pipeline.

As I neared the grade-intensive climax at Saufley, the CO, a non-Academy commander, announced that each officer, including the students, would be *required* to contribute to the United Way campaign. For some reason, this touched a nerve with me, and I refused to sign the payroll deduction form. Soon, I was in familiar territory—the CO's office.

The CO glared at me from behind his desk. "Nelson, why haven't you contributed yet? I was told that you refused. You Academy types think you can do your own thing. I want 100% participation in this squadron! What's your excuse?"

"Well, Sir, I feel charitable contributions are a personal choice. Contributions, by definition, should be voluntary. I have other charities in mind."

"Oh, really? I have news for *you*, Mister. You *will* contribute to United Way, or your graduation from Saufley will be held up. How do you like *that?*"

"With all due respect, Sir, if that occurs, I will be forced to appeal your decision up the chain-of-command, which is my right." *[Years later, I turned out to be a reasonably good appellate lawyer.]*

"*Get out!*" This scenario was becoming a frequent occurrence, I thought to myself, and left. A few weeks later, I still had not contributed, but still received orders to proceed to basic jet training at Meridian. The CO had transferred me to avoid hurting his statistics, and then publicly claimed victory with "100% participation" in the United Way campaign. I wondered what words of praise he would put on my Fitness Report.

I remember walking up the hangar stairs the day I checked in to Meridian, and seeing an angry lieutenant in full flight gear glaring down at me. "Are *you* scheduled to fly with *me*? If you are, you're late!"

"I don't think so, Sir. I'm just checking in."

"Well, *whoever* he is, he's in trouble!" I found out this was Lieutenant John S. McCain ('58), and the word among the students was that he was a difficult instructor and should be avoided if possible. A few years later, I was reading the message boards on *USS Ticonderoga*, and found a classified message announcing his shoot-down and capture by the North Vietnamese. Later, of course, he would become a U.S. senator and presidential candidate. It is truly a small world.

The flying at Meridian was demanding, but even more fun. There is something about the feel and sound of a jet that has no equal. I knew I had made the right career decision, because I loved every second in the cockpit.

During off-hours, we socialized with other married couples. However, our time in Meridian coincided with the nation's civil rights chaos. College kids and political activists from the North were traveling around the South to register African-American voters. While we were there, the Ku Klux Klan murdered three of the young activists. Many of the local cops were sympathetic (if not affiliated) with the KKK.

Two of our good friends were Ben Thomas ('64) and his lovely wife. Since they were African-Americans, we were constantly concerned for their personal safety in this tense environment, and tried to go out together as a group whenever possible. I frequently thought about what Ben and his wife must have been going through. Here he was, a Naval officer and Naval Academy graduate, and a student in jet flight training, but still having to use caution about where he went and how he talked to local Whites in this Mississippi town. The 1967 movie, *In the Heat of the Night,* captured the essence of this environment.

We all did well in basic jet training, and Ben went on to fly the A-4 Skyhawk. I then lost track of him. Some years later, I was a duty LSO on a carrier conducting flight ops near San Diego, when some A-4s came out to do some qualifying landings. I was standing next to the LSO from the A-4 squadron as one of his birds trapped. Instead of taxiing out of the wires to the bow parking area, the little jet began to roll ominously toward the starboard edge of the flight deck.
"I've lost my brakes!" radioed the pilot. Red hydraulic fluid gushed from his brakes.

His nose wheel hit the deck-edge wheel stopper, and then bounced over it, placing the aircraft nose-down in the catwalk, apparently headed for the water below. Thinking the aircraft was going into the water, the pilot ejected and narrowly missed the large radar antenna rotating above the bridge. His chute opened, and he nearly landed back on the flight deck, but wound up swimming in the wake of the ship. As the pilot drifted down in his chute, he was suspended only a few yards from the LSO platform. To my shock, it was Ben Thomas! "Hey, Ben!" I yelled. Ben seemed focused on other things, and did not return my greeting.

Ben landed in the water behind the carrier and was quickly recovered by the helo. He was returned to the ship, unhurt. His aircraft never did go over the side, and was still perched precariously in the catwalk with its engine running. Ben is one of the few pilots I ever heard of who had an ejection and parachute landing, but still did not lose the aircraft. Ben did exactly the right thing, but since the aircraft stuck in the catwalk, he probably wished he had not ejected. You just never know. Life is full of surprises, especially when you fly jets. I had found another link in the Chain, and an unlikely class reunion—on the flight deck of an aircraft carrier.

My friendship with Ben reminds me that the Naval Academy of the Sixties and the Naval Academy of today are different institutions in many respects. In our graduating class of nearly 1,000, there were no women, and only *four* African-Americans. Those men may not have realized it at the time, but their graduation from the Naval Academy helped to pave the way for other minority candidates in the future.

Just as the World War II military juggled the race issue by creating "the Tuskegee Airmen" 332nd Fighter Group (all African-Americans) and the Army's 442nd Regimental Combat Team (Asian-Americans), the Navy of the Sixties was slow to eliminate racial bias and open this elite institution to all qualified candidates. Wesley Brown, the first African-American graduate of the Naval Academy, received his diploma and commission with the Class of 1949, over 100 years after the Academy's founding. Why did it take 100 years to admit a qualified African-American? Obviously, there is no valid rationale for such barriers to exist.

Similarly, the "Tuskegee Airmen" of the all-black 332nd Fighter Group attained a World War II combat record of great distinction, fighting and risking their lives to defend a still-segregated society. In the same war, the "Go For Broke" 442nd Regimental Combat Team was primarily composed of Americans of Japanese ancestry, whose families were involuntarily held in *American* internment camps. The 442nd was the most decorated unit of the military, receiving 21 Medals of Honor and many other citations. Obviously, racial background did not prevent these racially segregated units from performing brilliantly in combat. President Truman formally desegregated the U.S. Armed Forces by Executive Order in 1948.

Today, women constitute about 20% of the Brigade, and racial minorities (non-white) about 35%. The intensive hazing, according to recent graduates, has been largely replaced by a much less physical and more intellectual approach, at least in part because of the admission of women since 1976. Some say this is a positive change, while others argue that the rigors of the "old" Plebe Year had an important role in preparing future combat leaders. A future war may tell us which approach was best.

In the case of my Academy class, the low number of African-Americans admitted is indefensible. Either there was bias in the admissions process, or the institution failed to reach out and actively recruit qualified African-American candidates, or both. One cannot ignore or explain away a statistical anomaly of this magnitude. The admissions process for the Class of 1964 (and other classes of that era) was skewed for some reason, as it related to race.

Our nation's values mandate that all qualified candidates have an unfettered, equal opportunity to seek admission to the Service Academies. However, because of the national security implications, Academy admission decisions must *always* be based on competitive merit, not a pursuit of filling demographic quotas. The Midshipmen and Cadets of today's Service Academies will be our military and naval leaders of tomorrow, and they *must* be the best. They will assume positions of great leadership responsibility, and much will be expected of them. A candidate's ethnicity should never be considered as a factor either *for* or *against* admission. These institutions *must* be completely "color-blind," as our country should be.

~ ~ ~

# Chapter 9: *A Flapping of Wings*

With each completed training flight in the T-2 jet trainer, our group became more cocky and self-assured. The competitive focus now shifted to *which* Fleet aircraft type would be the assignment for each of us. For some of the aircraft types, there was a minimum grade cut-off for qualifying. The F-8 Crusader required the highest grades, and several of us thought the shark-like charisma of this single-seat, single-engine fighter was irresistible. For others, the sheer muscle and grotesque beauty of the F-4 Phantom was the draw. In this Vietnam-era period, the only other choices available for jet "newbies," or "nuggets," were the A-4 Skyhawk or occasionally the A-6 Intruder, both attack (bomber) birds. There really were no "bad" choices in the jet universe. Each promised its own opportunities and special brand of action.

Our student group completed the Meridian syllabus and headed back to Pensacola for carrier qualification in the T-2. Life was good at Pensacola Beach, and we were riding high. I could not believe they actually paid us to have so much fun. Nevertheless, some students had difficulty around the ship, and were easily confused.

While one student was on final, struggling to stay on glide slope, the Air Boss asked, "On final, what's your fuel state?"

The student replied, "Ask me something in the middle [*of the instrument panel*]!"

Another one had missed the wires on repetitive passes, known as "bolters." The Air Boss was concerned about his remaining fuel and asked, "Two Zero Five, your state?"

The student stammered, "N-N-North Carolina, Sir."

The next stop was advanced jet training at either Beeville or Kingsville, Texas, flying the TF-9 Cougar, a swept-wing jet of Korean War vintage. This was a more demanding aircraft, and the syllabus involved a wider scope, including weapons delivery and Air Combat Maneuvering (ACM), traditionally called "dogfighting." In ACM, certain students began to demonstrate the beginnings of a killer instinct, and showed early tactical aptitude. One of these "hard chargers" became our first fatality—to be followed by many more.

I became good friends with Tom Wilburn, an ex-"Black Shoe" (term for a non-aviation officer) and graduate of the Merchant Marine Academy. He had been the engineering officer on a destroyer, and then successfully applied for flight training. We shared an obsession with mastering air combat skills. Over drinks, we would fantasize about shooting North Vietnamese MIGs out of the sky, as our wives listened politely and rolled their eyes.

On one sunny Texas day, Tom was chasing an instructor when one of our overly aggressive Ensigns tried to get to the "bogey" first. He lost sight of Tom below him and crashed into the tail of Tom's aircraft, killing himself instantly. Tom ejected, but his chute failed to open. Unable to locate the ripcord handle as he plummeted toward the ground, he literally clawed the chute pack open with his hands. The chute finally deployed, and he got one swing in his chute before he hit the ground between the burning aircraft. For years, Tom had frequent nightmares about falling toward the ground and struggling to open his chute.

Our student group—along with our wives—had a rude awakening, as we attended the dead pilot's memorial service and stopped by his apartment to console the new widow. At this young age, none of us knew exactly how to act, or what to say. There would be many more of these sad events in the future. We began to realize we were not as indestructible as we had thought.

We progressed to carrier qualifications in the TF-9. *USS Lexington* steamed around off the Texas coast, and we took off in a six-plane flight to meet her. Crossing the coast, we let down to about 3,000', when I got a surprise. A big Texas bumblebee started buzzing angrily around my face. I dropped my visor, and hoped he would not find a way inside. I radioed the instructor leading the flight, "Sir, I have a bee in my cockpit."

"Say *again*, Five?" I knew the other students had to be laughing, but I was concerned about ridding myself of this unwanted passenger. My carrier landings were not that great, and now I would have to worry about being stung all the way down the glide slope.

"I'm serious, Sir."

"OK, Five, detach and slow down to 150 knots, depressurize the cockpit, and open the canopy. That should blow him out. Don't forgot to close the canopy and re-pressurize. Then catch up to us."

"Will do, Sir." The TF-9 canopy was somewhat unique. Instead of opening like a clam shell, it slid back on rails and could be safely opened at slow flying speeds.

I split off to the right, pulled the power back, and slowed to 150 knots. Sadly, I forgot to secure my charts, which I would need to find my way back to Kingsville. When I depressurized and opened the canopy, there was a blast of air that almost took my helmet off. All of the charts and maps went overboard. *At least I got rid of the damn bee,* I thought.

I felt like a real celebrity, as I entered the break over the ship by myself. I broke left in a 4-g turn to downwind, dropped the gear and flaps and called the abeam position. *Damn, that carrier looks small.* Rolling onto final, I saw and called the meatball, which for a change, was nicely centered with the green datum lights. *Man, I'm doing great,* I said to myself. Then I became aware of some motion in my peripheral vision. *The bee!* The little bastard had survived, and he seemed very upset! Apparently, bees do not like to be depressurized. Now I had to modify my scan: meatball, airspeed, line-up, and now *bee position*! Luckily, I still caught a wire. After I taxied out of the landing area, I opened the canopy and the bee left to ride with someone else. I never heard the end of that incident. On later flights, I would frequently hear someone key their mike, with the sound "BZZZZZZZZZZZ." *Very unprofessional.*

Suddenly, flight training was over, and we pinned on our wings in a small ceremony. While the new Naval Aviators congratulated each other, I noticed a worried, somber look on the face of Wife #1. I wondered, *What does she know that I don't?*

In a few days, we learned of our Fleet aircraft assignments. Tom and I were going to the F-8 Crusader, our first choice. We felt like we had just won the lottery, and were on top of the world. Our wives, having heard stories about the many dangers of flying this demanding bird, were not as thrilled. I noticed they began to express new interest in our life insurance coverage.

Sometimes you have to follow your destiny, regardless of the risk. I was determined to live up to the legacy of my dad and his World War II exploits. He was obviously a thrill-seeker. *Good thing I am not like him,* I said to myself.

~ ~ ~

# Chapter 10: *Sharpening the Claws*

With the Training Command behind us, our group was sent to advanced instrument training. One of my instructors wrote in a flight evaluation: "Excellent hop, but this officer thinks he is God's gift to Naval Aviation." *Strange—I always thought humility was one of my strong points.*

As the war in Southeast Asia heated up, we expected to receive orders to some sort of jungle survival school, or at least the school in California. Instead, in a cold December, we were sent to the Survival-Evasion-Resistance-Escape (SERE) course in the rugged, snowbound mountains of Maine. The snow was so deep that we were required to wear snowshoes.

Within three days, we were all captured by the "enemy," who were actually a mix of U.S. Marines and Army troops, dressed like Russians, complete with fur  caps and AK-47s. The "prison camp" was adorned with signs in Esperanto, which many of them spoke instead of English (I never figured out why). A few of us taunted them by speaking "pig Latin." Russian, Korean, and Chinese music blared incessantly from loudspeakers. Guard towers were manned around a perimeter of barbed-wire and searchlights swept the camp during the night hours. It was very realistic, and with each passing hour, it seemed even more real. Several of the student pilots were beaten and subjected to hours of harsh interrogation in order to extract "war criminal confessions." One Marine student got severe frostbite, and several other students got sick.

Finally, I asked one of my Academy classmates, Bob Hinckley, if he wanted to try an escape. He agreed, and we planned a dive through the barbed wire into deep snow at one end of the camp, when the guards were distracted with a fake prisoner "fight" that we had arranged. It worked like a charm. We both slipped through the wire and made it into the woods. Our plan was to jog down the mountain road to the main highway (about three miles) and then break into the women's restroom in the gas station on the corner. We would then barricade ourselves in this unlikely place, figuring they would never look for us there, and raid the nearby vending machines for food. At the end of the training period, we would emerge victorious, having outsmarted these goons, and hold a press conference to pre-empt any retribution. *What a great plan!*

As Bob and I jogged down the mountain, we realized we had not eaten much for several days. Bob said, "Wait up! I put some bouillon cubes in my shoe before we were captured.....I'll share them with you." Ensign Hinckley's feet added a special gourmet flavor to those delicious cubes, but we ate them all anyway. This is another debt that must be repaid, which is why I always keep a Slim Jim in one shoe, just in case I bump into Bob again.

We thought we had made it, when suddenly we heard the tires of a vehicle coasting down the mountain behind us, with its engine and lights off. We dove off the road and sank headfirst into a deep snow bank. We fought our way back to the surface as we heard a loudspeaker: "OK, men, this is no drill. There is a blizzard coming, and you will not survive out here. You are ordered to come out now. If you don't, even if you live, you will not graduate!" Reluctantly, we came out. Death was one thing, but repeating the SERE course would be worse.

"You guys almost made it, huh?" said one of them, laughing. They drove us back to the camp, but made the mistake of placing us in *their own barracks* to warm up. We returned the favor by breaking into their lockers and kitchen, eating any food we could find. When they came back for us, their happy guards' home was a mess and they were furious.

They tied our hands and took us back to the camp. In the middle of a snowy Maine night and freezing temperatures, we were completely stripped and rolled around in a snow bank. We were then subjected to a harsh interrogation. When I was asked how we got out of the compound, I told them we were helped by a group of anti-Communist peasants that always vote Republican. I found myself naked again, back in the snow bank. All of this was certainly useful training, given that most of us were going to a *tropical jungle* environment in Southeast Asia. My friend Tom nearly died of exposure when they accidentally left him inside a frozen culvert and forgot about him. Two other students actually broke down and signed "confessions."

Finally, this lunacy was over and Tom and I reported to Fighter Squadron 174, the East Coast F-8 RAG (Replacement Air Group) at NAS Cecil Field, Florida, where we met the F-8 Crusader for the first time. For us, life would never be the same again. This was where it got deadly serious.

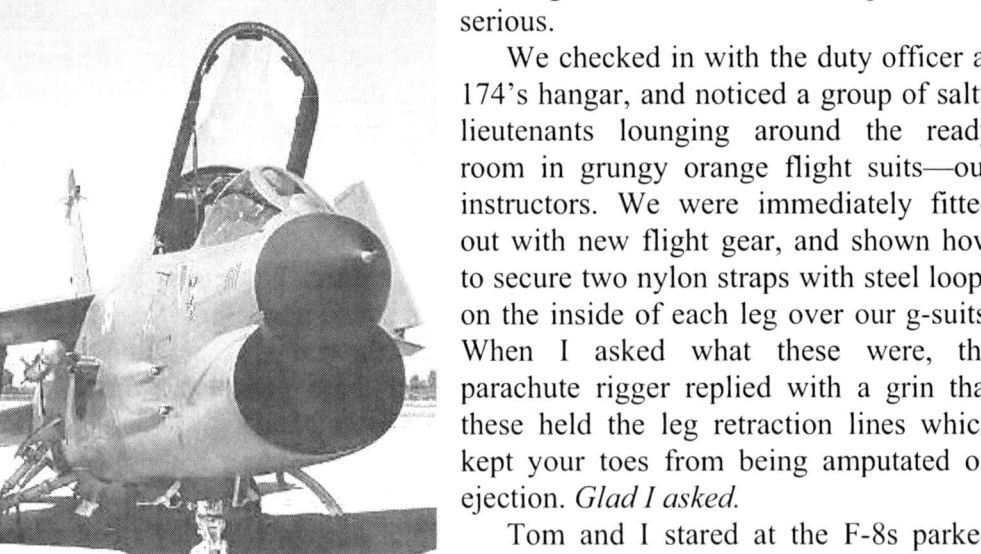

We checked in with the duty officer at 174's hangar, and noticed a group of salty lieutenants lounging around the ready room in grungy orange flight suits—our instructors. We were immediately fitted out with new flight gear, and shown how to secure two nylon straps with steel loops on the inside of each leg over our g-suits. When I asked what these were, the parachute rigger replied with a grin that these held the leg retraction lines which kept your toes from being amputated on ejection. *Glad I asked.*

Tom and I stared at the F-8s parked near the hangar. Even on the ground, the Crusader looked like it was going supersonic. It also *looked* angry, like a snarling junkyard dog. Thinking back to my Florida childhood, it also looked like a snake, poised to strike. Its big jet intake reminded me of a shark's mouth. As Tom and I would soon learn, it really *was* a man-eater.

The next day, we began an intensive ground school and simulator training for flying the Crusader. The problem for "nuggets" with this aircraft was that a two-seat trainer version was not available. The first time you flew it, you were all alone, with no one to look over your shoulder and tell you what to do. If you made a fatal mistake, no one could grab the controls and save you.

The F-8E, while now obsolete by the technological standards set by the F-15, F-16, F-18, and F-22, was a significant step forward in fighter aircraft in its time. It combined the best of all worlds for an air superiority fighter. It was highly maneuverable, with a fast roll rate and excellent rate of climb. It could almost reach Mach 2 in level flight. Its range of over 1,000 miles allowed operational flexibility and time over target. Best of all, it had an effective radar, full ECM (electronic counter-measures) gear, and a variety of weapons loads, including guns, bombs, rockets, and missiles. The standard fighter configuration was four internal 20mm cannon with two heat-seeking Sidewinder missiles, although it could carry four. Most of the F-8 MIG kills in Vietnam were accomplished with the two-Sidewinder load. With four Sidewinders, aircraft performance suffered because of the increased weight and drag of the added missiles and their larger fuselage pylons. Therefore, most of the squadrons that flew in Vietnam viewed the two additional missiles as a liability and unnecessary.

Although fighter pilots hated air-to-ground missions, the F-8E could also carry heavy loads of bombs and rockets: two 2,000 lb. bombs; or twelve Zuni 5-

inch rockets; or thirty-eight 2.75-inch rockets; or six 500 lb. bombs. This was a versatile combat aircraft that could fill a variety of missions. However, that was the *good* news. The *bad* news was that this 1950s vintage bird, in which astronaut John Glenn had set the coast-to-coast speed record, had some important peculiarities. If you disregarded them, you could be the subject of your own memorial service.

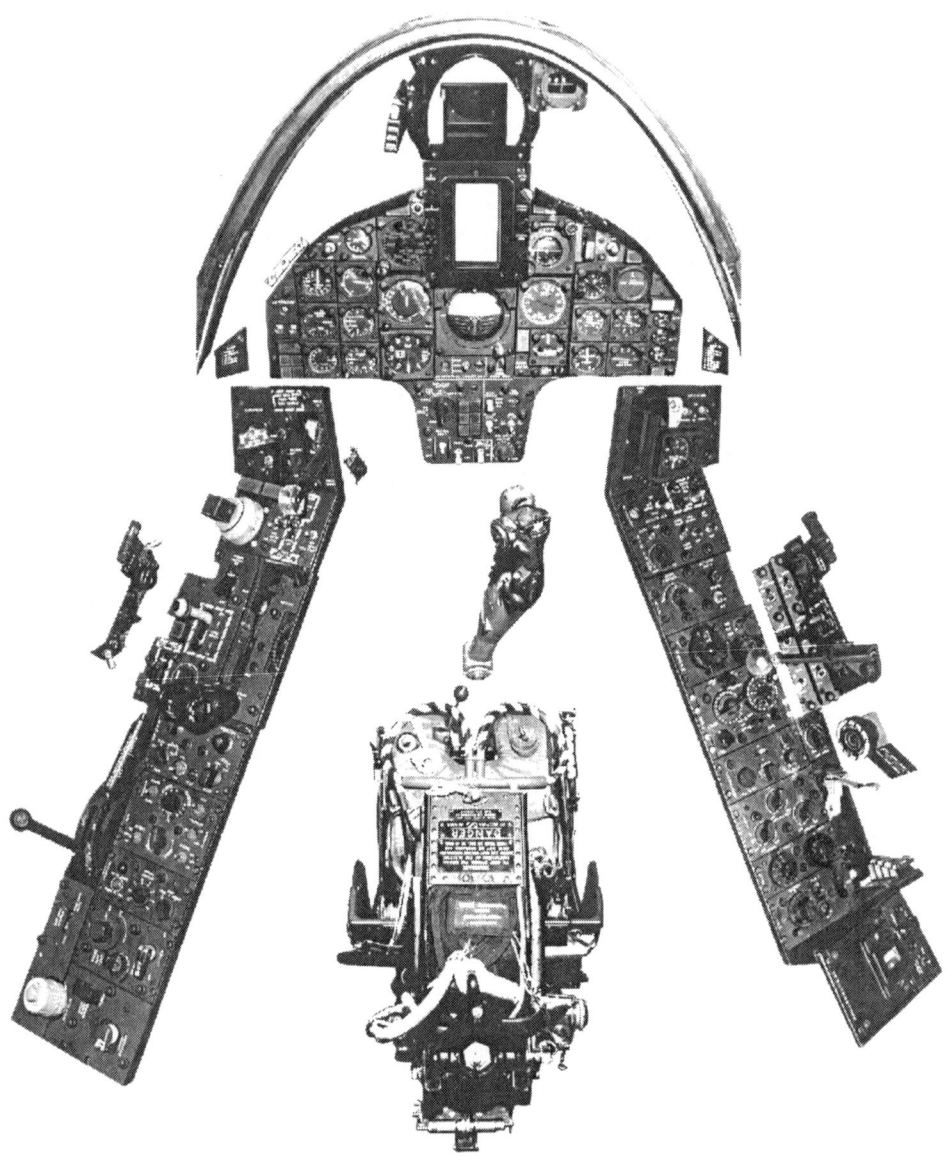

*Cockpit layout of the F-8E Crusader, showing the front and side panels, control stick, and ejection seat.*

When the LTV design team came up with this cutting-edge aircraft, they found that the pilot could not see over the nose to land on the carrier, and the nose gear would not withstand the high angle-of-attack landing. Ordinary wing flaps were also inadequate.

To achieve the necessary angle-of-attack and maintain visibility for carrier approaches, the engineers designed a unique wing-pivot system. They connected a hydraulic jack to the leading edge of the wing, which raised the wing angle for takeoffs and landings. They also added leading-edge wing "droops" and trailing edge "flaperons," all of which allowed the aircraft to fly slow enough to land on the carrier and not break a wire. However, for takeoff and landing, you had to think "wing UP" instead of "flaps down," as in conventional aircraft. After takeoff, the normal logic was also inverted: it was "wing DOWN" instead of "flaps up" as the bird accelerated to climb speed.

In the flight configuration, the F-8's high-performance wing tended to punish those who manhandled her by doing a snap roll ("departure") and entering into a dangerous spin, sometimes inverted. If a pilot could not learn to sense the F-8's symptomatic warning sounds and vibrations, this temperamental rattlesnake was probably going to bite him. If you entered a spin below 10,000', you had to eject immediately, or you probably would not make it. Either you bonded with *this* bird, or you would be a statistic. There were not many "casual" F-8 drivers in Fleet squadrons, when it came to flying this beautiful monster.

This unusual and seductive aircraft tended to change the personalities of the pilots who flew it well. The F-8 Crusader demanded intensity, mental independence and an aggressive attitude, and forced the men who sat in its saddle to become part of it—or bear the painful consequences. The Crusader was not separable into pilot and machine. To be successful, the two elements had to become a single, aggressive, killer organism with wings. The best F-8 squadrons had a swaggering, unruly culture that made the term "officers and gentlemen" laughable. The Navy establishment viewed F-8 pilots as sociopathic—but in wartime, temporarily, they were a necessary evil.

The forced solitude of the complex cockpit, combined with the technical challenges of flying this unique aircraft, pushed the F-8 pilot to develop levels of skill that he probably would never have acquired in another aircraft. You were riding your very own fire-breathing dragon, and you had to be in "synch" with it at all times. For me, this was the perfect aircraft. It made my naturally combative personality more of an asset than a liability, for the first time in my career.

Somehow, the F-8 and I seemed to understand each other. It reminded me of taming a wild animal, with lethal characteristics that deserved respect and awareness of its warning signs. With an expert pilot at the controls, we all believed that this aircraft was unbeatable. As expressed by one of the famous F-8 posters, the goal was to fear nothing and become "the meanest mutha' in the valley."

Within ten days, we were required to start and taxi the aircraft, with an instructor hanging on the side. Then we were facing the first flight—solo—with an instructor chasing us in another aircraft. The moment of truth had arrived.

The raw power of this bird, compared to our previous training aircraft, was shocking. As I rolled down the runway for the first time in the F-8, I realized this thing was taking *me* for a ride. After passing 125 knots, the roaring beast lifted from the runway, and things started to happen very fast. I raised the gear, lowered the wing and turned toward the Atlantic. *Looking good so far.*

The instructor joined on me, and he allowed me to do some aerobatics and get the feel of this complex machine. This must be how a baby eagle feels on his first flight. I felt a twinge of anxiety when the fun was over, and the instructor said, "OK, let's go back home." *Oops. Now comes the hard part.* This meant that I would have to *land* this thing.

We peeled off in the break over Cecil, with the instructor flying a close wing position on me. I dropped the gear and raised the wing—which also extended the flaps and landing droops—and then realized my sleek racehorse had become a bucking bronco. Unlike the other aircraft I had flown, it refused to stay on glide slope or "donut" approach speed. It seemed to require constant corrections of both aircraft attitude and power, and never stabilized.

This caused me to land fast, and have trouble slowing the bird down. I almost ran off the runway, giving the instructor a near heart attack. His comments at debrief: "Good hop, but you need to work on landings." I could not agree more.

Tom and I had many exciting experiences in the RAG, learning to cope with the F-8's peculiarities, most of which were dangerous. On one flight, my instructor, Lieutenant George "Jäger" [German for "hunter"] Talken took me on a low-level flight to strafe a shipwreck, a Navy target near Key West. Jäger was a real fighter pilot, and his love of flying this aircraft rubbed off on his students. This particular flight was a classic.

We launched from NAS Cecil and climbed to cruise at 31,000'. We began our descent after passing Orlando, crossing the coast near Clearwater. Dropping down to about 50' over the azure-blue waters of the Gulf of Mexico, we roared over the top of several fishing boats. This must have been somewhat scary for the anglers.

After about 45 minutes, Jäger called, "Tally-ho, target in sight. Follow my pattern." I looked ahead and saw an old destroyer, grounded on a reef.

"Jäger One, you have a fishing boat right behind the target," I radioed. There was a big sport-fishing boat about 200 yards from the wreck, apparently anchored.

"No problem, Two, watch this!" Jäger flew close by the boat, and then pulled up to a strafing pattern altitude. The boat was still not moving.

I thought Jäger was going to do another low pass, but to my shock, he fired a burst of 20mm into the wreck. Almost immediately, the fishing boat cut its anchor line, started its engines, and zoomed away at maximum speed. *Wow!* Although the boat was never in real danger, the experience was probably terrifying to the people on board.

"They're clear now, Two. They were inside a restricted area, which is well indicated on the charts. They like to cheat and fish near that wreck. That's what they get for breaking the rules! Commence your run on the target."

I fired out my guns in two runs, and we flew back to Cecil Field at high altitude. When I landed, I had minimum fuel remaining, enough for about 10 minutes of flying. I could not wait to tell Tom about *this* flight.

A few weeks later, we went out to the carrier for qualifying in the F-8. This required both day and night landings. Tom did well, but I had problems at night. I still had not mastered carrier landings in this tricky aircraft. However, I was not alone. Several of the other nuggets received criticism from the LSO. Finally, we all got the required landings, but our LSO probably needed a big martini that night.

As Tom and I completed F-8 training, we were directed to put in our choices for a Fleet squadron assignment. The two of us were itching to get into the air war over Vietnam, and to be in a squadron that was focused on killing MIGs.

After a lot of research, we learned of a squadron based at NAS Miramar, California, which had a big reputation. This unit had received the prized "E" (Fleet operational excellence award) several years in a row, and reportedly flew the F-8 to its limits. They had just returned from a combat cruise, and were in their training cycle.

This squadron only had spots for four "nuggets," which was unusual. Normally, there were more. Tom and I made them our first choice, and got the assignment. They were "The Legendary Red Lightnings" of Fighter Squadron 194, and in a matter of months, they were going again into harm's way aboard *USS Ticonderoga,* CVA-14. Their destination was the Gulf of Tonkin, just off the coast of Communist North Vietnam. The stage was set, and it would soon be our turn "in the barrel."

~ ~ ~

## Chapter 11: *Welcome to Hollywood*

In early 1966, San Diego was a classic California beach town, complete with multitudes of bikinis and surfboards. Upon arrival, I made a mental note to buy a surfboard as soon as possible. First, it was time to check in to Fighter Squadron 194, The Legendary Red Lightnings.

I met up with my friend Tom and we drove out to Naval Air Station (NAS) Miramar. We located VF-194's area, where a hangar displayed a huge sign: FIGHTERTOWN. Carrying our orders, we entered the ready room. In the first *Star Wars* movie, there was a scene in which Luke Skywalker and his entourage were searching for a pilot, and entered a bar containing a dozen or so bizarre creatures from various planets. This *was* that bar. Life often imitates art.

The duty officer, dressed in a dirty flight suit with unlaced boots propped up on his desk, was reading a paperback. A group of pilots stood in the back of the room, arguing loudly about who won the last "dogfight," or ACM engagement. Suddenly, all eyes were on us and the room fell silent. I felt like Gary Cooper in *High Noon.*

"Lieutenant Wilburn and Lieutenant Junior Grade Nelson reporting, Sir." The duty officer dropped his book and said, "Holy Christ, *nuggets*! Buzzard, go get the Skipper!" A tall, lanky pilot left the room. The ready room group became quiet and gathered around us for introductions. I felt like they were sizing us up, just as you do with potential adversaries before a fight begins.

This squadron was more like a professional sports team than a military unit. It had already set most of the operational performance records, which are based purely on flying skills, not gentlemanly behavior. It became clear they only wanted to be addressed by their call signs, not by their ranks or real names. In fact, we could not figure out the rank structure. There seemed to be only two officers who were addressed by other than their call sign—the Skipper (Commanding Officer) and the XO (Executive Officer). The rest treated each other as peers. Tom and I realized that as nuggets, we were going to be under intense scrutiny in this crowd.

Fighter squadrons in general are a strange warrior culture, and very different from the buttoned-down military mainstream. This was even truer in the Navy's F-8 fighter squadrons, where only three aspects of personal performance really mattered: excellence in air-to-air combat skills, accurate weapons delivery, and landing on the carrier. Everything else, including respect for rank, was not that important, and fierce flying competition with your peers was the daily norm. The Red Lightnings, however, took this culture to an extreme. Something told me I was going to fit in quite nicely—if I lived long enough.

As Tom and I stood nervously in the front of the ready room, a bear-like man in a flight suit came around the corner, followed by a gray-haired officer with steely blue eyes—the Skipper and XO had arrived. Commander Bob Chew (Naval Academy Class of '48) was the perfect CO for this squadron of hot-shot renegades. On the previous cruise on *Bon Homme Richard,* Chew's aircraft had been hit by North Vietnamese anti-aircraft artillery (AAA, or "flak") and had to punch out over the water, where he was rescued by the search-and-rescue (SAR) helo. His wingman—Buzzard—took several photographs of his ejection, which Chew had hanging conspicuously on the wall of his office. Buzzard could do no wrong, as far as Chew was concerned.

"Why aren't you men in your flight suits?" Chew asked. "You're strapping on an F-8 in fifteen minutes, and we need to know if you can fly." Tom and I looked at each other in shock. We were not prepared for this.

"Sir, our flight gear is still with the movers," Tom said.

"No problem—Maggot, get these guys fitted out, ASAP!"

"Roger that, Skipper!" Maggot ('61) was one of the more noteworthy pups in this orange-clad litter. He was a superb pilot, and the XO, Bill Conklin, usually assigned him to the diamond slot position in the squadron's air show team. His maniacal laugh penetrated the ready room, and he thought everything was funny.

In minutes, Tom and I were outfitted with new flight gear and found ourselves walking to the flight line. I remember thinking, *I hope I remember how to start this thing.* I did, and Tom and I were soon taxiing with four other F-8s to the runway. We were told to fly wing on our leader in a close section takeoff, and then we were climbing out eastward, toward the Salton Sea and El Centro.

The Skipper had chosen me as his wingman, and signaled me to break off into the Combat Spread formation. The Red Lightnings nearly always flew in this formation (sometimes erroneously called "Loose Deuce"), where the wingman flew directly abeam and slightly higher than the leader, about one mile apart. This made it nearly impossible for a bogey to get into a six o'clock firing position on either aircraft without being detected. Against the flexible Combat Spread, if you tried to "jump" one of the aircraft, the other would slide in behind you for the kill. Once a dogfight began, there was no "leader"—each pilot was considered equal and free to maneuver, but obligated to keep bogeys off the other pilot's six o'clock.

One of the distinguishing aspects of the Red Lightnings was promoted by the Skipper himself: "Never, *never* let anyone jump you and get behind you. God help you if they are able to sneak up on you and get your side number. If they do, you will stand the ready room duty the entire next weekend, because you have humiliated the squadron and stained our honor."

As a result of this official policy, as soon as Red Lightning pilots became airborne, they began frantically looking behind them and anticipating attack by unseen "bogeys," ready to do aerial battle. As the Skipper would say, "Gentlemen *[bad choice of words]*, no matter where we are, this squadron is *always* in the combat mode! And that includes the bar!" Their favorite trick was to hover just off the San Diego coast and pounce on unsuspecting F-8s and F-4s departing Miramar. These pitiful victims would then be publicly scorned and ridiculed at the next Happy Hour at the O'Club. The Red Lightnings were not popular and were considered arrogant and obnoxious, even by fighter pilot standards.

As we neared El Centro on our "introductory" flight, the Skipper called, "Break left, bogeys 7 o'clock high! Burner!" We pulled around in a 5-g turn as our afterburners lit with a boom, nearly doubling the thrust. We met the other four Crusaders head-on, with about 1,000 knots closure. The Skipper pulled up sharply in a left vertical maneuver, which spit me out behind him. I was trying to catch up, when one of the two bogey sections rolled over on me. "Tail-end Charlie" is often the first to be killed, since no one is guarding his six. However, I was not completely helpless, as the attackers found out.

As the Skipper got a "kill" on the first bogey section, which had overshot badly, I pulled down vertically under my two bogeys, baiting them into getting their noses down to follow me. This forced them to solve a severe vertical overshoot problem, with their noses pointed nearly straight down. Now the Skipper and I were both out of their reach. When they were committed, I pulled up into them as they shot past me in a vertical dive. I had learned this maneuver in the F-8 RAG, and found it very effective at blunting an attack, because it converts a defensive situation into a vertical or rolling "scissors" standoff, where you have a chance to win.

Unfortunately, I could not fly the F-8 close enough to stall speed, and my more experienced opponents quickly rolled over the top behind me after a few weaving turns, effortlessly controlling their birds at less than 200 knots "You're dead, nugget!" said the lead bogey. "And so are you, Buzzard!" said the Skipper, who had worked his way behind them when they were not looking.

The Skipper joined us up for the return to Miramar, where we did a six-plane "fan" break. This requires a precise, staggered "g" and deceleration differential between each aircraft in order to maintain landing interval. I screwed that up and wound up too close to the Skipper's bird on final, struggling to keep my bird from overrunning him. Luckily, he did not see my mistake.

Like the Blue Angels, the Red Lightnings *always* taxied in close section formation, another new concept for me. With overlapping wings, you had to be careful if the leader slowed down, or you would clip his wing. Finally, the hop was over, and Tom and I had survived the first day with the Red Lightnings.

Back in the ready room, the flight debrief was more like a barroom brawl than a professional discussion. The Skipper described with his hands and the chalkboard how he had killed all of the bogeys, while Buzzard and the others bragged about getting Tail-end Charlie (me). The Skipper looked sternly at me and said, "Don't EVER get sucked behind me like that again! You will get killed by a MIG, and worse yet, *I* might get killed."

One of the other pilots asked what I had done to sucker them in to the vertical over-shoot, and I said, "I could tell you, but it's classified." They all laughed.

"Does that maneuver have a name?" he asked.

"Yep, it's the Half Nelson. The Full Nelson is even better." More laughter.

The Red Lightning squadron, whose official squadron call sign was "Red Flash," was a ruthless, irreverent, and exclusive club, built upon flying skills. Its culture was more like Alan Alda's *M*A*S*H*, or John Belushi's *Animal House* than the Academy decorum that I had been taught. Their personal call signs said it all: Spanky, Buzzard, Devil, Maggot, Porky, Snake, Taco, Burger, Brillo, Sheepdog, Iron Mike. You could not give *yourself* a call sign—you had to earn it, the squadron originated it, and then it was painted on the side of your assigned aircraft. The typical call sign usually referred to some personal characteristic. Others memorialized an embarrassing incident, or were a humorous version of the bearer's name. Tom had impressed them with his testy personality and aggressiveness, and they gave him the call sign "Gator." I was still a nameless orphan.

Adding to my call sign superstition, the pilots who were never branded with call signs did not survive the cruises. One was the fourth nugget and my Academy classmate, Galen Gilbert. Another pilot ejected unsuccessfully from a burning aircraft, and did not survive. To my relief, I was finally baptized with my own call sign—"Hot Dog"—after some wild surfing during a squadron beach party in Hawaii, en route to Vietnam. The squadron immediately painted the name on my aircraft, my helmet, and all of my squadron nametags. A few weeks later, the veteran pilot who gave me the call sign—"Iron Mike" Newell ('62)—was killed by a SAM over North Vietnam. Mike was a super pilot and excellent officer, and seemed to know everything about the F-8. On the previous cruise, his roommate, Jeff Osborn (also Class of '62), had been killed after hitting the water during a night catapult shot. I remember wondering if my call sign carried a jinx.

As we completed our training cycle, the squadron won the prestigious "E" again. In 30,000' aerial gunnery, one pilot, Snake, actually hit the towed target with almost *every* round of 20mm that was loaded in the aircraft for the exercise. Since the gunnery run was actually flown at supersonic speed, this was even more remarkable. This would be comparable to getting a hole-in-one on each hole of a major golf course. The collective skill of these characters was intimidating. They were good at everything you could do with the F-8. For a lowly nugget, it was like being an extra on a Hollywood movie set, alongside a cast of super stars. The Red Lightnings were larger than life. The squadron was like a successful version of the New York Yankees, with a star-studded roster.

*The Red Lightning Squadron, aboard* **USS Ticonderoga***, 1967. We had already lost three pilots when the photo was taken. First row, from left: Snake, Ed Cichowitz, the XO, the Skipper, Burger, and Maggot; second row: Spanky, Buzzard, Brillo, Taco, Hot Dog, Porky, Sheepdog, Gator, and Devil. After Galen Gilbert's death, Gator, Spanky, and I were the only nuggets (newbies) remaining.*

Soon it was time to "CARQUAL" on our ship, *USS Ticonderoga*. My previous landings in the RAG had been on a "big deck" carrier. The other small carriers, to which F-8s were assigned, were *Bon Homme Richard, Oriskany, Hancock,* and *Intrepid*. On a perfect approach to these small ships (about 40,000 tons vs. 90,000 tons for the "big decks"), the F-8 tail hook only missed the flight deck edge (the "round-down") by 10.1 feet. There was little room for error, especially at night. You *had* to be good around the ship, or you would not survive.

One night, my Academy classmate, Galen Gilbert, was making a section carrier controlled radar approach (CCA). He was flying wing on Sheepdog, an experienced lieutenant. Galen got vertigo, rolled away from Sheepdog and flew into the water. No trace of him or his aircraft was ever found. I was devastated when I learned of his loss. One minute, he was there; the next, he was gone. His name vanished from the squadron roster as if he never existed.

The squadron had a memorial service for him at the base chapel, attended by his parents and all of the pilots. I tried to express my sorrow to his parents, but words failed me. His mom and dad stood bravely outside of the chapel, greeting the pilots and thanking them for coming. I could not help but think how terrible they must have felt. Not only did they lose their precious son, but he had just graduated from the Naval Academy and won his Navy wings, both significant achievements. After all that, he was taken from them by his own mistake, a momentary lapse in focus. I realized that I could easily be the next victim, because I was not doing well around the ship, a dangerous place for nuggets.

One of my contemporaries and a long-time friend, Lieutenant Junior Grade Jerry "Dog" Pearson, had just completed the RAG training, and had checked in to VF-24 aboard *USS Bon Homme Richard* (nick-named "Bonnie Dick"). For operational reasons, this carrier was recycled to return to combat operations without completing all of her overhaul repairs. Nevertheless, her air wing was directed to rendezvous with her in the area west of San Clemente Island and south of Catalina Island. Jerry launched from the carrier on a dark night to complete night carrier qualifications. His experience vividly demonstrates how the cumulative effect of bad command decisions can result in an airborne disaster.

Big sea conditions in the area were causing the small carrier's deck to pitch wildly, and very few pilots were getting aboard. Landing on a carrier at night is difficult enough, but with a pitching deck, it is beyond a new pilot's capabilities. In addition, one of the carrier's arresting gear systems was inoperative, leaving only three "wires" instead of the normal four. The carrier's radar and navigation (TACAN) system were also inoperative. This night should have been spent at the bar.

Because of the ship's proximity to the Navy airfield on San Clemente Island, a very low "bingo" fuel had been approved. This is the fuel quantity that allows an aircraft to fly safely to an alternate field and land. Unfortunately, the ship lost track of its position during the landing operations, and had moved far to the north without adjusting the "bingo" fuel quantity.

Finally, after several near accidents, the ship's captain finally decided the deck was pitching too much to land the F-8s safely. Jerry and his squadronmates were directed to head for San Clemente and land. Jerry was the last in a line of seven aircraft, all headed to the small Navy island field with emergency fuel states. Looking at his fuel gauge, he realized he could not make it, and would probably be forced to eject and parachute into the dark Pacific Ocean below.

Just as he had resigned himself to a dangerous night ejection, he spotted a lighted runway through a hole in the clouds! Realizing this was San Nicolas, another Navy island facility, he immediately descended to land before running out of fuel.

Jerry was unaware that rain had drenched the runway, and that a strong crosswind was gusting from the right. He landed with his hook down, hoping to catch the field arresting gear. To his surprise, the hook failed to engage the wire. He found out later that the field personnel had neglected to change the arresting gear to allow for his landing direction.

As he tried to slow the aircraft, the crosswind pushed him to the left. He knew he was going off the runway, so he followed proper procedures and blew the canopy off the aircraft. Jerry remembers vividly what happened next:

The instant I left the runway, the right main mount dug into the mud, which then dropped the right wing tip down low enough to dig into the mud, and the airplane shot back up into the air, and did a 360-degree roll, still headed sideways. I never in my wildest dreams thought it would do something like that. Before I could really get a grasp on what had just happened, it did another 360-degre roll, except it now did a partial pirouette on the nose, rather than doing a clean roll. I wondered during the second roll, is this thing going to come to a rest upside down, or will I get lucky, and come down right side up. As any aviator will tell you, it's better to be lucky than good, any day. This night I was lucky, and the F-8 came to a spine-jolting stop—right-side up.

Next, I had to get the hell out of the aircraft—and quick. I pulled the emergency egress handle, which was supposed to release me from the ejection seat, with the seat pan. I pulled the handle, pulled myself forward, and up. It felt jammed, and nothing happened. Very concerned, I tried it again, by grabbing the canopy bow and pulling myself up from the ejection seat. It still would not release. My next realization was that I just might be pulling on some loose firing cable on the ejection seat, and might accidentally fire the ejection seat. I sat down carefully, unhooked myself as I would do if I were just getting out of the airplane, and stepped down about three feet or so onto a nice soft grass and mud area. No fire, no nothing, other than a deathly silence.

I decided to put the safety pins in the ejection seat so that it would not fire unexpectedly if the emergency personnel accidentally pulled the actuators. There I was, on an unknown island, off the runway, with my beloved, but sorry looking F-8—wingtips shattered and broken, and the front quarter-panels all broken out. I walked around the wreck, mumbling how sorry I was to have literally destroyed a perfectly good airplane.

Soon I saw some lights on a big crash truck, which was now screaming down the runway toward me. Standing alongside the aircraft in the dark, I started to walk over to the truck to tell them all was well, and that there was no fire, nor any ordinance on board, and that I had already safety-pinned the ejection seat. In a flash, two guys ran toward the airplane, dressed in asbestos suits, carrying a hose attached to a long lance-like probe. They could not wait to poke the thing through the side of the airplane, and start spraying foam all over the interior. I jumped out in front of them to stop them from doing any more damage to my mortally injured F-8. They didn't see me at first, so I had to grab one of them on the arm, which must have scared him. The two men probably thought I was a ghost, coming out of the wreckage to haunt them.

Jerry had *his* fun; now my turn was next. After arguing with Wife #1 for hours during the previous night, and then standing the duty all day, I was scheduled for six night traps. I was tired, but I needed the landings to be qualified for the combat cruise.

At about 2100, I took off from Miramar and contacted the carrier approach control, which directed me to hold. "We had a crash, and we are clearing the deck," said the controller. I thought to myself, *Oh, wonderful—this is a real confidence-builder!*

After holding for an hour, I got low on fuel. I floundered through a night aerial refueling with an A-3 tanker, and was finally cleared for the approach. Now exhausted, I got high and fast, and missed the wires, "boltering" off the angle-deck. I also missed the next approach, and then got a wave-off from the LSO for being too high on the next pass. I decided, *The hell with this, I'm landing this thing.* Bad idea. When you got impatient with an F-8, you usually made mistakes.

I flew a close visual approach, to the consternation of the LSO. Determined not to go high again, I overcorrected by pulling off power and went dangerously low in close. The "meatball," which was supposed to stay centered between the green datum lights, went red, and then disappeared off the bottom of the lens. This meant that I was about to fly into the fantail at hangar deck level, nicknamed "the spud locker."

*A Red Lightning F-8 about to land. Three of the four wires are visible.*

*The Fresnel lens optical landing system, which gives the carrier pilot his glide slope information by aligning the yellow "meatball" with the row of green datum lights on either side. Here, the pilot would be dangerously low, as the "ball" is barely visible at the bottom of the lens, where it becomes bright red. With a "pitching deck" in heavy seas, landing becomes even more difficult.*

"Power, power, power!" yelled the LSO. I realized I was in big trouble, and hit afterburner. As the meatball rose from the bottom of the lens, I punched the nose over and caught a wire. I was lucky I did not dribble over the angle-deck into the water, as my spastic landing broke the tail hook mechanism. The maintenance people wired the hook up, and shot me off the catapult, sending me back to Miramar in disgrace. The next day, the Skipper said, "You are either going to be a *great* F-8 pilot, or you will be *dead* in six months. At this point, I don't know which." I silently agreed with him. *Humiliation.* Worse yet, no charisma.

~ ~ ~

## Chapter 12: *Take No Prisoners*

There were two types of fighters at Miramar in 1966—F-8 Crusaders and F-4 Phantoms. The two pilot communities could not have been more different. The F-8 had been developed and refined as an air superiority fighter. For close aerial combat over Vietnam, its AIM-9D Sidewinder heat-seeking missiles allowed the pilot to point and shoot while keeping his head on a swivel. If the dogfight became close combat, inside the minimum Sidewinder range, the F-8 could use its four 20mm cannon on the MIG.

The Navy F-4, on the other hand, was designed according to specifications of theoreticians in the Pentagon to be a pure Fleet interceptor, using missiles only. It had no guns. It had two engines that left highly visible smoke trails, and a Radar Intercept Officer (RIO) in the back seat to run the radar. In Vietnam, this meant it could not be as effective as the F-8 in close-range dogfighting. In spite of these problems, Lieutenant "Duke" Cunningham and his back-seater, Willie Driscoll, scored five MIG kills while flying an F-4 to become the only Navy "aces" (5 or more kills) of the Vietnam War.

The differences in the design of these two aircraft caused their pilots to be trained and think differently. In one incident, an F-4 pilot reportedly shot down his wingman with a missile, mistaking him for a MIG. The F-4s incurred so many losses by the MIGs that the Navy created Top Gun to address these deficiencies. Having a crewmember in the back seat also tended to overly "civilize" the flying of many F-4 pilots. The F-8 pilot only had to worry about himself and could fly his aircraft with wild abandon. Meanwhile, the F-8 amassed the highest overall kill ratio of the Vietnam War against the MIGs. The essential difference between the two fighter communities was that the F-8 pilots were trained to think like airborne *predators*, while the F-4 crews largely viewed themselves as Fleet *interceptor* pilots. *Animals* are predators and *gentlemen* are interceptors.

True to form, the Red Lightnings took fiendish delight in making the F-4 crews feel inadequate by mercilessly hunting them on almost every flight. The area west of San Diego, between San Clemente Island and the coast became "MIG alley," infested with bogeys waiting to jump the unwary driver. While the Navy hierarchy had strict policies against "unauthorized ACM," they knew very well what was going on offshore, and wisely looked the other way. The admirals felt it was better for the pilots to get embarrassed around San Diego than killed by a MIG in Vietnam. So far, no aircraft accidents had been attributed to the unauthorized ACM, so it continued. Commodore "Swede" Vejtasa, Commander Fleet Air Miramar, was a double "ace" from World War II, and the recipient of three Navy Crosses, the Legion of Merit, and the Bronze Star. He understood the need for this realistic training and quietly condoned it.

The Red Lightnings took this Wild-West practice to a new level, as usual. Every Friday, they would notify all Miramar ready rooms that they would be waiting for all challengers over the water near the 270-degree radial from

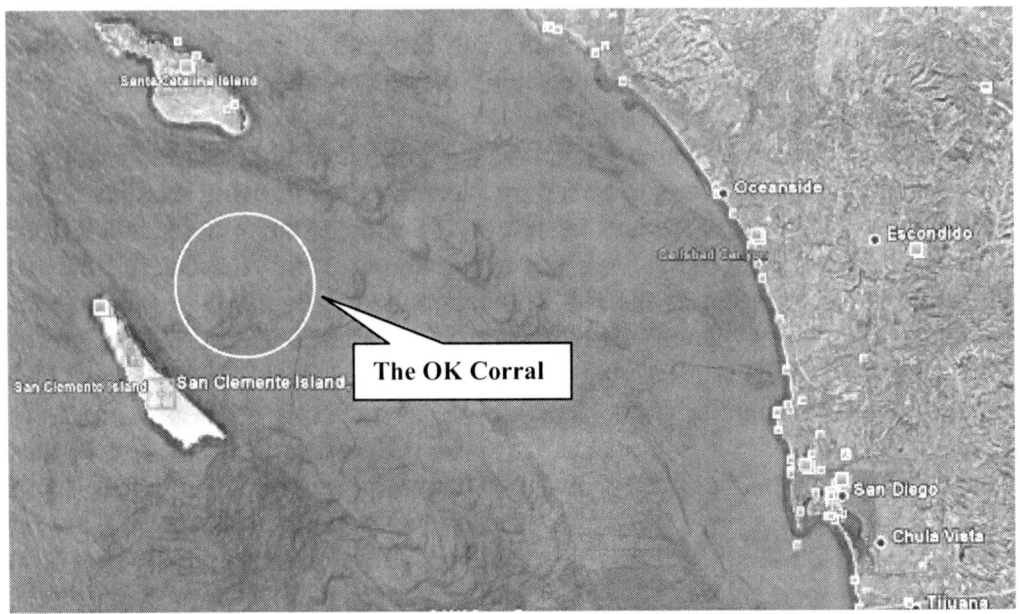

Miramar at 40 miles. This became known as "the OK Corral." At 1400, the area went "hot," and a giant "fur ball" of turning, twisting fighters would develop. It was not unusual to see 20 or more aircraft in a single battle. When the F-4s showed up, they would try to simulate the use of their Sparrow head-on radar missiles, which are quite useless in a "fur ball." This usually resulted in the Red Lightnings pouncing on the floundering F-4s as they decelerated and tried unsuccessfully to turn with the F-8s. Using gun cameras, the Red Lightnings acquired a huge inventory of documented F-4 "shoot downs." On one occasion, I set up a projector and played about fifty of these film clips at Friday Happy Hour at the O'Club, resulting in a near riot and lots of broken glass.

There was also vicious competition among the Miramar F-8 squadrons. Commodore Vejtasa issued an annual award to the best F-8 squadron at Miramar. With this award came a coveted trophy, known as The Mutha' Trophy. It was a glass-encased Japanese animal figure, Tanuki, with a hideous face and eyes that constantly flashed. At her side, a baby displayed what appeared to be an oversized set of testicles.

The Red Lightnings usually won this trophy each year, which became a source of intense envy and aggravation among the other F-8 squadrons. Finally, pilots from one of the other squadrons broke into the Red Lightnings' ready room one night and stole the Mutha'

Trophy. The Skipper immediately ordered a counterstrike to rescue Mutha' from the evildoers.

On a Saturday afternoon, Buzzard, Gator, and I executed a forced entry into the offending squadron's spaces, and after forcibly subduing the watch officer, left with Mutha'. We returned her to her proper shrine in our ready room, and locked her up. She seemed happy to be home. Gator got a bloody nose, but the mission was a total success. Sometimes you have to take casualties to win.

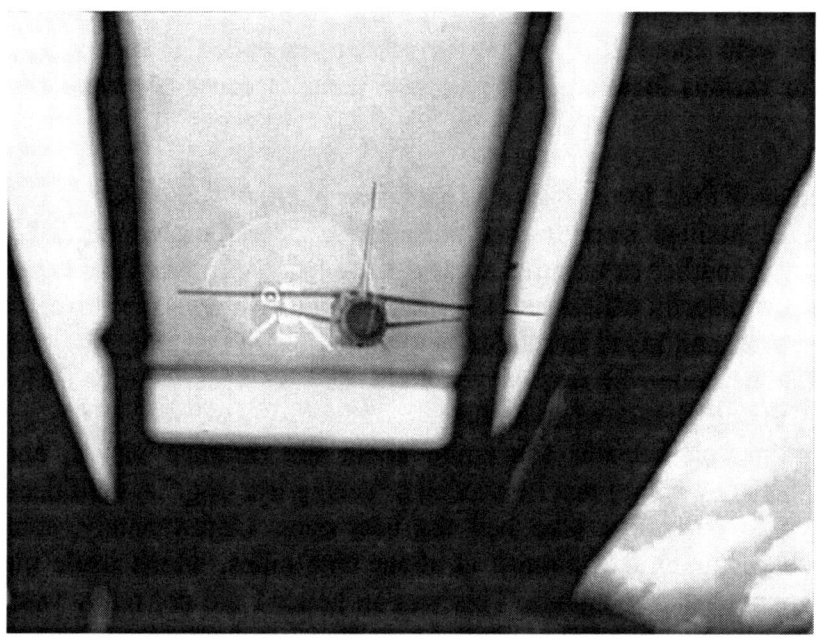

*View from an F-8 cockpit through the gun sight reticle. Note the visible "pipper," focused on the left wing of the F-8 leader. When pulling g's, the pipper floats to compute the proper lead solution for the cannon at a specified firing range.*

One morning, Maggot told me he was taking me on a sightseeing tour of the Grand Canyon. We launched from Miramar and flew east to the Tuba City area. We then started a low-level run *inside* the canyon, heading back west toward Las Vegas and Hoover Dam. The canyon became so narrow that Maggot had me fly directly behind him about 200' in "trail" so that I could instantly match his turns. Soon the limestone canyon walls loomed high above us on either side as we zoomed along at 350 knots.

It was great fun—until Maggot took a wrong turn and flew up a box canyon. Suddenly the canyon stopped, and a vertical wall was directly ahead. "Burner now!" he yelled and pulled straight up. I thought, *What a lousy way to die.*

The F-8's power saved us. We barely made the top of the canyon wall, and rolled inverted to float the nose over the rim, nibbling on a stall. Still in afterburner, we staggered over some horses and campers at the canyon rim as we struggled to keep the birds flying. It must have been exciting for those civilian sightseers.

After we recovered, Maggot dove back down into the main canyon again, determined to reach Hoover Dam. As we climbed out over the dam, I realized my fuel was dangerously low. We arrived at Miramar and my bird had about five minutes of fuel remaining. When I complained to Maggot, he replied, "No sweat. Fuel left after a flight is wasted. By the way, did you see the cables?" It seems that there were about 26 large power cables suspended from rim to rim of the canyon in various locations. I never saw them, because we were flying *below* them.

It was now time for a change of squadron command. Bob Chew ('48) handed the Red Lightnings over to his outstanding XO, Commander Bill Conklin. Conklin was another superlative aviator, with heavy Korean War experience. He also was a wonderful officer and leader. He had flown with the Royal Navy on an exchange tour, and loved formation aerobatics. There was only one problem with this handsome dude—he was 40 years old, and his eyes were bad. He had been secretly wearing glasses when he flew.

The squadron became concerned about his distance vision, and decided (without his knowledge) that he needed a "seeing-eye dog." A confidential survey was taken to determine who had the best eyes. Unfortunately, someone had noticed that I could spot aircraft at about nine miles, which made me the new Skipper's permanent wingman. This was an honor I did not really want, because this guy felt it was his duty to always be on the most dangerous missions. *No guts, no glory.*

Shortly after I was assigned as the new Skipper's wingman, he scheduled us for a night flight. "I need to know that you can stay on my wing, no matter what I do," he said. "We are going to do a few aerobatic maneuvers so you can get used to flying my wing." *Say again? At night?*

After we launched out of Miramar, we climbed out over the ink-black water to about 12,000', where he started a series of wing-overs, barrel rolls, loops, Immelman turns, half Cuban Eights, and even a split-S. With difficulty, I locked onto his wingtip, until the green wing light felt like it was close enough to touch. At times, I could not even tell whether we were inverted or right-side up. There was no horizon over the water, which was as dark as the sky. The only clue was the presence of a few stars—or were those boat lights? After we returned to Miramar, I was physically exhausted. "That was fun, huh?" said the Skipper, with a big grin. *Oh, yeah!*

His pet project was the squadron "air show" team. Leading a four-plane diamond, he would put Buzzard on his left wing, me on his right wing, and Maggot in the slot. On one occasion, the Skipper led a very low barrel roll over the carrier "to boost the troops' morale" and bottomed out with poor Maggot barely skimming the waves and screaming on his radio. His reply to Maggot was "Make sure your tail is black from my exhaust, or you are obviously not in position." *Jesus!*

I had become good friends with Porky and Buzzard, both of whom were great pilots and would have been good candidates for Pappy Boyington's Black Sheep Squadron in World War II. They were incorrigible products of the old Naval Aviation Cadet program, and neither Chew nor Conklin found it worth the effort to reform them. Besides, they produced "the numbers" when flying, and in the Red Lightning squadron, this was all that mattered.

For these two, every day was a new opportunity, as Buzzard would say, "to be VSH *[Very Shit Hot]*." Two of Buzzard's favorite quotes were "Better to bust your ass than look bad around the ship," and "I have never made an approach so bad that I couldn't salvage it." And Buzzard was our squadron LSO!

The squadron deployed to MCAS Yuma for its weapons training during that summer. Across the Arizona border from Yuma was Winterhaven, a small California town. It sported some sleazy bars and shady gamblers who liked to take advantage of the enlisted Servicemen from Marine Corps Air Station Yuma. Buzzard and Porky learned that some Sailors and Marines had been beaten up by locals at one particular bar, and vowed to administer some payback.

One night, with me in tow, they crossed into Winterhaven and located the guilty bar. After shutting down the bar's electrical power, they tossed some orange smoke flares through the door, causing the burly patrons to vacate the bar in a panic. As we escaped back to the base, Buzzard remarked, "Another successful mission. VSH!" Such was life in the Red Lightnings.

Porky was not only a great pilot, he was also an engineering genius. One of his creations was an analog launch-weight computer, which he built out of spare parts from our avionics shop. During cruise, the ready room duty officer used it to derive each aircraft's launch weight for the catapult settings, including any combination of ordnance or fuel. Porky offered its design to the Navy, but it was rejected as "unnecessary." The squadron used it anyway, and it prevented many errors on the launch weight calculation, which was a critical item.

As we prepared to go on deployment to Vietnam, our staterooms were pre-assigned by the air wing staff. Porky and Buzzard were roommates. They traveled to North Island where *Ticonderoga* was docked, and looked at their assigned room. It needed major upgrading.

Porky loaded up his tools, and he and Buzzard visited the San Diego naval base, where they found an old cruiser being prepared for the mothball fleet. Wearing hardhats and posing as "sand crabs" (civilian workers), they went aboard and checked out the cruiser's Flag spaces. The admiral's cabin had a beautiful teakwood door in immaculate condition. Porky dismantled it, and they took it back to North Island and installed it in their new stateroom. He then added matching wood paneling to the bulkheads, floor tile, and a marble vanity in place of the prison-like metal washbasin. They installed stereo speakers, along with recessed lighting and a built-in refrigerator. It was a cabin fit for a VIP. However, it still lacked one thing—air conditioning. These old ships only had minimal air conditioning, and you had to be senior to have that amenity.

Porky bought a window-style air conditioner at Sears, and installed it. He tapped into a fuse box for power, and with some of the ship's ducting, vented the hot air into the junior officer bunkroom down the passageway, where a group of ship's officers ("Black Shoes") lived. It must have been very hot in there, but the poor Black Shoes never caught on.

Porky had a girlfriend in Chula Vista, with whom he had a constantly stormy relationship. She had strayed off the reservation, and was seeing a *helicopter* pilot from North Island, a double insult. Porky learned the helo driver was going to do a low fly-over at the woman's house to impress her. With blood in his eyes, Porky talked the maintenance Chief into giving him an F-8 after lunch, and blasted off on a search-and-destroy mission. After orbiting over south San Diego Bay for a few minutes, he spotted a Navy SH-3 helo crossing the bay from North Island. He circled overhead, and watched as the ungainly craft headed for Chula Vista.

Porky had made illegal low passes over the woman's house before, and knew its exact location. As expected, the SH-3 began to hover over her house at about 200'. Porky added power and circled toward this interloper. Coming from behind the helo at about 400 knots, he dove to 100' and rolled inverted, flying between the girl friend's roof and the stationary helo. As he passed the helo, he hit afterburner and rolled upright, climbing vertically.

The terrified helo pilots nearly lost control of their clumsy machine, and headed at maximum speed back to North Island. The girlfriend, standing in her front yard, was so impressed that she dumped the helo pilot and reunited with Porky. Love (and the F-8) conquers all.

~ ~ ~

*Fighter Squadron 162 patch*

*Fighter Squadron 111 patch*

## Chapter 13: *The Black Max*

As the pre-deployment training cycle drew to a close and the departure for Vietnam grew closer, Red Lightning "social incidents" became more numerous. World War II "ace" Pappy Boyington once said, "Show me a hero, and I'll show you a bum!" The Red Lightnings often proved his theory.

Our squadron flight surgeon, affectionately nicknamed "Fighter Quack," once remarked, "When I leave the Navy, I am going into psychiatry. After closely observing F-8 pilots for three years, I know I can now deal with the mentally deranged. And I definitely would not allow my sister or daughter to marry an F-8 pilot!"

The new Skipper and his new XO, a grumpy, chain-smoking commander from the East Coast Navy, felt they were losing control of the pilots' social conduct and were nervous. I noticed the Skipper seemed to be getting more gray hairs. Then I had a brilliant idea which would give the Skipper and XO a discipline tool, yet keep the punishment light and consistent with Red Lightning culture. *[I was always a "big picture" guy. Hard to believe I never made admiral.]*

I came up with a novel concept patterned after Germany's top military award in WWI—the *Pour le Mérite* (For Merit) medal, known as The Blue Max. It was established by Frederick the Great in the 18th Century, and was inscribed in French because that was the "official" language of many European monarchies of the era. It was probably equivalent to our Navy Cross or perhaps even the Medal of Honor.

We copied the German medal's form, but changed the color from blue to black, and called it The Black Max. It was a velvet graphic of a black Iron Cross, with a red lightning bolt stabbing through it, beautifully framed. The legend at the bottom read: ***"For depraved social conduct, above and beyond the call of indecency."***

**The real "Blue Max" medal.**

The Black Max could only be awarded by the Skipper at an All-Officers Meeting. The ceremony followed the commission of a non-flying, indecent act which truly deserved discipline and general public revulsion. The recipient then had his name engraved on a plate beneath The Black Max, and a facsimile Black Max patch was sewn on his flight jacket, to be worn permanently to commemorate his atrocity. It was clear to me Buzzard was likely to be the first recipient. He did not disappoint me.

The Buzzard personified those Naval Aviators who only wanted to fly. He had no interest in any other aspect of being a Naval officer. If he could have worn only a flight suit every day, he would have thrown his uniforms over the side. His skill in an airplane, however, provided significant and offsetting value for his superiors. In wartime, operational excellence trumps nearly everything else.

Buzzard grew up in the San Francisco Bay Area, and began to fly airplanes at an early age. When he was 17, he was the Cadet Commander of his Civil Air Patrol unit. He was allegedly demoted after an unspecified incident with his adjutant, a cute 16-year-old girl. His college career ended abruptly after two years, when the Navy unwisely admitted him to Pensacola as a Naval Aviation Cadet.

Buzzard had a "trophy" girlfriend in San Diego. This voluptuous redhead even had her own call sign—"Big Red." Never one to ignore the importance of marketing his image, Buzzard carried an ample supply of business cards, featuring a large buzzard above his name. It read, "*Have parachute, will travel. Buzzard Jewell, Fighter Pilot.*" These cards seemed to be on the wall of every bar in San Diego and everywhere the carriers docked in Asia. The Buzzard was a large presence at Miramar, and a bad influence on an impressionable nugget like me.

On many occasions, Buzzard proved he truly deserved to wear the Black Max. During our weapons deployment to Yuma, Buzzard decided that we should get some target practice with our side arms, "in case we get shot down." As usual, the Red Lightnings took things a step too far. The Navy issued its pilots an ancient .38 revolver, which was intended for shooting flare rounds to be seen by the search and rescue units. Most of the pilots opted for more lethal weapons and rejected the old revolvers.

Porky, Buzzard, Maggot and I got in Buzzard's car with our "survival weapons" and drove from the base out to a remote bombing target area. Instead of the regulation .38 revolvers, each had his own special weapon: Maggot had a .45 automatic, Buzzard had a 9mm Browning Hi-Power, while Porky and I carried .357 magnums with hollow-point slugs. As we drove out to the Yuma bombing target, large jackrabbits began to scamper around the side of the road. They were a big problem at the base, because they often sat on the runways, creating a problem for arriving or departing jets.

This led to several broadsides of blazing pistol fire through open windows as we drove along, picking off the big rabbits as simulated Viet Cong. This might seem cruel, but they *were* trespassing on Government property, and were probably munching on federally protected plant species, or even causing a safety issue for pilots by sitting on the Yuma runways. I suspected that the other guys were testing me, to see if I could shoot straight.

Later that night, we went to one of the local bars in town. A grizzled guy with a crew cut and civilian clothes struck up a conversation. He identified himself as a Marine Gunnery Sergeant with the base Criminal Investigative Division. He casually said that he was investigating a new case.

He told me a rancher's cow had taken a large caliber hollow-point bullet in the neck, and had died out near the road to the bombing target. A number of dead jackrabbits were also found. The rancher had complained to the base. "Really?" I said in fake amazement. None of us ever saw any cattle during our shooting exercise, and we were quite sure that no people or livestock inhabited the restricted road area to the bombing targets. I suspected that the cow story was total fiction, and used to get my reaction. Obviously, even if it *was* true, they could not prove that *we* did it! One must always keep in mind that the interrogator may be bluffing.

"I was wondering if some of these crazy Navy F-8 pilots might have something to do with it. Especially those guys who have the red lightning bolt insignia on their birds." *This conversation is not going well,* I thought.

"I don't think so, Gunny. The Navy only lets us carry rusty old .38 pistols, with flare rounds. But I'll tell you what. As luck would have it, *I'm* in the Red Lightning squadron. I have a feeling that the *other* F-8 squadron in our air wing, VF-191, might be involved. They have some very unsavory and unbalanced characters in that squadron, and they can't seem to shoot straight when they're flying the aircraft. If you ask me, they should have their side arms confiscated and tested for a ballistic match with the cow bullet."

"Thanks, Lieutenant," said the Gunny. "Hey, if you ever need a favor, just let me know, OK?"

"Sure, Gunny." I was thinking, *The more cops you have on your side, the better. You never know what can happen. . . . .*

The last West Coast SERE survival school class was enduring "captivity" in the mountains outside of San Diego. Several pilots from VF-191 ("Satan's Kittens"), the sister squadron, were getting the "treatment" behind the camp's barbed wire. Competition between the two F-8 squadrons was always intense. VF-191 was actually an excellent squadron, but it was lost in the Red Lightnings' shadow. The Red Lightnings derisively referred to the VF-191 pilots as "Satan's Pussies." Adding to their misery was the ridiculous squadron call sign assigned by the Navy: FEEDBAG. Who, in their right mind, would want such a call sign, which is used daily on the radio? (Many years later, they wisely changed their call sign to HELLCAT.)

Led by Buzzard and Devil, we printed up several thousand leaflets, stating that the VF-191 pilots, each by rank and name, should *never* be subjected to harsh treatment, because they had a very low threshold of pain and might confess to *anything*. There were also several insults to the guards and their mothers contained in the message. These were taken to the flight line, where they were loaded inside the big speed brake compartment on the bellies of several F-8s.

"Operation Leaflet Drop" then took off from Miramar, and flew several low passes over the SERE camp at Warner Springs to get the guards' attention. Then right over the camp, the speed brakes were extended, raining the leaflets over the camp. Reportedly, the VF-191 pilots had a very rough night at the hands of the guards. We felt *really* bad about that.

Every day in the Red Lightning squadron was a true adventure. One morning, Buzzard walked up to me and said, "We're doing a low-level 'road recce' north of LA. I think you'll like it." Usually, this meant Buzzard was up to something.

We took off and headed north to the Channel Islands off Ventura. We then turned east and crossed "feet dry" at the coast at about 100' above the terrain. At Buzzard's direction, I turned my IFF [radar beacon] off so we could not be identified by radar controllers. After crossing several mountain ranges, we smoked along at about 350 knots over a flat desert landscape. At this low altitude, we would not be visible on radar.

I felt as if I could reach out and touch the big cactus plants which were zipping by. Suddenly Buzzard radioed, "Target in sight, 12 o'clock." I looked ahead and saw a large wooden structure coming up fast. "Hold your altitude," said Buzzard.

In a flash, we flew low over a group of fake Indians on horseback, and then over the walls of an old 19th-century cavalry fort. It was a Hollywood set, and they were filming a movie! The radio crackled, "Hey, maybe we'll be movie stars now! VSH!" As we pulled up, I looked back to see the horses stampeding in all directions. When we got back to Miramar and met in the ready room, Buzzard said, "If anyone asks where we were, tell them we were around Catalina Island. Since George Air Force Base is near that movie set, we can always blame it on the Air Force."

Like flying under bridges, the train prank had been done before by other Naval Aviators, but Buzzard decided to do it anyway. One night, he and Porky flew out to the desert. Between Yuma and Indio, there was a stretch of railroad tracks which marked a perfectly straight line in the desert. Buzzard spotted a long freight train heading south toward Yuma. "Time to see if the engineer is awake," he radioed Porky.

Buzzard dropped down to about 30' over the tracks, slowed down to landing speed, raised the wing and extended the landing gear. As the big train sped toward him, head on, he switched on his bright landing light. To the engineer, this must have looked like a train coming from the other direction, so he jammed on his brakes, throwing sparks from his wheels. He brought the big train to a grinding stop just as Buzzard flew over the top of him. "Yep, he *was* awake! VSH!"

Buzzard, Porky, and I went over to the Miramar O'Club one night for a nightcap. To our dismay, it was bingo night for the old folks, followed by sedate ballroom dancing for the retired officers and their wives. We hated this, because the dopey music and formal atmosphere discouraged the usual gaggle of smoking-hot local girls from coming to the bar to enjoy the normal dose of blaring rock music and the company of the young pilots.

After we had too many drinks, the club manager told us we had to put on a jacket and tie, because it was after 1800 and "we have retired senior officers present." Buzzard and Porky exploded, but we complied after a quick trip to the BOQ to retrieve jackets and ties. Upon our return, I noticed Buzzard's behavior was becoming more erratic than usual. Drinking multiple shots of tequila will do that to you.

As Porky and the club manager exchanged some insults, we suddenly heard Buzzard shout, "Whoo-hah!" We looked around and realized we were in real trouble. Buzzard had climbed up on a wooden railing which separated the bar from the dance floor, where twenty or so elderly couples danced to the sound of a Lawrence Welk tune. He then dropped his pants and *mooned* the dance floor. Women screamed and fainted, while their men cursed and shouted for Base Security. Buzzard started laughing, lost his balance, and fell into the dance floor with his pants around his ankles.

The next day, Buzzard was put in "hack" (base arrest) in the BOQ, while the chain-of-command tried to figure out what to do with him. I learned later from a direct source that the incident and Buzzard's fate got all the way to the admirals at FIRST FLEET, COMNAVAIRPAC, and their senior staffs. One day, according to the source, the admirals and captains were playing golf at North Island, discussing The Buzzard and his latest atrocity. "I think we should court-martial him," said one. Another favored pulling Buzzard's wings and transferring him to Thule, Greenland. COMNAVAIRPAC, a Vice Admiral, allegedly said, "He deserves it, but look at it this way. He's about to go to Vietnam and fly F-8s off a small-deck carrier over hostile territory. What can we do to him that would be worse than *that*? Keep him in the BOQ until the ship leaves, and tell his Skipper the kid is on permanent probation." Having been on an admiral's probation myself at the Boat School, I could relate to that.

Our Skipper told Buzzard, "You lucked out. The 'governor' called and stopped the execution. But you are on a very short leash, and you are getting the Black Max!" Then, in a solemn ceremony, The Buzzard's name was added to the Black Max, and the parachute riggers sewed the sacred patch on his flight jacket. *Many are called, but few are chosen.* (Matthew 22:14)

Meanwhile, Wife #1 had grown restless and tired of this testosterone-saturated lifestyle. In a rage, she confronted me: "*This* is no marriage! You need to decide what you want—running around with those squadron barbarians and flying that horrible airplane, or *me*!" *What was this woman thinking? I had already verified she couldn't pull 6 g's or go supersonic. Worse yet, she had just insulted the F-8! Blasphemy!*

"That's an easy choice. Pack your bags, Sweetheart." No doubt, she hoped the North Vietnamese would nail me and save her lawyer the trouble. The rest is history—our divorce became final some months later. *So this is what an ejection feels like,* I said to myself. *Better to eject at high speed than crash, burn, and die.*

Several days later, a Navy band played mournfully on the North Island dock as we watched from the flight deck. Friends, families, and girlfriends looked up and waved at us as the ship pulled away. I noticed there were many tears flowing from those on the dock. They knew, as we did, that some of us would not be coming back.

When a carrier left port for Vietnam, one thing was statistically certain. In each squadron of about 17 pilots, it was virtually guaranteed that *two or more* would not return—they either would be killed in combat or carrier operations, or would be shot down and taken prisoner by the North Vietnamese, to join other POWs at the so-called Hanoi Hilton. In some squadrons, the losses were as high as 50%. In my first tour, we lost three pilots.

Finally, the tugs began to move *Ticonderoga* away from the last safe and friendly territory we would see for many months. Buzzard was happy, however, as he was no longer in "hack." The warrior tribe was reunited, and we were back in business.

On the way to Vietnam, we stopped in Hawaiian waters for the standard Operational Readiness Inspection (ORI) exercise. We bombed and strafed the helpless Kahoolawe Island near Maui, did some aerial sight-seeing around the Hawaiian volcanoes, and then one night, we did an air defense exercise. They made the mistake of launching Gator and me together to defend the eastern sector, where the bogey threat was coming in. NAS Barbers Point was launching P-3 "bogeys" in an attempt to over-fly the carrier and cost us ORI "points."

For multi-motor "pukes," these guys were good. The big four-engine birds were zipping over the water at about 300' and nearly 300 knots. The carrier's old radar was having trouble tracking them. The F-8E had a fairly good radar capability out to 60 miles, but it did not have good "look-down" ability. You could lose a target in the ground clutter if you were above it. The ship's controllers were getting nervous: "Red Flash, this is Panther Strike. Bogeys are estimated at less than 1,000 feet altitude, on the Panther 080 radial at about 90 miles, inbound to Panther. Do you have contact?"

"Negative," replied Gator. "Hot Dog, you got 'em?"

"Negative, but let's use our Sidewinders." Each of us had dummy Sidewinder missiles, but the seeker heads were fully functional. This meant that if the

Sidewinder pointed within a few degrees of a heat source, it would growl in your headset. It was a beautiful, animalistic sound, suggestive of the missile's predatory desire to kill. This gave us our very own infrared (IR) heat detectors, so we just had to move the aircraft around until we got a growl, and then follow the signal to the source.

Gator understood immediately. We split apart and started pushing the nose of our aircraft down and around in search of a heat source. Because the P-3s had four big turbo-prop engines, they would give off lots of IR signal. Soon we each had a growl, about twenty degrees apart, from IR sources between the carrier and us. "Let's get 'em, Hot Dog! Keep on him and watch your altitude. They are probably down on the water."

"Roger that, I'm on the left guy." We were at 25,000', so we started descending at high speed while maintaining the Sidewinder growl on our respective bogeys. This kept the F-8's flight path zeroed in on the heat source, but we needed to watch our altitude carefully on this very dark night. The hungry ocean is always ready to swallow another Naval Aviator.

The growl got louder, and soon I could make out the shape of a large aircraft about 1,000' ahead of me, low on the water at around 500' altitude. "Tally-ho on my bogey, Gator."

"Rog, got mine too. These boys need a wake-up call. Turn your lights off and give them a surprise. Let's see if we can make 'em spill their coffee." I knew what he meant. When Gator and I flew together, we always knew instinctively what the other was doing and thinking. We were two gnarly branches from the same twisted tree.

We each flew directly under our P-3 bogey at about 150' over the water at around 400 knots. After passing under them with sufficient clearance, we lit our afterburners, turned on our lights and pulled up directly in front of the big P-3s. They probably thought the world had come to an end, or that they had been attacked by UFOs. We heard later that the pilots in one of them almost lost control of the aircraft, but they both turned around and headed back to Oahu without getting near the carrier. "Splash two bogeys, Panther," said Gator.

"Roger that, Red Flash! Come on home—your vector two five zero for home plate. You have Charlie [landing priority] on arrival. Switch now to Panther Approach, button seven."

It was a very good night, and we both got aboard on the first pass. The ship and air wing received excellent ratings on the ORI. Now we were going to find out what we—and the enemy—were *really* made of.

~ ~ ~

*Fighter Squadron 53*

## Chapter 14: *The Pre-game Show*

Behind the scenes of the Vietnam air war, there was intense competition between the Air Force and the Navy over which Service could deliver more combat sorties against North Vietnam. Such pointless facts are often used by the Armed Services to support their budget requests before Congress. Soon, it became more important to count sorties than to destroy meaningful targets.

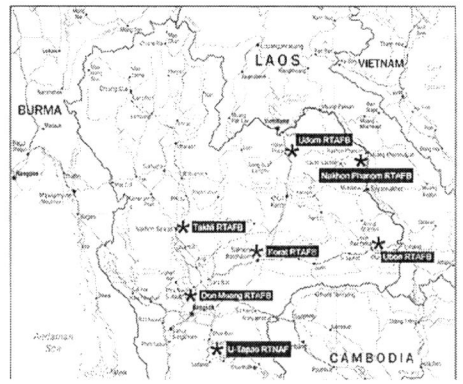

When the Navy was able to impress the White House with its ability to move carrier air power quickly into the Tonkin Gulf in 1965, the Air Force generals panicked. They quickly cut deals with Thailand and established huge air bases for their F-105s, F-4s, tankers, and support aircraft at Ubon, Takhli, Nakhon Phanom, Don Muang, U-Tabao, Udorn, and Korat.

The Air Force's main problem was that they had allowed their tactical air capability to stagnate, in favor of ICBMs and SAC bombers. In essence, they had forgotten how to use tactical air, which the missions in North Vietnam required until Nixon unleashed the B-52s against Hanoi near the end of the war.

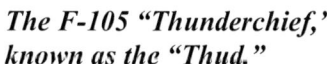

*The F-105 "Thunderchief," known as the "Thud."*

The Air Force's dogfighting skills had also languished for years. The Air Force generals viewed this activity in training as too risky, possibly leading to accidents. Like some in the Navy, they also had fallen in love with the air-to-air missile, such as the Sparrow and Sidewinder. Although the F-105s had internal guns, their F-4s lacked this close-in weapon until the F-4E was delivered late in the war. When the Air Force mounted a strike against North Vietnam, their aircraft flew in rigid, tight formations, not unlike the B-17s of World War II. They had forgotten how to fight.

*113*

Another problem was caused by the Air Force's decision to give some of their "desk jockeys" a little combat time. Instead of carefully controlling the training and rotations to and from the squadrons, they plucked hundreds of non-proficient majors, lieutenant colonels, and colonels from the bowels of the Pentagon, giving them a "career-enhancing" assignment to the Thailand tactical squadrons. With very little refresher training, it was a recipe for disaster. The F-105 squadrons began to experience devastating losses, resulting in the disparaging nickname for the aircraft—"Thud."

The Navy, for its part, was also not innocent. In the Vietnam era, there was a significant cultural and attitudinal difference between the East Coast and West Coast Navy. Similarly, the admirals decided the East Coast Navy ships and air wings needed some combat exposure instead of lounging around on those sun-drenched Mediterranean cruises. East Coast ships, like *America, Forrestal,* and *Independence* began to show up at Yankee Station for real combat duty. At the same time, senior pilots rotating out of the East Coast squadrons started arriving in West Coast squadrons about 1967, which had the dysfunctional effect of placing "newbies" in control of the air wings and combat squadrons. We often heard the cliché from senior officers: "It's not much of a war, but it's the only war we've got."

For the wrong reasons, the Navy was putting "second string" players into the lineup. Even worse, because of their senior rank, they were automatically designated as strike leaders and four-plane division leaders, creating an "upside-down" combat hierarchy. Some had been buried in staffs or non-combat assignments like utility or ferry squadrons, and now found themselves making carrier landings and dodging SAMs.

Adding to the chaos, the two Services began to arm-wrestle over "bombing rights" to North Vietnam, as each wanted to "own" the targets around Hanoi to demonstrate their force effectiveness to Washington. Finally, the Joint Chiefs mediated the territorial battle by splitting North Vietnam into "route packages," with the Air Force taking Packages 1 and 5, while the Navy got Packages 2, 3 and 4. The two Services were required to split Package 6 (see map). This had an important effect on the air order of battle which the NVA (North Vietnamese Army) positioned to defend each of these areas, causing unnecessary U.S. losses.

The Navy package areas were largely flat terrain, where the NVA ground radar was most effective. This led to the NVA massing its radar-controlled AAA and SAMs against the Navy threat. The North Vietnamese allocated their MIG resources mostly against the Air Force, coming in over mountainous terrain from Thailand. This is the reason for the larger number of air engagements between MIGs and the Air Force, as compared to the Navy experience. The North Vietnamese learned quickly the Navy was much better at air-to-air combat than the Air Force, so the MIGs picked the easier Air Force opponents to attack. They concentrated their SAMs and AAA against the Navy approach corridors in the eastern areas of North Vietnam, and positioned the bulk of their MIG flights to intercept Air Force strike groups.

Meanwhile, each Service engaged in a competitive, daily "sortie race," designed to impress the media and the McNamara "bean-counters" at the Pentagon. It was common to be launched from the carrier with a full bomb load, even if the weather made the mission impossible. You were then ordered to jettison the bombs over the water and return to the ship. It still counted as a sortie on the daily press release and the report to the Pentagon, and that was all that mattered to the Navy brass. Meanwhile, America was well on the way to losing 58,000 of its uniformed citizens, while the generals and admirals played their meaningless games of inter-Service rivalry.

Another shocking revelation involved the quality of air ordnance. While there were certainly technological bright spots, such as the Sparrow, Sidewinder, Shrike and Walleye, most of the bomb and rocket ordnance was of World War II or Korean War vintage.

Secretary of Defense McNamara decided it would be more cost-effective to use up the ordnance we already had in storage from prior wars before developing anything new, like "smart" bombs. As a result, we were relegated to crude bombing techniques which had been in place since World War II, trying to  estimate an invisible release point that depended on speed, altitude, dive angle and bomb sight millage, all while dodging AAA and SAMs, and an occasional MIG. Because these were manual calculations, accuracy was poor until the introduction of the A-7 Corsair II, which had a sophisticated weapons delivery computer system.

*Ticonderoga* reached Japan in November of 1966. In the port of Yokosuka, near the entrance to Tokyo Bay, the Red Lightnings were determined to have some fun before they got to Yankee Station. In a squadron "meeting" at the Yokosuka O'Club, things got predictably out of hand. Several pilots grabbed Buzzard and raised him quickly on their shoulders so that his head punched through the beautiful rice paper panels in the ceiling. The Japanese staff ran to call the Shore Patrol.

The Skipper yelled at the bartender, "Hay for my horses, beds for my wenches, and a bucket of stingers for my men, bartender!" A stinger was a nasty drink, which consisted of brandy and crème de menthe. Its arrival usually signaled that mayhem was not far behind. A silver champagne bucket was placed in front of Porky, containing about two gallons of stingers. Glasses were dipped into the bucket, and soon everyone had a full glass of stingers. "Now it's time for the nuggets to demonstrate a Flaming Hooker!" [The traditional recipe uses Drambuie, sometimes with rum. Fighter pilots are flexible.]

This is a particularly delicate maneuver. You fill your mouth full of stinger, and then someone holds a cigarette lighter in front of your face. You blow the liquid out over the lighter, and if you do it correctly, it becomes an impressive blowtorch but you avoid being burned. Gator and I passed the test, but Spanky, a very religious and shy kid, had already escaped and slipped back to the ship.

The ship pulled out of Yokosuka and headed to Subic Bay, in the Philippines. Five F-8 pilots, including me, were assigned to remain behind for a few days, and then to fly overhauled aircraft down from Atsugi Air Base to Cubi Point, with a fuel stop in Naha Air Base, Okinawa. I was told that this flight was "a good deal." I learned that when other pilots told you something was "a good deal," you should grab your wallet and run for cover. If it *was* a "good deal," *they* would be doing it.

By the time we departed Atsugi, we realized we had a big weather problem. A typhoon (the Western Pacific version of a hurricane) was threatening Okinawa. We had only a short window of time to get in and out of Okinawa before the huge storm arrived. The group was organized as a flight of three and a flight of two, in which I was the wingman.

We cruised uneventfully down the eastern coast of Japan at 37,000'. At Kagoshima, at the southern tip of the Japanese island of Kyushu, we turned south toward the Ryukyu Islands and Okinawa, several hundred miles away. So far, it was easy flying, even for a nugget like me.

As we neared Okinawa, the weather deteriorated. Soon, we were working hard to stay in sight of the other section of three, as the clouds continued to build. The first section started their descent at around 100 miles, as the radar controller vectored them toward Naha, at Okinawa's southwestern tip. As the first section descended, they advised us they were experiencing heavy turbulence and rain. We heard the controller switch them to approach control, and the frequency was quiet again.

Just as my leader and I were expecting clearance to descend, the controller came back up and said, "Red Flash Four Zero Two, continue to hold. An F-8 has gone off the runway, and Naha is closed." We found out later there was a severe crosswind, and the lead aircraft had been unable to brake to a stop on the rain-soaked runway. The other two had landed and blown tires. There were actually three F-8s sitting on or near the runway, making additional landings impossible.

I suddenly felt apprehensive. Naha only had one runway. My leader said, "Roger, we'll land at Kadena." I had studied the charts and felt relieved that he was taking this option. Kadena was a larger USAF field, about 13 miles north of Naha.

"Red Flash Four Zero Two, roger, you are cleared to Kadena. Contact Approach Control on 236.6 now." We both switched over to the assigned frequency.

"Approach, Red Flash Four Zero Two, with two F-8s for Kadena."

"Roger. Four Zero Two, descend and maintain five thousand, heading 220."

"Roger, five thousand, 220." As we leveled off at that altitude, we were completely immersed in a blinding rainstorm and were violently bounced around. I was having trouble staying on the leader's wing, and could barely see his wingtip.

"Red Flash Four Zero Two, descend and maintain two thousand. Four Zero Four, turn right to 350 for separation, maintain five thousand."

"Four Zero Four, roger, five thousand, 350." I turned right, glad that I no longer had to stay in close formation with the lead aircraft, which was hard work in this weather. I steadied up on the new heading, level at 5,000'. When I tried to communicate again with the controller, I realized my radio and navigation system, called TACAN, had suddenly failed. I was now deaf, dumb and blind, and flying around in a typhoon without visual contact with the ground. However, I was not totally lost.

At the Naval Academy, I had studied the World War II Battle of Okinawa in

some detail, and remembered that the 1945 American invasion force had landed in the western coastal area near Kadena Air Base. Just to the north, there was a large, unique promontory jutting out into the sea, called Cape Zanpa. I knew if I could find the west coast of Okinawa, I could find Kadena, which was about 10 miles southeast of Cape Zanpa.

Using my radar, I overflew the island, heading west. I turned my IFF to the emergency "squawk" of 7700 to alert the radar controllers, and started descending in a wide teardrop over the water, west of Okinawa. I dropped down below the clouds at 500' over the water, now heading east, and caught sight of the coast. I looked right and left, and spotted the cape. Aiming the aircraft at a point about 10 miles south of the cape, I looked at my fuel gauge. I now had less than 10 minutes of fuel remaining. It was time to get serious and not screw up.

Approaching the coastal point where I thought Kadena was, I slowed to 250 knots, and then spotted the long runway off to my left. I extended the landing gear, raised the wing, and turned my landing light on so the tower could see me. As I aimed for the landing point, I realized there was a strong crosswind from the right. The tower gave me a green light, which cleared me to land. I felt like I was flying sideways all the way to touchdown, where I straightened out the nose with the rudder to line up with the runway. As I rolled out, the wind pushed me further and further to my left. I stopped just before I was blown off the runway.

That night, the Kadena O'Club bar was a welcome destination for my leader and me. We had a rough time, but not as bad as the flight of three that went into Naha.

We learned that the carrier was north of the Philippines, and wanted us to land directly aboard, instead of flying to Cubi Point. As soon as the weather cleared, we proceeded to the rendezvous point and found the *Ticonderoga*. As luck would have it, the rendezvous point was an area of heavy seas, probably because of the passing typhoon. We landed aboard with a pitching deck and strong headwinds, almost out of limits. I was glad this so-called "good deal" flight was over.

Next, the carrier pulled into Cubi Point to take on fuel and munitions. There we were introduced to the famous Cubi Point O'Club, complete with its own Dilbert Dunker in the bar.  Someone had constructed a small cockpit and placed it on rails above a pond of stagnant water, filled with beer and God-knows-what. The contraption had a small tail hook, which the "pilot" could drop, and if lucky, catch a wire that kept him from being dumped into the pond. Buzzard made a bet with an A-4 driver, and the two squared off. Buzzard went first, and caught the wire. The A-4 pilot was not as good, and he paid the price by getting a bath in the stinking pond. The A-4 pilots bought the next round of drinks.

The pilots frequently got a few temporary rooms in the Cubi BOQ. It was a nice break to get away from the hot rooms on the ship. We would lounge around the BOQ pool all day, and then hit the club bar at night. It was almost like Club Med.

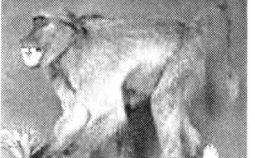

One day, we were out at the pool when Spanky noticed some movement near the garbage dumpster. "Hey, what's that?" asked a nugget from another squadron.

"That's one of those big baboons," another pilot said. "They're real tame, and come out of the jungle to raid the garbage for food." We watched as a big male baboon pulled the lid of the dumpster open and jumped down inside to forage for food.

The nugget whispered, "Watch this," and crept across the grass to the dumpster. The big baboon did not know anything was amiss until the nugget slammed the lid shut, holding it closed, and started banging on the dumpster with a stick. The baboon immediately went crazy and began shrieking loudly.

"Hey, man, I have a question. What happens when you let go of that lid?" asked Spanky, laughing. The prankster looked around with a worried look on his face. The lid was now bouncing up and down as the baboon pushed up from inside, determined to get out and attack his tormentor.

Suddenly, our hero picked his moment and sprinted for the safety of the nearby BOQ. The dumpster lid flew open and the baboon rocketed out with teeth bared, looking for revenge. He spotted the guilty party and ran after him, somehow getting inside the door just before it closed. As the enraged baboon scampered through the BOQ halls, officers poured out of the doors and windows of the building and ran in all directions. Those who did not make it barricaded themselves in their rooms. Finally, growling in disgust, the baboon returned to the safety of the jungle.

It was always interesting to find out what was happening with the other air wings, and the Cubi Point O'Club was a place where many good stories were exchanged. One of my Academy buddies in another air wing relayed an amazing episode that occurred during the evening movie in his squadron's ready room.

On all of the carriers, a movie was normally shown after the evening meal in each squadron's ready room. It was about the only "normal" entertainment that the pilots had, so there was considerable interest in the movie title each night. When the carrier started running out of newer films, they would pass out old films, with stars like The Three Stooges, Fred Astaire, Bela Lugosi, Boris Karloff, W.C. Fields, and of course, Shirley Temple.

In my friend's ready room, they had run out of good movies and the "natives" were getting restless. On the night in question, the boring movie starred Shirley Temple. This is not the type of movie that appeals to fighter pilots. As the cute little girl frolicked across the screen in one of her pre-pubescent adventures, one of the pilots decided to put his hands in front of the projector and do some nasty things to Ms. Temple with the shadows of his hands. It is always surprising to find artistic talent in a fighter squadron.

This immediately drew a loud outcry of moral condemnation from the audience. Even *fighter pilots* have their standards. However, the perpetrator continued his screen-shadow assault on Ms. Temple. He forgot that one of the pilots was a reclusive and extremely religious family man. This pilot did not swear, drink or partake of lustful temptations ashore. He was an unusual addition to an F-8 squadron.

Finally, the self-appointed morality officer yelled for the assault on Ms. Temple's image to stop. However, it continued, with the perpetrator giggling. "Hey, I mean it! Stop that right now!" said her protector. It continued.

"You were warned," said the evangelist aviator, drawing his .45 automatic at the rear of the room. Aiming at the outstretched hand shadow on the screen, the offended pilot fired a round. Everyone hit the deck, hiding under their seats, as the big slug ricocheted around the steel bulkheads. Luckily, no one was injured. However, the movie was canceled, and both pilots received a stern reprimand from the Skipper. The squadron Skipper's biggest problem was that the ready room movie screen now had a big hole that would require explanation. From then on, their Skipper required all pilot sidearms to be unloaded during the movies, which seems rather reasonable, not unlike a saloon in the Old West.

I thought, *Thank God we don't have any bizarre personalities like that in the Red Lightnings! Well—not many, anyway.*

"Dog Kicker," a member of the Class of '65, told me about an incident in his ready room on another carrier. An All-Officers Meeting was scheduled, and the squadron safety officer was going to give a lecture on ejection and water-entry procedures. My friend opened the door of the dark ready room to find the safety officer, a member of the Class of '64, hanging from the ready room ceiling beam by his parachute fittings, dressed in his flight gear. "What the hell are you doing, Jim?" he asked. "You scared the crap out of me!"

"I figured this is the best way to show how to release the torso harness fittings before you hit the water after an ejection," he replied. "A picture is worth a thousand words." *So true!*

Just outside the main gate to the Subic Bay Naval Base lay the urban squalor of Olongapo City, a grimy cluster of raunchy bars, bordellos, and cheap "one-nighter" hotels. Leaving the base gate, you walked across a bridge, which spanned the putrid waters of the Olongapo River, also known as "Shit River." Similar to the River Styx of Greek and Roman mythology, this is where the newly dead had to cross to arrive safely in Hell.

Little kids sat on the bridge railing, begging the Sailors and Marines to throw coins into the stinking water, where they would dive in to retrieve the money. On occasion, a drunk Sailor would take a dare, and dive off the bridge. The water was so filthy and contaminated that this often resulted in hospitalization and multiple diseases. While we were there, one Sailor went blind because of eye infections he got from the river.

On the other side of the bridge, local entrepreneurs urged the Servicemen to buy some San Miguel beer or delicious monkey meat-on-a-stick, one of the local delicacies. Others hawked their nightclubs or their wares, which were usually the bodies of young Filipina women. The most notorious establishment, where the most perverted activities took place, was unquestionably The East Inn Club. Only the hardest of hard-core connoisseurs could stand to watch what went on in this twisted Garden of Eden. Even fighter pilots were sometimes repulsed by what they saw. One of the delightful greetings from the female employees there was "Hey, fly-boy, I love you, no shit!"

One night, a group of us wound up in this lovely place, but left after a few "shows." I wondered if I was going to have nightmares and flashbacks from watching the anatomical contortions of the female pole-dancers. How does that saying go? *Too much of a good thing....*

**The infamous East Inn Club.**

For some reason, the ship left Cubi earlier than normal one morning. This was a problem, because Buzzard was comatose, trying to sleep off a hangover. We all thought he was somewhere on board, not realizing he was still in the BOQ. When he looked out of his window and saw *Ticonderoga* steaming out of Subic Bay, he knew this would be a problem with no easy solution. In the Navy, missing your ship is a very bad thing, indeed.

The only clothes Buzzard had were less than appropriate for reporting aboard. He had sandals, khaki slacks, and a Filipino *barong* shirt, complete with wine and food stains. The only solution was to get aboard by air.

Dressing quickly, he got a taxi to the flight line at the airfield, where the maintenance detachment was working on some broken aircraft. "Morning, Chief," said Buzzard to the maintenance chief. "I just got word that the ship wants me to test-fly this bird, and then land aboard. We'll need it for the strike tomorrow."

"Well, Sir, I don't have any orders to that effect. I was told they have too many birds on board right now."

"Nope, this is new info. Is she ready to fly?"

"Well, except that the radio is out."

"No problem. I just need a helmet and a torso harness, and I'm ready. Chief, you need to be flexible out here," said Buzzard. "This is wartime!" Buzzard called the tower by telephone and told them to give him a green light for takeoff. In minutes, he was speeding down the runway toward the departing carrier.

Buzzard knew that the carriers always had to take one or two last-minute aircraft aboard, and that the ship would be going to flight quarters as soon as it was clear of the channel. Orbiting over the ship, he saw it turn into the wind. Buzzard dove down to parallel the carrier on her starboard side to enter the break, wagging his wings. This was a signal to the Air Boss in the tower that he had no radio. The Air Boss was irate. He turned to Snake, who was the designated tower "observer" and said, "Why is this bird in my pattern? We really don't have room for another F-8 on board!" Snake pled ignorance.

Buzzard pulled left in the break, extended the gear and tail hook, and raised the wing. Making an A+ landing, he taxied forward to park on the bow. As he passed under the tower, the Air Boss said, "Hey, Snake—what kind of flight suit is this guy wearing? That looks like a *barong*!" Thinking quickly, Snake replied, "Boss, that's a special flight suit he had made for himself in Hong Kong. You know The Buzzard!"

The enlisted deck crews gaped in amazement as a guy in a *barong* and sandals climbed down from the F-8, puked over the side of the catwalk, and then slipped quickly below decks. The Buzzard had landed.

~ ~ ~

# Chapter 15: *Game Time!*

USS Ticonderoga (CV 14) underway 10 Nov. 1967. The ship was decommisisoned Sept. 1, 1973, and sold for scrap Nov. 16, 1973.
SDAN: 1129290   Date: 10 Nov 1967
Service ID:  CVA-14-3761

By November of 1966, *Ticonderoga* had joined the other two carriers on Yankee Station, a point about 100 miles from Haiphong, the main North Vietnamese port. One carrier usually conducted night operations, while the other two handled the day sorties.

Halfway between Yankee Station and the North Vietnamese coast was a guided missile cruiser or frigate, call sign "Red Crown," equipped with the Naval Tactical Data System (NTDS). This was a data-linked system that allowed the Task Force to coordinate its defenses and share data between ships and aircraft.

*USS Long Beach (CGN-9)*

Red Crown operated an important Positive Identification Radar Advisory Zone (PIRAZ) for the Tonkin Gulf area. This sophisticated picket ship, along with two others, protected the carrier battle groups and advised pilots of MIG activity and SAM firings. They also coordinated pilot rescues and kept pilots from straying into Chinese air space near the Vietnamese border or Hainan Island. Some of the ships that I remember serving as Red Crown were *Chicago, Long Beach, Jouett, Biddle,* and *Truxtun*. These surface warriors did an outstanding job, and saved many pilots with their expert radar control. However, they were still Black Shoes (non-aviators), so excessive praise would be inappropriate.

A former CO of the Red Lightnings, Commander Billy Phillips, led the Ticonderoga air wing, officially termed "CVW-19." The Air Wing Commander is traditionally called "CAG," from the old "Commander, Air Group" name. Phillips was a classic product of the Red Lightnings, with a cocky attitude and tremendous flying skills. When this non-Academy wild man was promoted to captain, his contemporaries could not believe it, thinking it must have been an administrative error. In spite of his aviating skills, flying with this egomaniac or being around him socially was no fun.

*CAG Billy Phillips*

Before the cruise, I flew with him on a bad weather day at Miramar, where we had to do a section (formation) ground controlled approach and landing. As we landed, with me on his wing, he immediately started maximum braking, which caused me to shoot past him on the runway. When he criticized me in the ready room for getting ahead of him on the rollout, I replied that it was because he had braked early and had not added the customary 3-4 knots to give me some flexibility on his wing. He exploded. This was a guy who never made a mistake, or so he thought.

As we started our combat tour on Yankee Station, Phillips began leading large bombing missions, known as Alpha Strikes. At the head of 16 or more A-4s, plus fighter escort, Phillips would lead meaningless attacks on the few authorized targets, such as "suspected truck parks," storage facilities, and highway "choke points." He would rotate the squadron COs and XOs as strike leaders to give them "medal opportunities." Most of the time, because the White House picked such pointless targets, we were bombing rice paddies. Nevertheless, whenever a senior officer led one of these big strikes, he was nearly guaranteed a Distinguished Flying Cross, Silver Star or Bronze Star. The commanders were waging an internal, competitive medals race, and it was a big joke among the junior officers: "Who's the only senior officer without a DFC? Answer: the chaplain!"

Meanwhile, the NVA and their Soviet and Chinese advisors continued to expand the SAM (surface-to-air missile) network and radar-controlled AAA, assisted by the highly restrictive Rules of Engagement that our senior command imposed on us. The air wing aircraft were outfitted with effective ECM (electronic counter-measures) gear, including warning and jamming systems and a chaff dispenser. You could even tell what was tracking you by a panel warning light, and an aural tone in your headset. A SAM lock-on triggered a steady red "SAM" light, with a tone in your headset. When a SAM was launched, the tone warbled and the SAM light flashed. This was a sound you learned to hate.

Porky and Buzzard had the electronic technicians obtain a SAM warning tone generator from the aircraft. They attached a small speaker, and wired the box for ship's power. One day, after a strike when air wing tensions were especially high, they keyed the squawk box intercom to all pilot ready rooms, and triggered the warbling SAM tone, while yelling "SAM! Break left!" Nervous pilots all over the ship leaped from their seats to dodge the imaginary SAM. Porky and Buzzard found that hilarious, with Buzzard's usual comment, "VSH!"

I was suiting up in the ready room before a flight, and noticed the Skipper watching me with amusement. Instead of the standard-issue .38 revolver, I carried a Smith & Wesson Model 19 Combat Magnum .357 in a tie-down hip holster, with a Walther PPK 7.65mm automatic in a shoulder holster as a back-up.

In place of the standard-issue knife, I carried a custom-made, 14-inch, razor-sharp "Arkansas Toothpick." Teddy Fox, my high school buddy, made it from a piece of steel he found on a Civil War battlefield. It was a beautiful weapon, with an impressive killing blade of tempered steel. He told me to wear it to bring good luck. Apparently it worked, because I never was shot down or had to eject. It was also good for opening beer cans.

The Skipper came up to me and pointed to the .357 magnum hollow-point cartridges on my gun belt. He said, "You may want to coat those with Vaseline, Hot Dog."

"Oh? You mean to keep the corrosion off of them, Skipper?"

"No, Hot Dog. I mean when the North Vietnamese capture you with those hollow-points, they are going to shove them up your ass one at a time. With some

Vaseline, it won't hurt as much." He walked away, laughing. I continued to carry them anyway. I had decided that the NVA were not going to take me alive, and I wanted to take as many of the little bastards with me as possible. When a hollow-point bullet hits a human body, it mushrooms and delivers a powerful shock, especially with the muzzle velocity of a .357 Magnum. A single bullet usually does the job.

During our first stay in Yokosuka, Maggot and I took our pistols over to the base gun range and qualified for the Navy Expert Pistol Medal. By this point, I had practiced many hours with the Magnum, and was an excellent shot. The range chief was surprised at my accuracy with the big Model 19, shooting Magnum loads. I had a feeling that I might need this skill before long, and I was right. I believe that my accuracy with ordnance delivery from the F-8 was significantly improved by the marksmanship principles I had learned with rifles and pistols. In essence, the F-8 was like a supersonic pistol, complete with gun sight and trigger.

We continued to have losses to SAMs and AAA. The squadron COs decided that we needed to have special teams to counter the SAM threat, and "flak suppression" sections to attack the 37, 57, and 100mm flak sites. These were not popular missions.

After losing Mike Newell ('62) and Commander Mel Moore to SAMs, morale was down. Iron Mike left a big hole in our squadron, and Moore was the XO of VA-192, an outstanding A-4E squadron. They called themselves "The World Famous Golden Dragons," but we called them "The Yellow Worms," a jab at their aircraft paint jobs. (We had great respect for them, but we could not let them know that. After all, they *were* attack pukes, not fighter pilots.)

Snake had circled above Moore after he had ejected from his damaged A-4, hoping to guide a SAR (search and rescue) helo in to recover him. Snake watched him parachute to the ground, where he was surrounded by North Vietnamese and taken captive. Since the North Vietnamese often shot pilots in their parachutes, or beat them to death after landing, we wondered if Moore was still alive. It would be six years before we found out.

Lieutenant Commander Mike Estocin was another A-4 pilot in VA-192, a rock-steady aviator, and a very quiet guy. He loved firing Shrike missiles at the SAM sites, and decided he was going to duel with them on one Alpha Strike. Near Haiphong, he engaged a site with his Shrikes just as it fired on the strike group. A SAM hit him head-on and his damaged aircraft went out of control and plunged into the water. It was the equivalent of falling on a hand grenade to save your buddies. He was posthumously awarded the Medal of Honor, the nation's highest decoration. Estocin was a true warrior, and his heroic act set a very high standard for the rest of us.

At that point, we revised our tactics. The A-4 pilots had to focus on their cockpit scope in order to fire a Shrike accurately, which took their eyes away from the incoming SAMs. The F-8 pilots were more accustomed to keeping sight of distant objects, because that was vital in ACM engagements. The answer was to put these attributes together in a team concept. The "Iron Hand" teams of two aircraft each consisted of an A-4E, with Shrikes, which would home in on the SAM radar; and an F-8E with 12 Zuni 5-inch proximity-fused rockets. The Air Force used a similar team concept against the SAMs, called "Wild Weasel." The concept was to kill any SAM radar with a Shrike when it illuminated us, and for the F-8 wingman to keep the flight clear of incoming missiles or MIGs. A visually acquired site would be attacked by the F-8 with the Zuni rockets.

Only volunteers and the best drivers from each squadron were assigned to fly Iron Hand, because the objective was actually to bait the NVA to shoot early and *run out of missiles* before the strike group aircraft were within range. This was a mission with an unforgiving learning curve, and it was not for everyone. The Iron Hand pilots became very skilled in dodging SAMs by using a variety of techniques. I was assigned to the teams, along with Buzzard, Snake, Gator and several other volunteers. *Lucky me.* I was either the Skipper's wingman, on a flight into dangerous territory, or flying Iron Hand. *What the hell—I* wanted *excitement, right? If you can't take a joke, you shouldn't have signed up.*

During my two cruises, I had at least 30 SAMs fired at me. I became quite good at out-maneuvering these monsters, which had a 500 lb. warhead and were 26 ft. long, with a range of about 20 miles. While the specific maneuvers probably remain classified, we developed a flying tactic that caused the big missile to over-stress itself and break apart, causing a spectacular but harmless orange fireball. After a while, it was almost fun. However, you had to *see* the SAM before you could out-maneuver it. This was the reason that we developed another rule for flying over the beach: "Never, *never* fly over a cloud layer in North Vietnam, and never fly over land in IFR [instrument] conditions, where you can't see a SAM coming." If you did, it was likely that you would meet a SAM in the clouds.

On one Alpha Strike into the Hanoi area, I was flying the Skipper's wing on a target combat air patrol (TARCAP). As we neared Hanoi, the SAMs were launching and the sky was full of flak puffs. Suddenly, an F-105 in a separate Air Force strike group was hit. The pilot ejected and floated down helplessly in the middle of our incoming strike group, dangling in his parachute. I thought, *Poor bastard—I wish I could reach out and pull him in.* As usual, no MIGs came up to challenge us, and the NVA continued firing SAMs. I wondered if anything had been accomplished that was worth losing this pilot. I never learned who he was or what happened to him.

On another day, the Skipper and I were assigned to a "coastal recce" to survey and attack any enemy shipping off the coast. We started our tour near the Chinese border and headed south, flying about five miles off the coast. As we passed Cam Pha, I flew abeam of the Skipper in Combat Spread and outboard of him, so that I was looking at him with the coast in the background. That way, I could see any threats coming at us from the beach, including MIGs. Suddenly, our SAM warning lights started flashing and that awful warbling tone began. I spotted two SAMs lifting off and heading toward us at their usual Mach 4, or approximately 3,000 miles per hour. "Skipper, they're locked on you!"

When a SAM is locked on you, there is not much to look at. You see little more than a black dot with a fireball behind it. Because it is coming right at you, it appears to be stationary. Every time you move your aircraft, the dot will move to head you off. If you can see the body of the missile, it is locked on someone else. "Hot Dog, I'm dragging them up!" The Skipper pulled high, with the two big telephone poles following him. He probably should have rolled and pulled down to get below the SAM radar envelope. I stayed below the cloud layer, in order to spot any new missile shots, because multiple SAMs can be a big problem. None came.

In the confusion, I forgot I was still in afterburner and still accelerating. As I passed low over Haiphong Harbor, I almost hit the mast of a Russian freighter that was waiting to dock at Haiphong to off-load more SAMs. According to the ridiculous Rules of Engagement, we were always forbidden from attacking any Russian or Chinese ships, even if they were bringing more missiles to the bad guys.

*A Russian freighter near Haiphong, with SAMs visible in deck containers.*

*A SAM exploding in the water off Cam Pha, North Vietnam. Note the unusual karst islands in the background.*

At the exact moment I crossed over the Russian ship, the Skipper's evasive maneuvers had caused one of the SAMs to break apart, with the big warhead tumbling down toward the water.

It hit and exploded about 200 yards from the Russian's bow, making him think I had bombed him. The Skipper and I joined up and returned to the ship.

We landed, and found an angry admiral's staffer waiting for us. "You people bombed a Russian ship! Now it has really hit the fan! Moscow has complained to the White House on the Hot Line!" The Skipper calmly said, "Well, Captain, the NVA shot SAMs at us and we were evading them. By the way, we were not carrying bombs. It must have been the Air Force."

The Navy's no-booze policy was carefully circumvented by the air wing pilots. Nearly every pilot stateroom had one or more small refrigerators concealed in their clothes lockers, along with precious supplies of beer and liquor.

After an Alpha Strike, the Flight Surgeon would visit each ready room and hand out officially authorized "medicinal" brandy in small bottles. This must have been the origin of airline "miniatures" that are currently sold to passengers in Coach. Some pilots would hoard these supplies until a squadron party was held, usually in the Skipper's stateroom, and then would make stingers out of them.

Because of the hot weather, we especially liked cold beer after a flight.

Heineken in cans was the favorite. However, it was difficult to smuggle it aboard because of the weight and size of a case of this precious nectar of the gods. Buzzard, however, figured out a clever solution—replenishment by air.

Periodically, the Skipper would rotate one pilot to Cubi Point from Yankee Station to ferry a damaged aircraft for maintenance and have "R&R" for a week. Buzzard's standing rule was that this pilot had to bring liquor and beer back aboard upon his return from Cubi. Finally, it was Buzzard's turn to make the trip. On this occasion, his "order list" consisted only of cases of Heineken. In preparation for his flight back, Buzzard had the maintenance crew load several cases of beer into the F-8's ammo compartment. The F-8 was a versatile aircraft.

Buzzard forgot that you need to stay below 20,000' to keep the contraband from freezing. Descending rapidly from 35,000', Buzzard spotted the carrier and entered the landing pattern. Making his typically excellent approach, he caught the target #3 wire.

Upon the shock of the arrestment, cans of frozen beer in the ammo compartment exploded, leaking white beer foam and bubbles down the sides of the F-8. As Buzzard taxied forward, the Air Boss spotted this, and asked the F-8 rep in the tower what it was. "Oh, that's just a small hydraulic leak, Boss. You know how leaky the F-8 is," said our rep. Quick thinking. Another near miss.

The Alpha Strikes became more frequent, and moved inexorably toward the most heavily defended areas of North Vietnam. One evening, we were informed that it was my Skipper's turn to lead a strike. Normally, one would expect that the F-8s would be configured for the MIG-killer TARCAP mission, with only guns and Sidewinders. However, some genius had decided to configure our F-8 division as *flak suppressors* instead of fighters. *Wonderful.* The pilots called this mission "flak absorbing."

We were saddled with six 500 lb. bombs each, and launched the next morning with about 25 other strike aircraft. The strike group target was a *one-lane bridge* over a muddy river near Hanoi. One of our four F-8s for the strike had a mechanical problem just before launch, so we led the strike with just three F-8Es—the Skipper, Gator and me. Approaching the target from the south, we could see the flash of large AAA guns in three circular sites around the target. These were radar-controlled 100mm guns, and they were very accurate, with long range. They had locked onto the slower moving A-4s just behind us and were filling the air with black puffs.

On the Skipper's call, we rolled in on the three big AAA sites, which were now getting the range on several A-4s. The Skipper assigned each of us to a flak site. As we got a bombsight solution, we each pickled our six bombs and pulled off. I rolled up on a wing and looked back to see how close our hits were. I was surprised to see that we had each gotten a bull's-eye! The flak immediately stopped, and the A-4s were able to destroy the bridge. When we returned to the ship, the A-4 drivers were ecstatic, and thanked us for "shit-hot bombing." I smiled grimly and thought, *Oh, great—I should be out chasing MIGs, and now the attack pukes will want us to be flak suppressors on every strike.*

After a long combat period, *Ticonderoga* pulled off the line for another R&R (rest and recreation) stop—first to Cubi, then up to Hong Kong! We could not wait to sample the bacchanalian treats of that exotic paradise. The night before departure, we all gathered in the Cubi O'Club for the usual night of drunken rowdiness. I was standing at the bar next to the Skipper, as CAG Billy Phillips walked up. *Just what I was hoping for,* I thought.

Billy was already smashed, and he was a mean drunk. He looked at us and said, "I'm Billy Phillips and I'm the world's greatest fighter pilot."

The Skipper smiled and said gently, in the tone that one uses to talk to a child, "I know."

Not getting the confrontation he was looking for, Billy spotted a quiet Marine 1/LT hunched over the bar at the other end. Approaching the man and thinking he was a pilot, Billy tapped him on the shoulder and said, "I'm Billy Phillips, and I can have your ass!"

Unfortunately for Billy, this happened to be a Marine Force Recon platoon leader who had just been through some bloody ground combat near the DMZ, and he was not in a good mood. The Marine spun around and punched Billy in the face, giving him a black eye. Billy dropped motionless to the floor, partially submerged in the usual bilge of beer and spilled drinks. The Marine went back to his bar stool.

The Skipper and I looked at each other. "What do you think, Skipper?"

"Charming.....just charming," he replied with a grin. While CAG was still unconscious, we bought the Marine a drink. We all hated Billy. The next day, Billy showed up for a flight to Hong Kong with a gorgeous black eye. He wore sunglasses to hide his pugilistic misfortune. We all envied that Marine 1/LT. I wonder where that hero is today, because I would buy him another drink. As the Marines say, *Semper Fi!*

In Hong Kong, we came up with a plan to de-flower Spanky. From his own admissions, we had concluded that Spanky was a virgin, or close to it. He was a good F-8 driver, but he was socially out of step in the Red Lightnings, and his purity was cause for concern. His parents had wanted him to enter the priesthood, not become a fighter pilot.

It was decided that we would kidnap Spanky, roll him up in a tarp and deliver him to an upscale brothel in Hong Kong's Wanchai District. We would pay the establishment to provide proper "care" for Spanky, and to take some appropriate photographs to memorialize the event for *our* subsequent viewing pleasure.

Like any clever prey, Spanky sensed something was afoot. We found out later that he had slipped off the ship early in a disguise and checked into a hotel under a false name. Some people do not appreciate what you try to do for them.

For all of his advanced knowledge of aviation, The Buzzard was surprisingly unsophisticated in other matters. This often led to amusing episodes that made life in the Red Lightnings even more interesting.

Buzzard, Porky, Gator, Maggot and I decided to tour Kowloon, across the harbor from Hong Kong. We were told to be careful, because many Communist Chinese sympathizers lived in the huge Asian city. It was more "Chinese" than the British-influenced Hong Kong on the other side of the harbor. We took a ferry across the harbor, and then a bus to the center of Kowloon. We went into a big department store, looking for unusual things to buy for family and friends back home.

We soon noticed that we were the only Caucasians in the store, and were getting hostile stares from the Chinese shoppers. Buzzard had consumed a few beers on the way over, and made some loud comments about the "cheap-ass" merchandise. Then, Buzzard  found what he was looking for. At the end of one aisle was a huge, stacked display of plaster busts of Mao Tse-Tung, the infamous Chinese Communist leader. Alongside were stacks of Mao's "Little Red Book," the self-promoting equivalent of Hitler's *Mein Kampf*. Porky was going to buy one, and then said to the horrified cashier, "How am I supposed to read this goddam thing? It's in friggin' Chinese!"

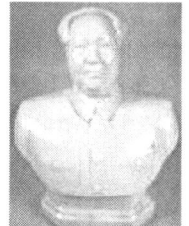

The Buzzard started laughing and then pulled a Mao bust from the bottom of the towering display, causing them all to cascade to the floor, breaking into pieces. The crowd of local shoppers became angry and hysterical, chanting "Yankee, go home!" and other insults in Chinese. We headed quickly for the exits and got a taxi back to the ferry depot. Another narrow escape. In a few days, we were back on the line, flying daily strikes, as if the Hong Kong stay never happened.

Sometimes the roulette wheel of life gives you a losing number. Upon arriving in the ready room one morning, I saw CAG Phillips, in his flight suit, talking to the Skipper. The Skipper looked worried. I tried to escape through the back door, because I had learned that being drawn into a conversation with CAG Phillips could only lead to problems.

CAG spotted me. "Morning, Hot Dog. You are flying with *me* today, so suit up!" said CAG. I wondered if they could hear me groaning and mumbling various curses and epithets, as I put on my g-suit.

This was supposed to be a "coastal recce," looking for enemy boat traffic off the coast. We were loaded with six 500 lb. bombs each, plus Sidewinders and the usual 20mm. We joined up off the catapult, and CAG headed straight for the Red River delta, the worst possible place. Although we were not supposed to go "feet dry," he crossed the beach and started flying toward Hanoi at about 4,000'. Not only was this a dangerous direction, it was a suicidal altitude. The NVA below probably thought, *Are these guys nuts?*

As I expected, the SAM warning light started flashing, and CAG dove down to the river, jinking wildly. The bomb load made our aircraft heavy and sluggish. In a few seconds, my SAM warning light started flashing and two SAMs zoomed by, just above our altitude. Finally, even CAG had enough. "Let's get out of here!" he yelled.

By this time, we were down on the deck, going like hell. I looked up just in time to see a pair of tall palm trees in the front yard of a large house. I rolled 90 degrees, stood the bird on a wing and flew between the trees, just missing them.

As we got to the coast, I thought the worst was over. *Wrong again.* CAG spotted a large boat in the river, and said, "Let's sink this guy!" He started into a racetrack bombing pattern, dropping one bomb at a time, violating another unwritten rule—*never fly repetitive runs on a target*. If you do, you become an easy target for flak gunners. He became quite angry when I pickled all six bombs and sank the boat on my first run, spoiling his fun. I joined up on him and we returned to the ship for uneventful landings.

When I got out of the aircraft, the maintenance chief told me that my bird had taken a hit. When I asked what it was, he said, "An AK-47 slug. You must have been pretty low." He was right. That was the only hole I ever got in my aircraft, and it was from a guy firing a *rifle. Thanks, CAG!*

During one of the day cycles, Snake and Porky were flying a BARCAP over Red Crown. These flights were usually uneventful, if not monotonous, and it was easy to get complacent. Snake was cruising along on autopilot, with Porky in

Combat Spread. Both were copying down information from the Red Crown controller on their kneeboards when Snake glanced up to see a big KC-135 tanker aircraft coming at him head-on, at about 600 knots closure.

Snake slapped the stick to the right, causing the F-8 to miss the big plane's fuselage, but his left wing clipped the vertical tail of the tanker. The horizontal stabilizer of the KC-135 creased the F-8's belly. The pilots of both aircraft called for assistance on guard channel, and were directed to head for the airfield at Da Nang. Snake was barely able to control his damaged bird, but somehow got it on the runway. Most pilots would have ejected. The KC-135 landed close behind him.

In the Navy's investigation that followed, they made Snake the scapegoat for the accident. The one thing you could count on with the Navy brass is that they would always avoid responsibility by attaching blame downstream to one of their subordinates, who in this case was Snake. The Air Force, on the other hand, proclaimed its KC-135 crew to be heroes and awarded each of them the Distinguished Flying Cross. Because of Snake's excellent reputation and support from CAG and the Skipper, the admirals finally backed off and Snake resumed flying, with his career intact. Years later, he even made Rear Admiral. The Navy had attempted to bury the fact that Red Crown was assigning the BARCAP fighters to 20,000', and not coordinating with the Air Force flights, which were also using that altitude for aerial tanking. In addition, the Red Crown controller had failed to alert Snake and Porky to the presence of the KC-135. This accident could have happened to any of us.

Snake's damaged F-8 received major repairs, and was then flown from Da Nang to Cubi Point for more inspections. Lieutenant Frank Harrington, who was an aircraft maintenance fanatic, volunteered to fly the bird up to Atsugi, Japan for major overhaul. He landed and refueled at Naha Air Base in Okinawa. So far, so good.

On takeoff, the top of the engine duct collapsed, dropping the main fuel cell into the engine compressor section. Apparently, it had been weakened by the mid-air collision and the inspections had not discovered it. At about 80 knots on takeoff roll, Frank ejected to escape the fireball. His chute failed to open, and he died upon impact with the runway, still in his seat.

I posed the obvious question to the Maintenance Officer: "Why didn't we leave that piece of junk in Da Nang, and let the Marines cannibalize it for parts? Was it worth losing Frank?" No answer. I became convinced that people on both sides of this war were trying to kill us, and some of the "enemy" wore our uniform.

During a Cubi Point port call, the Skipper asked me to fly one of our damaged aircraft up to Atsugi, Japan, where the Japanese had a fantastic re-work facility. I was scheduled to bring another repaired bird back as soon as it was ready to fly.

The flight to Atsugi was routine. The maintenance crew there told me that the other aircraft would not be ready for four more days, so I went into Tokyo for a few days. When I returned, the replacement bird was ready. I checked everything over, and all systems were good.

I started up, and started taxiing for the runway. The tower called me: "Red Flash, we have a problem. An ECM Whale is inbound and in trouble. The pilot has passed out, and one of the crew is flying the airplane."

From my LSO duties, I was familiar with this aircraft. I knew that it only had one pilot and a crew of three electronics specialists. There were no ejection seats. In an extreme emergency, the only options were to land or bail out manually through an escape hatch, just like in a World War II bomber.

"Tower, what do you want me to do?"

"Can you find him and lead him back to the field?"

"Roger, can do. I need clearance and a radar vector to his location."

"Roger, Red Flash. We have tied in a radar controller on this frequency. You are cleared for immediate takeoff, runway zero one. Squawk 3400 [the IFF setting]. Your initial vector is one two zero, and you are cleared to 25,000'. Contact Atsugi Departure Control after takeoff, and remain on this frequency."

"Roger, Red Flash is rolling." I taxied at high speed to the end of the runway, hit afterburner, and accelerated down the runway.

As I transitioned the bird to the cruise configuration, I turned right to the assigned heading. I raised the nose to the burner climb attitude of around thirty degrees. Almost immediately, I was immersed in thick clouds. I switched the radar to the 40-mile scale and looked for a contact. I saw one!

"Control, I have a bogey five left at twenty-five, slightly high."

"Roger, Red Flash, that's your bogey. Cleared for intercept."

As I was closing the contact quickly, indicating he was coming almost head-on, I switched to the 20-mile scale and locked the radar on him. At a range of five miles, I popped out on top of the clouds, and spotted the Whale, lumbering along on a westerly course. I de-selected burner, and did a left yo-yo maneuver to join on him, with my speed brake extended. When I came up on his wing, I adjusted power and retracted the speed brake. What I saw was amazing.

The bombardier-navigator (BN) normally sat in the right seat, while the pilot sat in the left. When I got in close to the Whale, I signaled the frequency with hand signals, and the BN came up on the radio. "This is Reno Three Zero Eight. Our pilot is unconscious. I'm flying the airplane with the autopilot. We are getting low on fuel. We pulled the pilot out of his seat."

"Roger, Reno, this is Red Flash Four Zero Three. We need to get you down below this cloud layer, lined up with the Atsugi runway, and on glide slope. You're going to make an arrested landing to get stopped. Can you guys do that?"

"Affirmative. I'll stay in my seat and fly the autopilot as long as possible, and then be ready to flare it."

"Rog. OK, I'll stay on your wing. Control, what heading for the runway?"

"Red Flash, Control. Turn right to zero one zero. Tower has given you priority and you and Reno are cleared to descend to 2,000'. You are also cleared to land, runway zero one. Call runway in sight."

"Reno—you are cleared to land. Runway ahead—you got a visual?" I asked.

*Pilot's view of Atsugi air base, on final approach for runway 01.*

"Rog, got it," came the hesitant reply.

"Just do your landing checklist. Your gear and hook are down. Check your landing flaps. Just keep it lined up. I'll watch your glide slope."

"Rog, Red Flash."

I did not know it then, but the BN was a real pro, and very knowledgeable about his aircraft. Apparently, many of the squadron pilots had even allowed him to fly the aircraft on occasion, so he knew where all the switches were.

About a mile from the runway, the EA-3 started to go low. "Little power, Reno—don't overcorrect, now," I advised. Now I was an airborne LSO, flying wing on a bird with no pilot. *Life is truly strange.*

He got back on glide slope, and was lined up perfectly. As he flew it down to touchdown, that beautiful field arresting gear was waiting, about 2,000' from the end. He touched down, and bounced a little. I added power to level off and flew low alongside him without touching down, in order to watch his rollout.

Suddenly, I saw the hook go up, then down again! Just as they were going to catch the arresting gear, the pilot woke up and said, "Hey, the hook is down!" and *raised* the hook. The crew member behind the pilot held him back and the BN slapped the hook back down just in time to catch the wire. The big EA-3 caught the arresting gear, and was pulled to a safe stop.

I landed after they got the big bird off the runway. I went into the terminal and met the EA-3 crew. They still looked terrified. It seems that the pilot had been drinking heavily the night before, and had taken his oxygen mask off at high altitude after their mission near the North Korean coast. He then passed out.

I wrote an incident statement, and identified the BN as the real hero of the day. Without his cool professionalism, a valuable aircraft and four men would have been lost. The pilot lost his wings after the investigation, but at least he was still alive, thanks to his BN.

Back on the line, we were hitting North Vietnam with daily Alpha Strikes. The atmosphere was tense. Everyone was showing the strain, and tempers ran hot. During day operations, an A-4 hit the ramp and the pilot was killed.

Returning from a BARCAP, Porky and his section leader broke over the ship and entered the landing pattern. I was the LSO. Just behind Porky, a flight of A-4s arrived in the break, led by CAG Billy Phillips: "Chippies, let's take an extra interval—this F-8 is long in the groove." That does not sound like much, but to a carrier pilot, it is like a comment about your mother's chastity. Moreover, to have such a comment broadcast on the radio was highly insulting. At that moment, Porky gave the mandatory call to let the LSO know he saw the glide slope "meatball."

"Red Flash Four Zero Nine, Crusader, ball, two-point-three [fuel remaining]. *And you can bite my ass!*"

The reply was quick. "This is CAG. When I get on deck, I *will*!"

I could not believe what I was hearing on the radio. As expected, Porky was reprimanded, grounded, and assigned to be the permanent ready room duty officer. Within a few days, CAG sent him on the COD aircraft back to Cubi to run the maintenance detachment, apparently thinking this would be viewed as punishment. As Porky departed, with a big smile on his face, he said, "Well, boys, while you poor schmucks are flying Alpha Strikes and getting your asses shot off, I'll be in the Cubi O'Club, sipping a martini and thinking about you! Please, *please* don't throw me in that briar patch!"

I wondered if he had planned this all along. Porky was a very smart and devious guy, and one of my heroes.

~ ~ ~

# Chapter 16: *Targets of Opportunity*

The *Ticonderoga* cruise wore on, and the pilot losses continued. An F-8 nugget in VF-191 lost his oil pressure, and tried to land back aboard before the engine froze up. It quit on short final, and he ejected. He drowned when he became tangled up in his chute before the helo could get to him.

I became convinced that I was not going to survive this environment. Too many experienced pilots had gone down, and I was still in the learning stage. I had played enough Klondike, the pilots' favorite dice game, to know that the odds were against me. I began to spend money ashore as if I had struck oil, on the theory that I would never be required to pay off the credit card bills.

After I concluded that I only had a few weeks to live, I actually became a much better pilot. There was nothing more to be afraid of. In fact, the shakiest pilots were the ones that thought too much about their family, wrote melancholy letters home, stared at their wife's picture, and worried about surviving. It was becoming apparent that you had to have lots of *attitude*, and even more *luck*. Fortunately, I was well supplied with both.

One of the most deceptively dangerous missions was "photo escort." The Navy had an unarmed photo reconnaissance version of the F-8 with fantastic camera capability, which was utilized for bomb damage assessment and target selection. These were the birds that took the dramatic low-level photos of Soviet missiles in Cuba, setting off the Cuban Missile Crisis in 1962.

 Usually, three photo F-8s were attached to each carrier and were flown by their own specially trained pilots. To remind them that they were not real fighter pilots, we referred to them as "photo weenies." On a typical mission, an armed fighter F-8 flew with the photo bird in case of MIG engagement, or to warn of SAMs. Too often, these guys tended to fly with their head in the "boot," aiming their cameras. The really bad part was that they always made their camera runs at low altitude over the most heavily defended territory. Japanese Kamikaze pilots would have been quite comfortable with this mission.

We continued to receive reports about the North Vietnamese killing downed pilots. We became aware that the ever-present fishing boats in the Gulf of Tonkin were armed and just waiting for an opportunity to take out an American pilot. Nevertheless, we were given strict orders to leave the fishing boats alone, because they were "innocent civilians." One of the reasons that we lost in Vietnam was that our leaders failed to understand that a totalitarian society, like Communist North Vietnam, Nazi Germany, or World War II Japan, really has no innocent civilians. War has no boundaries or sanctuaries, if the intent is to win.

On a typical monsoon weather day, I was launched with one of the more experienced "photo weenies," who used the call sign, "Corktip." We were directed to start at the DMZ and fly north up the entire North Vietnamese coast to Cam Pha, just below the Chinese border. We were to report ship traffic and weather, because the admirals were itching to launch an Alpha Strike into any hole in the clouds. God forbid—we were falling behind in the Navy-Air Force sortie race!

After launch, we found the weather to be impossible for visual bombing. Cloud tops were about 20,000', solid down to the bottoms at around 500'. Visibility over the water was restricted to about two miles in haze and fog. The photo pilot took the lead, and we dropped down to about 200' to keep sight of the coast. We cruised north at a leisurely 300 knots, enjoying the picturesque sight of the fishing boats that were scattered over the coastal waters. At this low altitude, we were below the SAM envelope.

We cruised along on our "sight-seeing" tour, and finally reached the Hourglass River area, just northeast of Thanh Hoa. Numerous fishing boats were directly in our path, as we dropped down to 100' to stay below radar coverage of the numerous SAM sites in the area. I was flying a loose wing on the photo bird on his right side. Suddenly, tracers flashed just over my canopy, and I heard the staccato hammering of bullet shockwaves. This meant that the stream of bullets was coming *extremely* close to the cockpit.

I looked down to the right and spotted a fishing boat with two guys manning a machine gun, blazing away at me. I have often wondered how they could have missed at such close range.

We added full power. "Helo trap!" radioed the photo. The NVA had started mixing heavily armed boats within the fishing fleet, hoping to take out a low-flying helo or A-1 prop aircraft. Combined with all the other nasty behavior by the North Vietnamese, this cheap shot caused me to lose my cool.

"*I have the lead*," I told the photo. The gunners wanted to fight, so I decided to accommodate them.

I turned seaward in a wide right 270-degree turn, flying on the instruments. Even though I knew I would lose sight of the culprit boat because of the bad visibility and low ceiling, I figured it would have to be directly ahead of me when I rolled wings level.

I checked MASTER ARM—ON, and selected GUNS. I heard that beautiful "clunk-clunk" sound as the four cannons each rammed a big 20mm high-explosive round into their chambers. The gun sight reticle was illuminated and I leaned forward, hoping to place the "pipper" on the boat gunners before they saw me. *Time to reach out and touch someone* . . . .

Out of the haze appeared a line of six small boats, apparently tied together. Their occupants saw me and a barrage of machine-gun fire erupted, now coming from *all six boats*. The bullets were kicking up water geysers around me, and I quickly realized, *I have to get them before they get me!* As I got closer, I felt like the tracers were going right down my engine intake duct, but somehow they were missing. Head on, the F-8 does not give you much to shoot at.

The six-boat line had me in deep trouble. I was coming in perpendicular to their line, allowing them all to shoot at me simultaneously. I had stupidly crossed "the T" on myself, even though at the Academy I had studied the historic Battles of Tsushima, Cape Esperance, Jutland, and Surigao Strait, where this mistake resulted in tactical disaster. I was now in a simple contest that would be determined in favor of the one that landed the first knockout punch. *Time to get creative.*

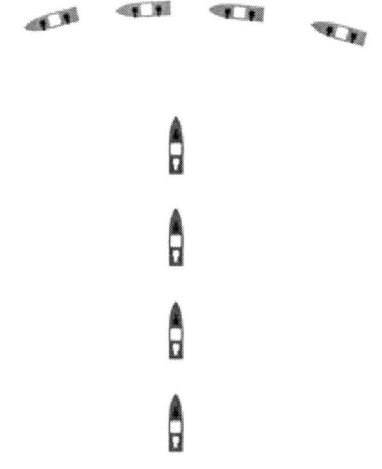

I knew that if *any* of the gunners remained alive, there was no way they could miss my bird's exposed belly when I pulled out. At about 3,000' distance, I pulled sharply up to the 500' ceiling, and then jammed the nose down, putting the fixed pipper on the center boats. This caused them to lose their bead on me, momentarily. Holding the trigger down, I alternately pushed the rudder pedals and yawed the aircraft several times left and right, making my tracers slash across the line of boats. The boats disintegrated and the high-explosive incendiary rounds vaporized the gunners. It was the luckiest shot I ever made. *[Career tip: Never use up all of your luck (or your ammo) in one phase of a battle. Save a little for the unexpected.]* Watching the center boat break apart, I almost flew in the water and then overreacted by pulling up hard into the overcast. I believe they call that "target fixation." Some call it stupidity.

While hyperventilating in the clouds, I sensed something was very wrong. In my frantic pullout, I had failed to focus on my flight instruments as I entered the thick clouds. I looked at the attitude and vertical speed indicators and then the altimeter, and realized I was now in a steep dive, with my nose aimed at the water in a near 90-degree angle. The altimeter was unwinding rapidly. Focusing on  my instruments, I slapped the stick to bring the wings level and pulled back hard, nearly entering a stall. As I popped out below the cloud deck, the dark water came rushing up. *This is going to be close,* I told myself. The bird began to shudder violently on the edge of a stall as I pulled even harder to keep her from hitting the water, which would cause her to disintegrate.

What they say is true about a near-death moment. Everything goes into slow motion, while your life's most important images flash through your mind at high speed. Scenes of my childhood, my mom, and my dad zoomed through my brain, like a video player in fast-forward. The water seemed to be reaching up to grab me, as my last thought zipped through my mind: *This is a really stupid way to die!*

Just as I accepted the fact that I was dead, the groaning bird leveled off and somehow gradually flew out of the stall, with the water surface just inches from her belly. The photo pilot, who was trying to join on me, later said I was creating a huge rooster-tail of white water behind me. My bonding with this beast was paying off. In my imagination, the abused Crusader whispered to me—as women often did—"Don't do this to me again! *Ever!*"

My brain had melted down. I told the photo pilot, "Take me home—I can't think straight." In my mind, I was sure I was actually dead, and simply dreaming the rest of the flight from my watery grave. I flew along on the photo bird's wing, in a mindless daze. When we got back to the carrier, I landed on the first pass, but could not remember the landing. I found myself sitting in "the pack" parking area on the port bow of the carrier, not knowing how I got there. The maintenance crew had to help me out of the aircraft, because my knees would not work. The photo pilot was so certain that I had actually hit the water, he went back to inspect the tail cone of my bird to see if it was flattened.

The Skipper was not happy when he heard the story. "Great! You almost traded a multi-million dollar aircraft for six lousy boats! And I don't have time to break in a new wingman!" I was thinking, *It's nice to be needed.*

I had nightmares about hitting the water for months. Since I slept in the top bunk, I would wake up in a sweaty panic and hit my head on the pipes overhead. I am sure this caused permanent brain damage, which excuses most of my inappropriate behavior since then.

From that day on, I always saved some ordnance to use on the Hourglass fishing fleet, which I now considered my personal enemy, trespassing on *my* turf. I figured that if they could not behave like law-abiding fishermen, they should lose their fishing privileges. Besides, the waters of the Gulf were *mine*. I noticed they were now staying much closer to shore because of my "friendly visits." I suspect that the price of fresh fish in Hanoi went up considerably because of my personal vendetta.

I now realized *everyone* in North Vietnam was the enemy, regardless of gender, occupation or age. Everyone carried an AK-47 or other weapon. There were no innocent civilians north of the DMZ. The transformation was complete. I had become an expert killing machine. The American taxpayers were finally getting what they had paid for.

One day the weather broke, and the Alpha Strikes began. I was assigned to Iron Hand, to prevent the SAMs from being launched against the strike group. I teamed up with A-4 driver Rick Millson (who later became a Blue Angel). We flew well together. The  big Shrike missile, carried by Millson's A-4E, was a wonderful payback to the SAM operators. It locked on their radar and flew directly into the control van, which often contained Soviet advisors. When Millson was out of Shrikes, I still had my 12 Zuni rockets, which were accurate and deadly to personnel and light vehicles. We fused them to explode about 50' above the ground, where they would spray a vicious cone of shrapnel. Being in a Zuni's path would not be pleasant—or survivable.

*Gator, sitting in aircraft 410 on the flight deck, loaded with 12 Zuni rockets, ready to launch on an Iron Hand SAM-killer mission. Across the flight deck, F-8s and A-4s are lined up for the launch. This launch process is repeated 8-10 times each day, followed immediately by the recovery of airborne aircraft from the previous launch.*

On this strike, the air wing deployed four Iron Hand teams in a semi-circular screen up the Red River ahead of the strike force, and we started hunting. It did not take long for the NVA's reaction. Our SAM lights started flashing, with that hideous tone in our headsets. "Tally-ho, SAMs at 10 and 12 o'clock!" yelled Millson. He immediately locked his first Shrike on the southern site, and pickled the missile off. He then swung around to point at the other one, firing another Shrike. His missiles flew directly down the SAM L-band guidance beams and hit the control vans, undoubtedly killing everyone inside.

Just as I was telling myself how much fun this was, two more SAMs lifted off from different sites, tracking toward us from opposite directions. Millson dodged the first one, but we both had to go into a high-g spiral to escape the second missile. I lost sight of Millson in the frantic pullout, and he failed to answer on the radio. I thought he had been shot down, and that put me into a rage. Now I *really* wanted to take somebody out.

At that moment, through a hole in the scattered cloud layer, I saw the distinctive rosette pattern of a big SAM site, reloading its missiles. I rolled into a steep dive on it and ripple-fired all 12 Zunis in a direct hit on the control van. Later reconnaissance photos showed the van and missiles were all destroyed by the Zunis. Pulling off, my aircraft was nearly smothered by big black puffs of AAA fire from 100mm guns. The NVA did not seem to be happy about the loss of a SAM site.

I finally found Millson, who had experienced radio problems and had joined up on our big A-3 tanker about 30 miles from the ship. We both tanked and landed back aboard, feeling very good about this day. Between us, we had destroyed three SAM sites and the strike group had no losses. *It doesn't get much better than that.*

*Hot Dog—mounting up for Iron Hand SAM-killer mission. Zuni rockets are visible on the fuselage launcher.*

The weather went bad again, and only a few birds were launched each day. The Buzzard came up to me in the ready room and said, "I got one of my buddies in Strike Ops to launch the spare with us on a coastal recce. We're going to have some fun." On each flight, there was normally a back-up aircraft, called the "spare." On this launch, Buzzard was the lead, I was the wingman, and *Gator* was the spare. Each aircraft was to be armed with 38 2.75-inch rockets, in addition to two Sidewinders and 20mm ammo. *Oh, shit. This was not a trio that the Skipper would want flying together.* When Buzzard talked about "fun," there was usually a price to pay.

Buzzard had us meet him in his room. "How do you guys feel about watching Soviet and Chinese ships carry SAMS and ammo into Haiphong?" Buzzard asked.

"It sucks," replied Gator.

"Big time," I added.

"Well, do you want to do something about it? I've been working on a plan. But I need to know you are both on board."

"Buzzard, we are fed up with these 'rules of endangerment' that are getting our people killed and captured. What do you want to do?" I asked.

Buzzard went over the procedures, and what to expect. We reviewed a map with Buzzard to make sure we all understood the tricky geography involved. His plan was to loft our rockets into the port of Haiphong, where the ships were off-loading SAMs and ammo for the NVA. It would be critical to fly a perfect track to the rocket release point in order to avoid the deadly ground fire around the city.

Usually, the big 19-shot rocket pods we carried were set to fire one rocket at a time. Buzzard told us to change the pod settings to RIPPLE and our cockpit switches to BOTH, which would shoot all 38 in close sequence.

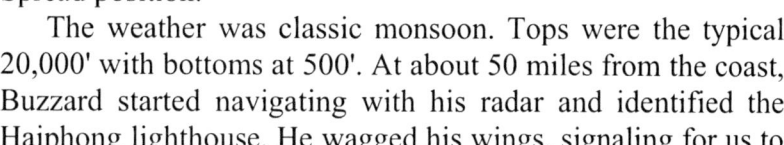

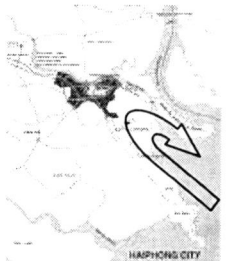

The Admiral wanted more sorties, so—just as Buzzard predicted—the spare (Gator) was launched with us. We joined up in Combat Spread with Buzzard in the lead, me in a loose tactical wing, and Gator in the Combat Spread position.

The weather was classic monsoon. Tops were the typical 20,000' with bottoms at 500'. At about 50 miles from the coast, Buzzard started navigating with his radar and identified the Haiphong lighthouse. He wagged his wings, signaling for us to join close on him, with Gator on his left wing, and me on his right. We switched to a pre-arranged frequency, and turned our IFF systems off so that Red Crown could not identify us. There was no need to provide evidence for our own court-martial.

In a tight "V" formation, we started descending through the clouds, heading directly for Haiphong, the heavily defended port. Everyone knew that the Soviets and Chinese were resupplying the NVA through Haiphong, but Washington's ridiculous Rules of Engagement placed Haiphong and their ships strictly off-limits. It would certainly be unfortunate if we hit some Soviet or Chinese ships, but we would not be specifically aiming at them. Besides, they had assumed the risk by entering a hot combat area. *Sometimes you have to pay the freight, Comrades.*

The clouds got thicker, and Gator and I closed in tight on Buzzard's wing to keep sight of him. If you screwed up and lost sight of that wingtip, you had to pull away and reverse course to avoid a mid-air collision in the clouds. I was so close, I felt as if I could reach out and touch Buzzard's wingtip, which was only about five feet from my cockpit. Even then, I could barely keep sight of it.

Finally, the three of us popped out together at 400' over the water, with the Haiphong lighthouse passing to our left. We descended to about 50' to avoid their radar and SAM shots. Buzzard had correctly predicted that the gunners on either side of the harbor entrance would be unable to fire at us for fear of hitting their buddies on the other side. They probably were not expecting an F-8 air show, either.

The Buzzard had carefully plotted this attack. At an exact spot and heading, he pulled up with us in close formation to a 30-degree nose-high angle, and said, "Stand by…….FIRE!" A salvo of 114 rockets from our three birds arched toward the Haiphong docks, where the NVA stashed their SAMs and ammo, and where the Soviet and Chinese ships were tied up.

Buzzard then did a smooth right wing-over reversal, with Gator and me on each wing. The trick was to get back down on the water before the NVA could fire at us. At the top of this maneuver, our SAM lights illuminated, first steady, then flashing, indicating a launch. The SAM radar lost lock when we reversed our track and zipped back through the harbor entrance at 50' altitude. Out of SAM range, Buzzard climbed us back through the clouds, again in tight formation. When on top, we switched back to Red Crown's frequency and turned our IFF back on, as if nothing had happened. *See no evil, hear no evil, speak no evil . . . .*

During debrief with the intelligence officers, which occurred after almost every flight, we were asked if we had gone anywhere near Haiphong. Apparently, the rocket barrage had hit several Soviet ships and started multiple fires and explosions in the ammunition storage around the port area. The Russians were furious, and complained to Washington. *How dare we interfere with them delivering SAMs and ammo to our enemy!* Buzzard replied, "No, but we did see some Air Force F-105s in that area. It must have been them." As Buzzard left the room, he whispered to me, "VSH!"

Early in the cruise, CAG Phillips became obsessed with getting a MIG before he gave the air wing over to his replacement. He abandoned what little good judgment he had, and each time he flew an F-8, he took his flight toward Hanoi to bait the MIGs into fighting. On one flight, he led Burger over a low overcast toward Hanoi, resulting in multiple SAMs being launched at them. On another, he nearly got Devil shot down with his foolishness.

CAG then came up with a rather brilliant plan. Knowing that the MIG ground controllers were listening to our radio frequencies, and that they knew our squadron call signs, he put together a bait-and-switch plan to ambush the MIGs.

He planned to launch a gaggle of 16 F-8s and lead them to the west of Hanoi, where the Air Force usually came in from their Thailand bases. They would use A-4 formations and A-4 squadron call signs. How could the MIGs resist this easy target? When the MIGs jumped the formation, they would find 16 F-8s, loaded with guns and Sidewinders instead of slow, defenseless A-4s. It actually sounded like it might work.

The hitch came when the air commanders in Saigon told Billy he would need to come down and brief them on the plan, because it involved using an Air Force route package area. Billy left for Saigon immediately, loaded down with charts and diagrams. He returned, confident that he would soon be leading his MIG sweep.

It was amusing to watch the political maneuvering among the F-8 pilots, because everyone wanted to be on that flight. I expected to be on it, because my Skipper rarely flew with anyone but me on his wing. The senior F-8 pilots were lobbying CAG vigorously for a spot, since he was personally approving every pilot on that flight.

We waited for the final "green light" from Saigon, but it never came. Billy sensed something was going on, and he was right. Once again, politics overruled common sense in the Vietnam War.

The Air Force denied Billy permission to fly into their package. Instead, they passed Billy's plan to Air Force COL Robin Olds, commander of the 8th Tactical Fighter Wing at Ubon, Thailand. Olds adapted Billy's plan to his F-4C aircraft and induced the MIGs to attack his group of fighters, pretending to be vulnerable F-105s. "Operation Bolo" destroyed half of the North Vietnamese Air Force MIG-21 inventory in one flight. Billy nearly had a stroke, contending that his plan had been hijacked by Olds and the Air Force. He never got over that.

*COL Robin Olds preflighting his F-4C aircraft. A West Point graduate, Olds was a double-ace in WWII (12 kills) and then added four MIGs to his total in Vietnam, making him a rare triple-ace.*

If someone deserved to steal CAG's MIG-sweep plan, it had to be COL Robin Olds. A star football player at West Point, Olds exhibited the same forceful skills and aggressiveness in the cockpit of a fighter. His criticism of the Air Force's senior leadership hurt his career, preventing him from rising above the rank of Brigadier General. In a candid interview with *Airman* magazine, he discussed the Air Force tactical problems and lack of ACM training during the Vietnam War:

"We weren't allowed to dogfight. Very little attention was paid to strafing, dive-bombing, rocketry, stuff like that. It was thought to be unnecessary. Yet every confrontation America faced in the Cold War years was a 'bombs and bullets' situation, raging under an uneasy nuclear standoff. [The Vietnam War] proved the need to teach tactical warfare and have [trained] fighter pilots. It caught us unprepared because we weren't allowed to learn it or practice it in training."

This great air warrior retired in 1973 when the Air Force leadership refused to allow him to go back to the Tactical Fighter Wings and retrain the pilots in aerial combat tactics. He died in 2007.

I looked at the flight schedule one evening and found that the Skipper was leading another strike. That meant that I would be flying his wing. This time, it was even closer to Hanoi. The target was actually *a wooden footbridge,* which had been selected by Secretary of Defense McNamara himself. I was fed up. The White House and McNamara were micro-managing this conflict into a needless defeat. There were plenty of good targets, but this was not one of them. For every real target we did *not* hit, more American troops in South Vietnam would die and the war would last longer.

Even more upsetting was the revelation that we would be the lead bombers, because the F-8s could each carry two 2,000 lb. bombs. Gator and I were again flying wing on the Skipper. He seemed to like having both of us around on difficult missions. *How nice.*

*A Mark 84 2,000 lb. bomb.*

We were strapped in our birds, sitting on the catapults, and waiting for the target weather to improve. I was on the starboard catapult, feeling a growing resentment for those idiots who constantly launched us against worthless targets in heavily defended areas, even in bad weather. Out of the corner of my eye, I noticed two men approaching my aircraft. I looked down to see the Admiral and his chief of staff standing by the cockpit, looking up at me. "Good luck, son," said Rear Admiral Tom Walker ('39).

"Yeah, pray for good weather, Admiral," I replied curtly. His chief of staff glowered at my insolence, and they walked away, wondering why this lowly lieutenant did not embrace their morale-building encouragement. I think they had watched *The Bridges at Toko-Ri* too many times.

The Admiral and his staff ran a spooky place below decks, called "The War Room." There were big maps on the bulkheads with hundreds of little colored pins. The only thing missing was Dr. Strangelove himself. Basically, the Admiral and his staff were useless and contributed nothing of value to our operations. They were simply justifying their own existence, like sea-going bureaucrats.

This is the same admiral that actually dozed off during a briefing for a visiting VIP, when I had been ordered to attend as a "representative" junior pilot. He was not much of a leader, so I wondered how he became an admiral. The Navy's byzantine politics at the senior level were a mystery.

Finally, the flight deck erupted in activity and we were told to crank it up. We blasted off the catapults in afterburner, carrying a partial fuel load because of the heavy bomb weight. We then had to top off our fuel at the tanker, struggling to plug into the basket with our probe. We frequently had to tap afterburner to keep control at this slow speed and excessive weight. After fueling, we rendezvoused with the strike group and headed for our coast-in point, the junction of the Hourglass Rivers, the Cua Day and Cua Lac Giang.

On the way in, the flak was heavy and the SAMs were flying at us from every direction. We came up on our miserable little target, and I noticed a large town just southwest of the bridge. Tracers and heavy flak were spewing up at us from the town itself. I decided that I had been jacked around enough for one day. Besides, with my newly acquired bombing accuracy, I now enjoyed killing flak sites. It was sort of my "thing." There is a certain primitive exhilaration in killing someone who is trying to kill you.

The Skipper and Gator rolled right to bomb the little bamboo bridge, and they both missed it. Out of their field of vision, knowing the Skipper would not approve, I rolled left to put my aim point squarely in the center of the big town. This was obviously a supply staging area and the source of the monstrous flak barrage. If any traffic was actually going across the measly little bridge, it was undoubtedly traveling through this town. They certainly had plenty of flak gunners, and those guys were just begging to die. They would get their wish.

Gator and I had worked hard to perfect a high angle, high altitude bomb release technique from about 10,000'. At that altitude, we could pull out well above the bulk of the ground fire, which—except for the big 100mm guns—was only accurate up to about 6,000'. This technique was surprisingly effective because of the high dive angle, and very hard for the flak gunners to hit an aircraft in such a high, steep dive.

I placed my bombsight on the center of the town, using the 70-mil ring. I pickled and felt the huge bombs drop off, followed by the shock waves from the detonations as I climbed out at full power. I looked back to see that the two bombs had obliterated the town and started multiple secondary explosions, indicating the presence of fuel or munitions. Obviously, the town was storing something more sinister than rice and monkey meat. The residual fire and explosions indicated that it was a disguised ammo dump. The flak abruptly stopped. The stinking town was guilty as charged. *How did that feel, Comrades?*

During the intelligence debrief back on the carrier, we stated that we were desperately dodging flak, and did the best we could to get that pesky, important little bridge. However, someone noticed that the town was conspicuously missing in the new reconnaissance photos, replaced by two huge bomb craters. Gator looked at me and smiled. "It must have been the Air Force again," he said. No thanks to McNamara and the other pinheads in the Pentagon, a real target had been hit. The attack pukes were happy, because I had eliminated most of the flak. One of the little bombers actually hit the bridge after we pulled off. Naturally, the North Vietnamese repaired it within 48 hours.

Life on the carrier during these times was strange and schizophrenic. We would go to the wardroom and have a nice breakfast, complete with uniformed stewards and white linen tablecloths and napkins. Then we would go out and sweat through two hours of combat, while several million North Vietnamese tried to kill us. After we landed back aboard ship, we would go down to the wardroom for lunch. Uniformed stewards, white linens again. Then back in the aircraft to let people try to kill us all over again, day after day.

Gator had a weird sense of humor. Few people—except me—knew when he was joking. Knowing how the Black Shoes disliked the air wing, Gator loved to elbow his way into a seat at the senior officers' table in the wardroom, wearing his sweaty flight suit. Gator's table manners were bad enough, but he always had to say something inflammatory to upset the Black Shoes. I found this somewhat amusing, since Gator had *been* a Black Shoe prior to flight training. I loved to remind him of this whenever possible, just to set him off.

On one occasion, we returned from a mission in time for lunch. Gator announced, "Flight priority! Make way for fighter pilots! Hide your women and children!" as he pushed his way to the head table, populated by the ship's senior officers.

"Gator! Not a good idea! Abort, Gator!" My warning fell on deaf ears.

We were seated in the midst of lieutenant commanders and commanders in spotless uniforms, who clearly disliked our smelly flight suits at their table. Gator said loudly, "Hot Dog, I can't believe I missed that target today with my bombs, and hit a stupid hospital!" All eyes turned toward us and the table became quiet. I squirmed in my seat, kicking Gator's leg under the table.

"Well, *why* did you miss it, Gator? What were you trying to hit?" I asked innocently. My facial contortions and winks were lost on Gator, who was now on a roll. He continued.

"Dog, I was actually trying to hit a school bus, but the gooks parked it right in front of that hospital. What a mess! Body parts everywhere. I ran out of bombs before I could nail that school bus, so I had to strafe it with 20mm." With horrified looks, the Black Shoes abandoned the table in disgust. Apparently, they did not know that the North Vietnamese did not have any school buses, and had purchased Russian tanks instead.

Gator laughed loudly, saying, "Hot Dog, I don't think anyone wants to have lunch with you!" I wondered if he had gone over the edge. I was sure that *I* had. Gator munched happily on his sandwich and said, "Pass the ketchup," as if nothing had happened. I wondered if anyone would notice if I quietly strangled Gator with my cloth napkin.

*Gator and Hot Dog, aboard* **Ticonderoga**, *1968.*

The East Coast F-8 drivers were not the only ones having trouble with the Tonkin Gulf environment. Some of the East Coast F-4 squadrons were also having adjustment problems. While grossly undertrained for this new environment, they were overly aggressive in their desire to shoot down a MIG and prove their manhood, which culminated in a huge fiasco one sunny day.

The Air Force had been using pilotless jet drones, equipped with cameras, to conduct high-risk photo-reconnaissance runs around Hanoi. The drones were launched from a multi-engine aircraft and flew a programmed flight profile into the target area, then flew back over the water for recovery by a specially equipped C-130. On electronic command, the drone would shut down and jettison its camera capsule, which would descend from high altitude in a parachute. The recovery aircraft would snag it before it hit the water, and reel it in to retrieve the camera films. It was quite a procedure.

On this particular day, the Air Force had neglected to tell the Navy that it was launching a drone. Normally, Red Crown would clear all aircraft out of the way.

The drone was launched and flew its profile perfectly. As it reversed course over Hanoi, the drone began to climb to its egress altitude, which was about 50,000'. When the drone crossed the coastline without showing a friendly IFF signal, Red Crown announced that a MIG was heading toward the carrier group at high altitude.

On one of the big carriers, a well-known lieutenant commander was sitting in his F-4 on Alert Five. He was immediately launched, along with his wingman, to intercept the bogey. The wingman got radar contact and was given permission to fire on the bogey. However, he misjudged the bogey altitude and could not get into firing position.

The leader then hit afterburner and climbed into firing position, saying, "Red Crown, I have a positive ID on a MIG-21! Am I cleared to fire?"

"This is Red Crown. You are cleared to fire!"

The F-4 fired a Sidewinder, which exploded near the drone's tail. Immediately, the drone's recovery chute opened and its camera package started descending. "Red Crown, splash one bogey! And we have a MIG pilot in his chute! We are following him down!"

Everyone dreamed of capturing one of the MIG pilots, because we knew the Russians, Chinese, and possibly the North Koreans had been flying missions with the North Vietnamese. Capturing one of the foreign pilots would be a huge prize, and a great embarrassment to the other side. I had been thinking about this. Maybe it would be fun to have our very own MIG pilot at Happy Hour! We could keep him as a squadron mascot, and chain him to a seat in our ready room! After the war, we could get him political asylum, and he could run a 7-11 or drive a taxi in New York City.

Gator had his own fantasy. He wanted to surround a MIG with several F-8s, then force the pilot to fly back to the carrier with us (similar to a scene in the movie *Blue Max*). Then, Gator would shoot him down alongside the carrier, and with a little luck, we would recover the pilot unharmed. Gator would say, "Who cares about the Mutha' Trophy when you can have your very own MIG pilot? We could use him to clean our rooms, run the movie projector, and make coffee in the ready room."

However, the "MIG pilot" capture of the moment had electrified the Fleet. Immediately, several destroyers and frigates were detached to proceed at flank speed to the anticipated splashdown of the "MIG pilot." The two F-4 crews watched as the drone camera package hit the water, triggering its automatic flotation devices.

"Red Crown, the MIG pilot appears to be in his raft!" said the lead F-4.

"Roger, we have a destroyer nearby—return to home plate. Good job!"

When the two F-4 crews returned to their carrier, their on-board admiral and the ship's captain were proudly waiting. The lead crew reportedly received the Navy Cross, amid the cheers of the crew.

Meanwhile, the Air Force could not find its drone. A terse message was issued to Task Force 77: "Urgent--- recce drone missing, ser. no. _____. Advise if drone is in radar contact, or last known position."

About the same time, the on-scene destroyer fished wreckage from the water. One piece contained the same Air

Force serial number. The "MIG" was actually one of the Air Force's drones. *Oops!*

When this information reached the big-deck carrier, the admiral canceled the press release and instructed the F-4 crew to return the Navy Crosses. After that, the F-8s were given more opportunities to engage airborne MIGs, since the F-4s had embarrassed their senior Navy supporters.

Gator had decided that he was tired of the intolerable heat in our stateroom, mostly caused by a huge steel duct that supplied steam to the catapults. These small carriers had been built in a hurry during World War II, and they did not even have catapults in those days. The steam catapult was an "add-on," which required some makeshift plumbing to supply the necessary steam. We were unlucky enough to have a room with this hideous thing running from the deck to the overhead, adding about 25 degrees to the ambient temperature. After several hours of flight operations, you could fry an egg on this duct. I agreed with Gator—we had to do something to reduce the temperature in this room.

Gator vowed to duplicate the engineering achievements of Porky and Buzzard and install the air conditioner he had smuggled aboard in Hawaii. Because of his Black Shoe engineering knowledge, he quickly got it installed and vented. Now it was time to hook up the power. Gator found that the ship "snipes" [engineers] were doing some serious wiring on the fourth deck. One night, he "borrowed" about 50' of heavy-duty power cable from their work site. Gator said, "Hey we're all just trying to modernize the ship, right? The Black Shoes should thank us!"

Gator was almost as clever with tools as Porky. One night, he dragged out his huge power drill and said, "We are going to wire our air conditioner to the water-tight fuse box in the passage way." He found that the box was sealed, so he drilled it open. He was hooking up his wires to achieve a 110v. solution in a 220v. circuit when the ship's Engineering Officer rounded the corner. This was very bad timing.

"What are you men doing??? Who *are* you? My God, you are *officers!*" said the shocked Black Shoe.

Gator replied matter-of-factly, "I'm Gator, this is Hot Dog, and we're just drillin' into this fuse box to get some power for our air conditioner."

The head snipe, a commander, went crazy. "You men are sabotaging my ship! You are going to the Captain!" I thought, *This could be a really good thing. I actually haven't met the Captain yet, and personal relationships are important in the Navy. The more senior officers you know, the better your chances for promotion.* We were called to the bridge.

"Hot Dog, I think we're going to get some kind of engineering award," Gator speculated. I was not so sure. Gator was an eternal optimist. If Gator were being dragged to the gallows to be hanged, he would think he was going to a knot-tying class.

The Captain was visibly upset. He glared at us from his big leather bridge chair and said, "You men have violated our engineering integrity. You have done what the enemy has *not* been able to do. You have damaged our ship." I silently thought, *Hey, you should see what I do to your ship with some of my landings, if you think this is bad. Wow, he has a nice view from up here!*

Back in the squadron ready room, our Skipper had a hard time keeping a straight face. "OK, boys, keep your hands off the ship. Play with your own toys. The F-8s belong to you, but the ship belongs to the Black Shoes. We are guests here. Consider yourselves reprimanded."

"Aye, aye, Sir," we chorused. Back to that miserable hot room. Time to think about tomorrow's Alpha Strike. More death, more destruction. Hopefully, death will be the fate of the North Vietnamese, and not us.

~ ~ ~

# Chapter 17: *Threading the Needle*

The Buzzard was the personification of a paradox. On the ground, he was out of control and a constant embarrassment for the Skipper. When it was time to get serious in the air, however, no one was more professional, courageous, and mission-focused.

Running with The Buzzard could be dangerous, whether on the ground or in the air. His ground-based exploits had become legendary at Miramar, if not infamous. On the other hand, Buzzard's overall aviation technique surpassed any other F-8 pilot that I had known. In the aircraft, Buzzard delivered the complete package. As I saw it, the trick for me was to learn *how* and *why* he did things in the air, while trying to stay with him on his shore-based escapades without being killed or court-martialed.

His cardinal rule was to focus on flying the aircraft *first, last, and always,* and not to become distracted by a peripheral detail, especially in an emergency situation. In two combat cruises, he never had to eject and he had never been hit by a SAM or AAA, even though he flew more than his share of the most dangerous missions.

Early in the cruise, I could see that none of the other pilots understood how to fly in the Vietnam combat environment as cleverly as Buzzard. He knew every detail of the SA-2 SAM performance, and how to keep from being hit by one. He also knew the entire AAA inventory, including the lethal envelope of each type of gun.

Each of the North Vietnamese MIG types (17, 19, and 21) had its own weaknesses and strengths, and Buzzard had come up with F-8 tactics that were tailored for each type.

Around the ship, no pilot was better. That is probably why he was selected to be the squadron LSO, or Landing Signal Officer, a position of enormous individual responsibility. When the LSO is "waving" aircraft (a term that goes back to the early days when flags or paddles were used instead of radios), even the Air Boss and the ship's captain defer to him on judgment calls and pilot instructions for landings.

*An LSO "waving" an aircraft aboard a carrier. He has the radio handset in his left hand, with the "pickle" light controls in his right.*

I guess it was a natural evolution for me to become interested in serving as an LSO, since it was something that The Buzzard did. I spent every spare moment on the LSO platform, learning how and why everything worked. Soon, my own landings began to improve as I watched the mistakes of other pilots, especially at night.

Night operations on a carrier are extremely dangerous. All of the things that can go wrong during daylight are still lurking, and you also must contend with the darkness. You have no horizon for orientation and are completely dependent on your instruments. If you are unlucky enough to have a generator failure on the catapult shot, you might not react  quickly enough to deploy the RAT (ram air turbine—the emergency generator) and regain your instruments. This kind of bad luck has resulted in more than a few Naval Aviators flying into the water at night.

The adrenaline starts to pump the minute you walk into the ready room to brief for your night flight. Everyone seems a little more serious. At the appointed moment, you proceed to the flight deck and climb into your aircraft, where the "plane captain" (ground crewman) straps you into the seat. I always had the feeling that if this young enlisted man had been a priest, he would have given me the Last Rites after strapping me in. The plane captains never said it, but I am sure that they were always wondering if we would be coming back.

After start-up, you taxi out of your spot, guided by ghostly figures with lighted wands, while steam rises from the catapults on a deck awash in an eerie red glow. The first time that you see this from the cockpit, you think, *I made it to Hell after all.*

You work your way forward toward one of the catapults in a continuous line of aircraft. Finally, the aircraft director stops you behind the jet blast deflector (JBD), a massive metal shield that rises magically from the deck to keep the jet blast generated by the bird on the catapult from hitting you.

Approaching the catapult, you must pay extremely close attention to the aircraft directors, who use small head-nods, twitches, and various body language to "fine tune" your approach to the catapult shuttle. Over-controlling the nose wheel steering, actuated by a button on the stick, can get you a bad reputation with the flight deck crew—and they *do* know who you are, by name!

If you are off lineup or position by even a few inches, you cannot be attached to the catapult. With the F-8, you had to roll the nose wheel directly over the catapult shuttle and immediately stop, while the bridle and "hold-back" fitting were attached. Even while the aircraft is moving, ground crewmen are doing final safety checks to

make sure the ordnance is on tight; panels are closed; there are no hydraulic leaks; and the wings are spread and locked. Out of nowhere appears a man with a lighted digital panel, which announces the estimated weight of the aircraft. If you agree with the number, you give a thumbs-up. The number must be right, or you will not get sufficient speed off the catapult and will crash into the water, with a good chance that the carrier will run over you.

Finally, the catapult officer turns to you, and gives the "rev up" signal. You go to 100% power, put your head back against the seat, and lock your left elbow to keep the throttle at full power. If your instruments are all normal, you either salute (daytime) or turn your exterior lights on (night). The cat officer visually clears the bow, then touches the deck, and the cat operator fires the cat.

You go from zero to 150 knots in about 1.5 seconds, and the aircraft is suddenly flying. *Check rate of climb, attitude, altitude and airspeed; gear up; wing down and locked; switch frequency; check IFF; look for your wingman; radar on; turn to rendezvous heading.* Soon you are climbing at 350 knots, joining on the other aircraft.

For the F-8 squadrons, the typical night mission was BARCAP (Barrier Combat Air Patrol). This was a racetrack pattern just off the coast at about 20,000' to protect the task force, including Red Crown. Sometimes Red Crown did not need much protection, as these ships occasionally demonstrated by shooting down MIGs with their long-range Talos or Terrier missiles. It was bad enough that we had to share the MIG opportunities with the Air Force and other Navy squadrons—now we had to share them with the trigger-happy *Black Shoes*!

After about an hour and a half, it would be time to return to the ship. Night landings are a nasty side of carrier flying. I had about 100 (out of 300 landings), and I can remember every one of them, as if they were a bad dream. You start out by separating from your wingman for spacing on a radar-controlled approach. At about one mile, you call the "ball" (meaning you see the glide slope), which is acknowledged by the LSO. Ahead of you, in the middle of blackness, all you can see is a tiny runway light picture and the meatball. You have little or no visual depth perception at night, particularly over dark water with no horizon.

All the way down the glide slope, you fight to keep on optimum angle of attack, or "donut" speed. You simultaneously work to stay on the centerline and keep the meatball centered in the row of green lights. A few hundred yards out, you usually feel some turbulence, caused by the ship's own airstream, or sometimes from the stack gas.

In close, the LSO gets tense. Your aircraft is approaching him faster than a Wimbledon tennis serve. He may give you various corrections, which you must follow carefully. A good LSO can see trends developing (change in speed, drift, settling or climbing, or problems with a pitching deck) well before the pilot can.

As you pass over the "round-down," it is critically important to keep your eyes locked on the meatball until your wheels hit the deck. The optimum wire to catch is #3, although #2 and #4 are acceptable. However, #1 is *never* acceptable, because it places your tail too close to a ramp strike, which is nearly always fatal. The LSO grades every pass, and debriefs the pilots after the recovery. Failure to pay attention to the LSO can get you a deadly ramp strike.

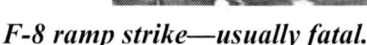

*F-8 ramp strike—usually fatal.*

***Red Lightning F-8E approaching the carrier. The wing is in the landing configuration, with the tail hook down. The amber approach light on the nose gear door is illuminated, showing the aircraft to be "on speed."***

After an arrestment, you are thrown violently forward in your harness, but you add full power anyway, in case the hook drops the wire or you miss all four. Better to bolter than dribble over the angle deck. As the arresting cable pulls you backwards, you are in a frenzy of activity: *Power to idle, hook up, tap the left brake on roll-back to swivel the nose gear, unlock and fold the wings, add power and follow the "yellow shirt" as he directs you out of the landing area.* The next bird is only 45-60 seconds behind you, and there is no time to waste. It is a cardinal sin to become snarled in the arresting gear and cause the next aircraft to wave off. This is crudely referred to as "shitting in the gear," and is duly recorded by the LSO on your landing grade.

When the "yellow shirts" taxi you forward, you are squeezed within inches of parked aircraft. The F-8s normally parked at a 30-degree angle on the port bow. At night, the F-8's long nose placed the pilot directly over the edge of the flight deck, making you feel like you were going over the side into the black water. It was always a relief to get back to the ready room after night flying. Every ready room has a closed-circuit TV, showing each landing and catapult shot. If you had a bad night, there were always plenty of self-appointed critics that would comment on your lack of flying skill.

In our squadron, it was customary for the LSO to write the daily flight schedule, as an additional duty. This was a critically important document, because you could get someone killed if you put the wrong pilots together. On this cruise for the Red Lightnings, Buzzard wrote the schedule. This was like handing a loaded gun to a bank robber. Contrary to expectations, Buzzard showed excellent judgment by carefully pairing compatible pilots together, and making sure that two weaker pilots did not fly together. This would be a skill I would need in a few months, although I did not know it yet.

During a period of daytime operations, I noticed Buzzard and I were paired together for a "weather recce." For Buzzard, this type of flight was a chance to have some fun, because it was a non-specific mission, or as Buzzard would say, "a free-lance opportunity."

On the day of the flight, he managed to talk the maintenance Chief into changing the ordnance load to a pure fighter configuration, removing the rockets, and loading each aircraft with two Sidewinders and full 20mm. "No reason not to be ready for a MIG," he mumbled. "It's a jerk-off mission anyway. Here's the deal. Last time I was over Vinh [a large city in southern North Vietnam], the bastards shot at me! Time for payback. We'll go high over the city, dive straight down in burner, droops in. Then we empty our 20mm directly into the city, and pull out. Just do what I do. If we get lucky, this might make some MIGs come out to fight, and we will still have our Sidewinders."

This may sound harsh, but Vinh—once a beautiful city—had become nothing but a military staging area, loaded with SAMs and AAA. It had become a legitimate military target, by any standard. If there were any civilians left there, they were supporting the enemy war effort and they had made their choice.

I banged off the cat right behind Buzzard, and we joined up. He gave me a hand signal to switch to our unauthorized tactical frequency. "Hot Dog's up."

"Rog."

We climbed to 25,000' and cruised over Vinh. Then we did the last thing the heavily armed city of Vinh was expecting. We rolled inverted, hit burner, clicked the droops in for supersonic flight, and pulled the birds straight down, accelerating fast. We went supersonic in a few seconds, just as we started firing the cannons into downtown Vinh. We did a 6-g pull-out and headed straight out to the water at around 600 knots, completing the "split S" maneuver.

Back on the carrier, I asked Buzzard the purpose of this maneuver. He said, "Well, imagine you are a driver in an NVA convoy going down the street in Vinh. The first thing you know, the entire downtown is lit up with high-explosive incendiary rounds raining down, penetrating buildings and vehicles. Then, two supersonic shockwaves hit, and you dive under your truck! How funny is that? VSH! You would think they might have the balls to launch their MIGs after us, but they didn't." As the mayor of Vinh found out that day, Buzzard did *not* like to be shot at.

The Buzzard was a very precise and disciplined instrument pilot. While most pilots paid no attention to obsolete equipment like the ADF (Automatic Direction Finder) receiver, Buzzard had required me to demonstrate a proper ADF approach to various fields *and* the carrier. On the carrier, this involved descending in a teardrop pattern from overhead the carrier to final approach. It was another way to find the ship.

Buzzard had tremendous insight into the F-8 weapons systems, including the radar. He emphasized the necessity of being able to navigate with the radar, and to recognize geographical points on the North Vietnamese coast, using the 60-mile scale. "If you can do this, it will someday save your ass," he commented after a flight. On the way in to targets, I began to study the radar display of the coast, as compared to the visual picture. Soon, I felt much safer in knowing where I was, especially at night or in bad weather. At night, you needed every advantage.

Buzzard also emphasized the unique radar blip of a carrier on the F-8 radar display.  "If you lose your radio at night or in bad weather, you can usually find the large blip of the carrier on your scope. Then, you just need to know the ship's approximate heading, so that you can get set up astern on final. You do that by looking at your radar and maneuvering to final lineup. You fly a course that will place the blip of the plane guard destroyer behind the carrier blip, which is where it always will be, and slightly to your left. That's because you are lining up right to account for the angle deck of the carrier." The plane guard destroyer is a ship that trails behind the carrier, ready to pick up pilots who wind up in the water.

This made no sense to me, until one day I actually did lose my radio and TACAN navigation system after a photo escort mission. The photo driver descended through the overcast and left me before I could join on him (typical photo "weenie"), leaving me lost over a solid overcast. I had no idea where the carrier was. I began to wonder how I was going to find the carrier—any carrier! Although landing on the wrong carrier is a terrible sin, it is still better than ejecting and going for a swim.

I turned on my ADF, and surprisingly, it still worked! Using the technique Buzzard had taught me, I did a teardrop descent when the needle spun in the "null," overhead the ship, and then started scanning my radar display. I flew a course that placed the destroyer blip aft of the big one, and slightly to the left. I popped out of the clouds exactly on lineup! What could have been a disaster was averted by one of Buzzard's tricks.

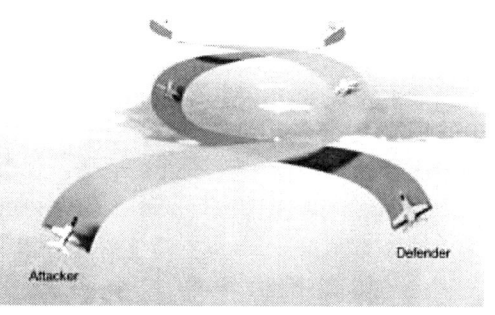

During our many practice dogfighting engagements, I noticed that Buzzard rarely lost a slow-speed scissors maneuver. In a classic scissors, the two adversaries find themselves abeam of each other, with each decelerating to minimum flying speed in an attempt to get behind the other. Invariably, he would be able to get slower than his opponent, and then slide behind him for a simulated guns kill. I asked how he did it.

"Simple. I use only my rudder to make the turns into the bogey. If you deflect your ailerons at such low speed, you will have a departure stall and spin. However, you still have to make your reversals fast and violent, without stalling. You do that by trimming the nose down so you don't accidentally spin it during the reversals, then holding it carefully back up with stick pressure, against the trim. Whenever you get a few knots excess, you pull up to a stall buffet, and then release stick pressure before it spins. This will make you stand still, compared to the other guy, who will usually slide out in front of you. Most guys are afraid to fly that close to a stall."

This was interesting stuff, because the F-8 would enter into a vicious spin if you pulled it into a stall in a nose-high attitude. Frequently, the spin would be inverted, compounding the difficulty in recovering. With each turn in the spin, the aircraft would lose thousands of feet of altitude. Theoretically, there were specific procedures that would enable the pilot to regain control, but if you reached 10,000' over the ground, ejection was *mandatory* because that was the lowest safe altitude to exit the aircraft and have your chute deploy. Thanks to Buzzard's teaching, I never experienced a spin in the F-8, but I came close several times.

"Remember—if you do get in a slow-speed scissors, you can't let the bogey get 'in synch' with your turns, or he will work behind you. You have to reverse before *he* does, and get 'in synch' with *his* turns instead. This is a guns-kill situation, so make sure all your gun switches are hot, or you will miss your chance to nail the bogey if he goes in front of you for a few seconds.

*North Vietnamese MIG-17*

*North Vietnamese MIG-21*

"Just make sure that the bogey stall speed is higher than yours, which eliminates using this against the MIG-17 and 19. They can definitely 'out-slow' the F-8. You can probably beat a 21 with a scissors, but you are hung out like a grape if other bogeys come up behind you while you are engaged. It's actually a stupid maneuver, and should be avoided. You should always work to maintain your energy and ability to accelerate away from a MIG to attack him vertically, with high-energy slant-loop maneuvers and close coordination with your wingman. *Never* get into a horizontal, turning fight, because you will get slow and their MIG birds will out-turn you.

"Remember that the MIG-17 controls are poorly boosted and turn to concrete over about 400 knots, so you want to keep him fast and pulling lots of g's where he has control and stability problems. With the 21, he has elevator deflection limits in pulling high g's below 15,000', affecting his ability to pull out of verticals. You also want to keep the 21 in a high-speed vertical fight, forcing high-g pull-outs. Don't let the 21 get his nose around to point at your six when you go high, because you are a sitting duck for an Atoll [Soviet-made heat-seeking missile] shot, which the 21 will always be carrying. If you can get him into a vertical scissors, that should suck him into a vertical overshoot eventually. Use the same techniques on the 19 as you apply to the 17, but they don't have many 19s anyway, and you are not likely to see one.

*MIG-19, firing heat-seeking Atoll missile*

"Be aware that the North Vietnamese like to tie you up in a turning fight with MIG-17s, and then run some MIG-21s in on you from your blind side, doing a 'slash and dash' attack. So if you get slow or forget to check your six, especially when slow at the top of a vertical maneuver, you may get an Atoll from a MIG-21 up your ass. If you don't have a sore neck from looking behind you after every practice dogfight, you probably are getting sloppy and complacent, and not acquiring the necessary skills."

Buzzard had just delivered a five-minute analysis that would be worthy of Top Gun. Some pilots may disagree with his tactical analysis, but it all seemed to work for him. That was good enough for me. He had done all of this research himself, and thought through every type of potential MIG engagement and tactical situation to arrive at this basic approach. This analysis proved to be essentially correct after the U.S. obtained and test-flew several MIGs that the Israelis captured in the 1967 Middle East war.

I noticed that most of the senior pilots used traditional fighter tactics, in which they would normally find themselves in a slow, turning fight— exactly what The Buzzard was preaching *not* to do. Buzzard's tactics against MIGs emphasized maintaining "energy"—altitude and speed advantage—while *avoiding* a decelerating, turning fight. This was foreign to most senior pilots, especially outside of the Red Lightning squadron. Most of the "old-timer" F-8 pilots loved to defeat their opponent in a grinding slow-speed scissors, filling up their windscreen with the other aircraft for an undisputed guns "kill."

For me, one of Buzzard's most impressive tactics involved the concept of the "alternating lead." The essential concept was an adaptation of the Thach Weave from World War II, using a spherical maneuvering "bubble" concept. The invisible "bubble" was dynamic and changed throughout an engagement, defined only by the flight paths of the involved aircraft, within three dimensions. In a fighter engagement, the entire fight would occur within the moving "bubble." To my knowledge, Buzzard was the first pilot to conceptualize a dogfight by using the "bubble" idea. It made you think of the fight in *three* dimensions, instead of two.

This tactic used the two-plane "section" as the maneuvering unit. When a tactical engagement began—whether defensive or offensive—the section immediately determined which of the two aircraft was the "key," or engaged fighter. Whether on offense or defense, the section fighters would maneuver within the spherical "bubble," providing mutual support to each other. Even when the section aircraft appeared separated, they were still tactically coordinated.

For example, beginning in a Combat Spread formation, in an offensive situation, one of the two fighters will always be in a better position for a kill on the bogey. That places the other fighter in an automatic defensive cover role, to prevent a surprise attack on the engaged "key" fighter. This allows the "key" to focus on achieving the kill, knowing his partner is protecting their "six." This is automatic, but always confirmed and coordinated by radio calls.

If the bogey turns into the attack to prevent a missile or guns solution by the "key" fighter, the "key" avoids bleeding energy in a turn and pulls high, followed by a fast vertical reversal at the top to be ready for another attack. This is because an aircraft at the top of a vertical reversal is nearly inverted, and can pull down with a faster rate of turn inside the bogey turn radius, taking advantage of the one "g" of gravity to increase the longitudinal acceleration. In laymen's terms, you could turn faster than the bogey by this maneuver, and you were positioned to drop down on his vulnerable six o'clock with overtaking speed.

The covering fighter, according to Buzzard's tactics, could also do a displacement roll over the top to the outside of the bogey's turn and pull down vertically into the bogeys' six o'clock cone of vulnerability. Then, if the angle still could not be solved, *that* fighter would pull off high, while the other rolled in.

The result of this tactical procedure was the forced deceleration of the bogey(s) in the turn, caused by the continuous, alternating attack from a high advantage position. Invariably, we found that even experienced pilots from other squadrons that tried to defend against this tactic would leave one aircraft vulnerable in "trail," and not defensible by the other. It was like two wolves making high-speed slashing attacks on an elk. No matter which way the elk turns, a wolf tears at his hindquarters, until he is down.

*LT Jerry Pearson of VF-24 in his F-8C, with cannons firing. Note the muzzle flashes below the cockpit and gun vent doors open on the belly.*

If the section was attacked first by a bogey, the same alternating procedure would be used. The first priority was to force the bogey to pick his target and commit to one of the two fighters. At that instant, the engaged fighter would maintain his energy in a nose-low, high-g turn, sufficient to prevent a missile or guns solution by the bogey. The other fighter, having pitched up, would be rolling across the top of the turn radius, waiting for the opportunity to drop down on the bogey's six. This would result in either a kill, or a high-g defensive turn by the bogey, releasing the first engaged fighter to go vertical and repeat the high, rolling attack profile. This tactic worked well, because the bogey could not afford to ignore the "free" fighter. Whichever fighter he engaged, the other would be aggressively attacking him within seconds. Even with two bogeys, the system was effective and usually resulted in victory, if done correctly.

Repeatedly, against a variety of different aircraft of that era, I saw this tactic work to perfection. The only time it did *not* work as well was when it was used against other Red Lightning pilots. Then, since the aircraft all had the same performance capabilities, and the pilots thoroughly understood this tactic, the fight usually degenerated into some sort of "Mexican standoff" scissors maneuvers with a close-in simulated guns kill as the final result. Most of the Red Lightnings would not fall for the trap created by Buzzard's "alternating lead." As I look back on this time, flying with The Buzzard was like attending Crusader post-grad school. However, the price of tuition was sometimes quite high.

The Buzzard pounded the nuggets with several tactical rules: (1) Never go below 6,000' unless it is absolutely necessary, and *never* go below 3,000', because of ground fire; (2) never duel with a flak site; (3) never make more than one air-to-ground run on a target; and (4) never fly more than a few seconds on the same heading and at the same altitude—keep "jinking," so the flak gunners are not able to get an aiming solution.

On one occasion, just before the end of the cruise, several of us got sloppy and decided to disregard these well-accepted rules. We wound up with four F-8s airborne on the very last launch of the cruise. I was given the lead, and decided that a nasty flak site near the Hourglass River needed a special farewell. We all knew this site, which was an aggressive cluster of 37mm AAA guns. They were very effective below 6,000', with a high rate of fire. We rolled in, with me strafing them first, followed by Gator, Devil, and Maggot.

By the time Maggot rolled in, the NVA were ready and let loose a barrage of exploding 37mm shells that engulfed Maggot's aircraft with deadly gray puffs of shrapnel. The normally jovial Maggot developed a sense of urgency in his voice, calling, "They're all over me—let's get out of here!" Back in the ready room, Maggot confronted me. "Dog, you almost got me killed!"

*North Vietnamese 37mm anti-aircraft guns.*

As a Red Lightning, I had learned that you *never* show mercy or remorse, and the best defense is a vigorous offense, especially when you debriefed a flight in the ready room. "That's payback for the Grand Canyon trip, Maggot. Hey, those gunners liked you best—what can I say? If you had been good enough with your guns to hit those guys, they would not have been shooting at you!"

Maggot never forgot that one, and still complains about it to this day. He did get even with me, however. He introduced me to future Wife #2. Some guys have a mean streak.

~ ~ ~

## Chapter 18: *Change of the Watch*

*Ticonderoga* pulled off the line for the last time and headed to Yokosuka. The Red Lightnings were still agonizing over the fact that they had never seen a MIG, unlike VF-191's "Pirate" Nichols, who won his place in air wing history with a great MIG kill during a photo escort mission. Surfer, the photo weenie, was attacked by a MIG-17. He pulled so many g's evading the MIG that he popped rivets off the wing. His hard turn enabled Pirate to damage the MIG with a Sidewinder, and then close in for a guns kill. Pirate's aircraft was nearly hit by  flying debris from his own cannon hits on the MIG.

*"Pirate" closes in on a damaged MIG for a guns kill.*

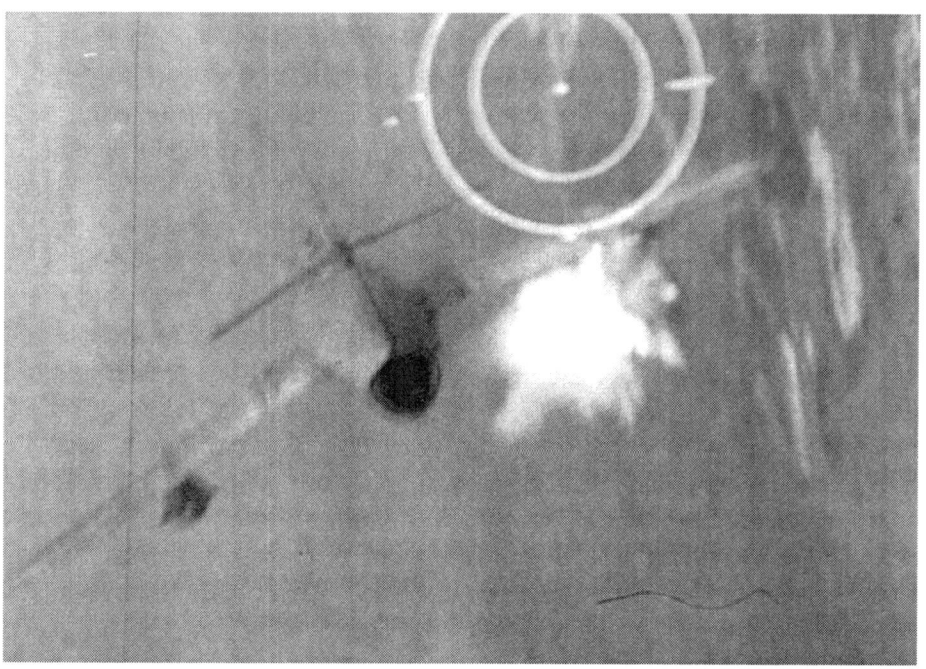

*A guns kill on a North Vietnamese MIG-17. Cannon shells are hitting the MIG's right fuel tank.*

On the way home, we stopped and anchored in Hong Kong, always a welcome event. After I slept through an All-Officers Meeting, the XO put me in "hack," restricting me to the ship, and gave me the squadron duty for the entire port call. I never liked this XO, primarily because I thought he was a marginal combat pilot and did not trust him as a flight leader. He was leading the flight when "Iron Mike" Newell was lost to a SAM. I wondered if he had been using good lookout doctrine, especially on Mike's piece of sky. Who knows? Maybe Mike screwed up and failed to counter the missile. I knew one thing for sure—senior drivers like the XO never checked the wingman's six, because they felt *that* mundane duty was beneath them. A MIG could have flown up the XO's six, painted graffiti on his fuselage, and he would never have known it. Like many of the senior officers of his vintage, he was oblivious to the realities of his airborne environment.

During one night of my restriction to the ship, as I stood sullenly on the flight deck and admired the beautiful lights of Hong Kong from a painful distance, it struck me that I had actually beaten the odds and survived the cruise. *Now I would have to pay my credit card bills!*

I reflected solemnly on the fact that our squadron had lost *three* pilots, and two were Academy graduates—three fine young men, with promising lives ahead of them. The oldest was about 26. They deserved better, or at least to die in the pursuit of victory, not a contrived "political solution." The other squadrons on *Ticonderoga* lost an additional half-dozen pilots between them, with three confirmed as POWs: LCDR Dick Stratton and CDR Mel Moore, both from VA-192; and LCDR "Moon" Mullen from VF-191. Each was an excellent officer and pilot. However, sometimes being good was not enough. Between combat and

operational accidents, the air wing lost 17 aircraft out of 90. These losses were mostly the result of the restrictive Rules of Engagement issued by the Johnson administration and our senior military commanders. Had we been able to apply our air power in an appropriate manner, North Vietnam would have been forced to give up its subversion of the South. The best evidence of this is Nixon's "Linebacker" series of B-52 air assaults on Hanoi, which finally forced the North Vietnamese to negotiate an end to the war. This resulted in the Paris peace agreement and the release of our POWs.

Unrestricted air warfare against the North could have saved many thousands of American and South Vietnamese lives, but what do *we* know? We in the military simply *fight* the wars—someone else, usually a civilian sitting safely behind a desk, *starts* them and then issues restrictive rules of engagement, which, militarily, often make no sense.

During our port calls, we heard some spectacular stories from the other air wings. On one carrier, the air wing leadership and tactics were fundamentally bad. Their losses were horrendous, with one A-4 squadron losing half of its pilots and virtually all of its original aircraft by the end of the cruise.

According to one story that was circulating about that air wing, two replacement nuggets came aboard as passengers on the COD (logistics) aircraft one day. They were told to leave their bags in the ready room and put on their flight gear to fly in an Alpha Strike, because their A-4 squadron was short on pilots. During the strike, both were shot down. The squadron took their unpacked bags back up to the flight deck and sent them back to their next of kin on the COD aircraft. They never even had a chance to unpack before they were blown out of the sky.

One of my Academy classmates in another air wing got a night catapult shot in an F-8 before he was ready, and the throttle was slapped back to idle power by the rapid acceleration of the catapult. His aircraft splashed into the water ahead of the carrier, which was barely able to avoid running over him. As his aircraft sank, he realized he had only one chance, because the increasing water pressure prevented him from opening the canopy. At about 50' depth, he ejected through the canopy and actuated his life vest. He then became entangled in the parachute shrouds, but was able to cut himself loose and pop to the surface, where the helo recovered him. "Tarzan" lived up to his call sign. He only had a sore neck the next day.

An RA-5C Vigilante reconnaissance bird from the *Kitty Hawk* was hit by ground fire. The RAN (reconnaissance attack navigator), Lieutenant Junior Grade Frank Prendergast, ejected just before the Vigilante crashed in shallow water near the mouth of the Hourglass. The pilot was killed. Local militia began shooting at the navigator as he landed in the surf and then ran out from the coastal village and tried to capture him.

One man held an AK-47 on him, while another took the navigator's .38 revolver and pointed it at him. For some reason, this young officer had only loaded four out of six chambers, unknown to his captors. When several A-1 RESCAP (rescue) aircraft arrived, all of the militia ran back to the village except for the two aiming weapons at the navigator. After the A-1s had exhausted their ammo to keep the militia away from him, two F-4s came in and started firing unguided Sidewinders and Sparrow missiles in a desperate attempt to keep the militia from capturing him.

As the SAR helo came in to pick up the navigator, the man holding the .38 pulled the trigger, but hit an empty chamber. At that moment, the RIO pulled out his back-up weapon, a .25 automatic, and killed the North Vietnamese that had taken his .38, and then punched the other man in the face. As if in a Hollywood movie, he sprinted for the helo sling and was swept away to rejoin his squadron, while the helo machine-gunned the last pursuing militiaman.

Because of the amount of classified equipment on the Vigilante, combined with the shallow water of the crash site, the Navy launched several bombing strikes on the wreck to prevent enemy retrieval of the equipment. We finally had a good target—one of our own aircraft! LTJG Prendergast received the Navy Cross, the Purple Heart and three Air Medals.

*Ticonderoga* proceeded to Yokosuka, Japan to make final preparations for the trek home across the Pacific. I realized I was having problems coming off of my adrenaline highs from daily combat flying and making the transition to nearly complete inactivity. There is nothing more tedious than being a pilot aboard an aircraft carrier when there is no flying. My personal solution was to study German and Japanese. Fortunately, we arrived at Yokosuka within a few days, before I acquired a permanent foreign accent.

From Yokosuka, most of the air wing was flown back to San Diego on chartered airliners. The rest of the squadron personnel arrived a few weeks later by ship, when *Ticonderoga* docked at North Island. Everyone went on leave and scattered to see their families and loved ones. I noticed that, except for occasional war protestors, people back home were mostly oblivious to the war and it was "business as usual" in stores, bars and restaurants. This was very different from World War II, my dad's war, when everyone seemed to be involved in some way, and supported the war effort.

I initiated my divorce proceedings with Wife #1. One of her settlement demands was that she wanted a life insurance policy on me. Apparently, she shared my pessimism about surviving the Vietnam War. *Just more combat, and a different enemy,* I decided.

The squadron returned from leave, went back to work, and had another change-of-command. Skipper Conklin handed the Red Lightnings over to a sour-faced commander from the East Coast, Al Ostrand. The XO was certainly no loss, and he was replaced by a commander with a great fighter pilot attitude, but no Vietnam experience—Robbie Roberts.

We received yet another East Coast commander to replace Snake. This new officer's leadership inadequacies were exceeded only by his severe lack of piloting skills. Trading Snake for *this* guy truly epitomized our rotation problem. Reputations are rapidly communicated in the fighter community, and "Cuffs" had a bad one.

During one of his flights on a Mediterranean cruise, Cuffs was #3 in a flight of three F-8s. The leader gave the standard hand signal for the #2 wingman to cross over to the other side of the leader. This meant that the #3 pilot was to make room for #2 to slide underneath the leader's belly. Instead, this idiot misinterpreted the signal to mean that *he* was supposed to cross under the leader. The two wingmen met in a mid-air collision underneath the leader, and both ejected. I wondered how long he was going to last in a real combat arena, where there was little room for error.

We also took on two additional "re-tread" lieutenant commanders and an East Coast lieutenant, who all had marginal operational experience and were in a combat squadron for the first time. To complete the puzzle, we also received a batch of nuggets.

The problem with many of the pilots from East Coast squadrons was their easy-going attitude. They seemed to lack the necessary intensity. You could hardly blame them, as they had no combat exposure on their Mediterranean cruises. The East Coast flying environment seemed to produce less aggressive pilots, who flew their aircraft as if they were safely boring holes in the sky over Florida or the Mediterranean. As my mom used to say, *you are a product of your environment.* However, after one combat cruise to Vietnam, most of them made the necessary attitude transition and were as good as anyone from then on. For them, the trick was to survive the first Vietnam cruise. MIG killer "Pirate" Nichols of VF-191, for example, was originally from the East Coast, but was one of the best F-8 drivers that ever flew the aircraft.

After the pilot rotation was complete, I looked at the roster in dismay. We only had a few pilots with Vietnam combat experience, and all but one of those was a junior officer: Burger, a lieutenant commander; Devil, a senior lieutenant; Gator; Spanky; and me. *Oh, this is going to be fun!* Only one of us (Burger) was technically a division (four aircraft) leader, which normally went by rank, and the squadron was now very top-heavy with three commanders and three lieutenant commanders. In many types of military organizations, this may not be a serious problem. In a combat fighter squadron, having *inexperienced* seniors and *highly experienced* juniors is not only awkward, it is actually dangerous for all concerned.

The military rank structure is predicated on the assumption that "If I am senior to you, then I know more than you, so I give the orders." In combat flying, having "command" of a flight only lasts until the first shot is fired, or the dogfight begins. Then, everyone is (or should be) on an equal footing, somewhat like two cops who are partners on patrol. The pilot with the best tactical position calls the play, not the most senior pilot. However, this tactical philosophy was not shared by all senior pilots, especially those from the East Coast.

The new Skipper, though stiff and aloof, was a good man. The problem was that he was not much of a fighter pilot. He was in the wrong line of work. Like many of the East Coast F-8 pilots of that era, he liked to be *called* a fighter pilot—he simply did not know how to *be* one. Being a fighter pilot had little to do with the aircraft that you flew—it was a state of mind, an attitude, a culture.

One morning, I received a call from Maggot, who was dating a flight attendant. "Hey, Hot Dog, you gotta help me out. I need someone to go out with my girl's roommate and keep her occupied, because The Buzzard is too hung over to show up. Look, Hot Dog, you owe me for draggin' me over that flak site!" For a brief moment, I actually had a guilty conscience, and reluctantly agreed.

So here I was playing "backup" for The Buzzard. *What an insult!* Against my better judgment, I went along, and met Jan, the woman of my dreams. She was beautiful, smart, feisty and able to hold her own around The Red Lightnings. I was not only in love, but awestruck. She became Wife #2 about a year later.

***Jan, checking out Hot Dog's aircraft on* Ticonderoga *(San Diego, 1967).***

In the meantime, Maggot left active duty to join the airlines, along with another experienced pilot, Taco. Our squadron experience and talent level became weaker with each veteran pilot's departure. Buzzard and Porky already were scheduled for separation at the end of the training cycle, and both had airline jobs waiting. I knew the cumulative effect of these departures was going to leave a huge gap in our operational capabilities as a squadron.

If these personnel issues were not bad enough, we also got a new CAG—from the East Coast, of course. He looked and acted more like a CPA than a fighter pilot. Short, pudgy and balding, he had recently commanded an East Coast F-8 squadron. Now the formula for disaster was complete. Except for our new XO, the leadership structure was contaminated with incompetence from the top down.

In order to force-feed all of our newbies, I developed a demanding and realistic combat training syllabus. It was like an expanded Top Gun training, using informational briefings, simulated SAM evasions, MIG engagements, and carrier procedures. To give the nuggets confidence in night instrument flying, I would give them the lead, and require them to fly at 200' over the black water from San Diego all the way to the Channel Islands near Ventura. This was admittedly dangerous, but it provided the necessary "pucker factor" to make them rely upon their radar and instruments in navigating to a particular island in the chain.

Everything in my syllabus was designed to look, sound, and feel like you were flying over North Vietnam. We even had simulated Red Crown calls, announcing that MIGs were airborne: "This is Red Crown on guard. Blue bandits [MIG-21s] airborne—Bull's-eye [Hanoi], 180 at 20, heading south." At the end of the flight,

the newbies were required to fly an instrument approach down to the "meatball" and a touch-and-go at San Clemente Island's runway, which was situated with water at both ends, similar to an aircraft carrier. This gave the newbies a scary and realistic feel of how a carrier-based mission ends—with a carrier landing.

I wanted them to hear the Tonkin Gulf "noise" in their headsets before they had to experience it for the first time in combat. When you heard that for the first time, with pilots screaming things like, "I'm hit!" or "Break right—SAM at 2 o'clock!" it can be very disconcerting. At the end of the cruise, one of them came up to me and said, "Hot Dog, when I started flying in the Tonkin Gulf, I felt like I had been here before, thanks to that training." For the first time in a *long* time, I felt like I was making a positive difference in something.

One warm San Diego morning, the new CAG showed up, and announced he wanted to fly one of my syllabus flights, a "road recce" over simulated hostile territory. He had heard about the syllabus and how demanding it was. CAG and his selected wingman (poor Spanky) took off ahead of the "bogey" section, which I led. They were required to navigate over a designated highway in the desert, looking for simulated truck convoys, MIGs and SAM sites, which had been designated on the charts during the briefing.

Gator and I orbited north of their track and waited. We picked them up on radar and then acquired them visually. I started my attack out of the sun, and Spanky called "Tally-ho! Bogeys at 8 o'clock, break left!" The CAG failed to break and went into a lazy left turn, allowing us to call a Sidewinder shot on them and then close in to gun range. I could not believe it. CAG "Newbie" made no defensive maneuvers and allowed his section to be "killed." I made a mental note to make sure our nuggets never flew with him in combat.

I became formally certified as an LSO by COMNAVAIRPAC, and started getting the pilots ready for the required CARQUAL landings on *Ticonderoga.* Predictably, the nuggets had the usual problems doing practice "bounces" at the field. The "re-tread" lieutenant commanders were not much better. At least the Skipper was good at doing *this,* which is probably the one thing he did well with the F-8, and the reason he was still alive.

The air wing went next to MCAS Yuma for the usual weapons training. One of the most challenging phases was aerial gunnery, firing the four 20mm cannon at a moving target. The target was a large banner, towed by another aircraft, called the "tractor." Each pilot's aircraft carried ammo that was painted with a certain color, which left marks on the banner when it was hit.

There were two types of aerial gunnery—at 20,000 and 30,000 feet. The tractor flew straight and level at the base altitude, while the "shooters" lined up about 10,000' above and abeam on a parallel course, known as "the perch." The shooters would roll in toward the tractor, reversing their course about halfway down. As they tracked the banner in their sights, they fired at about 1,500-1,000' range, pulling around 4 g's. At the last second, the shooter would roll wings-level, zip over the banner, and then pull hard to parallel the tractor at his altitude. It was a wild ride, and pilots loved to do it.

While it was fun at 20,000', the 30,000' gunnery was another story. The tolerances were very tight, and it was difficult to get hits because of the speed of the firing run. The run began off the perch at about 40,000', and the aircraft was supersonic at the low reversal and while shooting. Only the best shooters got hits in this gunnery phase.

One day, I was flying the tractor and towing the banner for the shooters at 30,000'. One of the nuggets forgot to compensate for the control pitch-up that occurs when the aircraft goes from supersonic to subsonic flight. This phenomenon sometimes results in stalls or spins if the pilot does not release back-pressure on the stick immediately.

As the nugget rolled in, I noticed that he was "acute," or too far ahead of the proper perch position. This usually results in excessive g's and an impossibly high angle off the target. However, this nugget added something special as he fired wildly, missing the banner completely. As he slid behind me, I saw him pulling hard to stay close-aboard.

His aircraft experienced the subsonic pitch-up at that moment, resulting in a violent "departure" stall. His aircraft actually cart-wheeled by me, end over end. I had never seen anything like this before. Luckily, he did not spin, and recovered about 5,000' below me. "That was spectacular, but don't try that on a MIG," I radioed to him.

If Buzzard was out of control during the *last* Yuma visit, his short-timer attitude now made him even worse. One night, Buzzard led a three-man covert ops team (including me) to let the Marines know we had arrived. I went along, merely to provide a stabilizing influence.

Our ground crews had prepared a large stencil of a lightning bolt and the squadron numbers for us. After parking our car by the base perimeter fence, we made our way to the runway. Buzzard renumbered the field runways with red spray paint to read "VF-194." He then climbed up and stenciled a huge red lightning bolt on the base water tower. Completing the mission back in the BOQ, he caught some of the VF-191 pilots in their rooms, and soaked them down with a blast from a fire hose.

In a few minutes, the base MPs surrounded the BOQ and arrested the Skipper, who had unwisely identified himself as being in command! *Welcome to the Red Lightnings*, I thought. The next morning, the base CO, a Marine Colonel, placed the Skipper in "hack" in the BOQ, and told him, "This is the last straw. After this deployment, VF-194 is *exiled* from MCAS Yuma. You guys can never come back here! You are maniacs!" Obviously, you *must* be bad, if *the Marines* kick you out. The following year, the squadron had to go to El Centro, somewhat like being sent to the leper colony on Molokai.

That is when I started liking the new Skipper. He stood up for his men, and took the punishment. I decided I was going to keep this man alive, whether he deserved it or not.

Buzzard and I were off the schedule one day at Yuma, with nothing to do. It was always dangerous when Buzzard had time on his hands. This day was no different.

"Hot Dog, go over to the Navy Exchange and buy some plastic lawn bags, rolls of toilet paper and some balloons. Don't ask me what the stuff is for—you'll see!"

I returned to the BOQ with the materials, and Buzzard told me to start filling the balloons with water and to then tie them off and place them carefully in the lawn bags. "Now, I'm going over to the civilian side of the field and rent a Cessna 150. I'll pick you up on the ramp, at the side of the civilian passenger terminal. Just bring that stuff and jump in the airplane. I don't want the rental place to see us loading it."

As directed, I loaded our cargo in the Cessna, and then jumped in. Buzzard radioed for takeoff, and we launched. It had been a long time since I had been in a prop aircraft, and it felt strange. "Buzzard, so what's the deal? What are we doing here?"

"I found out that the XO, Burger, and one of the nuggets are going out to the fields north of the base to shoot doves. They rented shotguns from the Navy Exchange yesterday. We just need to find the XO's green Austin-Healey and follow it."

*173*

We climbed to 3,500' and set up a holding pattern over the main Yuma gate. Soon we spotted the XO's distinctive vehicle leaving the gate and traveling north to the farm areas. We followed, S-turning to stay behind them.

After about 30 minutes, the XO's car pulled off the road and parked in a field, surrounded by irrigation canals. We could see three individuals leave the car, wearing the red squadron baseball caps. "Wait until they're clear of the car," Buzzard said. "And get ready to drop a water balloon on my mark." The Buzzard pulled a black grease pencil from his pocket and drew a near-perfect F-8 gun sight on the Cessna windscreen. Now I knew what he was doing. We were about to do an Alpha Strike on the XO's car! I wondered what would happen to the thin metal of an Austin-Healey when it was hit by a water balloon, dropped from several thousand feet. *Oh, what the hell. I hadn't been in hack for a while, and I needed the rest anyway.*

The Buzzard pulled the nose of the little aircraft up about twenty degrees and pulled the throttle to idle. I always hated the sound of a prop aircraft at idle—it seems to sputter and cough like an old lawn mower.

Buzzard rolled smoothly to place his pipper on the Austin-Healey. "Whattaya think, Dog? How many mils lead?"

"I'd use about 100 mils—but what do I know, Buzzard? I've never bombed with a Cessna before."

Buzzard adjusted to 100 mils, and said, "Stand by—DROP!"

The Cessna had a little window on the side that you could open. I pushed a red balloon out into the slipstream, and we pulled out at about 2,000'. Buzzard rolled the Cessna up on a wing to watch the hit.

A big dust cloud erupted about twenty feet from the car. Buzzard said, "Shit! I forgot to crank in the wind. I need to correct about twenty mils right. Let's give 'em another one!" This is when I knew I was probably not going to enjoy this episode as much as Buzzard. Instead of climbing back to a safe altitude, he immediately pulled the power to idle and rolled in on the car from about 2,000'. "Stand by........DROP!"

I pushed out another balloon, and cringed as the ground came rushing up at us. This time, it was quite easy to see the hit, because we were so close—too close! Buzzard missed again, with the balloon impacting the ground about ten feet from the car. "Damn! There's a big crosswind. I need about ten mils more correction." He went into a series of bombing runs until we almost ran out of balloons. Our worst hit was about twenty-five feet, and our closest about five feet from the hood of the car. "We won't get the bombing 'E' for this one!" Buzzard mumbled. He was disappointed that we missed.

Meanwhile, the three hunters could not believe their eyes. They were being attacked by *an aircraft*! They had each taken refuge behind a canal berm, while they watched the XO's car being used as a bombing target. We spotted the XO hunkered down near one canal. Then I realized we still had three balloons left. Buzzard said, "OK, let's get the XO. I'll come up the canal from behind him, and on my mark, give him all three."

The Buzzard dove the little airplane down to just above the surface of the canal, downstream of the XO. We zoomed along, skimming the surface of the water, doing pylon turns through the twisting canal. We came around a bend, and there was the XO, looking the other way. "Stand by………DROP!" said the Buzzard. I tossed out all three balloons, which skipped across the canal surface right up to the XO, drenching him with stinking canal water. "VSH!" roared The Buzzard, laughing as he left the target with a hard turn.

This model of the Cessna has a rear window, which was nice, because I was able to see the XO aiming his shotgun at us. "Jesus, Buzzard, he's going to shoot at us!" Buzzard began to jink wildly and hopped over the canal berm, staying below the XO's line of sight.

"Now, let's give 'em an air show," said Buzzard. "When I get to about 3,000', throw out some toilet paper rolls."

When we reached 3,000', I started tossing the rolls out of the window. Buzzard proceeded to slice and dice the paper streamers with the prop, causing a blizzard of white confetti to descend on the nearby farmers' fields. "OK, that's enough—let's get rid of those plastic lawn bags. I don't want any evidence for the rental manager to find. Toss 'em out."

I threw the plastic bags out of the window, but one folded perfectly across the vertical stabilizer of the Cessna. Buzzard was not happy. "I have to get that off, because the rental guy will see that for sure." He started yawing the Cessna back and forth with the rudder. It only partially dislodged the bag.

"Well, Hot Dog, we need to spin it. That will get it off." Buzzard had casually mentioned that this model of the Cessna is not certified for aerobatic maneuvers—and that obviously includes spins. Before I had a chance to comment, Buzzard pulled the power to idle, raised the nose up thirty degrees, and put in cross-controls. The little bird groaned, flipped over, and started a nasty spin. My heart was in my throat as the landscape below rotated fast to the right.

As he pulled out at about 1,500', Buzzard said, "Damn it, it almost came off. I need to spin it the other direction." Instead of climbing back to altitude, he immediately put the little Cessna into another spin. Now I knew we were going to die, as we spun toward the fields below. Buzzard recovered from the spin and pulled out at about 500'. "That got it! VSH!" Luckily, the bag had dropped off. Down on the ground, the XO and his hunting partners saw the bag drop off and one of them said, "My God, the airplane is coming apart!"

We returned to the base, and turned in the abused Cessna to the rental company. "Did you guys have fun?" asked the rental guy. "Oh, definitely," replied Buzzard. I was still unable to speak. Flying an F-8 off the carrier at night was more fun than this.

When we joined up with the three erstwhile dove hunters at Happy Hour, the XO told us that he almost fired his shotgun at us, until he realized that it had to be some Red Lightnings in the airplane. The XO said, "I should have blasted you out of the sky, Buzzard, but I spared you both because you are the only LSOs that we have. However, if you had hit my car, you would be dead!" It *is* nice to be needed. *Life is all about leverage, and how you use it.*

Porky was detaching from the squadron, and we decided to give him a rousing send-off. Gator made the mistake of volunteering his house for the party. Even worse, Gator's mom was visiting. Wisely, she hid in her room during the party with the door locked.

Things began to get out of control when The Buzzard climbed a tree in Gator's backyard. This was too tempting a target, so the entire squadron started pelting him with large chunks of ice, finally knocking him out of the tree into the shrubs below. He was motionless, lying on his back in Gator's flower garden, so we checked to make sure he was still breathing by holding Big Red's makeup mirror in front of his mouth. "Yep, he's fogging it pretty good," said Gator.

"Hey, Gator, I know this will arouse you, but I think you should give him mouth-to-mouth CPR anyway," I suggested, which got a few laughs.

"No way! I don't know *where* his mouth has been! He's on his own!" said Gator.

We then heard a piercing scream. Gator's mom came running out, frantically yelling—"Porky is fighting with his girl friend!"

We all ran into one of the bedrooms to find Porky pinning his girl's arms to the bed, as she tried to punch and kick him. Apparently, she had expected to leave town with Porky as he went to his new civilian job, but he had decided to go alone. She decided to express her disappointment with her fists and feet. Love is a wonderful thing, but Porky needed to minimize his baggage.

Although this was quite typical of the relationship between Porky and his girl, the new Skipper did not know that, and decided to ride to the fair damsel's rescue. In reality, this "damsel" could probably hold her own in an alley fight.

The Skipper grabbed Porky and said, "Leave this young woman alone, Lieutenant!" Porky immediately responded with a punch that knocked the Skipper unconscious against the wall. Gator and I jumped Porky and subdued him before more damage occurred. Gradually, everyone settled down. The Skipper woke up, stood up tall, and told Porky in a stern voice, "Lieutenant, be at my office at 1000 tomorrow for Captain's Mast!"

"You can meet with yourself, pal. I'm a civilian." It seems that Porky had signed his release papers that morning, and he was no longer in the Navy. It was a fitting end to a fine Navy career.

The remaining time in San Diego began to fly by, as we tried to get the squadron ready for what lay ahead. A few days before the ship pulled out, Buzzard detached and went to an airline job. For some reason, I had a very ominous feeling about his departure, which would later be justified. Buzzard always kept a large magnum bottle of expensive Piper Heidsieck champagne in his room. During the cruise, he had told me, "If I get a MIG, we will open this bottle and drink it dry. If I bust my ass, I want the squadron to open it and drink it. And don't forget to make an eloquent toast, because I'll be listening!"

This was a much shorter period at Miramar for the squadron training than I had experienced before my first cruise. There was not enough time to get everyone trained adequately. Sometimes Gator and I would exchange glances and shake our heads at the spastic flying by some of the pilots. *God help them,* we thought.

One day, I led a flight of six, including four nuggets, into the break at Miramar. This was the notorious Red Lightning "pencil formation." Not surprisingly, this was The Buzzard's creation. Although six aircraft are generally too unwieldy in a "fan break" landing pattern, we had found that it worked because of the required "Mission Bay Entry" to Miramar's pattern. We crossed Mission Bay at 12,500' in a right echelon formation. Each pilot opened his oil cooler door manually, which created a siren-like wail when we broke over the field at 450 knots, getting the attention of everyone on the ground. It is very important for fighter pilots to be noticed, and frequently.

*F-8s in the "break" over the carrier, with tail hooks down. The aircraft on the left is an RF-8A photo bird; the one on the right is a Red Lightning F-8E fighter. The leader will pull hard in a decelerating turn to the left, and then extend his gear and raise the movable wing. The photo bird will be approximately 45 seconds behind him for landing.*

After crossing Mission Bay, the leader would ease into a left turn, letting his nose drop to about 15 degrees down. Each of the other pilots then tucked their aircraft's nose close under the tail of the bird ahead of them, creating the appearance of a long "pencil" of aircraft, coming down at high speed.

The leader would keep the turn in and pull away hard to the left, decelerating in the turn. Each aircraft pulled in a "fan" with incrementally less g-force. It was a spectacular display, *if done correctly*. On this occasion, it did not go well.

We arrived in the break with two F-4s chugging leisurely on their downwind leg, clogging our pattern. This caused our fan break interval to fall apart, because the leader must make a very fast approach to keep separation with the aircraft that follow him. Only one bird out of six actually was able to land on the first approach, and the Tower Chief gave me a flight violation as the flight leader for "causing chaos in the landing pattern." I responded, "But Chief, you have to admit that we *did* look shit-hot in the break!" The Chief laughed and tore up the flight violation.

Gator, Spanky and I continued to refine our section air-to-air tactics. We worked hard to make the "bubble" concept second nature, so that an engaged bogey never had a chance to go on the offense. We gave the nuggets as much practice at this important concept as we could, given the limited training time available. We also taught them two other essential maneuvers. In typical fashion, I put my own labels on these, in the hope that history would give me full credit for their origination.

The first was a refinement of my defensive move, when a bogey was attacking from behind with altitude advantage. It required a nose-low, accelerating turn into the vertical plane of the attack, flying the aircraft directly below the oncoming bogey. This "over-bank" turn created a visual illusion to the bogey, as it appeared that you were doing a split-S—a fatal tactical error. Instead, just as the bogey tried to capitalize on this, and committed with his nose down and accelerating, you suddenly rolled wings level and pulled directly up into him. This created an impossible angle for the attacker. It also gave you the opportunity to gain separation and make a vertical-reversal turn. The objective was to be pointed back at him as he pulled out of his dive, neutralizing his original advantage. This was the Half-Nelson.

The other maneuver is known to many fighter pilots as a "displacement roll." When you are on the attack, it is designed to prevent you from over-shooting the bogey, to keep separation, and to maintain energy. It amounts to a modified barrel roll to the outside of the bogey's turn, instantly eliminating an excessive attack angle, maintaining energy, and permitting a possible Sidewinder shot. New pilots found this to be counter-intuitive, because it did not seem logical until you flew it correctly for the first time. I called this one the Danish Roll. It was important to have this in your "bag of tricks," because few pilots knew how to do it correctly or defend against it.

We got everyone qualified on the carrier, and then it was time to leave again. *Ticonderoga* pushed away from North Island with the usual band playing the usual tunes, while women and children cried. I thought to myself, *Some of them will be crying again before <u>this</u> stinking cruise is over.*

By the time we left San Diego, the squadron had seen the departures of some of our best talent: Skipper Conklin, Snake, Buzzard, Taco, Porky, Brillo, and Maggot. In the previous cruise, we also had lost Mike Newell ('62) and Frank Harrington, both outstanding aviators and leaders. These were all big shoes to fill. Unfortunately, they did *not* get filled.

This time, Gator and I had a better room, with real air conditioning. We were moving up in the world. During the transit across the Pacific, I made it my personal mission to give as much preparation as possible to any of the newbies that would listen. Since I was slightly senior to the nuggets, I drilled them relentlessly on everything, whether they wanted it or not: North Vietnam geography, weapons delivery, SAM and AAA threats, MIG tactics, lookout doctrine, ECM operation, and carrier procedures. I did not want to lose any of these young pilots simply because they were not properly trained. Suddenly, here I was, acting like a mother hen, trying to protect her chicks. It was no longer "fun and games," like the previous cruise. I felt personal responsibility for the newbies, and it weighed heavily on me. I did not like to attend memorial services.

The egos of the senior newbies, however, seemed to prevent them from engaging in this beneficial process in a serious way. Because of their rank, they adopted the attitude that they had acquired enough knowledge to get by, and did not like the idea of a mere lieutenant telling them how to fly. Except for XO Roberts, they lacked the proficiency that was necessary to survive this environment. I think half of them would have been lost, if it had not been for President Johnson's lack of will in Vietnam, and the North Koreans' surprise aggression, each of which would occur separately and intervene to determine our fate.

There was also a change of command for *Ticonderoga*. The very prim and proper Captain Miller turned the ship over to a crusty old salt from Louisiana, Captain Norman K. McInnis. Because this was his last command before retirement, he had nothing to lose and had decided to enjoy himself.

"Captain Mac" loved to wear a special workout suit while on the bridge. It had eagles on each shoulder, and across the back it said, "USS TICONDEROGA." He had a chinning bar and parallel bars welded to the side of the bridge so he could work out while conning the ship.

Many of the young pilots tried to stay in shape by lifting weights and jogging on the flight deck. The Captain also liked to jog, and was frequently joined by a group of pilots. His Marine orderly was not as enthusiastic, as the poor kid had to jog behind the Captain in his dress uniform, complete with pistol belt. The Captain was very popular with the ship's crew and the air wing.

The Admiral saw the pilots jogging on the flight deck, and decided it was unsafe. He ordered the jogging to stop.

Captain "Mac," however, politely informed the Admiral that this was *his* ship, and he would continue jogging on the flight deck, if he so desired. When the pilots learned of this, they would wait for the Captain's jogging time, and then run behind him on the flight deck, while the Admiral, our unwelcome guest, glared down from the Flag bridge.

Completing our journey across the Pacific, we were approaching Subic Bay when we learned that the Cubi Point base CO had prohibited *Ticonderoga* from tying up at the dock. Our air wing's reputation had preceded us. Instead, we were ordered to anchor in the harbor, which made it very difficult to get ashore and commit the necessary mayhem. Captain McInnis was furious. We also learned that the Cubi Point CO and our Captain had been enemies for years, which probably had sealed our fate.

"Don't worry, boys," said the old captain. "My air wing is going to be in that bastard's O'Club tonight for Happy Hour, one way or the other."

At around 1400, the squawk box blared alive: "All ready rooms, this is the Captain. Stand by for flight quarters and an air wing fly-off. Your destination will be the adjacent runway at Cubi Point." McInnis knew that a thunderstorm was coming, and that the wind speed would be enough to launch aircraft, even though the carrier was anchored. The ship went into a flurry of activity.

At about 1500, with a 25-knot breeze, the catapults started blasting aircraft off the bow. The pilots did not even raise their landing gear, turning left to land on the nearby runway. In an hour, most of the air wing was ashore and heading for the new Cubi Point O'Club. The barbarians were at the gates.

The Cubi Point CO had decided that the old O'Club was a bad influence on pilot behavior, so the base tore it down and built a new club, with a more formal atmosphere. We were not happy to see that our old watering hole had been destroyed.

Almost immediately, the trouble started. A band played "civilized" dance music from the Fifties, as base officers and their wives waltzed around the dance floor and ate dinner. The air wing pilots were upset to find their "Dilbert Dunker" contraption from the old club was also missing. I thought, *Wow, The Buzzard would love to be here now!*

To compensate, some pilots located an expensive dining-room chair with casters. The "aviator" was placed in the chair, blindfolded, and with the "catapult officer's" signal, was pushed rapidly by several pilots toward the stairs leading to the dance floor. If he hit at the bottom on all four rollers, he had a chance to get an "OK" pass from the LSO. Crashing into the band's bass drum was the best possible landing, a #3 wire. Otherwise, any fall was considered a "ramp strike," and a high-velocity trajectory into the dining area was a "bolter." One A-4 pilot broke his arm, but "attack pukes" were always expendable.

In a few minutes, the club manager called Base Security to stop the damage. Before they got there, our ship's Captain arrived. He had flown off the carrier with the helo crew. He surveyed the damage with a smile as the Cubi Point CO and Security arrived. The two four-stripers went nose-to-nose and exchanged insults. "Your men are out of control and not fit to use our Officers Clubs!" said the base CO.

"We're your best customers, and you are lucky to have us, Frenchie!" said our Captain.

"Not anymore, Norman! Your ship and air wing are prohibited from using this O'Club and the Subic Bay Club—permanently!"

"OK, Frenchie, you asked for it," said McInnis, who took the microphone from the band leader. "*Tico* Tigers, this is the Captain. These people don't want us here, so let's leave this damn club *now!*" All of *Ticonderoga*'s officers got up and left their dinner and bar bills unpaid.

Another officer went to the microphone. "All officers from the *Constellation*—if this place isn't good enough for the *Tico*, it's not good enough for us either!" Another 30 or so officers got up and left the club.

A young Ensign grabbed the microphone. "I'm the only guy here from the *Intrepid*, but I'm leaving, too!"

The base CO had forgotten there was one other club, a small one normally used only by the resident base officers and their dependents—the Kalayaan Club, which was about to receive a new and more playful clientele. The word was passed to meet up on the hill at the Kalayaan Club.

When I finally got up there, the world's biggest Klondike dice game was already underway. Several pilots sat on the floor, making bets, while one player shook the cup with the dice. A big pile of money lay in the center of the circle. In one game, a pilot actually won a new car! The club manager was busy trying to order more booze and ice to keep the party and his surprise revenue stream going. The scene was more like a fraternity party than an Officers' Club.

Our squadron Skipper, who already had consumed too many martinis, decided he would go back to the dock and get a water taxi to the ship. He called the base motor pool, and asked for a car. "Sorry, Commander, we only provide cars for captains and above." The Skipper became irate.

"Do you realize *I* am the CO of the Red Lightnings?" he fumed.

"Sorry, Sir, you are still not getting a car." Looking around, the Skipper spotted a base police vehicle in the driveway with the engine running. The cop was chatting with one of his buddies in another patrol car. The Skipper quietly slid behind the wheel of the empty patrol vehicle, and gunned it.

Immediately, the other cops gave pursuit. Sirens blared and lights flashed. The Skipper became lost on the winding roads of Kalayaan, and found himself back in the club driveway, with the cops behind him. While trying to make a hard turn at high speed, he lost control of the car and it crashed through the thin wall of the O'Club, nearly hitting the players in the Klondike game. As the dust settled, everyone stood up to see who the driver was. There sat the Skipper, behind the wheel with his gold-braided cap on sideways and one shoulder board hanging loose, in a wide-eyed daze.

The Skipper bolted from the car, ran down the hill and jumped into the club swimming pool to hide. The base CO was having a busy night. Along with security reinforcements, he now arrived at this club to survey the damage. "Who was driving this vehicle?" he demanded.

"Well, Captain, we never saw him before. I think he may have been an Air Force guy," said one pilot. Getting a tip from the club manager, the base CO walked to the back of the club, facing the pool.

"Is anyone down there?" he shouted. He then heard splashing. *Someone* was in the pool.

The reply was shouted back. "No-o-o-o, there's no one down here!"

The Skipper was hauled from the pool and arrested, placed in a base paddy wagon and returned to the ship, in "hack" once again. On the way back, the Skipper and some other air wing pilots decided to harass the driver to protest their

arrest. They began rocking the van violently, nearly causing it to flip over on its side. The base security officers were more than happy to give the Skipper and his pals over to the *Ticonderoga* Officer of the Deck.

This was something different—we finally had a pilot who had been in "hack" more times than I, and it was *the Skipper*! I turned to Gator. "Gator, I think I love this guy. Anyone with balls that big needs to survive this cruise." Gator agreed. The Skipper now had *two* guardian angels. What more can you ask for in life? The Skipper had passed the test—he *was* a Red Lightning!

~ ~ ~

## Chapter 19: *Great Balls of Fire!*

Being a Landing Signal Officer was a great job. Unlike many of the onerous collateral duties that normally were assigned to junior officers, the LSO job made you feel that you were doing something that counted—keeping your buddies in the air wing safe. On the small carriers used in the Vietnam era to which the F-8s were assigned, that was easier said than done. Even on a perfect pass, the F-8 tail hook crossed the fearsome ramp with minimum clearance. At night, with a pitching deck and minimum fuel, even the best pilots were at risk. A good LSO could significantly enhance safety and improve the odds.

I got into the LSO business after almost hitting the ramp at night as a nugget, and then getting reamed by my squadronmates, including The Buzzard, the squadron LSO at the time. I remember his words to this day: "Hot Dog, the best way to learn something is to teach it." Buzzard allowed me to "wave" field carrier landing practice sessions, and then the squadron sent me to LSO school. By the end of the first cruise, I was fully air wing qualified, day and night, which is a big accomplishment for an LSO. This means that an LSO can "wave" all of the carrier's aircraft types without supervision. Usually, there were only about three LSOs (including the Air Wing LSO) that were fully qualified, primarily because of the unusual landing difficulties with the F-8 and the A-3 tanker, a huge aircraft known as the "Whale."

Every third day, I went off the flight schedule and staffed the LSO platform. On my flying days, I usually took two missions each day, to make up for the LSO day. The LSO "tools" consisted of a "pickle"—the wave-off and "cut" light controls—and a hand-held radio set.

*Another Red Lightning Crusader, at the instant that the tail hook caught a wire. All four arresting cables ("the wires") are visible. As always, parked aircraft are only a few feet from the landing area. Photo taken from the LSO platform.*

*F-8E on short final for landing. This is the most dangerous phase of the carrier approach, where tolerances are minimal, and any mistake can be disastrous.*

You also needed some type of earplugs to keep the jet noise from damaging your hearing. The jets would hit full power when they caught a wire, always in close proximity to the LSOs. Most ex-LSOs, including me, have some permanent hearing loss in one ear because of the landing jets hitting full power on touchdown.

There were usually about eight "cycles" of launches and recoveries during the carrier's operating schedule, either day or night. After each recovery of aircraft, the LSO visited each pilot ready room, and debriefed the pilots on their landings. It was one of those rare situations where a junior officer had the authority to criticize a senior officer's performance. Obviously, a prudent LSO would be as tactful as possible when telling a senior officer that his landing was terrible.

On approach, a carrier pilot must worry about three factors simultaneously: glide slope, airspeed and right-left lineup. More than a small deviation from the correct parameters will result in a potential accident. Being more than a few feet above glide slope means a "bolter," or missed arrestment. Below glide slope, you risk a ramp strike and fatal crash.

The airspeed must be maintained very close to the ideal approach "angle of attack" point (around 140 knots for the F-8, depending on landing weight), or an arrestment can break the tail hook or the arresting cable, with fatal results. The LSO can see whether the aircraft is on speed by a set of three lights, displayed on the nose gear or other visible location and duplicated in the cockpit. A red light means "fast," a green light means "slow," and amber means "on speed." Lineup is also critical, because an off-center arrestment can put the aircraft over the side of the ship on the left side, or into parked aircraft or the carrier "island" on the right side.

The best LSOs developed almost a psychic ability to sense when an approaching aircraft was going to deviate from the glide slope. This came from knowing the proper sound level of the engine, the ability to sense relative motion, and knowledge of the aircraft. This enabled them to talk to the pilot with preventive guidance before problems developed, such as "Little power.....don't go low," "Don't climb," or "Check your lineup." This was enormously helpful to new or below-average pilots, who needed all the help they could get—especially after a stressful combat mission.

Part of the LSO's "art" was the ability to sense the energy of the aircraft in terms of airspeed, rate of descent and power setting. A good LSO could read not only where the aircraft *was* on the approach path, but also where it was *going*. Listening to the engine RPM and watching the exhaust smoke were important clues as to the stability of any aircraft on approach.

When a pilot got in real trouble, the LSO had the responsibility (and the authority) to make an instantaneous, independent decision whether to allow him to land or to "wave off" the aircraft and make him go around. Only the "Air Boss," the Air Operations Officer, also had the authority to "wave off" the aircraft, but that was extremely rare. The LSO's responsibility to control landings efficiently, but safely, is crucially important to the carrier's operations. The carrier has only limited time to recover aircraft from the previous launch, "re-spot" the deck, and supply the aircraft with fuel and ordnance for the next launch. Thus, a pilot that has problems catching an arresting gear wire and makes multiple landing attempts will affect the entire carrier combat operations. Although it sometimes seemed overwhelming, I enjoyed having this responsibility.

While waiting for the recovery to begin one day, I looked down at the water alongside the ship and spotted a huge raft of what appeared to be seaweed. "Wonder where that comes from," I asked the other LSO.

"Hot Dog, those are sea snakes. It's their mating season and the horny little devils clump together like that. I guess you call that a snake orgy. By the way, their bite is more poisonous than a King Cobra."

*The good news never stops coming.* I decided that I would try to avoid ejecting over the Tonkin Gulf. I wondered if a snakebite kit was contained in our survival gear.

On the small carriers of the *Ticonderoga* class, the LSO platform was

dangerously close to the landing area. On the *Ticonderoga*, the F-8's left wingtip passed close to the LSO, even when on a perfect pass. The wingtip of the A-3 "Whale" passed almost overhead. If an aircraft was going to hit the ramp, there was little time to react. There were only two places to go: into the "net," a trampoline rigged outboard of the platform; or across the flight deck, which was so dangerous a move that no one would seriously try it.

An LSO's decisional dilemma was captured by the attached sequence of photographs taken of a ramp strike by an F-7U Cutlass, a notoriously under-powered aircraft. In the sequence, the F-7U began to drop below glide slope and to its left, in the direction of the LSO platform. The LSO correctly sensed the left-to-right drift (as seen by the LSO) and the impending ramp strike. He dropped the pickle and radio and sprinted across the flight deck, directly in front of the approaching aircraft. Some of the platform crew stayed on the platform and were reportedly killed. The LSO had a fireball licking at his heels, but he made it. *[Career tip: At critical moments in life, you often come to a fork in the road, and are forced to make a big decision with limited information.]*

*The LSO sees that the F-7U will hit the ramp, and is drifting toward the LSO platform. He makes an instantaneous decision to run <u>across</u> the flight deck, in the path of the oncoming aircraft. This quick reaction saved his life, when the aircraft hit the ramp and slid into the LSO platform. The pilot was killed. The fate of the men in the catwalk is unknown.*

*Ticonderoga* launched aircraft one dark night during terrible weather. I had the bad luck of being the LSO. The cloud layer bottomed out at about 200', with one-fourth of a mile visibility in fog. We got all the pilots back aboard except Devil, in the last F-8, just as the visibility dropped to one-eighth of a mile.

These conditions were too much—even for a pilot with Devil's skills. By a strange coincidence, Devil had been one of my instructors in the jet training command. He was a superb aviator. I thought, *how ironic that I am now the guy standing between him and disaster. I'll bet he wishes he had been nicer to me back at Meridian.*

He made several good radar-controlled approaches, but on each pass, he was slightly off glide slope or lineup tolerance when he popped out of the cloud deck. At this in-close position, the deviation tolerances are extremely tight, and I had to wave him off.

Devil was getting low on fuel, and we had already recovered the A-4 tanker, which had given away the last of its fuel to other thirsty aircraft. Everyone was having trouble getting aboard in this weather. If we did not get Devil aboard, he would probably not make it to Da Nang, the nearest "bingo" field, and would have to eject.

I pulled the protective earplugs out of my ears, and concentrated on his engine noise on the next pass. I told the platform crew not to talk. "Devil, you sound like you're lined up slightly left [thinking backwards, like reading in a mirror]—give me five degrees right. . . . OK, now five degrees left and hold that heading." Devil suddenly popped out of the cloud deck, almost on centerline and close enough to the glide slope. I let him land, and he caught the #2 wire. I was nearly as relieved as he was. We were all lucky that it was Devil that was dealing with those conditions, and not one of the nuggets.

On another night, I was the duty (primary) LSO running the platform. Just before dawn, the Air Wing LSO ("Moon Pie") showed up, even though he was not on duty. We had been having trouble getting the last aircraft of the cycle on board because of arresting gear problems and a "fouled deck." The unlucky crew of four aboard a "Q-Spad," an ECM version of the Skyraider prop aircraft, had already been airborne for several hours, and were naturally anxious to complete their flight.

The Spad also had electrical trouble with its external lights, including the one that indicates "gear down" to the LSO. This light, as I recall, is in the left wing edge, near the fuselage. It normally flashes when the tail hook is not down, and is green when the landing gear is down and locked. With this particular bird, there were no lights showing at all.

Moon Pie said he wanted to wave the last bird, and took the lights and radio. "OK, you've got it," I said. *What the hell—he was senior to me.* I did not like to have my concentration disrupted on the platform.

When he gave the Spad the "cut" lights [a set of green lights that signal a prop aircraft to cut power to idle], the Spad's power came off and he swooped down for the wires. As he passed the platform in the dark, I mumbled, "No gear!" Too late. He caught the #3 wire, landing gear up, with his prop carving divots in the deck. No one was injured, and the Spad only needed a new prop! This was a very durable aircraft.

I remember wondering if I would have diagnosed the gear problem before he landed. Nevertheless, *my* "cherry" was intact—still no accidents or ramp strikes on *my* watch. I remember thinking, *That's what Moon Pie gets for hogging the pickle! Now he gets to explain why he landed an aircraft with its gear up.* [Career tip: *when you take the "con," make sure you know and understand the tactical environment for which you are assuming responsibility!*]

A few weeks later, I was waving the day shift. Two F-8s zoomed into the break, and the first one turned on approach and called the ball. "Red Flash Four Zero Two, Crusader, ball, two point zero." It was one of my squadron's birds, but I did not recognize the voice or know who the pilot was. I assumed it was one of our nuggets. Because he omitted the words "manual ball," I knew he was using APC, and that his fuel was 2,000 lbs. remaining.

Because of its landing difficulty, the F-8 was equipped with an Approach Power Compensator, or "auto throttle," for approaches. It was roughly similar to cruise control in a car. When engaged, its primitive computer would move the throttle, adding or reducing power automatically in order to maintain the optimum angle of attack, or airspeed. I personally disliked using it, because you had to move the nose too much, and there was always a lag in the response. However, for some reason, the East Coast F-8 pilots loved it, day or night.

At the in-close position, the F-8 started to rise above glide slope because of the up-draft from the ship's fantail, and the pilot dropped his nose. Since he was in APC, his nose dropped and the power came off abruptly. He failed to anticipate his needed counter-correction, and then finally jerked the nose up at the ramp, while still settling in a nose-high attitude. I needed to bust him out of APC, so I keyed the radio and yelled, "Power, power!" in order to flatten him and prevent an in-flight wire engagement and broken nose gear. He complied, missed the wires, and boltered.

Often, as in this case, a bolter occurs because the pilot was high on glide slope or flat, making the touchdown occur beyond the last wire. While somewhat embarrassing, the pilot merely adds full power and goes around for another try.

Just as I was dictating a nasty grade on his pass to the log writer, the radio came alive: "Don't *ever* do that to me again!" *Those are familiar words,* I thought. *Was Wife #1 flying that F-8?*

I replied, "Don't honk your nose up at the ramp, and I *won't!*" *Who does this damn nugget think he is?*

On the next pass, the pilot successfully landed. A few minutes later, I saw the Air Wing LSO sprinting across the deck between landings. "Hot Dog, you've really *done* it this time. That was the *CAG* in that F-8. You are to report to his office immediately. I have the paddles [meaning he had control of the LSO platform]."

I knocked on CAG's office door. I assumed he wanted a private debrief of his landings. "Good morning, CAG," I said. "Moon Pie has the log, but I remember your passes. On the first one . . . . ."

The angry little man yelled, "Stand at attention, Hot Dog! I am sick and tired of your insubordinate and disrespectful behavior! I've heard a lot about you from the senior officers in your squadron."

"Why, thank you, Sir. That's very kind of them," I replied with a grin.

"*See?* That's exactly what I mean! You're a wise guy! What you did today was totally unprofessional. You are GROUNDED! Now get out!"

I then located the Air Wing LSO. I told him CAG had grounded me. I also told him that, as a result, I was retiring my LSO "paddles" until the grounding order was rescinded. I said, "If I'm not fit to fly, then I'm obviously not fit to wave. Sorry about that. By the way, Moon Pie, maybe I should have kept quiet and let the little bastard catch an in-flight engagement and bust the nose gear—but I remembered that we are short on aircraft right now, so that would not have been the right thing to do." Moon Pie's jaw dropped.

Giving up the paddles does not sound very threatening, until you learn that this meant double-duty for the other LSOs, especially the Air Wing LSO. At that time, only the Air Wing LSO and I were qualified to control all aircraft in the air wing, day and night, without supervision. One of us had to be on the platform at all times.

Since my "wings" were clipped, I stood the ready room duty every day, ran a very spiffy watch, and I became quite good at it! My telephone etiquette improved dramatically, the coffee was always ready, and there was plenty of chalk for the heavies [senior officers] to write their meaningless directives and pithy sayings on the blackboard. I was like the equipment guy on a football team, making sure that there was enough Gatorade, towels, and jockstraps for the players.

After about four days of this diplomatic impasse, I heard that some of the pilots were complaining through their Skippers to the CAG that they wanted me back on the LSO platform, especially during night ops. Moon Pie was an A-4 driver by background, and he made the F-8 pilots nervous at night when he was running the platform. He clearly did not understand the F-8's peculiarities in the landing configuration. Whether senior or junior, pilots are funny about such things—they want the best people in key positions when they are airborne. CAG was forced to relent. One afternoon, Moon Pie stopped by the ready room and said, "OK, Hot Dog—you've made your point. CAG says you are no longer grounded."

I told him, "Moon Pie, if you think this is an 'Aw, shucks, CAG didn't really mean it' moment, you are wrong. CAG needs to put it in writing. And there better not be *anything* about this incident in my file or fitness report. CAG is lucky I am not demanding a *public* apology! Do you know what General Patton had to do after slapping a soldier in World War II?"

Look, I admit it—by normal, civilized standards, I <u>was</u> a *prima donna.* That was part of my charm. I was one of those characters that the senior officers loved or hated, depending on where we were at the time. I was one of the pilots who they always wanted on their wing in combat, or acting as the LSO when they returned to the ship. However, as the newly designated XO, "Cuffs" (the fourth XO in 18 months), told me at the end of the second combat cruise, "Hot Dog, if I had been the Skipper, you would have been court-martialed for insubordination."

I replied, "Well, XO, thank you for that inspirational talk. I guess that's why *you* were not the Skipper." I never understood why some of the heavies thought I was insubordinate. I always thought they would *want* to know when they were about to get shot down, or crash, even if it bruised their egos. I felt they owed me at least a "thank you" for keeping their fat asses alive. *But that's just me. . . . .*

~ ~ ~

# Chapter 20: *Voyage of the Lambs*

In a few short months, the Red Lightnings had been transformed from a powerhouse of fighter aviation talent to what football teams call "a rebuilding roster." We were like a college bowl team that graduated most of the starters, and then replaced them with freshmen and second-stringers. Even the "coaches" (i.e., senior officers) were rookies in the Vietnam combat environment, regardless of their basic flying experience. In a matter of a few weeks, Burger, Gator, Devil, Spanky and I found ourselves in a different world. The only thing that had not changed was the red lightning bolt logo, painted on the aircraft tails.

It did not take long for me to figure out that the composition of the daily flight schedule assignments would have a large impact on pilot survivability. I made *sure* that I had the assignment of writing the schedule. I did not trust anyone else to put the section teams together, particularly since many of the new flight leaders were so inexperienced. Because I had put the new pilots through my combat training syllabus and was the squadron LSO, I knew their individual capabilities better than anyone. I secretly dreaded the inevitable first Alpha Strikes. I wondered how many pilots we were going to lose, and how quickly. I knew one thing for certain—most of our pilots were not ready for "prime time."

While the nuggets had a great attitude, they simply lacked flying experience. Through no fault of their own, they had been placed in a dangerous situation, with "newbie" senior officers and a short training cycle. That alone is enough to get you killed in combat. The senior "newbie" pilots, on the other hand, lacked an appreciation for the environment facing them, and except for XO Roberts, did not have the necessary skills for flying the F-8 in the Tonkin Gulf.

The night before we left Cubi Point for the first online period, I received word that we would be launching two Alpha Strikes in sequential cycles as soon as we reached Yankee Station. CAG "Newbie" assigned our squadron a variety of missions, all of which were going to be very difficult and dangerous for most of the new pilots. We did not have enough experienced drivers to pair up with the newbies and keep them out of trouble. In addition, because Alpha Strikes drain pilot resources quickly, I was concerned about the necessity to assign the experienced pilots to fly in *both* strikes.

There simply were not enough combat-experienced pilots to spread around, and assigning an experienced driver to double-duty was unfair. This presented me with an ethical dilemma: Should I give extra combat exposure to a pilot because he is experienced and/or a good driver, or do I try to make the exposure equal? I wrestled with the scheduling puzzle for hours, and finally decided that I had done the best I could. The schedule was signed by the Skipper and printed, just as *Ticonderoga* left port. The outcome would now be decided by a Higher Power. I looked forward to a sleepless night.

*A typical daily flight schedule for the Red Lightnings.*

At about 1900, a messenger arrived from Strike Ops, asking who our Ready Alert pilots were, and why they were not in their aircraft on the flight deck. When a carrier is steaming in hostile territory and not conducting air operations, two fighters are normally ready for immediate launch, with pilots strapped in the cockpit in two-hour shifts throughout the night ("Alert Five"). Since we were barely out of the Subic channel, the North Vietnamese MIGs were some 900 nautical miles away and not capable of striking at such a range. Moreover, the North Vietnamese MIG pilots rarely flew at night, which told me they were smarter than we were. I asked who the idiot was that set Alert Five, and was told with a grin, "The Admiral, Sir."

I became angrier than usual with our incompetent leadership. This arbitrary order would require us to have two pilots strapped in their cockpits, ready for instant launch, around the clock. Every two hours, we would have to relieve the pilots in the cockpit and substitute another team, which effectively eliminated about four hours of sleep for each of the pilots involved. This heavily impacted the pilot rest factor, and made the impending missions even more dangerous, as they would be flown by tired pilots when the Alpha Strikes began. Carrier operations are a marathon, not a sprint, and you need to use your pilot resources carefully—as the Japanese learned the hard way in the Battle of Midway. *Every bastard up the chain-of-command is trying to kill us,* I thought. With this incident, I reached my "red line." I guess the stress of combat will do that to you after a while.

I knew where to find the culprits—the War Room. Without thinking it through, I proceeded directly to that sacred lair, clad only in a green t-shirt, camouflage pants, and shower shoes. This is not how you normally do a social call on senior officers, especially the Admiral.

Finding their Bat Cave, I barged into the room, and demanded loudly, "Who in the hell set Alert Five?" I had incorrectly guessed that some junior staff officer was the guilty party. I expected to find a small office area, but instead found a large room with wall-to-wall maps and men placing little pins to represent targets and threats. It was a very formal atmosphere.

Several enlisted men in crisp white uniforms turned away from their map-keeping tasks, and surveyed my appearance in horror. From an inner sanctum to the right, I noticed the Chief of Staff, complete with gold shoulder braid, coming through the door. "*I* did! Who the hell are *you*?" he demanded.

*Oh, shit! Time to stand tall, and not blink.* "Captain, I'm Hot Dog Nelson—the guy who wrote the schedule for tomorrow's strikes for VF-194. I have to put a bunch of inexperienced pilots over the most heavily defended territory in the world, chasing the usual Mickey Mouse targets. Some of these guys may not come back. I want them to be as rested as possible, not sitting on the flight deck playing Alert Five games for MIGs that can't fly this *far*, and that can't even *fly* at night. I request that you cancel the Alert Five, immediately."

There was a long silence. Without realizing it, I had just laid a pre-emptive guilt trip on this officer. If we lost pilots the next day, he knew I would be blaming him for it. The four-striper said quietly, "You have a point. We will reconsider the Alert Five. But don't ever come down here again, dressed like that. Do you read me?"

"Yes, Sir. Thank you for reconsidering your decision." I left, wondering what would happen next. Thinking back to the Boat School piranha incident, I realized I had a rare talent for upsetting admirals and captains. One thing for sure, I knew they could not afford to ground me and take me off the flight schedule, and Gator and I had a big laugh about the irony of their dilemma. I had already learned that when you are a volunteer, and willing to be *expendable*, you are also *irreplaceable*. The reason for that paradox is that most *sane* people are *not* willing to be expendable. That gets you special treatment—temporarily. During his career, The Buzzard played this paradox masterfully for all it was worth.

Within 20 minutes, the Alert Five was canceled for our ship, and assigned to another carrier already on Yankee Station. Perhaps I saved one or more of our pilots that day—who knows?

Several years later, Wife #2, an airline flight attendant, was serving meals on a trip to New York. She noticed a young Sailor in uniform, with a shoulder patch that said "*USS Ticonderoga.*" She said, "My husband was on *Ticonderoga.*"

"Oh, really, Ma'am? What was his name?"

"You probably wouldn't know him. He was a junior F-8 pilot."

"Oh, I might. What was his name?"

"Lieutenant Dick Nelson, VF-194."

"*Hot Dog* Nelson?? Oh, I remember *him!* I was on duty in the War Room on *Ticonderoga* when he busted into the room and demanded that we release the Alert Five! That really shocked the Admiral and Chief of Staff! We thought he was going to be court-martialed or something for a while. Tell him I said 'good job'!"

"I will—I'm sure he will enjoy hearing from you."

It is truly a small world. That is why *[Career tip!]* you must always be careful, as I was, not to offend your superiors.

It was another hot and humid day when CAG "Newbie" decided he would descend like a god from Mount Olympus, and lead an Alpha Strike. He was planning to lead a group of about a dozen A-4s to a worthless target just north of Vinh. This was a much safer and less-defended part of North Vietnam, which is probably why he decided to lead this particular strike.

Gator and I had each "adopted" a couple of nuggets and made them our assigned wingmen, whenever possible. This was to make sure that the nuggets would not get any bad habits from the weak senior "newbies," and that they would learn how to fly "smart" in this demanding environment.

On this particular strike, we were using two F-8s from VF-191 (call sign "Feedbag") and two from our squadron. CAG assigned our four birds as TARCAP for his strike group, but he made the same tactical mistake that the Luftwaffe made during the Battle of Britain.

In that epic air campaign of 1940, Hermann Goering ordered the German fighters to fly co-speed within the slow bomber formations, resulting in large losses while they were pummeled by the RAF's Spitfires and Hurricanes. Similarly, CAG wanted the F-8s to stay co-speed, within the strike group formation, instead of acting as free-lance hunter-killer sections. This meant that the F-8s had to fly at the slower speed of the A-4 bombers, severely handicapping our ability to engage MIGs, which was our mission. Learning of this stupidity, I assigned myself to lead the Red Lightning section with one of my nuggets as wingman. Better to control the chaos than to be a mere spectator.

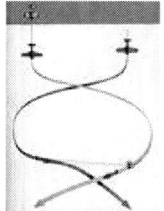

I privately conferred with the Feedbag section leader, and told him to do a Thach Weave with us over the top of the bomber formation, giving us at least a little speed advantage. This meant that the F-8 sections would cross over the bombers with symmetrical, opposing S-turns, which also kept us moving to avoid the NVA flak solutions. The maneuver was originated in World War II by Admiral John ("Jimmie") Thach, Naval Academy Class of '27, as a defense to the maneuverable Japanese Zero. On the way in to the target, the weather cleared and the entire North Vietnamese coast was visible. I was about to learn that CAG could not read a map.

There are two significant islands near the coast of North Vietnam: Hon Mat and Hon Me. One, Hon Mat, marked the coast near Vinh, a more lightly defended area. The other, Hon Me, was just off Thanh Hoa and south of the Hourglass river area, a hotbed of SAMs and AAA. You did not want to poke your nose in that hornet's nest unless you had to.

The mission plan, briefed by CAG, was to "coast in" over Hon Mat and attack the target a few miles inland. As we approached the coastline, CAG picked the wrong island, even though they are miles apart. He was leading the strike group directly toward Hon Me and the Thanh Hoa area, and we did not have Iron Hand SAM-killers on this strike to protect the bombers.

I kept thinking, *He must know where he's going. He'll turn to the correct "coast in" point any minute.* Finally, at 30 miles from the coast, I could not wait any longer. "Chippy lead, recommend left 40 degrees." No answer. "Lead, coast-in point is at your 10 o'clock."

"Roger," was the terse reply. The strike group finally turned left to aim at the correct island, Hon Mat. *This is going well,* I thought.

The strike itself was predictably uneventful. No SAMs were fired, and the AAA was almost non-existent. As usual, no MIGs came up. The strike group dropped their bombs on the target and exited "feet wet" to the safety of the open water.

Back on the carrier, several of the A-4 drivers came up to me. "Thanks, Hot Dog. I thought we were hallucinating on the way in. He was going right at Thanh Hoa until you made him turn left! This guy is dangerous!" I thought, *I'm sure CAG really appreciated me pointing out his navigational screw-up. I guess I've been insubordinate again!*

*LTJG Bob McMahan*

Nugget Bob McMahan was a solid and dependable young pilot, and learning fast. He was a handsome kid, and looked like he belonged on a Naval Aviation recruiting poster. When a photo escort mission came up, I assigned him to fly with an experienced photo weenie. At the time, I thought he was ready for this type of mission, but I was wrong.

He apparently got confused when his SAM warning system lit up, and he failed to take the proper evasive action. The SAM hit him from the side, and his aircraft disintegrated. He left a young wife behind. We now had our first casualty of this cruise.

For some of our pilots, this was a jarring wake-up call, which Bob McMahan paid for with his life. For my part, I had to live with the fact that I was the one who scheduled him for his last flight. I wish I had put *my* name in that fatal spot on the flight schedule, instead of his. I had the experience and knowledge to have evaded the SAM that got him, and it probably would have been a "non-event." I still have feelings of guilt about losing this young pilot, after more than forty years. Should I have given him more training and briefings about dodging SAMs? Was he making mistakes during training that I failed to notice? *Lots of questions, but no answers. . . . .*

I began to notice personality changes in some of the pilots. Spanky, who was a naïve, shy, and wide-eyed kid on our first cruise, became very focused and grimly resolute. When in the aircraft, Spanky now was a no-nonsense guy. His relentless mission obsession almost got him killed one day.

During an armed reconnaissance, Spanky and his wingman found a small bridge near the Ho Chi Minh Trail, on the Vietnamese border with Laos. In his determination to nail the bridge, Spanky pressed his last run down to 3,000' before pulling out. As he bottomed out, he noticed a stream of tracers following him. He heard a metallic "thud," followed by a vibration. He knew that he had been hit.

I was the duty LSO as Spanky made his approach, announcing that his engine was "running rough." Jet engines do not "run rough," unless they are about to fail. As his aircraft passed by the LSO platform, I heard several compressor stalls, and he was trailing smoke. Luckily, he caught a wire.

When the maintenance crew inspected his aircraft, they found a hole in the bottom of the fuselage. As they followed the trajectory of the bullet through the hole, it disappeared in the top of the intake duct, which apparently caused debris damage to the engine blades. Then they found the bullet itself—perfectly centered, on a course to castrate Spanky and deny him his rightful descendants. The bullet stopped short only because of the thickness of his fiberglass seat pan.

"Must have been your lucky day, Lieutenant," said the maintenance chief to Spanky, with a big grin.

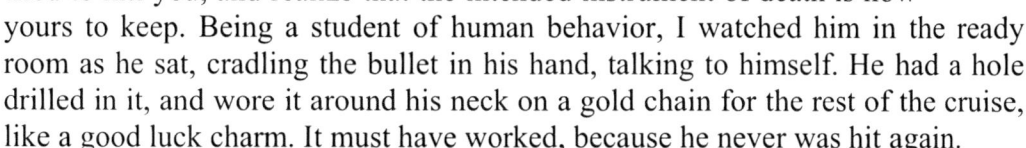

Spanky took possession of the big bullet, obviously from a 12.7mm machine gun. It truly is fascinating to be able to look at something that tried to kill you, and realize that the intended instrument of death is now yours to keep. Being a student of human behavior, I watched him in the ready room as he sat, cradling the bullet in his hand, talking to himself. He had a hole drilled in it, and wore it around his neck on a gold chain for the rest of the cruise, like a good luck charm. It must have worked, because he never was hit again.

It is often said that the aircraft carrier flight deck is the most dangerous workplace on earth. This is true for the flight deck crew as well as for the pilots that fly the aircraft. These young Sailors, whose average age is about 19, spend many exhausting hours on the flight deck and do not receive the so-called "glory" enjoyed by the flight crews. On almost every cruise, a flight deck crewman walks into a spinning propeller, is blown over the side by jet blast, has a foot run over by a moving aircraft, or is sucked into a jet intake. One of the worst events of all is the breaking of an arresting gear cable.

When an aircraft lands successfully, its tail hook snags one of the four cables, which is programmed with a hydraulic pressure for the speed and weight of that type of aircraft. The repetitive stress on these cables requires them to be replaced after every 100 arrestments or so. Even then, a cable sometimes breaks without warning, and becomes a huge, high-speed whip that cuts down everything in its path. During one of these incidents, flight deck crewmen are often cut in half, decapitated, or have their legs severed. These are gruesome accidents.

A story was making the rounds on all the carriers. On a certain carrier, a senior enlisted man was standing near the "foul line" close to the carrier island, when the arresting gear cable broke. The aircraft went over the side and the pilot successfully ejected. The cable whipped around to the right, like a huge lawnmower blade, releasing the energy of the arrestment. From his years of flight deck experience, the man knew instantly what had happened and what was coming. He ducked, and the cable zipped just over his head, cutting the man next to him in half.

On this man's next cruise, the incident happened again. This time, for reasons he could not explain, he sensed the cable was coming in a much lower arc. He jumped as high as he could, tucking his feet up under him. The cable clipped off the heels of his shoes, flipping him in a somersault, and severed the legs of the man next to him. It took him a few minutes to figure out why he was walking "funny." His shoes were missing heels. If he had ducked, as he did on the first cable incident, he would have died.

*Ticonderoga* was a proud old ship, and was blessed with diligent crewmembers that operated the arresting gear and the catapults. In two cruises on that carrier, we never had a cable break or a catapult malfunction. It is hard to believe that this old ship was so good at her job, which is attributable to her fine crew. For history buffs, this was the lead ship of the World War II *Essex*-class carriers. She was actually hit by Japanese Kamikazes in 1945, and lost 140 Sailors. After Vietnam, she was decommissioned and sold for scrap—a sad fate for such a proud warship.

Burger was an extroverted personality, and an above-average driver. He had been awarded the Black Max in Yokosuka for an incident in the O'Club when he was recovering from a sprained ankle. That was an award that any lieutenant commander could be proud of, and none had achieved, especially with a sprained ankle.

Every now and then, he would make a dumb mistake in the air, which had earned him the uncomplimentary call sign. After one of his airborne *faux pas,*

Buzzard told him, "You're a *hamburger!*" Burger had a wife and kid that he adored, and he tried to hide his fear that he would not survive to see them by exhibiting artificial bravado and a phony "Let's go get 'em" attitude.

During a TARCAP mission, Burger took a direct hit in the nose of his aircraft from a 37mm shell. This is about as close as you can get to being blown out of the sky. The explosion set the magnesium-alloy radar dish on fire. Limping back to the ship, he caught a wire on the first pass. As the aircraft sat in the arresting gear, a larger fire erupted, blackening his face. The fire crews went into action, spraying the aircraft and pumping CO2 into the nose to contain the fire.

We became concerned that the fire would start cooking off his 20mm ammo, which would probably result in multiple fatalities, including Burger. The "Tin Man," a fire crewmember in an asbestos suit, climbed bravely up on the burning aircraft and pulled Burger from the cockpit. Down in the ready room, Burger told the story of his narrow escape and was visibly shaken. He never seemed right after that.

Gator, who had a beautiful wife and two small children, also began to show uncharacteristic signs of stress. Unlike his cocky, unflappable attitude on our first cruise, he was now moody and spent his personal time writing melancholy letters to his wife. I began to worry about him, because the "family syndrome" is very distracting and can get you killed. I decided to shake him out of it. Everyone needs a "Dr. Phil" sometimes, and I had just read a book on abnormal psychology, which definitely applied to Gator.

As we got ready for an Alpha Strike one day, I noticed he was abnormally quiet. "Gator, what's bugging you?" I asked.

"I don't know—just worried about Ann and the kids, I guess, and what would happen to them if I get smoked out here."

"Gator, not to worry. Let's assume you get blown away. As soon as we have your memorial service—and I'm not sure I will even go—I'll marry Ann, treat her like crap, and sell your kids into slavery."

"Dog, I may kill you while you're sleeping, you bastard!"

"Too late, Gator. Take a number and get in line. Besides, I'm already dead. And by the way, what size uniform do you wear? Your whites are in better shape than mine. What about your sword? Shall I have a garage sale with the rest of your stuff? It ought to be worth *something* if you go down in a blaze of friggin' glory! I want you to think of some famous last words to say on the radio before you hit the ground, like 'I'm going in—God Bless McNamara!' or 'Hot Dog for president!'" For a while, this teasing worked on him. Then he went flying with Burger on a fateful BARCAP mission.

Burger was a lieutenant commander, so he had the lead on this flight. The flight of two F-8s did slow laps over Red Crown for an hour. They were about to come back to the ship, when Red Crown came up on Guard frequency: "This is

Red Crown on Guard. Bandits, red bandits [MIG-17s], 120 at 40 from Bull's-eye 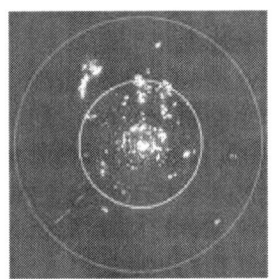 [Hanoi], heading 130." This put the MIGs southeast of Hanoi, over the Hourglass, heading approximately toward Red Crown and the two F-8s. Gator went GUNS hot, and selected his left Sidewinder. He waited impatiently for Burger to ask for an intercept heading.

This was the opportunity that we *all* had been waiting for. Our squadron was weary from being teased about not having any MIG kills. Even the VF-191 "Feedbags" had one, which made our pain even more severe. The MIGs had never flown during *any* of our strikes, and except for the dogfight with Pirate, never came up to confront our air wing. One of the intelligence officers ("spooks") said that was because NVA intelligence had us pegged as dangerous air-to-air opponents. We knew they listened to our frequencies, just as we listened to theirs. They obviously knew our squadron call signs, so that explanation was plausible. Perhaps the "spook" only said it to make us feel better.

Red Crown radioed Burger, "Red Flash, you have multiple bandits 300 at 30. Take angels 25, your heading 310 for intercept." Burger continued his lazy racetrack pattern, still at 250 knots loiter speed. Gator was about to explode.

"Burger, take the heading! Let's go burner now!" Burger did not answer. Burger had lost the edge. The previous flak hit had really affected him.

"Red Flash, this is Red Crown—did you read my last?"

"Roger, Red Crown. We're low on fuel. What's our vector back to Panther [the carrier]?"

Gator replied, "Burger, I've got four point five [four thousand five hundred pounds]! We have plenty of gas! We can do it!"

"Roger, Red Flash, your vector to Panther is 150, 75 miles. *Have a nice day.*" The Black Shoe controller seemed as irritated as Gator was at Burger's lack of aggressiveness. After all, Black Shoes are warriors, too. Now our squadron reputation had been damaged with the *Black Shoes!* The reputations of squadrons, ships, pilots and air wings spread through the Fleet faster than the speed of light.

When Gator got to the ready room, I wondered if I should take his 9mm pistol and his knife away from him. I really think he would have attacked Burger physically if I had not been there. He screamed, "Burger, you *&%$# pussy! You let some MIGs get away, and we'll probably never have another chance!"

Burger shrugged, and said meekly, "Well, I just thought we were too low on fuel to be chasing MIGs, and the smart move was to come home." All of the pilots stared at him in disbelief. That is why we have tankers airborne. Burger had broken the faith and lost the respect of his squadronmates. VF-194, even with its long history of operational excellence, remains one of the only F-8 squadrons of its era that never had a MIG engagement and never shot down a MIG. Now I know how Dan Marino felt without a Super Bowl win. Gator and I often wondered what would have happened if he and *I* had been together on that BARCAP, instead of Burger. *The fickle finger of fate . . . .*

No matter how hard I tried to get Skipper Ostrand to fly like a fighter pilot, he continued to have a casual attitude about flying in the Tonkin Gulf. My coaching efforts were sometimes less than subtle, and viewed by other senior officers, including the CAG, as disrespectful and out-of-line. Nevertheless, I had decided that I would do and say whatever was necessary to keep the Skipper safe, because a life was involved. I tried to assign Gator or myself with him as wingman whenever possible to keep him from getting in trouble in a combat situation. I juggled flight assignments to prevent the nuggets from flying with him. On one typical flight, we were droning along at 20,000' in a BARCAP holding pattern. I had noticed that he was a chain-smoker, and frequently smoked in the aircraft while airborne.

The Skipper, always a laid-back personality, was feeling very relaxed on this day—something that should never happen in a combat area. He switched on his autopilot, and from my wing position, I watched him light a cigarette. Suddenly, I noticed his arms flailing wildly, and his aircraft wobbled as he bumped the stick.

"Skipper, you OK?" I asked.

"Negative. . . . .got a problem."

"What's the problem?"

"Just had a fire. I need to get back to the ship."

It seems that he had taken off his gloves and oxygen mask, but had neglected to shut off the oxygen flow completely. When he lit up his cigarette, his mask became a blowtorch, burning his face and hands before he could secure the oxygen switch. His mask was almost completely melted.

Luckily, he got aboard on his first pass. They took him to sickbay, where they treated his burns. He was unable to fly for several weeks, which was probably just as well. I saw him as an airborne disaster, just waiting to happen.

Just when I thought there was no hope for some of our pilots, God and the North Koreans intervened. Seven months before, *USS Liberty,* an unarmed intelligence ship, was attacked by Israeli Air Force jets in the eastern Mediterranean, and nearly sunk. She lost 34 of her crew. Senior Navy leadership refused to let a nearby U.S. aircraft carrier defend her, and to this day, the Navy will not disclose why *Liberty* was sacrificed, or why our Israeli "allies" attacked her.

Now, in early 1968, another intelligence-gathering ship, *USS Pueblo,* was cruising in international waters off the east coast of North Korea. According to the *USS Pueblo* Veterans Association Web site:

> **The USS PUEBLO's first operational mission was conceived by and was tasked through the Naval Security Group Command. This first mission was primarily a period for training and testing. With no current information available on hostile activities by North Korean forces, the officer in charge**

at US CINCPACFLT assigned the mission a risk assessment of "minimal." All attempts by PUEBLO's commanding officer to upgrade this assessment to hazardous were rebuffed.

Like the USS LIBERTY, AGTR-5, PUEBLO operated under the assumption that help would be available if needed. The US 7th Fleet, US Forces Korea, and the US 5th Air Force, Fuchu, Japan were informed of PUEBLO's mission, but because of the minimal risk assessment, the US Navy made no specific requests for support. The tasking for similar USS BANNER missions had been rated as hazardous, and fighter aircraft had been made available on a strip alert status and two US Navy destroyers had maintained station within 50 miles of BANNER. When 5th Air Force personnel questioned the lack of request for strip alert status for PUEBLO's mission, they were verbally informed that they would not be needed.

In addition to the lack of ready protection, the US Navy maintained the same communications procedures and methods for the PUEBLO mission as LIBERTY had operated under during her fateful mission of June 1967. The PUEBLO's inability to establish reliable communications with a higher command authority would be a similar repeat of the problems that contributed to the lack of help for LIBERTY. Unfortunately, it appears nothing was learned from the LIBERTY incident.

While in international waters, *Pueblo* was attacked by North Korean MIGs and gunboats. One of her crew was killed and others were wounded. She was loaded with highly classified documents, electronics, and code-breaking equipment, and before they could be destroyed, she was boarded and captured. Typical of our Navy's inept leadership in that era, *Pueblo* had been assigned to cruise in the hostile waters off North Korea with no air or surface protection. When she radioed for help, the responsible local commanders were afraid to engage the North Koreans without "cover your ass" authorization from the president, which never came. Rather than protect the little ship, its top-secret gear, and its crew, these senior commanders were more concerned about avoiding personal criticism for acting too aggressively.

Finally, realizing the impact of what they had allowed to occur, the admirals dispatched Task Force 71 in an empty show of force, consisting of the carriers *Enterprise, Ranger* and screening vessels. *Ticonderoga* was ordered to Cubi Point to take on cold weather gear and special munitions, and then join the Task Force in the Sea of Japan.

With a few days before departure, I decided to contact Jan, future Wife #2, and have her meet me in Manila. I knew she could fly standby from New York, using her airline employee passes. I sent her a telegram, and she responded that she would arrive in Manila on Pan Am on a specified date, which would coincide with my arrival at Cubi Point.

Before the ship arrived to dock at Cubi Point, the squadron decided to send several F-8s to Langley Field (an auxiliary field in Manila Bay) for maintenance work and I was allowed to fly one off. I was able to meet Jan at Manila Airport, and we had several wonderful days sightseeing and traveling around Manila.

On one trip, we visited Camp O'Donnell and the POW Memorial near the town of Capas. This was the Japanese prison camp for the survivors of the Bataan Death March, and where many thousands of American and Filipino POWs suffered and died. To see it and walk its grounds is a very personal and depressing experience. I felt like I could almost hear the screams of thousands of starving, tortured ghosts. I realized that we were standing on the sacred ground where our

POWs were beaten and killed by their Japanese captors. I was not afraid to die, but for some reason, I had an irrational fear of being captured alive. Although I did not express it to Jan, I was thinking, *There is <u>no way</u> I am becoming a POW and checking into a place like this—better to go down in friggin' flames, with my finger on the trigger.*

One morning, I was contacted by our squadron maintenance chief, who asked if I could fly a maintenance test flight from Langley. I agreed. Jan and I caught a Navy boat from Manila to Langley, and I showed her around the aircraft and sat her in the cockpit. Giving a girl a cheap thrill is often a smart thing to do.

I then got permission from the tower to have Jan stand out near the runway so that I could put on a little air show for her. After I got airborne, I did a loop, barrel roll, half Cuban Eight, and some other low pass maneuvers over the field. She *said* she was impressed, but women often lie to boost our male egos.

*At Langley Field, Philippines, ready to give Jan an air show.*

While I was burning off the excess fuel, I made several low passes over the historic island of Corregidor, which appears like a big, rocky tadpole at the mouth of Manila Bay. From the air, I could see the entrance to Malinta Tunnel, where our forces held off the Japanese until forced to surrender, with the peninsula of Bataan to the north. The pier from which General MacArthur made his escape to Australia in a PT boat was plainly visible. I was reminded of MacArthur's feeble promise: "I shall return!" This place was an important piece of American history, and I felt fortunate to have seen it from the air like this.

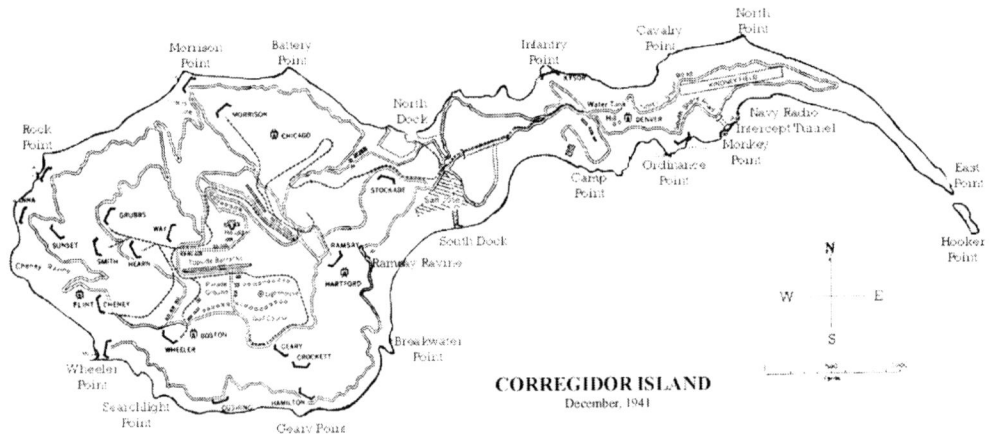

**CORREGIDOR ISLAND**
December, 1941

During that flight, I flew over to Subic Bay and buzzed the *Ticonderoga* at masthead height. That got me a flight violation from the Air Boss. My response was, "So what are you going to do? Ground me? Send me to Vietnam on an aircraft carrier and let me get shot at? Come on, Boss—I was only trying to raise the troops' morale!" I never heard anything more about the incident.

As our time together in Manila ended, Jan and I said an emotional goodbye. Both of us were thinking the same thing—this could be the last time that we would ever have together. Jan left on the next Pan Am flight back to New York. I flew an F-8 out to the carrier, which had just left Cubi Point. Now it was back to business.

*Ticonderoga* steamed north at high speed and joined the other two carriers off the coast of North Korea. There was a higher level of tension within the air wing. When dealing with the psychotic North Koreans, we had to be prepared for anything. Some of our senior officers had seen combat during the Korean War, and knew what we might be facing if the shooting started.

At that time of year, the weather conditions in the Sea of Japan were brutal. Freezing rain coated the flight deck and the aircraft, and the seas were huge. The air wing pilots were required to wear uncomfortable exposure suits, called "poopy suits," to get a few more survivable minutes in the frigid water in the event of an ejection. While our politicians equivocated and tried to find their courage, we did nothing. The net result was that we abandoned a Navy ship to the enemy, along with her crew and top-secret equipment.

The Task Force steamed in tense formation off the North Korean coast, waiting for orders that never came. The *Pueblo* crew languished in captivity for 11 months, while our country still did nothing. If there was ever a case where war *was* the proper option, this was it. A U.S. Naval vessel had been taken by the armed forces of North Korea, a crewmember had been killed, and they even refused to return the ship and its remaining crew. Under international law, that is a clear act of war.

During the presidential campaign of 1968, Richard Nixon harshly criticized Lyndon Johnson for not retaliating against the North Koreans and getting the *Pueblo* back. Sensing that Nixon might be inclined to do something about the *Pueblo,* the North Koreans kept the ship, but released the crew, following his election.

A few months later, in another political debacle, North Korean MIGs shot down an EC-121 aircraft with its entire crew of 31, about 100 miles at sea. Although *he* was now the president, Nixon also did nothing. Our country had become a paper tiger, having no credibility with friend and foe alike. It seemed that our nation's leaders had lost their backbone, and could always find a diplomatic or political rationale for avoiding confrontation—even when it was necessary.

When we were detached to return to Vietnam, with our tail between our legs, we stopped in Yokosuka. I paid a visit to the Japanese company in Tokyo that produced our various squadron patches, and gave them a new design. As squadron mess treasurer, I was always on the lookout for a new way to improve the financial position of our squadron nest egg. I decided that a special patch should commemorate the national disgrace of the *Pueblo* incident. Although I was not much of an artist, I came up with a graphic design that expressed our feelings about the capture of the *Pueblo.*

The design featured a map of Wonsan Harbor, showing the *Pueblo.* The legend around the outside proclaimed, "What's One Little Ship To A Big Country Like Ours?" At the bottom, it read, "USS Pueblo Recovery Team, 1968-?" Near the center was a familiar quote for all Naval Academy graduates: "'Don't give up the ship'—Lawrence, 1813". The final touch was a *large yellow stripe*, right down the center, to portray the cowardice of our senior leaders, including the President of the United States.

I had one sewn on my flight jacket, and put out the word that they were available to all flight crews in the Pacific Fleet for $5 per patch. I sold out my stock several times, and had to keep re-ordering from Japan. Even the Black Shoes were buying them. The mess treasury grew larger. I was considering whether to invest the surplus funds in CDs, stocks or bonds. I thought that when we got back to Miramar, we might have enough funds to build our own squadron O'Club near the hangar, complete with a bar, live band, and pole dancers. Another Red Lightning first!

My financial venture for the squadron came to a sudden halt, when the admiral commanding Seventh Fleet saw a patch on the jacket of an *Enterprise* pilot, and demanded to know where he got it. "I got this from VF-194 on *Ticonderoga,* Admiral. If you want one, I'm sure they still have some left over," said the pilot.

*The* **Pueblo,** *still sitting in Wonsan Harbor, North Korea. It is still used as a propaganda tool and tourist attraction, complete with uniformed tour guides. The Top Secret code and electronics equipment was removed after the ship's capture, and sent to an unknown destination—probably the Soviet Union.*

The visual message conveyed by this patch really got under this admiral's skin. I concluded that he must have had something to do with the *Pueblo* screw-up and subsequent timidity shown by the chain-of-command in failing to stop the capture. Sometimes the truth really hurts. This admiral sent an order to our CAG, demanding that he confiscate all of these patches immediately, and that further production and distribution would be grounds for harsh discipline. Furthermore, they were banned and could not be worn on flight jackets. Naturally, I secretly kept a few, but surrendered the rest to the CAG staff. We still made a pile of money, and after the confiscation, the value of the patch went up dramatically.

Perhaps the North Koreans would like to purchase a few hundred patches. It would be quite amusing to see one of these on Kim Jong-Il's jacket. This *could* be the diplomatic breakthrough with North Korea that the White House has been waiting for, similar to Richard Nixon's ping-pong tournaments with the Chinese.

After steaming in circles, we left Korean waters with a sense of betrayal, as our nation wrote off our fellow Sailors on the *Pueblo*. If I did not have a bad attitude about our chain-of-command before, I *really* had one now.

As we returned to Yankee Station off North Vietnam, President Lyndon Johnson, Secretary of Defense McNamara, and the rest of that dysfunctional administration decided to show even *more* "restraint" toward Hanoi, in the hope of negotiating a political settlement. This resulted in a stupid series of bombing halts, designed to entice North Vietnam to join peace talks in Paris. All it really did was give North Vietnam time to re-arm, re-supply, and train their MIG pilots, SAM crews, and AAA gunners. Nevertheless, it did keep our "newbie" pilots off the beach, and—for the moment—safe.

Following the capture of the *Pueblo*, the Communist Chinese took a cue from their North Korean comrades. Two unarmed A-1 Skyraider props were transiting the South China Sea between Cubi Point and Yankee Station, en route to *USS Coral Sea,* when they got off course and were intercepted by Chinese MIG-19s. Lieutenant Junior Grade Joe Dunn was shot down, and parachuted into the water about seven miles off the Hainan coast. He was alive when he landed in the water.

**Chinese Air Force MIG-19**

*A-1 Skyraider ("Spad")*

According to unofficial reports within the Fleet, a Navy destroyer was nearby, had him in sight, and asked for permission to pick him up. The chain-of-command reportedly held the ship outside the 12-mile limit, and *allowed* the Chinese to take Dunn captive.

Dunn has never been heard from since, and the Chinese refuse to discuss his fate. His status was changed from MIA to "presumed dead" in 1982, and he received a posthumous promotion to commander. His wife, Maureen, still waits and prays for his return.

It was now abundantly clear that our senior military leaders would rather sacrifice our own people than incur the wrath of their superiors in Washington. We had arrived at a despicable place in our military history where leadership priorities were focused more on senior officers preserving their careers than taking care of their troops and winning the war. Joe Dunn was another casualty of that selfish mentality.

Through *nine* presidents, we have allowed the Chinese to stay silent on what they did to Joe Dunn. How can a Serviceman trust his government officials and chain-of-command, when they are so willing to write him off, in order to pursue endless diplomatic strategies? Joe Dunn's case should *never* be forgotten. As long as the Chinese refuse to return him alive, or even return his remains, *our* government has no honor or credibility.

Dunn's fate and abandonment was sadly typical of our leaders' general attitudes during this period. The lives of American Servicemen and women were subordinated to the Rules of Engagement and the administration's fear of confrontation with the Russians, North Koreans, and Communist Chinese. This was the basis for the timid strategies and tactics that have prevailed and emanated from the White House ever since the Truman capitulation in the Korean War.

Aggressor nations have learned that while the U.S. may growl and bark, or even show its teeth, it will ultimately turn tail and run if you can inflict some serious casualties or bluff with a threat of nuclear war. A nation cannot win a war by imposing restrictions on *its* forces, while the enemy employs *no* restrictions.

Since Korea, the world has watched our retreat from Vietnam, the failure to respond to numerous terrorist attacks, and hasty withdrawals from Lebanon, Somalia, and Iraq. The world's aggressors have concluded that we lack commitment to our principles, and have no stamina for prolonged conflict. Allies feel they cannot rely on us, and our enemies do not fear us. This will guarantee that we *will* be attacked and our people killed, as in the 9/11 strike on the World Trade Center and the Pentagon.

As a final insult to Joe Dunn and his family, there is no body beneath his lonely headstone. His country and its leaders not only lacked the courage to save him, but also to account for his fate and bring him home.

All who have served in our nation's military know and understand how important it is "to leave no one behind." When dead, wounded, or captured warriors are abandoned and effectively written off by America, as occurred with Joe Dunn, the *Pueblo* crew, the Vietnam POWs, and many others, this breeds an atmosphere of cynicism and distrust in the minds of our warriors. This ultimately affects every man or woman in a combat situation, and diminishes the effectiveness and fighting spirit of our military. America betrays her lost and wounded warriors at her own peril. An old poem, written in the bloody nightmare called World War I, expresses this frustration:

> *In Flanders Fields the poppies blow*
> *Between the crosses row on row,*
> *That mark our place; and in the sky*
> *The larks, still bravely singing, fly*
> *Scarce heard amid the guns below.*
>
> *We are the Dead. Short days ago*
> *We lived, felt dawn, saw sunset glow,*
> *Loved and were loved, and now we lie*
> *In Flanders fields.*
>
> *Take up our quarrel with the foe:*
> *To you from failing hands we throw*
> *The torch; be yours to hold it high.*
> *If ye break faith with us who die*
> *We shall not sleep, though poppies grow*
> *In Flanders fields.*
>
> ---LCOL John McCrae—written during WWI

~ ~ ~

## Chapter 21: *Rules of Engagement*

As Lyndon Johnson found out, the negotiating techniques that work at a Texas barbecue are worthless when dealing with hard-line Communists. In a panic to preserve his presidential legacy, Johnson tried to tempt the North Vietnamese to negotiate a peace deal by adopting a unilateral bombing halt in the North. As a result, the North Vietnamese gained valuable time and attack-free supply lines to increase their military pressure on South Vietnam.  When this insane gambit was combined with the micro-management of Robert McNamara and the doomed attrition strategy of General Westmoreland, the result was inevitable defeat for the United States.

Serious students of American history know that the American public, unlike that of Asian or even European countries, cannot seem to tolerate wars that last longer than about four years. After that, public support begins to wither and political opposition grows stronger. It is difficult to harness the independent spirit of America to support a conflict in which its uniformed sons and daughters are being maimed and killed, unless the enemy has committed acts so atrocious that Americans' thirst for justice or vengeance overrides all else. Even that scenario has its time limits, as Washington, Lincoln, Wilson, FDR, Truman, and George W. Bush learned after the four-year milestone was passed in their respective conflicts. It took Pearl Harbor to push us belatedly into World War II, and 9/11 to wake us up—temporarily—to Islamic terrorism and Saddam Hussein's threats.

The American psyche today is dominated by a desire for personal convenience, instant gratification, and a "What's in it for me?" mentality. Fighting a protracted war, even for sound foreign policy reasons, will not be tolerated for long by the self-centered American public.

America's resolve began to wither in 1968, a year of historic national turmoil. After the slanted media coverage of the Communist Tet Offensive, the American public lost its will to continue the fight to save South Vietnam. This was tragic, because we actually were now winning on the battlefield, in spite of the many political restrictions. However, the media declared the war lost and demanded an "exit strategy." In mid-year, Bobby Kennedy and Martin Luther King were assassinated, further diverting America's attention from the war.

Johnson, always a crafty domestic politician, knew he only had a few months to extricate the U.S. from Vietnam before his administration would be swept away by a tsunami of political opposition, even from within his own party. Johnson pulled out of the presidential race, but the Democratic convention in Chicago became a pitched battle in the streets between anti-war protestors and the police. The desperate moves of bombing halts and other restrictions were part of his failed diplomatic strategy, and they made the Tonkin Gulf operations ineffective.

Air Wing 19 had just returned to the Tonkin Gulf from our national disgrace with the *Pueblo* capture when the most restrictive Rules of Engagement were announced. We could not believe what we were reading. There was so much opposition to these rules within the air wing that CAG "Newbie" decided to call a meeting of all officers in the wardroom. Big mistake—never try to promote a stupid policy unless you really believe in it, and know how to explain it. A dumb idea cooked up in the Oval Office of the White House will not necessarily work in the theater of operations, no matter how much the local commanders faithfully try to implement it.

As we gathered in the *Ticonderoga* wardroom, I noticed an abundance of grumbling and critical comments from the pilots. We all had been affected by our recent humiliation with the *Pueblo* incident, and there was a growing lack of confidence in the chain-of-command, beginning with our air wing and reaching all the way to the White House. CAG was about to experience the depth of these feelings by trying to promote the new Rules of Engagement to a very hostile audience.

Using a series of maps and charts, CAG described the latest bombing restrictions. A no-fly line was drawn across North Vietnam at the 20th parallel, and 12 miles off the coast. CAG announced that any intrusion into this vast protected area, which contained 95% of the military and industrial targets in North Vietnam, was prohibited. Then he made a statement that I could not tolerate.

"If any of you go into the no-fly area, and are shot down, we are under orders *not* to come in to rescue you," said CAG. There was a stunned silence in the room.

I raised my hand. "Yes, Hot Dog?" CAG glared at me.

"Sir, I was just wondering—what if I am flying *outside* of the protected area, and take a flak hit. I punch out, the wind blows me in my parachute across the no-fly line, and I land *inside* the protected area. Obviously, it would not be my fault that I landed across the line. Will you come in to get me, or will you abandon me because of this arbitrary line? Do these rules take the prevailing winds into account?" I always loved to test new theories with a problem hypothetical, and I had not even been to law school yet. All eyes were on CAG, and he looked very upset.

"I'll get back to you on that," he said. The chatter from the crowd became louder. "OK, dismissed," he said. I could feel his eyes boring holes in the back of my head as I left the room, but I knew that I had made my point and had exposed the stupidity of the new restrictions. As usual, the enemy gets a free pass, and we have to fight with one arm tied behind us.

*[Career tip: Always look for a "silver lining" and find a way to manipulate a bad situation for your benefit.]* The *good* thing about this situation was that I no longer had to worry as much about my newbies. It was going to be just like an East Coast Med cruise, and our guys could handle that. The *bad* news was that our Commander-in-Chief, President Johnson, had just voluntarily surrendered his air power, which enabled the enemy to become stronger.

The fact that our troops in the South were being killed by enemy troops, weapons, and ammo coming down from the North was apparently not important to President Johnson. Worse yet, our senior military and naval commanders went along without even a whimper. No admiral or general resigned in moral protest against this ridiculous restriction. So much for personal and professional integrity. As Matthew Maury cautioned many years before, "When principle is involved, be deaf to expediency." Perhaps our admirals had lost their Reef Points, or never had a Plebe Year.

In the midst of all this moral confusion, I decided that I needed a break from the Navy and its continuous command failures. I still wanted to stay in for a career, but my second combat cruise would soon be over. I would be facing some unpleasant assignment possibilities for my next tour.

All of the air wing lieutenants who had completed two combat tours were expecting non-flying assignments on a carrier, like Catapult Officer, Hangar Deck Officer, Arresting Gear Officer, or—if they were lucky—a staff or the Training Command. While these jobs were obviously very important, they were also tedious and unpleasant. For an aviator, it was like going to Siberia. You had to watch everyone else fly, while you walked around in a grimy yellow sweatshirt and were under constant pressure from the Air Boss and Aircraft Handling Officer. Except for the Training Command, these assignments were non-flying, grueling, and miserable. We had talked with the officers on our carrier that held these billets, and they hated their jobs, primarily because they were not flying and felt they were not acquiring important skills that prepared them for more senior command assignments. The Navy should never have assigned combat aviators to these billets.

I learned that I would probably be assigned to an air wing staff as an LSO. After thinking it over, I applied to the Bureau of Naval Personnel (BUPERS) for Air Force exchange duty, which would give me a third combat tour. Specifically, I wanted to fly either F-4s or F-105s out of Thailand and have a chance to bag a few MIGs. I felt that I had presented my case effectively, and anticipated a

 positive response. From my naïve perspective, I could see no reason why BUPERS would deny my request.

Not long after that, I received the bad news. Instead of Air Force exchange duty, I was being assigned to the Miramar F-8 RAG, VF-124, to train new F-8 pilots. I went ballistic. I felt that I had paid my dues, and had earned a slot with Air Force exchange and more combat duty. If an officer wants to continue flying in combat, why not give him what he wants? This was the same situation that had occurred with my dad, when the RAF sent him to a non-combat assignment in Canada. His reaction was to switch Services from the RCAF to the USAAF, in order to get back into combat. I was effectively trying to do the same thing.

It turned out that my first Skipper from VF-194, Bob Chew ('48), was now the head detailer (assignment officer) for aviators at BUPERS. After I learned of my fate, Chew came through the Fleet to meet with officers in my status and give junior officers "career counseling." When he came to our ship, I met with him in the ready room for a one-on-one showdown, thinking I could use my Naval Academy and squadron connections with him to get what I wanted.

"Skipper, I put in for Air Force exchange. I don't understand why I didn't get it," I said. "I request that you reconsider that decision."

"Needs of the Service, Hot Dog. You may not realize it, but you have acquired a wealth of experience and knowledge of the combat arena. Also, you are a fully qualified air wing LSO. You are needed in the F-8 RAG, not flying with the Air Force. Assigning you to the RAG was not even a close call."

"But Skipper—I'm a fighter pilot, not a teacher. I want to be in on the MIG action, and that means I need a tour with the Air Force. You've *got* to let me have this one!"

"Sorry, Hot Dog. I hear you are actually an excellent teacher, even if you are a little difficult for your superiors to deal with. Welcome to Miramar, son!"

I was really pissed. If there was ever a lame excuse for an incompetent or unfair decision, it is that old "needs of the Service" rationale. It really means, "We are too lazy to figure out a way to give you what you asked for."

The word was out that the standards for assignment to F-8s had been relaxed for nuggets, in order to keep the pipeline full. Most of the top newbie pilots coming out of the Training Command now wanted to fly F-4s or A-7s, because the F-8 was perceived as becoming obsolete, with a limited remaining service life. In addition, junior pilots were leaving the Navy in ever-increasing numbers, causing even more pressure to find replacements for empty F-8 slots. The F-8 RAG was being forced to pump out new F-8 pilots prematurely, so the training standards were being lowered. The term *cannon fodder* comes to mind.

For the first time, I began to think about leaving the Navy. The elite F-8 fighter community was slowly crumbling, and we were hearing that the F-8 squadrons would be decommissioned in favor of F-4s and the new F-14s. This made my assignment to the F-8 RAG even more harmful to my career. I needed to swallow my disdain of the F-4 and become part of that community. That would give me an opportunity to get into the new generations of fighters, like the F-14.

Tragic news circulated through the F-8 community. Buzzard, who had been flying with the Los Alamitos Reserves while working for Continental Airlines, had been killed in an A-4 crash at NAF Crows Landing, California. He had obtained permission to practice for an upcoming air show, and was doing solo aerobatic maneuvers. He had given his own camera to a ground crewman, and requested that the man take photos of his spectacular "loop to a landing."

This is a maneuver that neither the Blue Angels nor the Thunderbirds will attempt. It requires a low pass over the runway, then a 4-g pull-up to a loop. When the bird is on its back at the top of the loop, the gear are extended and the flaps deployed, while the power is reduced to idle. The aircraft is then effectively "dead-sticked" at idle power in a screaming dive to a landing on the same pass. There is no room for error in this maneuver. To make it more spectacular, Buzzard decided to add a "dirty" (gear down) aileron roll after touching down, followed by another touch-and-go. Every pilot I know considered this an impossible combination for the underpowered A-4, doomed to cause an accident.

As Buzzard came down from the high point of the loop, he touched down, added full power, and tried to roll the little jet. Coming out of the roll too low, he struck his right main wheel on the runway while still rolling. The A-4 has long, spindly gear struts for its size, making the problem worse. His right main landing gear collapsed and he rolled inverted, skidding to a fiery stop. The ground crewman captured the entire incident on Buzzard's own camera. During the subsequent investigation, the Officer-in-Charge of Crows Landing and his immediate superior were disciplined and relieved of duty.

The Buzzard's luck had finally run out. Gator and I got a bottle of champagne, toasted The Buzzard, and drank it all. At least Buzzard died doing what he loved—flying. Whatever you thought of The Buzzard, he achieved his life's goal. He was truly a legend in his own time.

It may have been the bombing halt and the general morale problems, or it may have been simply laziness on the part of our squadron Skipper. His failure to react to a NAVAIR maintenance directive cost us a valuable aircraft and produced the only accident of my aviation career.

One summer day, I went out with Surfer, one of my photo weenie friends, on a do-nothing photo recce of the North Vietnamese coastline. We came back together and broke over the ship. It felt like it would be just another day landing, which—at my current level of experience—was actually fun.

When I dropped the landing gear, I got a "barber pole" on the right main gear, indicating that it was not down and locked. The Air Boss directed me to climb to 2,000' and recycle the gear. Surfer was told to wave off and follow me to visually check the gear. I recycled the gear, and still got an unsafe indication. Surfer flew up close to me and said it looked like one of the "black boxes" was jamming the gear in the up position. The F-8 wheel wells were crammed with various avionics boxes, which had been added as the F-8 continued to receive modernized avionics equipment. Using my last option, I initiated the gear "blow down" system, to no avail. We found out later that the box had come loose on the catapult shot, and jammed the wheel in the "up" position.

The Air Boss told me that I would be taking the barricade, which is always a dicey proposition. The only other alternative was to eject alongside the ship, equally problematic. In the meantime, I was instructed to go to the tanker and take on fuel. The Air Boss wanted to recover all of the other aircraft before rigging the barricade. After flying in circles for about 30 minutes, I watched the last aircraft

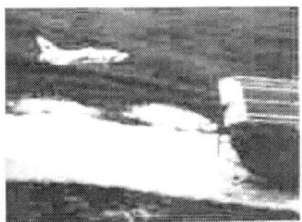  

## RIG FOR BARRICADE LANDING !

land and the deck crew begin the process of raising the huge barricade. If I had not been so personally involved, it would have been fun to watch this activity.

The barricade presents a difficult problem for the unlucky carrier pilot. You must discipline yourself to concentrate on the meatball, and ignore the fact that you are about to fly into a big volleyball net that will probably destroy the aircraft. Even worse, the Fresnel lens glide slope angle is flattened to make the #2 wire the target, instead of #3. This change puts you even closer to a ramp strike, if you get low. No one likes the barricade, even when you need to use it.

The crackle of the radio, with the Air Boss's booming voice, woke me up. "Red Flash, you have a Charlie [landing priority] now! Call the ball." The Boss wanted to get me aboard and clean up his flight deck for the next launch.

As I passed the 90-degree position, I picked up the meatball, centered with the row of green datum lights. *Hey, this isn't so hard!* Then I saw the monstrous barricade, waiting to wrap me in its spidery embrace. As I lined up, I kept telling myself, *Don't look at it—pretend it isn't there—it's only a net, right?* However, I could not resist looking at it periodically, which was screwing up my scan. Carrier pilots do not train for barricade engagements. You know about the barricade, but you pretend it will never happen to you.

*On short final. Note the absence of the right main landing gear. The plane guard destroyer is visible in the background.*

Carrier approaches in a jet go by in a hurry. Before I knew it, I was crossing the ramp. The ailing bird's nose gear and left main gear contacted the deck, and—with no right gear—she immediately fell off on her right wing tip. Sparks and flame burst from the tip as it plowed down the deck. I caught the #1 wire, which did not make the LSO too happy. However, I was determined to get this hog aboard on the first pass.

As I careened down the flight deck, the friction of the wing tip caused the bird to veer toward the carrier island structure. Luckily, the barricade straps held, and snagged me like a second baseman catches a line drive. When I stopped, the nose of the aircraft was only six feet from the carrier island. My neck hurt from the violent stop, but I was able to climb out on my own.

Remembering how important it is to keep a cool demeanor in front of the troops, or in the event there is press coverage, I said to the maintenance crew, "This bird seems to have some minor problems, boys. Check the oil and clean the windshield." In reality, the landing broke the wing spar and the keel, and the net straps put a big slice in the tail and wing. The aircraft was a "strike." I was told it was cannibalized for parts and never flew again.

*Sliding in to home plate!*

During my approach and barricade engagement, Surfer—a fanatical photo weenie—flew off to my right and took sequential photographs. If that was not bloodthirsty enough, Spanky ran up to "Vulture's Row" near the tower and took videos of the entire approach and landing. Now I know how celebrities feel when pursued by *paparazzi* with cameras. These photos appeared in newspapers all over the country, with my name directly below. My mom actually found out about the incident by reading the morning paper! Somewhat like a televised football game, it was one of those "Hi, Mom!" moments.

When I got to the ready room, I got a few cheers and a lot of backslapping. "Hey, Hot Dog, you almost hit the island!" said one nugget.

"No, numb-nuts, I planned it that way. I didn't want to walk too far to get to the ready room, so I stopped it right there next to the hatch." That got a few laughs. I thought, *I sure hope they don't notice my knees are wobbling.* Gator and I went down to our stateroom for a few beers. Mission accomplished. Any landing you can walk away from is a good landing.

I became very upset when I learned that the Skipper had a directive in his pile of in-box papers that required F-8 squadrons to strengthen the black box mounts in the wheel wells. This malfunction had occurred before. The Skipper had received the notice over a month ago, but he had not read it or forwarded it to the maintenance officer. I privately told him, "Skipper, with all due respect, *that busted bird belongs to you.*" I made sure that this information was contained in the official accident report.

In another odd twist of fate, the photo weenie that took the spectacular pictures of my barricade arrestment—Surfer—went to work for Continental Airlines, as I did later. He was the Second Officer in a B-727 one summer day, taking off from Denver. A microburst wind shear hit the aircraft just after lift off, and drove it into the ground alongside the runway. The pilots performed brilliantly, and were cleared of any pilot error. There were only a few minor injuries to the crew and passengers. Surfer had a small head wound, and was admitted to the hospital. I sent him a "get well" card, saying, "I only wish I had been flying alongside you with a camera to record your accident. Signed, Hot Dog." Another "small world" incident.

The nuggets were doing well, and becoming more confident every day. However, every now and then, one of them would make a mistake that reminded me they were still learning.

On one flight, the ship wanted us to delay our "ramp time" to allow for some shuffling of the aircraft on deck. This would place us low on fuel, so I asked for the tanker. "Roger, Red Flash. Contact the Whale on this frequency. He's at your two o'clock at nine miles."

"Roger, Panther—Tally-ho on the tanker. Four Zero Five, I'll tank first."

"Roger," the nugget responded.

We joined on the A-3 tanker, which had extended its large basket, called a drogue. I flipped the air-refueling switch to extend the in-flight refueling probe. The door on the left side of the fuselage opened and the probe extended. I plugged in on the first try, having done it hundreds of times.

Unlike most Navy aircraft, the F-8 probe was behind the pilot, and not visible when looking straight ahead. You made a successful "plug" by lining up on the basket, and then flying toward a spot on the tanker aircraft without trying to look at the probe. If you did it right, the probe plugged into the basket and you started receiving fuel through the hose. At nighttime or in turbulence, this was another demanding aspect of flying the F-8 off the carrier, where "tanking" was a very frequent occurrence.

After taking on about 1,000 lbs. of fuel, I saw the tanker's green "fill" light go to yellow, and I reduced power and unplugged. Moving over to the right of the tanker, I said, "Four Zero Five, it's your turn." The nugget moved behind the tanker and began stabbing wildly at the basket with his probe. *Wow, they're going to need a new basket,* I thought to myself.

I could sense that he was becoming frustrated. After about ten attempts, he still had not plugged in. Then, in a moment of misguided determination, the nugget added too much power and stabbed aggressively at the basket. His probe caught the lip of the basket, kinking the big hose. The lateral stress broke his probe at the elbow, making it point straight down. It now looked like the injured genitalia of a big racehorse, dangling limply at a crazy angle. *Ouch! That hurts!* I thought, squirming in my seat.

"Panther, Red Flash Four Zero Eight. We have a problem with Four Zero Five's probe. He is unable to take on fuel, and we need to return to the ship."

"Roger, Red Flash, proceed inbound to Panther and call ten miles for a Charlie time."

"Roger that."

However, the fun was not over. The nugget came up on his radio: "Red Flash lead, my fuel is running out! I only have 1,000 left in my main."

I thought, *Now what?* "OK, Four Zero Five, check your probe switch to OFF." With the fuel probe switch in the wrong position, transfer between the fuel tanks was suspended.

"Ahh, roger. It's going now."

When he landed, he actually ducked down low in the cockpit, nearly disappearing from view. The LSO later asked him what he was doing.

"I was afraid the broken probe was going to swing around and hit me in the head when I landed," he replied. I decided I had some more work to do with this lad.

I was flying with one of the sharpest nuggets one day when I lost my radio. I passed him the lead, which was standard procedure. On that day, there was a low cloud layer over most of North Vietnam, obscuring the coastline, and we were over the water just north of Vinh. We were supposed to fly up the coast and then turn back toward the carrier just east of Haiphong.

I kept looking at my radar, and then the heading he was flying. He had forgotten that the North Vietnam coast curves toward the northeast. He had taken an inadvertent short cut, and was about to overfly the Red River delta, which is loaded with SAM sites, over an overcast. I flew up alongside him and tried to motion him toward a new heading to the right. He looked at me blankly.

At about that time, my AAA warning lights and SAM light illuminated. We were just seconds from receiving a barrage of flak and SAMs. I selected AUTO on my chaff dispenser and hit the actuator button. (Chaff consists of individual "squibs" of tin foil, cut to a length that confuses ground radar and electronically shields an aircraft.) Bursts of chaff shot from the belly of my aircraft, placing false targets on the NVA radar scopes below. Adding power, I pulled ahead of him and gave him the hand signal that I had the lead. I added full power and broke down to the right, heading fast for open water. He followed.

After we returned to the ship, I showed him on a map where we were going. "You were about to become a ball of fire, man! Don't fly over *that* piece of real estate unless you have to!"

"Yeah, I *wondered* why you were dumping chaff!"

"Well, now you know!" I replied.

Another of our best nuggets was launched at night on the usual BARCAP over Red Crown. After the section returned to the ship, his leader landed first. "Young Ben" was intercepting the glide slope when his horizontal tail trim failed and ran full nose down. His emergency trim would not work. He was able to hold his altitude only by pulling the stick to the full back position. Obviously, this is not the way that you want to attempt a carrier landing, especially at night.

After several wave-offs, Young Ben and the LSO were both becoming concerned. He was running low on fuel, and getting tired. His right arm was starting to shake from the strain of holding so much backpressure on the stick, while his left hand was busy with the throttle to keep on speed and glide slope. The LSO finally used a little psychology to lighten everyone up. "Ben, just remember—busy hands are *happy* hands!"

For some reason, a little humor did the trick. Young Ben caught a wire on the next pass. When he got to the ready room, he looked like he had been through the wringer. *Welcome to the NFL, son. All's well that ends well.*

One day, XO Robbie Roberts reached his own redline. He was fed up with the restrictive Rules of Engagement. He put together a four-plane division of F-8s and launched on a fake "coastal recce." The White House bombing restrictions placed the North Vietnamese air base at Thanh Hoa off limits. Red Crown and other radar monitors were seeing increased MIG activity at the base, now that the North Vietnamese knew we were not allowed near it.

The XO took his division south of the 20th parallel, which was the no-fly "dividing line." He ordered his division to turn off their IFF, turned right, and accelerated to 500 knots in a Combat Spread formation. He illegally penetrated the restricted zone, and overflew the Thanh Hoa MIG base at low altitude, in an effort to make the MIGs get airborne and chase him. The MIG pilots, unfortunately, were too smart and stayed on the ground. They were probably laughing and sipping a Heineken in their O'Club.

The bombing restrictions and no-fly zones made the remainder of the cruise relatively easy. Soon, this dysfunctional phase of the Vietnam air war came to a close. Richard Nixon was elected as the next president, and promised to end the war "with honor." It took him five more years to end it, and the "honor" was nowhere to be found.

I was designated as a Double Centurion, with more than 200 landings and combat missions on *Ticonderoga*. I returned to Miramar along with my squadronmates, wondering how life would be as an F-8 RAG instructor. I called Jan and arranged to meet her at San Diego Airport. It was time for life to return to normal—whatever *that* was. On several fronts, my future was now more uncertain than ever. As Forrest Gump would say, "Life is like a box of chocolates. You never know what you're gonna get."

~ ~ ~

USS Ticonderoga, just after recovering aircraft from her last launch. The A-3 "Whale" tanker is usually the last to land. The deck will now be "re-spotted" to clear the catapults for the next launch.

# Chapter 22: *Mutiny on the Bounty*

A few months after I returned to Miramar, I married Wife #2 in a small chapel ceremony at Miramar, with Gator as my "best man," a term that seems odd for describing Gator. True to form, Gator let loose with a psychotic giggle when I lost my voice at  the sacred moment of saying, "I do." A few days later, Gator left the Navy and went to work for TWA.

It occurred to me that I had been around this wild man since 1964, when we started training in Pensacola in the same class. Life was going to be different and not as much fun without him, because he was the closest thing to a brother that I ever had. If I were flying into combat again, and I could pick my wingman or my leader, it would be Gator. He was fearless and always ready for anything. He was a true warrior. However, our combat days were over, and we had to go our separate ways.

I reported to the F-8 RAG, and found about a dozen of my combat-experienced junior officer peers from the F-8 community were also there as instructors. This was a very belligerent group of junior officers. A few of them even exhibited a worse attitude than mine. One was a MIG killer, and all had in excess of 200 carrier landings and 1,000 to 2,000 hours in the F-8. Several were my Academy classmates. The years of negative experiences in the Tonkin Gulf had left them with a simmering distrust of senior officers, and they showed it rather openly. Totally disillusioned, bitter, and cynical, most could not wait to leave active duty and join the airlines. The Navy was about to lose an entire generation of expert combat pilots, largely through its own incompetence and cavalier attitude about officer retention.

At the same time, the ranking officers in the RAG hierarchy were cut from a very different cloth. They were senior lieutenants, lieutenant commanders, and commanders who were very career oriented, and had their eye on future Flag  rank, or at least command of a carrier. One of the best of them, Jerry Unruh, actually did get command of a carrier, and ultimately was promoted to Vice Admiral. He was a great officer and pilot, and a real pleasure to work with, unlike the rest of them. The junior officers dubbed this group "the Lifers." These two groups, with dramatically different goals, attitudes, and priorities, were destined to clash—and they frequently did.

I was in my first week with VF-124 when I learned how ugly this experience was going to be. The Lifers decided to take an instant dislike to two of my Academy classmates, John Sande and "Moose" Myers. They had prematurely and unwisely announced that they were going to leave active duty. Instead of trying to persuade them to stay in the Navy, the Lifers opted to punish them by assigning them to the San Diego Shore Patrol, a shocking assignment that was perceived as

*222*

a real insult for Miramar aviators. Up to that point, I had never heard of a Naval Aviator being assigned to the Shore Patrol. *How <u>dare</u> they! Don't they realize pilots don't <u>do</u> such things?*

I carefully reviewed my career plans and consulted some trusted senior officers at Miramar outside of the RAG. It became obvious from these discussions that being an LSO was not a good career path. Few LSOs had achieved carrier commands or Flag rank. It was too specialized, and you missed key career assignments while waving aircraft. The longer you served as an LSO, the more valuable in that job you became. This tended to land you in air wing staffs in a non-flying, overly specialized assignment. I decided to resign my LSO certification, which, like being a Naval Aviator, was a voluntary status. I wanted to remove myself from this assignment category before I was "kidnapped" again by BUPERS. I intended instead to push for assignment to NAS Patuxent River, the Navy test facility, or try again for Air Force exchange duty.

When I informed the RAG heavies of this decision, they were irate. They became even angrier when the Vice Admiral at COMNAVAIRPAC backed me up and pointed out to the RAG Skipper, in writing, that being an LSO was purely voluntary. When the Admiral took that position, I viewed that as confirmation that I was doing the right thing.

A minor factor in my decision was the inadequate field training the squadron was giving to the RAG students for simulated carrier landings. Apparently, this was caused by budget factors and aircraft availability. The shortage of F-8J aircraft made the RAG a replacement parts depot for the entire Pacific Fleet. Every time a Fleet squadron lost an aircraft, we shipped one of ours out to them, further diminishing our resources.

If that were not bad enough, the underpowered F-8J was a flying coffin, even for experienced drivers. It was criminal negligence to put such a defective aircraft in the hands of a student, and then tell him to land on a carrier with minimum training. The Navy had decided to "modernize" the F-8Es by converting them to F-8Js without the normal testing. This was an idiotic decision that would needlessly cost lives and aircraft.

The RAG Ops Officer, a former Blue Angel and pompous commander that was detested by all of the junior officers, told me, "OK, Hot Dog. You want another career path? I'm going to give you one. I'm sending you to the Shore Patrol like your two Academy buddies."

"Respectfully, Sir, if you do that, you will have my letter of resignation within 24 hours."

"Get out! I'm going to inform the Skipper of this conversation, and you will be hearing from us."

The RAG Skipper was a wimpy, reclusive captain who, in my opinion, was a below-average pilot and ineffective leader. Unlike other Skippers I had worked for, this one kept an aloof distance from his junior officers. None of us had much respect for him. On top of that, he had absolutely no sense of humor. I could just imagine his reaction at my refusal to continue as an LSO.

The next day, I was called in to the Skipper's office, accompanied by the Ops Officer. "Hot Dog, you are making a very bad impression on your superiors so far. I understand you are unhappy with your assignments. I'm going to give you a chance to excel, Mister. I'm assigning you to be the Aircraft Division Officer. *That* should keep you busy!"

"Aye, aye, Sir." *Life in the RAG was going to be a terrible experience,* I thought. An image of Captain Bligh berating Mr. Christian in the original *Mutiny on the Bounty* flashed through my mind. Now that I think about it, I *do* look like Clark Gable.

The Skipper's assignment was intended to give me a job that would cause me to fail. I was a lieutenant, and that was supposed to be a lieutenant commander billet in this squadron. This division had four Chief Petty Officers and 200 enlisted, and was the largest division in the squadron. It was well known that the Aircraft Division was the RAG's version of *McHale's Navy*, complete with an active drug distribution ring, constant discipline problems, and a declining re-enlistment rate. It was the worst division in the RAG, and perhaps all of Miramar. The leadership and morale problems in this division had caused the squadron's aircraft readiness to decline significantly.

The Aircraft Division was responsible for maintaining critical infrastructure systems on the squadron's F-8s: hydraulics, airframes and engines. It was obvious what had to be done. It was time to shake things up, which was something I did quite well. First, the "bad apples" had to be surgically removed.

I worked closely with NCIS, and we discovered that the paint shop personnel were operating a drug ring from a storage trailer near the hangar. We busted the perpetrators, who were then prosecuted. I made it clear that drug use or distribution would have "zero tolerance" in this division.

Next, I formed up the division in the hangar. *Memories, memories—just like noon meal formation on Tecumseh Court at the Naval Academy.* I could see that standing in a military formation was a new experience for this crew, as they tried to figure out where and how to stand, where to stow their coffee cups, and whether to wear their hats or not.

I introduced myself and announced that there was a new sheriff in town. I told them that the Chief Petty Officers were responsible for the daily workload and maintenance objectives being met. "Gentlemen, the senior Petty Officers run this Navy, and run this division. If you screw up, you answer to them—if *they* screw up, they will answer to me. Our work in this division is critically important. The squadron can't fly if we don't do our job right. And trust me, we *will* do it right! Those who *don't* support the rest of the team and work diligently to keep these aircraft in the air will be assigned to landscaping and janitorial duties, and I don't care what rate or rank you are. For those who are confused by what I just said, I'll put it this way—you can work on these beautiful Crusaders and get promoted, or you can clean the head, pull weeds, and sweep the hangar deck. Those who *do* produce will be promoted and be given more responsibility as fast as I can make it happen. You can always talk to me, but go through your Chief first. Senior Chief, dismiss the division and report to work stations."

In the next few weeks, I made sure that each department had a smoothly operating command structure within it. Where I found problems, I juggled assignments and counseled Petty Officers until the unit worked compatibly. I instituted a system of "triage" for correcting maintenance "gripes" on the aircraft returning from flights, using portable radios. By the end of the month, aircraft readiness increased exponentially.

When one of the troops went up for a Captain's Mast (a Navy disciplinary hearing), I went with him. In nearly all Mast cases, I asked the Skipper to withhold punishment and place the Sailor on probation, with me being personally responsible for his good conduct. The Skipper went along with this approach, primarily because he saw another opportunity to set me up for criticism. Outside in the hallway, I would take the Sailor aside, and tell him, "Now, *your* ass is *mine*. If you screw up, *I* will be in trouble, and you have no idea how bad life can be if you get *me* in trouble. The next time, you will be on your own, and I will help them throw the book at you and I'll hang you myself from the flagpole." This was extremely effective, and I never had a Sailor fail me after that.

I also tried to be as helpful to the troops as possible. I got one of my Petty Officers promoted to warrant officer, and another admitted to the Naval Academy. I reviewed their career advancement requirements, and made sure they were focusing on the next promotion. Re-enlistments increased, which shocked the Skipper and the other Lifers.

When it was income tax time, I even offered to help the troops with filing their tax returns, which I emphasized was something (unfortunately) that they had to know how to do. The other officers in the squadron began calling me "H&R Block." Around the first of April, the troops would line up outside my office with their tax forms. It was another devious way to make them dependent on me as their division officer.

Because these were young kids, I also felt it was important to help them when they got into personal or family problems, which ultimately will translate into poor squadron performance. When one of the junior Petty Officers was badly burned in a home fire, my wife and I visited him frequently in the hospital to make sure he was receiving proper care, and to see if he needed any special assistance.

In another situation, a young Sailor was convinced that his wife was having an affair while he was at work. I found her sitting in a steaming-hot car in the squadron parking lot one day, holding a small baby in her arms. When I confronted the Sailor, he said, "Well, Lieutenant, that's the only way I can really keep an eye on her." I convinced him to go to the base chaplain with her for marital counseling, and their problems were eventually resolved. His squadron performance improved greatly.

I arranged with the Skipper to shut down the entire division one morning and have the troops report to the base auditorium, where I showed movies and slides of F-8s on the carriers and in combat operations. "This is *why* you do what you do every day," I told them. "Without each one of *you*, these aircraft could not do such spectacular things." I also asked the Skipper to appear and give the troops an inspirational talk, which he did. This was the first and only time, as far as I know, that he ever talked to a large group of his enlisted men, as he normally considered himself above such contacts.

The morale steadily improved, and the Aircraft Division became the best unit in the squadron, much to the chagrin of the senior officers who had originally sent me to the "salt mines" to suffer. I confess—I took great delight in turning the tables on them and rubbing their arrogant noses in a success story they could not ignore. *Take that, you bastards!*

Our lack of confidence in the Navy's senior leadership was continually reinforced. We had watched in dismay while the Navy was fumbling around in an attempt to adapt the TFX, a McNamara-inspired swing-wing fighter-bomber, to carrier operations. Finally, when the huge aircraft was found incompatible for carrier operations in 1968, as predicted, it became the F-111, a troubled Air Force project. The Navy had wasted millions of dollars and years of valuable design and development time for producing a new fighter.

Our experienced pilots were shocked to learn that all of the F-8Es, a proven carrier fighter, were being "modernized" as the F-8J. This entailed the addition of new radar, a larger horizontal tail and a boundary layer control (BLC) system that was like a Rube Goldberg contraption. Air was bled from the engine and blasted over the surface of the wing flaps to prevent boundary layer separation at lower approach speeds, which were reduced to about 120-125 knots. This caused the "J" to be horribly underpowered and heavy, with decreased dogfighting performance and problems during wave-offs on a carrier approach. This "new" aircraft was not given the normal aircraft-testing program, and was rushed into service in carrier-based squadrons, including the Red Lightnings, who became the Navy's "guinea pigs."

The worst feature of all was the insidious boundary layer control switch, which was magnetically held in the OFF position. If aircraft electrical power was momentarily interrupted, the switch silently clicked to the ON position, activating BLC, whether desired or not. The BLC mode was supposed to be used only for landings. On takeoff, the pilot was required to ensure that it was turned off manually, or the aircraft might not get airborne.

On a landing approach with BLC, the "J" flew below the minimum speed for the Ram Air Turbine (RAT), which provided emergency electrical and hydraulic power in the event of a generator or engine failure. The people running the "J" project had forgotten about the RAT. If the main generator failed on approach, the RAT was useless, because the "J" aircraft was already too slow for it to operate. This would result in a complete electrical failure, and at night, this could be fatal.

I wrote up an urgent evaluation, which was forwarded to senior Navy officials. Nothing was done. I also noticed that my criticism of the "J" aircraft was viewed negatively by the Lifers, as a form of insubordination.

The "J" had serious problems with carrier wave-off and glide slope performance. Around the time that I was instructing in the RAG, one of the students hit the ramp so low that only the tip of his radome wound up on the flight deck. When the "J" got to the Tonkin Gulf, the high temperatures resulted in insufficient power to execute a safe wave-off. Shockwaves went through the Navy Air establishment, as one air wing grounded its "J" birds in the Tonkin Gulf. This is what happens when you cut corners on testing and evaluation of weapons systems.

The "J" also seemed less forgiving in low speed maneuvering. The modifications appeared to have changed the aircraft's flight characteristics (especially at low airspeeds) and made it more susceptible to spins. These hazards were not limited to inexperienced pilots. One of my best friends nearly lost his life because of this.

In December of 1968, Norm McCoy, one of Miramar's junior officer MIG killers, was practicing his dogfighting skills with a squadronmate near El Centro. The fight wound up in a slow-speed scissors, as each pilot maneuvered for the "kill." Suddenly, his F-8J snapped into a departure stall and went into an *inverted* spin. Unable to recover, he was forced to eject.

The negative g's of the inverted spin had pulled his legs away from the seat, resulting in compound fractures in both legs when the seat fired. He landed in his parachute in a sandy desert area, and was dragged by high winds, exposing his wounds to further injury and soil contamination. An off-duty enlisted man spotted him and transported him to the hospital. His wounds became infected and he nearly lost both legs, but recovered and completed a very successful Navy and civilian career. The treacherous "J" bird nearly got one of our very best drivers. In a story-book ending, Norm married one of the Navy nurses that cared for him in the hospital.

One of our more aggressive RAG students decided that he could see better in a dogfight if he *detached his parachute riser fittings*, enabling him to twist around in the cockpit and look behind him. None of the instructors knew he was doing this, although it turned out that some of his peers were aware of it. On his last flight, the young pilot unsnapped his parachute fittings as he started a practice dogfight with an instructor. In trying to out-turn his more skilled opponent, he stalled and the F-8J went into a violent spin. His aircraft hit the ground before he could get his harness hooked up again to eject. The crash investigators found his torso fittings were not secured to the ejection seat. Another life had been needlessly lost.

While I was attempting to adjust to the hostile RAG environment, my old squadron, VF-194, was having more problems. This once-great squadron was about to become "legendary" for the wrong reasons. It was truly a "canary in a coal mine," symptomatic of the problems occurring in the F-8 community.

As before, a large number of inexperienced pilots filled the holes left by the transferred veterans. "Cuffs" became the Skipper, which I found unbelievable. For some reason, the Navy apparently could not find senior pilots who were competent and qualified for command. "Cuffs" got his call sign when he passed out at the O'Club bar during Happy Hour, and was handcuffed to the Mutha' Trophy by one of the junior officers. No one would supply the key, so he had to call the San Diego Police to remove the handcuffs.

Under his incompetent leadership, some of the junior pilots then assigned to the squadron had significant problems in flying the F-8. To make matters even worse, the squadron was transitioned from the high-performing F-8E to the ponderous F-8J, compounding their operational difficulties.

One of the nuggets became what pilots call "snake-bit." This means that bad luck was following this individual wherever he went. This nugget had the distinction of personally destroying more U.S. Navy aircraft than perhaps any other U.S. citizen in history. He was a poster-child for what experienced F-8 drivers all knew—you *had* to become part of this bird, or you were headed for disaster.

In his first incident, the "snake-bit" nugget hit the ramp on the carrier and then ejected, with the loss of the aircraft. In the second, he had an oil pressure failure, and even though established on final for the Miramar runway, he decided to eject. The aircraft continued to fly and went directly into one of the huge maintenance hangars, killing about a dozen maintenance personnel and destroying several multi-million dollar F-4s and their support equipment. In his last debacle, the nugget had a mid-air collision with a squadronmate, resulting in their ejections and the loss of both aircraft. If this unlucky nugget had kept flying, the Navy would have run out of parachutes. I heard that he turned in his wings.

Another VF-194 pilot landed at night at Barbers Point, Hawaii with his landing gear up, wiping out another aircraft. Altogether, the Red Lightnings went on to lose nearly half of their assigned aircraft during their next training cycle and cruise. This was not the squadron that I had known, and I was glad I was not present during this chaos, particularly with Cuffs as the CO.

I heard that Cuffs himself hit the ramp on a carrier approach, resulting in a destroyed aircraft. Robbie Roberts had been relieved of command early because he refused to allow his squadron to fly the "J" in hot temperatures, due to the unsafe wave-off characteristics. Apparently, Robbie was right, and as usual, he stood up for what he believed. Robbie passed away a few years ago, and we will all miss him. He was a true fighter pilot.

Nevertheless, three of the nuggets I had trained became excellent F-8 drivers, and had very successful careers—"Slug" Bates, "Skip" Giles, and "Young Ben" Franklin. From what I heard, they were the backbone of the squadron, which was no surprise. These three had "the right stuff." They provided solid leadership in a squadron plagued by faulty aircraft and an incompetent commanding officer.

Finally, my time to leave the RAG was approaching. With a nasty, non-combat assignment looming just over the horizon, I opted to submit my resignation letter. Instead of being smart, and merely stating I was resigning "for personal reasons," I felt compelled to elaborate, in my typical fashion. In a two-page letter, I  cited the dismal record of the Navy's latest fighter development programs, and the fact that I did "not want to lead men into battle, if victory was not the objective." As with my peers, the Vietnam experience had a profoundly negative effect on me.

My resignation was accepted, but the Navy froze me on active duty status for one additional year—another example of our love-hate relationship. This cost me dearly with my next career in the airlines, where pilot jobs are based on date of hire. The Skipper of the RAG and his fellow Lifers became extremely hostile to those who were left in this "freeze" status with a release pending. Instead of maintaining a professional relationship, they treated us as hostages—who needed to be punished.

One of the senior Lifers seemed to look for new and innovative ways to make life miserable for those junior officers that were scheduled to leave the Navy. While undeniably a good F-8 driver, this lieutenant commander had a reputation from his Fleet squadron for treating junior officers badly. He also was quite good at self-promotion and protecting his inflated image.

The schedules officer notified me that I would be taking a group of students to El Centro, along with four other lieutenant instructors. The detachment would be led by our favorite Lifer, the self-important lieutenant commander. This promised to be an interesting trip.

Almost immediately, the four lieutenant instructors noticed that this lieutenant commander was placing himself on the flight schedule three or four times each day, and not letting the lieutenants fly. Finally, two of us confronted him about this out on the ramp. He was very direct: "You people are leaving the Navy. We don't need to waste any flight hours on *you*. You're just using the flight time to get a job with the airlines, anyway." All of that—even if true—was irrelevant. We were still on active duty, and we had a job to do as RAG instructors.

As you might suspect, this was not the end of it. I had another blowout with him in the ready room, when I needled him about "hogging" the flight schedule. I suggested that the nuggets needed to fly with the rest of us, before they adopted some of *his* poor flying techniques. He came unglued. "Lieutenant Parlette, crank up the T-28 and take Lieutenant Nelson back to Miramar ASAP. Hot Dog, you're *fired*."

I now had risen to a very unique and privileged status. I had my own personal pilot and aircraft to take me home. Usually, you must make four-star admiral to have such a perk. The next day or so, this egomaniac fired another instructor, and the T-28 prop did another round trip to Miramar. I was told he grounded yet another instructor pilot before the detachment was over. If he could only have fired two more junior officers, he would have had five "kills" and been an ace.

To this day, I have never forgotten nor forgiven what I believe was a flagrant abuse of authority by this arrogant man, and I still consider him a prime example of the poor leadership that permeated the senior officer ranks of my era. This was a major reason why so many good junior officers left the Navy.

Looking back, I can think of only a few senior officers of that vintage that I would follow to the *bar*, let alone into combat. As a group, they were a pitiful lot, and mostly incompetent. In some years, the grape harvest produces bad wine. There were some stellar exceptions, such as my former Skipper Bill Conklin, XO Robbie Roberts, Jerry Unruh, Snake, and Pirate, but the good ones were badly outnumbered. I knew I had made the right decision in leaving the active duty Navy.

Naturally, this ugly situation resulted in even more unruly behavior among the junior officers, who felt they were being treated unfairly. One fall day, the "short-timers" held their usual lunch meeting at the BOQ. The RAG Skipper and another commander sat at a table nearby, and were visibly irritated by the raucous laughter and loud story telling that was typical of our little band of merry men.

Upon leaving the BOQ, the junior officers all piled into one vehicle, a Scout. The lieutenant who was driving decided to pass the Skipper's slow-moving car, not knowing that two of our more ill-mannered colleagues had dropped their pants and were mooning the Skipper from the rear windows of the Scout as we sped by his car. This gave the term "body language" a completely new meaning. I can still see the shocked and horrified look on the Skipper's face, as he stared through his windshield at the pimpled posteriors of two of his junior officers.

In this caper, I was innocent—a rare occurrence. However, the Skipper was unable to identify the butt owners from his limited view, so a shadow of suspicion was cast over my role in the mooning episode. When we got to the parking lot, the Skipper drove up to us, and said, "Well, I hope you men think that was funny, because you are all in trouble. You will muster twice a day with the duty officer, and before you leave each day. I hear some of you have been playing golf during working hours." He was misinformed. In my case, it was surfing—part of my water survival training regimen. Obviously, he was not referring to me.

One of the two perpetrators was worried. "What if he calls NCIS, and they take butt prints from the vehicle back windows? Could they identify us?" he asked fearfully.

"What do I look like, a butt-print expert?" I replied. "Find yourself a lawyer who specializes in defending mooning cases!" After I became a lawyer, I learned this is a *very* specialized field, indeed, and not very lucrative. Those who moon their superiors rarely have money to pay lawyers.

Meanwhile, Wife #2 and I were enjoying our time together in San Diego in the off-hours. Jan approached everything logically, and she found the animosity of the RAG Lifers toward the junior officers hard to understand. She was glad that I was getting out. She was unaware that I had tried to get a third combat tour with the Air Force exchange program, and it took me about twenty years to tell her I had made that request.

F-8 incidents continued to occur at Miramar. One pilot forgot to close his canopy before takeoff. On takeoff roll, he realized it was a little noisier than usual, and instead of aborting the takeoff, he continued down the runway in afterburner, trying to hold the canopy down. As the bird reached flying speed, the clamshell canopy ripped out of his hands and blew off the aircraft. He went around the pattern and landed uneventfully, minus his canopy. Some drivers prefer convertibles.

On another flight, the pilot forgot to spread and lock his folded wings in his rush to take off. He flew a wide pattern, and successfully landed, demonstrating that the F-8 had more wing area than it really needed! *Who knew?*

One of our RAG students became overly imbibed at Happy Hour. As he approached the main gate at Miramar, he took one hand off the wheel to salute the Marine guard, swerved and crashed into the Marine guard shack, leveling the helpless building. When I heard about this, I thought, *No one ever said being a gate guard on Friday afternoon would be easy!* In spite of this and other early fiascos, that pilot went on to have an outstanding reputation in the Fleet as an LSO, and wound up flying A-4Es. On a training flight off San Diego, he experienced engine failure and ejected. He apparently died in the ejection when he struck the tail of the aircraft. It turned out that one of the ejection seat explosive charges was defective. An award is presented annually in his name during the Tailhook Association gathering in Las Vegas, and a room in the Pentagon has even been dedicated to him. His name was "Bug" Roach.

Rick Amber ('67), another of my former RAG students and an Academy graduate, had completed about half of his first combat cruise when he hit the ramp in an F-8J. I firmly believe he was another tragic victim of the "J" bird's inadequate power. He ejected, apparently hitting the steel catwalk, which rendered him a paraplegic. After leaving the Navy, he started a charitable organization, dedicated to assisting disabled people in learning to fly. He died of cancer in 1997.

One of my most talented students in the RAG, Lieutenant Junior Grade L.C. Green, was lost after reporting to his Fleet squadron. He experienced a catastrophic control surface failure while flying around his carrier. The aircraft crashed in the water before he could eject. This also was an F-8J.

As November of 1969 arrived, our time in this miserable squadron was finally over. My contemporaries and I left the RAG for various civilian careers, mostly in the airlines. I joined Continental in Los Angeles, and started in a class with several other Miramar "refugees." Continental had several Naval Academy graduates: Gene Chancy ('60), Dave Hicks ('61), John Sande ('64), Bob Hulse ('61), Frank Corah ('65) and Mike Quaintance ('64).

However, some habits and addictions are hard to break. For me, flying F-8s was one of them. I joined the Naval Reserve, and was assigned to VF-202 at NAS Dallas. A new adventure was about to begin.

Only one of our junior officer RAG instructors, Skip Umstead, stayed in the Navy. Skip was a very likeable guy, and an excellent aviator. Prior to joining the F-8 RAG as an instructor, he flew 202 combat missions with VF-53 and had a total of 284 carrier landings. During his two combat tours, he was awarded 13 Air Medals, the Navy Commendation Medal with Combat "V", the Navy Unit Citation, and the Vietnamese Gallantry Cross.

Skip and I used to fly test flights on the weekends, in order to build our flight time. He used to laugh when he saw me on the weekends, saying, "You're getting hours to join the airlines, and I'm getting hours to join the Blue Angels!"

Skip flew his first tour in the Blue Angels, and then transitioned to F-14s in VF-2. He was well on his way to a fast-track Navy career, but was called back to the Blue Angels to be Team Leader in 1972, flying the F-4. He died in a crash during a practice show at Lakehurst, New Jersey, in 1973.

I never heard *anyone* make a negative comment about this man, which is rare in the fighter pilot universe. All who knew him will continue to mourn his loss.

Skip now rests in the Escambia National Cemetery, in the company of many other heroes. Skip, you will not be forgotten.

~~~

## Chapter 23: *Weekend Warriors*

I left active duty and three days later began training with Continental Airlines. It was a radical transition. I was assigned to the Boeing 707/720 as a flight engineer, the #3 pilot in the cockpit. *How far I have fallen,* I thought. It was an easy job, but very boring, compared to the excitement of military flying. I was grateful that I could still fly F-8s in the Reserves.

At the end of my first year, the airline furloughed over 100 pilots from the bottom of the seniority list, including me. I had already begun flying with the Ready Reserves at NAS Dallas while I was working on an MBA, so I had plenty to keep me busy.

Among those furloughed by Continental was a close-knit group of former Miramar aviators from both the F-4 and F-8 communities. We compared job strategies, and decided to apply to go back on active duty. The air war in Vietnam had begun to heat up again, and the Navy belatedly realized it had lost too many junior officers to the airlines. This might be my opportunity to get a MIG!

One of my F-4 contemporaries, also an LSO, went back on active duty and became an air wing LSO on a big-deck carrier. Billy Foster was assigned to a plush tour at NAS Glynco, flying the T-39 Sabreliner (left) for training radar operators. John Sande, my Academy classmate, was assigned to the Pensacola Dilbert Dunker crew and the swimming pool as a lifeguard. Since our civilian jobs were protected by federal law, I decided to try my luck and apply for active duty.

I submitted an application for the temporary recall program to BUPERS. In a few weeks, I received a letter rejecting my application. I felt my qualifications were as good as the pilots who had been accepted, so I traveled back to BUPERS in the Washington area to review my file and to find out what had happened. What I found was amazing and a real insight into how the Navy hierarchy holds a grudge, not unlike a vicious ex-spouse.

When I arrived at BUPERS, I filled out a form requesting my file from the archives. After 45 minutes, an attractive female lieutenant walked in to the visitors' room and called my name. She looked very serious.

I introduced myself, and mentioned that I was trying to figure out why I had not been accepted back on active duty, when my contemporaries were. She said, "Well, your personnel jacket has a red flag on it."

"What is *that*? Some kind of special award?"

"It means the Navy considers you to be……well, a problem. The letter of resignation that you wrote was passed around to all of the Navy's senior admirals

233

to demonstrate why the junior pilots were leaving the Navy. They didn't like what you said, which resulted in your being 'flagged.'"

"I think *'flogged'* is more like it," I said. She smiled. It struck me as a little odd that you are required to state the reason for your resignation in the letter, but they really did not want to hear it, and got mad when they did. *When in doubt, kill the messenger.*

I sat down and read my Fitness Reports (performance evaluations), hoping to find some helpful material to use in getting back on active duty. Even with my escapades in the Red Lightnings, they were all excellent—until I got to the RAG pages. As expected, the RAG Skipper had really hammered me. He characterized me as "disloyal to the Naval Service, because he is a Naval Academy graduate and he has resigned from active duty." That was an odd rationale, particularly since this officer was *not* an Academy graduate. The stupid mistake I had made was to forget that I was no longer irreplaceable, as before. I was only another junior officer in the RAG. In fact, I gave away my leverage and ability to defend myself the minute I announced that I was (1) not going to be an LSO, and (2) not remaining on active duty. From those moments on, I was a "dead man walking."

I called my BUPERS detailer at the time and tried to get around the "flagged jacket" problem. Captain Harry Post, whom I knew from Miramar, was no help. He was always a very cautious politician, and never liked to make waves. He said, "My hands are tied. You really upset the top brass." Obviously, this was one of my special talents. I concluded that it was time to move on. I turned my attention to flying with the Reserves in Dallas.

VF-202 was a diverse group of aviators, each with thousands of flight hours, acquired in many different aircraft. Nearly all were airline pilots in their "day" job, and flew the F-8H at NAS Dallas as a sort of "flying club" activity. All of us were there for one reason—we all loved flying jets, and the F-8 in particular. The "H" model, flown by the Reserves, was now the best performing F-8 flying, while the active duty Fleet squadrons were forced to fly the treacherous and under-powered "J". Life is often full of ironies.

I reported in to VF-202, and walked into the ready room. It was another *déjà vu* moment. Although I did not know any of the pilots, they knew me. "Hey, guys, Hot Dog is here!" exclaimed the duty officer. As they introduced me to everyone, I was certain that this was going to be a good time. In retrospect, I have never been around a more likeable group of people than the pilots of VF-202.

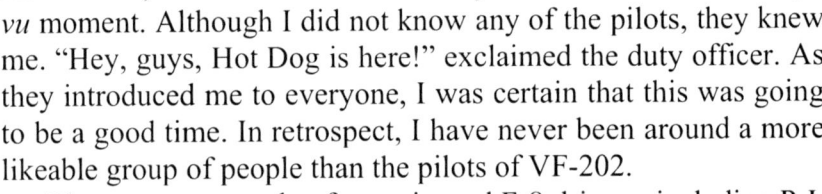

There were a couple of experienced F-8 drivers, including P.J. Smith and Ken Fox, but most had flown a different aircraft in the Fleet. They had transitioned to the F-8 to fly in the Dallas Reserves. One lieutenant commander was actually an inter-service transfer from the Air Force, where he had flown F-86s! Nevertheless, they all were experienced jet pilots.

During the *Pueblo* incident, this squadron had been called to active duty and was actually scheduled to be deployed on a carrier. They were very colorful when they first arrived at Miramar. They taxied in to their line after landing and simultaneously extended their fueling probes, each decorated with a Texas state flag. They got out of their aircraft wearing ten-gallon cowboy hats and cowboy boots. Every week, they flew cases of Lone Star beer in from Dallas for Happy Hour, and would not drink any other brand.

When the Navy tried to qualify the squadron on the carrier, several of the pilots had problems, especially at night. As one nervous pilot was sitting at full power on the catapult one night, ready for launch, the Air Boss announced on the radio that the squadron had just been deactivated and would be returning to Dallas. Without waiting for the catapult to be properly secured, he shut down the engine and jumped down to the flight deck. *No point in tempting fate. . . . . .*

After this experience, the Navy decided to enhance the Reserve capabilities with better aircraft, more flying time, and a requirement to maintain annual carrier qualifications. Now I understood why I was able to get into this squadron so easily, in spite of a long waiting list. They needed an LSO. *Here we go again.*

We soon deployed to MCAS Yuma for weapons training. After we returned, I decided I could contribute to the squadron's success if I picked up the LSO "paddles" again. Now I had come full circle—or had I just grown up a little?

For the next few months, we incorporated Field Carrier Landing Practice (FCLP) into the daily flight schedules. The squadron's performance was improving each month. Still, I had concerns about actual carrier landings for some of the pilots, who had few carrier landings in *any* aircraft. I had the most F-8 carrier landings in the squadron, so I felt it was up to me to get the squadron ready. Everyone was rusty at doing carrier landings, so we needed a lot of practice.

FCLP "bounces" are normally done at night, when there is less runway traffic. One spring night, it was my turn to get some practice from the cockpit. I took off with a light fuel load, and returned to the base traffic pattern, entering the break at about 300 knots

Just as I passed over the runway, the aircraft shook with a loud bang, followed by an engine FIRE light illuminating. Instinctively, I reached for the face curtain to eject. Then I realized that if I ejected, the aircraft would probably drop into the LTV factory complex to the west of the field. That would be newsworthy, because this is the factory that actually built the F-8.

Since the engine was still running, I kept one hand on the face curtain and flew the bird with the other. So far, so good. *I can make the runway,* I thought. I notified the tower that I had an emergency and a fire light. I then requested clearance for a full-stop and for fire equipment to meet me. "Roger, you are cleared to land. Fire trucks on the way!"

I popped the RAT in order to keep hydraulic pressure and electrical power if the engine quit. Maintaining 180 knots, I rolled onto final and aimed the nose at the end of the runway. Even if the engine quit, with this speed I could glide in to the runway—theoretically. Approaching the close-in position, I pulled the power to idle. I remembered the field runway was a relatively short 8,000', and I did not want to run off the other end of the runway onto the busy highway. I dropped the tail hook.

I braked the aircraft successfully to a slow speed, not needing an arrestment. I raised the tail hook, turned off the runway and shut down the engine. Our maintenance crew and the fire truck personnel immediately met me and helped me get out of the cockpit and secure the ejection seat safety pins.

The next day, after the maintenance crew had worked all night on the sick aircraft, they found that I had flown through a flock of night-flying ducks. Three had been sucked down the engine intake and damaged the compressor blades, which had caused the fire light. The engine was full of "roast duck," as the Chief put it. They found body parts of three ducks. I had two more strikes on the wing and tail, which gave me a total of five. The squadron declared me an "ace," and painted five little ducks below the cockpit of my aircraft. The maintenance chief estimated my engine would have failed in a matter of minutes. *Wonderful.* The next night, when I tried to catch up on my landings, I hit three more ducks! One of the pilots threatened to turn me in to the Audubon Society for excessive cruelty to birds. *Very funny.*

We qualified most of the pilots on the carrier, but it was obvious that the few flight hours authorized for Reserve squadrons were insufficient to maintain proficiency for carrier operations. I constantly worried about a carrier landing accident with our group, particularly if we had to do night landings. I was spending over two weeks per month with the Dallas squadron, trying to get all of our pilots proficient in carrier landing techniques.

During the winter of 1970-71, I continued training with the Dallas Reserves. This required commuting from where I lived in Los Angeles to Dallas. On one trip, I was in uniform. I shared a cab from the DFW airport to Dallas with a tall, older man in a cowboy hat. He introduced himself as "Joe Foss." Being a student of World War II history, I knew this was one of the top fighter pilots from that war. We immediately found common ground in talking about fighter aviation. I felt embarrassed because at the time, I did not know the full details of this man's incredible life. It is worth reviewing, because he is one of the greatest air warriors produced by our country in World War II.

Major Joe Foss (later a BGEN in the Air National Guard) racked up 26 Japanese kills with Guadalcanal's "Cactus Air Force" in the incredibly short period between October 1942 to January 1943. He was a master tactician and the leader of VMF-115's F-4F Wildcat flights, known as "Foss's Flying Circus." After receiving the Medal of Honor and doing a public relations tour back in the U.S., he returned to his squadron only to be stricken with malaria. He never again saw combat. After leaving active duty, he served in the South Dakota Air National Guard, the South Dakota legislature, and then won election as Governor.

Foss held various other positions, including Commissioner of the AFL, president of the National Rifle Association, and a stint as a TV sports commentator.

As the old warrior left the cab, he looked at me and said, "Fly safe, and check your six, son."

"Roger that, Sir," I replied.

This great fighter pilot, who is listed by the Marine Corps as its leading World War II ace with twenty-six kills (Pappy Boyington's twenty-eight kills included six from his tour with the Flying Tigers), died in 2003 at age 87. In his later life, Foss became friends with Japan's leading living ace, Saburo Sakai (64+ kills), with whom he

made several public appearances, recounting wartime experiences. If Joe Foss had been able to continue combat flying, he could have become the leading American ace of the war, surpassing P-38 jock Major Richard Bong's 40+ Japanese kills. *(below at left)*

The Marines had a Reserve squadron of F-8Ks at Dallas, and there was considerable animosity between the two Reserve communities. One of the Marine pilots considered himself to be the best dogfighter at the base, and during every

Happy Hour at the O'Club, was quick to announce this belief. We grew tired of hearing this noise, so we decided to turn the heat up a few notches.

The next week, I went over to the Navy Exchange on the base and bought a Marine khaki dress shirt, together with Marine captain bars and gold wings. I had the laundry press it to put in the three Marine regulation vertical creases in the back. Then we cut out large 20mm-size holes in the back, and painted them with simulated bloodstains. The less than subtle message was that we had shot down a Marine pilot.

Just before the next Happy Hour, we hung the shirt above the table that the Marines normally used. They came in, looked at the shirt, and then threatened a fight with the Navy pilots, including me. A burly man by the name of Smokey Tolbert ('62) separated the combatants before a punch was thrown. Smokey had been one of the solo pilots in the Blue Angeles before he left active duty to join the airlines. He missed the military flying and had gone back on active duty. He had flown a TA-4 in from the East Coast and was spending the night at Dallas.

Smokey said, "OK, boys. I'm neutral, because I am not from around here. If both sides will agree, we will settle this like true warriors. The Marines will pick their champion to represent them, and the Navy will pick theirs. We will get airborne tomorrow at 1000. I will be the official referee and observer in my TA-4, and will score the fights. The losing group will pay for an open bar for the winners at the next Happy Hour." Both sides agreed. The Marines picked their guy, and the Navy picked me.

The next day, we took off together and headed south to the normal operating area after obtaining FAA clearance. We separated at about 30,000' on parallel courses, and Smokey called "The fight is on!" from his TA-4. The Marine and I turned in toward each other. The important thing in a head-on engagement is to maintain your energy, and not let the opponent get any angle on you. The Marine knew this also. We met head-on, canopy to canopy at 1,200 knots closure and the high-g turns began. This guy was good. The first fight was called off when we reached 5,000', the minimum altitude for the joust. Neither of us had been able to work off any angle. No winner.

I won the next fight, using the Danish Roll, a displacement barrel roll to the outside of his turn radius. It was clear that if either of us got within 30 degrees angle off the opponent, it was going to end in a kill. The Marine won the last one when we both were low on fuel. Since he was flying a lighter F-8K, he staggered over the top of a severe vertical maneuver, and I was unable to follow him in my heavier "H". A rolling scissors resulted, and he carefully guarded his energy advantage. I finally had to break the "hard deck" of 5,000' to evade him, which resulted in a win for him.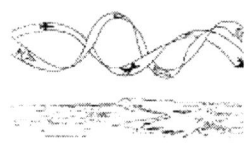

Smokey declared the overall joust a draw, at a score of 1-1-1. At the next Happy Hour, the two sides had more than a few drinks together, and the bitter rivalry was set aside, but only temporarily.

After two years of great flying and good times with the VF-202 pilots, I learned that two more F-8 Reserve squadrons were being activated at Miramar, my old home base. Somewhat reluctantly, I transferred to VF-302 at Miramar, which was closer to my Redondo Beach home. It would turn out to be a questionable decision, as politics and big egos dominated the two F-8H squadrons there. However, being a very diplomatic and humble guy, I expected to fit right in. After all, as you know by now, I try to bring harmony wherever I go. In the meantime, the Navy screwed up again. I made Lieutenant Commander!

~ ~ ~

## Chapter 24: *Back to Fightertown*

In those halcyon days of the F-8 Crusader, Miramar was to fighter pilots as Bethlehem is to Baptists, or Mecca is to Muslims. It was a cherished place where we learned our trade and established our reputations, good or bad. It was where the followers of this strange warrior culture called their home. I was glad to be back.

I checked in to VF-302, and found many familiar faces. Unlike the diverse backgrounds of the Dallas Reserve pilots, these pilots were purebred Crusader drivers, except for the XO. The Skipper, Bill Kiper, was a well-known presence in the F-8 community and was an expert tactician. In his "day job," he was a United Airlines pilot.

His XO was a "TAR" (Training and Administration of Reserves) officer, who had been an F-4 pilot. The XO had a high opinion of himself, having shot down a MIG in 1967 when attached to an F-4 squadron on the *Constellation*. Right away, I could see that there was considerable friction between him and the Skipper. There was no doubt that F-4 pukes and F-8 drivers saw the world through different lenses. As a person, I thought that the XO was actually very likeable. However, with his lack of time in the F-8, managing a squadron like this was an impossible assignment. He seemed constantly stressed out.

*CDR Bill Kiper*

Bill Kiper had amassed approximately 3,000 hours in the F-8, and had been flying it since the early Sixties. His tactical prowess in a dogfight was well known in the F-8 community. For his shore rotation, he had been assigned to the Miramar F-8 RAG as an instructor, during the time that Bill Conklin was receiving F-8 training, before reporting as the VF-194 XO.

One day, Kiper returned to the RAG ready room after an exciting practice dogfight with students. As usual, Kiper won. Peeling off his g-suit, he exclaimed, "What a great day! Flying the F-8 is better than *sex*!" Conklin was taking a sip of coffee nearby, and choked loudly when he heard this statement. Everyone looked at him.

Conklin always knew what to say, no matter what was happening. "Kiper, either *I* don't know how to *fly*, or *you* don't know how to *screw*!"

Spanky had left the Red Lightnings to join Northwest Airlines, and then was furloughed. He had gone back on active duty, and was now a TAR officer in the squadron. Another airline "refugee," Tom Corboy ('61), was also a highly credentialed F-8 driver and the third TAR. The TARs were the only active duty officers, and ran the squadron on a daily basis. The rest of the pilots were "weekend warriors" like me, with at least two combat cruises and hundreds of carrier landings in the F-8. Most were airline pilots.

This squadron, along with its Reserve sister squadron, VF-301, looked more like a group of handpicked RAG instructors than a typical Reserve squadron. Many of them were the same rebellious junior officers who had just left the RAG.

Like the squadrons in Dallas, nearly all the pilots worked for airlines in their "real" jobs. They were quite a crew, and displayed the typical F-8 squadron attitude. I decided to continue serving as an LSO, since we were slated to do carrier qualifications in the near future.

*A Navy F-4B--the "Phantom II"*

The XO was having big problems adjusting from the more orthodox behavior and culture of the F-4 community to the "screw you" attitude of the F-8 drivers. Remembering my experience with the culture clashes in the RAG between senior and junior officers, I could see that there was going to be big trouble—and I had just arrived!

One of the monumental dilemmas of many senior officers within the Naval Aviation community—especially in the combat air wings—was their ability to lead. The Marines, Surface Warfare, and Submarine Force officers grow up in a more structured command system with many early leadership assignments, while Naval Aviators tend to be more cloistered and operate separately, even from the enlisted men who maintain their aircraft. While the insignia and levels of rank gave the senior aviators the *authority* to be leaders, most pilots would not genuinely submit to their authority unless the senior officer *earned* their respect.

For below-average officers and marginal pilots at the senior levels, leading a squadron or air wing in an operational environment demanded more than they had to give. Some could not measure up. When those officers were placed in command positions within the F-8 community, conflict was inevitable. The Crusader pilot's attitude is well defined by the unofficial Crusader Pilot's Creed:

> **I am a United States Navy Crusader pilot. My life is dedicated to protecting the skies of America between sunrise and sunset. Nothing shall deter me from performing my duty except clouds, darkness, or lack of wind. My country has invested in me the faith of its people, by**

training me to fly faster while doing less than any other pilot in the world. I shall always do my utmost, provided the weather is clear, to ensure that this sacred trust has not been placed in vain. I shall never forget, nor allow anyone in my general area to forget that:
- I can fly 1,000 miles per hour.
- I can carry a Sidewinder missile.
- My wing goes up and down.

I do hereby solemnly swear to observe faithfully the following code of professional ethics:

1. Whenever Naval Aviators congregate in drinking establishments, I shall conduct myself in a loud and obnoxious manner, especially if less fortunate pilots of low-performance aircraft are present.
2. While deployed (and not yet off-loaded), I shall strive to maintain the long-cherished tradition of daylight fighter pilots by attending every nightly movie, regardless of whether I can follow the plot.
3. I shall not permit interruptions of occasional flights to prevent me from maintaining my proficiency in Acey Deucy at fighter pilot standards.
4. I shall never go ashore without my F8 lapel pin and my F8 baseball cap.
5. I will not bolter.
6. If I should bolter, I will have readily available an assorted variety of colorful excuses.
7. I will wear my space suit and helmet for all air shows, Dependents' Day cruises, and those operational flights which do not require any movement in the cockpit (providing someone helps me in and out of the airplane).

This is my Creed and these are my ideals. With the help of God and my afterburner, I shall do my best to justify the confidence that has been placed in me, even if I have to fly during lunchtime.

The XO decided it was his mission in life to make the squadron conform to his notion of a proper behavioral model. As many senior officers had learned the hard way, you cannot "herd cats," and you cannot make F-8 drivers act like officers and gentlemen. He went on a tirade about spilling coffee in the ready room and putting feet on the furniture, both of which are part of standard F-8 pilot behavior. He finally published a set of rules for ready-room conduct, which instantly made him the squadron joke. Some disrespectful prankster, who shall remain anonymous, published an alternative set of rules for ready room etiquette and placed them on a large sign on the ready-room wall:

"The following rules are hereby promulgated by the XO, effective immediately. Rules for conduct in the squadron ready room:
- No beverages are permitted, unless they contain alcohol
- No placing feet on furniture, especially the XO's chair

- **No laughing and scratching**
- **No talking with hands**
- **No bull-shit story telling**
- **No slanderous remarks about F-4 pilots and their manhood**
- **No comments about senior officer erectile dysfunction**
- **No urinating in the XO's coffee cup**
- **No flatulating or belching during the All-Officers Meetings**
- **In addition, there will be no promotions, leaves, or liberty granted until the morale improves."**

As police Captain Renault (Claude Rains) said in *Casablanca*, "Round up the usual suspects." Naturally, I was unfairly accused of producing this fake set of rules, but there were no witnesses and the sign had been wiped clean of fingerprints. The sign was removed, by order of the XO. This became another joke within the squadron, similar to the hilarious strawberries incident in *The Caine Mutiny* or the palm tree scene in *Mr. Roberts*.

After his experience of flying the stable F-4, assisted by an RIO in the back  seat, the XO had difficulty flying the unpredictable F-8 to the edge of its flight envelope, where a dangerous spin was always waiting. This was understandable, because he had the lowest number of F-8 hours out of all of the squadron pilots. During our impromptu dogfighting, he was usually ravaged by his more experienced opponents, which the junior officers enjoyed.

There were also deliberately offensive discussions in his presence about the many inadequacies of F-4 pilots, who "needed a guy in the back seat to help them fly." Instead of calling the big birds F-4s or Phantoms, the junior officers would refer to them, because of their two engines, as "double-barreled shit cans" and their pilots as "multi-motor pukes." Some even made nasty comments to the XO, like "How in hell did *you* ever get a MIG?" The XO would become visibly angry at these insults, but they continued unabated. We noticed with amusement that he kept a bottle of Mylanta handy on his desk. With a little luck, the junior officers hoped to give him an ulcer. Sometimes, but not often, I actually felt sorry for him.

One of the problems I noticed in the F-8 Reserves was aircraft maintenance. The maintenance departments in Miramar Reserve squadrons were not staffed adequately, and aircraft readiness was often the victim. In addition, the Navy was planning the phase-out of the F-8, which meant spare parts were increasingly difficult to obtain.

I personally found out how bad this situation had become in two incidents. In the first, I was out dogfighting with Spanky over the water when I heard a loud *bang* in the engine. Looking in my rear-view mirrors, I could see that I was trailing black smoke, suggesting that the engine was coming apart.

I told Spanky I had an emergency and was heading back to Miramar. He said, "Yeah, you're smokin' bad, Dog." I was lucky, because it was a clear day and I could see Miramar easily from 30 miles out. The important thing was to move the throttle as little as possible to avoid unnecessary stresses to the engine, so I reduced power to a conservative 80% for the approach.

I decided to shoot a precautionary, high-speed approach with the RAT out, in case the engine quit. The area around Miramar was heavily populated, and I did not want to be flying a pattern where an ejection would drop the aircraft into a residential area. I asked the tower for a non-standard, right downwind leg with a

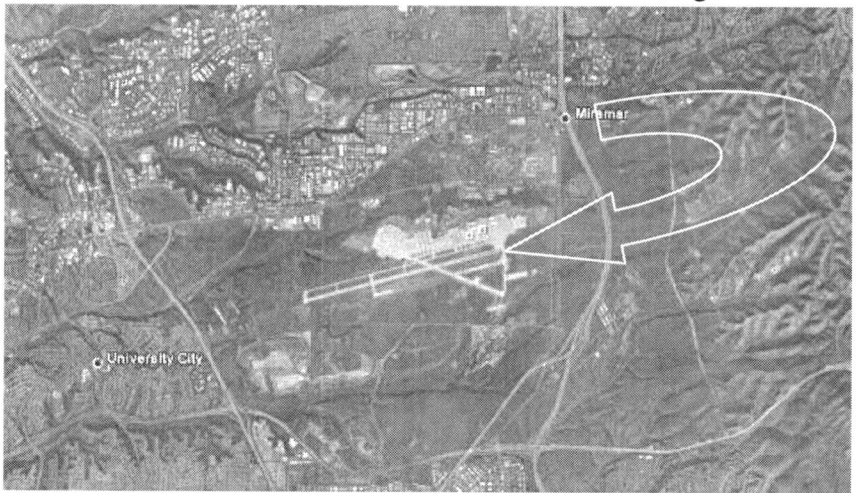

right turn to runway 24R, the long runway. If I had to eject, this would give me slightly more of a chance to aim the dead bird at the mountainous area northeast of the field, and across the freeway. Crossing the freeway on an easterly heading, I extended the landing gear and raised the wing. I turned right at around 190 knots, and dropped the tail hook to engage the field arresting gear.

After crossing the freeway out of the turn, I went to idle power and allowed the aircraft to decelerate in a glide. I touched down and then caught the arresting gear, stopping abruptly. The fire trucks surrounded me. *Wow, that was fun!* I got a ride back to the squadron, as the maintenance crew hooked up a tug to the aircraft. I learned later the engine had spit out a few turbine blades, and was definitely going to fail in a matter of minutes. In nearly 2,000 hours in the F-8, this was the first time, other than the Dallas duck ingestion, that I had ever experienced a problem of any kind with the reliable Pratt & Whitney J-57 engine. As one of my friends said, "Roll those dice enough times, and you will eventually get snake eyes."

The second incident nearly got me. One of the aircraft had just come back from an overhaul at the re-work facility. I was assigned to fly the customary test flight, which is usually a non-event. It was always fun to have an F-8 all to yourself for a couple of hours.

After looking the bird over carefully, I started up, completed post-start checks, and taxied out for takeoff. *Looking good so far.* When cleared for takeoff, I stood on the brakes and ran the engine up to 100%, making the bird squat down on the nose gear, rearing to go. Everything looked good, so I released the brakes and hit afterburner.

At 125 knots, I rotated the nose. I noticed a pull to the left. I wondered, *Where did that wind gust come from?* As the main gear wheels lifted from the runway, I raised the gear and lowered the wing. Then all hell broke loose.

The aircraft started rolling uncontrollably to the left, and I could not stop the roll with *full* right stick deflection. At only 100' above the ground, it was time to make an instantaneous decision—eject, or try to regain control. There would be no second chance if I picked the wrong answer. I knew that an ejection would drop this bird, full of jet fuel, into the University City residential area west of the field.

I always used a lot of rudder in tactically maneuvering the F-8, which was one of The Buzzard's unorthodox tricks. Instinctively, I jammed the right (top) rudder, and the aircraft slowly rolled wings level. As the speed increased, I gained more control. I notified the tower that I had an emergency flight control problem, and that I would be returning for a precautionary approach and field arrested landing after I dumped fuel.

Playing the rudder and using full right stick and aileron trim, I flew out over the water. Now I could eject without dropping the aircraft into a residential area. I climbed to about 8,000' and started experimenting to find out where the loss of control would occur. In the "clean," or cruise configuration, I lost control at about 210 knots When I went "dirty," dropping the gear and raising the wing, I found that I had to fly above 175 knots to maintain control, about 35 knots above normal approach speed.

When the high-wing F-8 is in flight, the pilot cannot see what the ailerons are doing. This made it impossible to diagnose the problem, other than to know there was a serious flight control failure of some sort.

After dumping most of my fuel over the water, I proceeded back to Miramar. This time, I made a very wide and deep approach to avoid losing lateral control in the turn. When activated, the F-8 RAT pops out on the right side of the fuselage, where the airflow drives the little turbine. Although I did not anticipate needing the RAT for this type of emergency, I figured it would produce a certain amount of additional lateral drag on the right side, inducing a yaw to the right. This would give me some additional control to counter the tendency to roll left.

*Gear down, wing up, RAT out, tail hook down.* When lined up on final, I had to jam the stick full right and push full right rudder to keep the wings level. My mind was racing, as I tried to figure out how I was going to slow down enough to land, without making an uncontrolled left roll into the concrete runway. Although The Buzzard had been one of my heroes, I did not want to end up as he did, grinding my head off on the runway.

As I got down to short final, I became aware of a number of crash vehicles with flashing lights near the runway arresting gear. I knew I had to catch a wire in order to stop, and until then I had to stay fast enough to keep control. Otherwise, the aircraft would roll over on its left side.

I eased the sick Crusader to a point just above the runway, and added power to hold the minimum control speed, which now appeared to be about 160 knots. I watched the runway markers go by, and then spotted the wire ahead. *Time to commit!* If I missed the wire, I would go off the end of the runway, with probably fatal results. It would be impossible to go around for another try. *Roll the friggin' dice, Hot Dog!* I sawed the power to  idle, and gently pushed the aircraft down where the wheels were slightly above the runway. Just as it started to roll left, I caught the wire and was jerked to a stop.

After a ride back to our hangar in a crash vehicle, I told the maintenance crew I was not leaving the area until I knew what had caused the control failure. After about 45 minutes, the Chief found me. "Hot Dog, I don't know how to tell you this. I feel terrible."

"Let's hear it, Chief. What was it?"

"It seems that the overhaul facility left out some control link components, which finally jammed and completely disabled the left aileron. Then the linkage to the *right* aileron was partially jammed! We didn't notice it on our pre-flight checks because it probably was still working and looked normal. You could roll left, but not right. I don't know how you kept your wings level!"

"Because of a guy named Buzzard, Chief. I'll tell you about it sometime."

When the Reserve Air Wing CAG sent the squadron and me a personal "well done" message, I noticed the XO reaching for his Mylanta bottle. The last thing he wanted was for the CAG to be on my side.

The squadron gathered one Saturday morning for the monthly "drill weekend," for which all hands were supposed to show up.  Driving down from Los Angeles, I was late because of traffic. I zoomed down the base road from the west gate, trying to make muster on time. The base police caught me on radar, and followed me in their police truck with their lights flashing.

I turned into the squadron parking lot, with my surfboards on the roof rack of my vehicle. I could not find a parking place, and orbited the lot several times, with the police truck escort close behind me. I noticed that the squadron was standing in formation next to the parking lot, with the Skipper standing out front, watching my version of O.J. Simpson's slow-speed Bronco chase around the parking lot. I finally found a spot, and got out of the car. The cops stopped and approached me. "Sir, we clocked you at 70 in a 45 mph zone," the base cop said.

Remembering my Red Lightning training, which always called for taking the offense, I said, "Actually, I was going *quite* a bit faster. Be advised, Officer, that our squadron is responding to an emergency national security directive, and I was ordered to get down here from Los Angeles, as a key member of this important unit. [Snickering from nearby formation.] If you look over there, you can see the squadron has been called in and is waiting in formation for further orders from the chain-of-command. They are also waiting for me to brief them on certain highly classified information. I could tell you what it is, but then I would have to kill you. Time is of the essence, and I need to get over there ASAP! Wasn't your security unit notified about this?" [More snickering.]

"Oh! Sorry, Sir....I didn't know," said the base cop. I was hoping he did not notice the giggling and obscene middle-finger hand signals coming from the adjacent squadron ranks.

"Quite all right, Officer, you were doing your job, and doing it damned well," I added. "Who is your boss? I would like to send over a commendation letter for you and your partner here."

"Why, thank you, Sir!"

"No problem. We need more good people like you, because things may get a little sticky around here. Now, Williams [reading his name tag], I need to get over there with the squadron and see what is going on, OK?"

"Yes, Sir. Sorry to have delayed you. I hope your mission goes well," said Williams.

"Thanks for that, Officer. Take care." Williams saluted and left in his police truck. I never got a ticket for speeding. I slipped into ranks with the XO glaring daggers at me.

The XO could hardly wait to pounce on me and get even. His opportunity arrived when early one morning, I discovered I had been switched on the schedule to fly the night hop. The XO insisted that the officers sign in and out on a ready room status board. Since I did not need to be at the squadron until evening, I signed out by my name: "GONE SURFING." *It's always better to be honest. [Career tip!]*

I changed into my swim trunks and drove with my surfboards to Black's Beach in La Jolla, also known for its nude female beach-goers. The waves were

perfect, as was the beach scenery between waves. However, I did not realize that an All-Officers Meeting had been convened in my absence. It would have been nice if they had given me an RSVP invitation, which is only common courtesy.

My absence was noticed, along with my sign-out note. The XO had caught me red-handed, SWOL (surfing without leave).

*After catching a few good waves, there is nothing like taking a ride in a Crusader. Surfing is very much like flying. This was a custom surfboard by Mike Eaton, master board shaper of the famous Bing surfboard company. It was a great board, which I named "Excalibur," after King Arthur's magic sword. Like the F-8, its superior design got me out of many dangerous situations. A few months after this photo was taken, the two of us were hit in a "close-out" by a monster wave at Hermosa Beach, breaking the board neatly in half. There is a lesson here somewhere. . . . .*

I returned to Miramar, changed into my flight suit, and went to the Navy Exchange for dinner. I saw two of our TARs, Tom Corboy and Spanky, going through the line.

They both started laughing. "What's so funny?" I asked.

"Hot Dog," said Spanky, "I have some good news and some bad news. Which do you want first?"

"Hmmmm....I'll try the good news," I replied.

"Dog, you are *not* going to night fly," said Spanky with a grin. Happy visions of the wild O'Club Bar, known as the W0X0F Room, danced through my head.

"Fantastic! So what's the bad news?"

"Hot Dog, for missing the All-Officers Meeting, the XO has placed you in hack in the BOQ for the entire weekend, and you are grounded."

Well, you *know* what I am going to say. This is starting to become a pattern, or as Yogi Berra said, like *déjà vu* all over again, or like Bill Murray experienced in *Groundhog Day*. I had finally achieved the impossible. I was in a category all by myself. I had become the only Reservist *in history* to be put in hack, going all the way back to the Revolutionary War! That should be worth some kind of medal or award.

The next morning, I called the squadron from my cruel imprisonment in the BOQ and spoke with the XO. When you are dealing with senior officers [*Career tip!*], it is always advisable to get the day off to a good start. I decided to turn on my charm, which was always irresistible. "Goo-o-o-o-d morning, XO," I said cheerily.

"What do *you* want, Hot Dog?"

"Well, I have an administrative question."

"OK, what is it?"

"XO, am I getting paid for my time in hack?" The phone went dead. I suspect he needed another bottle of Mylanta after that.

Shortly after this sordid episode, the entire air wing did carrier qualifications. The Air Wing LSO was really into metrics, and he set up a numerical grading system to rank every pilot in the air wing on the carrier landings. He then published the names of each pilot in the air wing, with his numerical grade. To the XO's chagrin, he was ranked *last* in the squadron, and I was ranked *first* in the entire air wing. Being an LSO and having a few hundred carrier landings in the Crusader is very helpful. Now the XO *really* had me on his target list. As I used to tell my ex-wife, *It's better to be hated than ignored.*

The active duty squadrons at Miramar became increasingly aware of the incredible talent and experience we had in the two F-8 Reserve squadrons. Even Top Gun and the F-4 RAG began using us for "dissimilar aircraft" opponents in their tactics training. The MIG-21 and the F-8 had performance similarities which made for a good, realistic dogfight practice for the newbies. In addition, our F-8

Reserve pilots were often former RAG instructors and/or MIG killers, which made the dogfights even more exciting for the students.

It seems the Air Force heard about our Weekend Warriors, and wanted to introduce some of their pilots to more realistic training. One day, a half-dozen F-106s from Minot AFB arrived with their support crew. We briefed with them and launched a section of F-8s against a section of F-106s on each flight. It was fun to watch these big delta-wing birds trying to do orthodox "by the book" section tactics against our freelancing, "wolf pack" style of fighting.

On one of the flights, I launched with the VF-301 XO, Commander Ren "Hornet" Stedman, an excellent driver. I had a tape recorder hooked up to my radio so that we could debrief the pilots after the flight. This would turn out to be an important coincidence.

The GCI (radar) controller set us up with about 50 miles separation in the area between San Diego and San Clemente Island. He then vectored the two sections toward each other for a head-on engagement. The "knock-off" altitude was 10,000'. We noticed that a low cloud deck blanketed the entire area, which was normal for this time of year in the San Diego coastal zone.

We picked up the F-106 section on our radars at about 30 miles. They were flying in a loose tactical wing, while we were in the more flexible Combat Spread. At about eight miles, the fun began.

"Hornet, tally-ho, 10 o'clock level, break left!" I called. We hit burner and pulled into a climbing left turn, waiting for the 106s to commit. Their leader called a break and they turned hard into us, which spit the wingman to the outside of their turn, pulling hard and decelerating in order to stay with his leader.  The smart move would have been for the wingman to extend a few seconds, and then pitch up over the top in a slant loop, which would have put him behind us. However, this maneuver requires teamwork and coordination, because the leader must be prepared to quickly reverse and cover his wingman if the attackers do a switch.

In about two turns, our alternating attacks wore down the wingman and he radioed, "OK, you got me. Knock it off." Being in a continuous hard turn across the circle from us, the leader never was able to get back into the fight. That is why it is necessary to do a separation and re-entry maneuver over the top of "the bubble," defined by the turns of the engaged aircraft. The GCI controller then took the sections apart for another engagement.

On the next engagement, the wingman tried to extend and loop back behind us, thinking we were focused on his leader. The instant that we saw him detach and extend for separation, we did a "head fake" toward the leader to keep him turning and pretended to press the attack for a few seconds. After a few degrees of turn, we let the leader continue his decelerating turn and then we quickly reversed to go after the wingman instead. We caught him in our sights at the top of his vertical. "You're *dead,* Number Two—guns, guns, guns!" said Hornet. We pulled back around and attacked the leader, who, having lost sight of us, was out of energy and lasted only a few more turns. The leader's voice on the radio suggested that they were getting very frustrated. When you fly fighters and get frustrated, you will usually do something stupid.

As we detached again, heading south toward the Coronados Islands, I looked back and spotted the wingman diving his 106 at high speed behind us. He apparently was trying to gain an overtake speed, so he could fly up our six and claim a kill, even though the fight had been called off.

We later speculated that this young pilot misinterpreted the cloud deck below to have plenty of "air" between him and the water. Where this squadron was based in the Midwest, you do not see low surface cloud decks like we had around Southern California. This caused him to misread his altimeter.

The wingman punched into the low cloud deck in a steep dive, going at least 500 knots As he entered the clouds, he radioed, "F-8s, I'm lost in the clouds. . . ." That was his last transmission. The controller called "lost contact" and the wingman no longer responded on the radio. He impacted the water in a near-vertical dive at around 600 knots. The aircraft completely disintegrated and he was killed instantly.

We set up a SAR (search and rescue) orbit. Hornet went below the overcast and located the debris field. I stayed high to relay information to the controller, who had already launched a helo from North Island. When the helo arrived, there was little more than an oil slick. The helo crew dropped their basket and fished out some pieces, including a piece of the pilot's helmet. This was all that was left of him. The helo advised us the crash site was swarming with big sharks, so they could not put a diver in the water.

The Air Force reacted predictably, and convened a formal accident board. Stedman and I had to testify, and the tape, which corroborated our description of events, was confiscated by the board. We learned that the lost pilot had a wife and several kids. We felt very bad for his family and squadronmates. In my opinion, the accident was caused by obvious pilot error, but there was a larger problem. The Air Force did not allow its fighter pilots to practice dogfighting without imposing excessive safety rules. That is over-protective and not a realistic combat environment. It leaves the pilots vulnerable to basic mistakes when they do it for real, such as occurred with the lost 106. They failed to heed the words of Karl von Clausewitz: "To secure peace is to prepare for war."

Dogfighting in a jet fighter is more like a rough contact sport than a "professional" activity, if done correctly. It is violent, physically and mentally intensive, and requires situational awareness at all times. If you do it any other way, you will inevitably kill *yourself* or someone will kill *you.*

While still flying at Miramar, I learned of a great story involving World War II fighter pilots. During the Pacific War, a Navy F-6F pilot was flying fighter cover on a strike near the Japanese fortress of Rabaul. He caught a Japanese Zero

pilot looking the other way, and fired his guns on a belly-side deflection shot, hitting the Zero in the engine oil cooler. The Zero's engine stopped, and the pilot ditched in the water. The Navy pilot watched him swim ashore, apparently to his own lines. The aircraft sank in shallow water.

*Navy F-6F Hellcat*

The Navy pilot made a promise to himself. If he ever had the funds, he vowed to come back, salvage the Zero, and return it to the U.S. In fighter aviation, it is not often you are able to retrieve one of your kills for a souvenir.

In the early Seventies, this retired pilot had acquired the money to hire a salvage crew and retrieve the Zero that he had shot down some thirty-five years before. The Zero was located, placed on a barge and inspected. It was in excellent shape, considering it had been submerged in salt water for so many years.

The old veteran shipped his prize back to San Diego, where it was cleaned of sea growth and beautifully restored. The original paint job and squadron markings were still visible when I saw it at Miramar.

*Mitsubishi A-6 "Zero"*

He then had a great idea. He would contact the Japanese Defense Ministry and find the pilot whom he had shot down, if the man was still alive. In a few weeks, using a few U.S. Navy and diplomatic contacts, the Zero's pilot was located in Japan. The Navy pilot traveled to meet him and tell him that his old Zero was at Miramar. The two of them came up with the idea of bringing the two leading aces from each side (who were still living) to Miramar to see the Zero: David McCampbell, U.S. Navy, 34 kills; and Saburo Sakai, Japanese Navy, 64+ kills. According to what I was told, the four had their picture taken, standing in front of the salvaged Zero. I have never been able to locate this photograph, which would be a priceless collector's item to serious "war bird" fans, including me.

I was able to get permission to climb up on the Zero and sit in its cockpit. All of the instruments were identifiable, even after years under water. It was truly amazing to realize this primitive little aircraft, with its cramped cockpit, struck terror in the Allies throughout the Pacific in World War II.

Like the Germans in World War II, the Japanese kept their aces flying, usually until they *died*. Unlike the Americans, they did not pull their pilots back to the homeland for public relations and war bond tours. This is the main reason for the comparatively high numbers of kills amassed by the German and Japanese aces. They did not limit their pilots on combat exposure.

Japan's leading ace overall was Tetsuzō Iwamoto (right), with 94 kills. He survived the war, but because the Occupation Forces Command considered him unrepentant and a pro-militarist, he was blackballed from employment in post-war Japan. He died in 1955, bitter and impoverished, after complications with appendicitis. Unlike Sakai and other Japanese aces, he never had any interest in befriending his American counterparts. Some warriors carry their feelings to the grave.

David McCampbell ('33) was a junior pilot aboard *USS Wasp* and an LSO. Pictured here in his Naval Academy photo, and then waving aircraft during operations off Guadalcanal, he survived the sinking of the *Wasp*. He later formed VF-15 as its CO, and then served as Air Wing 15 CAG aboard *USS Essex,* flying the dependable Grumman F-6F.

McCampbell scored 34 confirmed kills. He still holds the record for the number of kills in a single flight. During operations in 1944, he shot down *seven* Japanese aircraft in one flight, then *nine more* in a subsequent flight.

Before his 1960 retirement as a captain, he commanded *USS Bon Homme Richard*. He died in 1996. During his career, he received the Medal of Honor, the Navy Cross, the Silver Star, the Legion of Merit, the Distinguished Flying Cross (3 awards) and the Air Medal, among other decorations.

Excellence in fighter aviation knows no national boundaries. In the bitterly contested conflict of World War II, every major nation—including our adversaries, Japan and Germany—had its own fighter aces and treated them as celebrities and heroes. After the conflict, many of them became friends and shared their wartime experiences. For others, their hatred of a former enemy would not go away.

*The photo above includes two of Japan's top aces in the famous Tainan Air Group: Saburo Sakai (64+ kills) [second from left, second row] and Hiroyoshi Nishizawa (87 kills) [last row, on left]. This elite group provided fighter escort for the 12/8/41 destruction of MacArthur's air force on Clark Field, Philippines, and then flew long-range raids from Rabaul to fight the Americans' "Cactus Air Force" on Guadalcanal, a 1,000-mile trip. Although these were naval aviators, most of their flying was land-based during the war.*

Of all the German Luftwaffe aces of World War II, one young pilot became legendary for his partying lifestyle, as well as his brilliant flying. Hans-Joachim Marseille was considered one of the most expert marksmen in the Luftwaffe, as well as a tactical genius. In only two years, he amassed 158 Allied kills, including eight in one flight, and 17 in one day. However, because of his rebellious attitude, he was given a disciplinary transfer from France to North Africa.

His squadron CO, Eduard Neumann, remembered: "His hair was too long and he brought with him a list of disciplinary punishments as long as your arm. Of the seven kills he had claimed fighting along the English Channel, four had not been confirmed – a large percentage. On top of it all, he was a Berliner [party boy]… In trying to create an image, he wasn't averse from talking about the many girls he had been to bed with, among them a famous actress. He was tempestuous, temperamental and unruly. Thirty years later, he would have been called a playboy." Nevertheless, Neumann quickly recognized Marseille's potential as a pilot. He stated in an interview: "Marseille could only [become] one of two [things]—either a disciplinary problem or a great fighter pilot."

If he had personal problems, flying fighters was not one of them. Marseille was awarded the Knight's Cross with Oak Leaves, Swords, and Diamonds (roughly equivalent to our Medal of Honor) by age 22. In one month, he shot down more than 50 Allied aircraft. After receiving early promotions, he was killed in September 1942, while trying to bail out of a Messerschmitt Bf-109G, an aircraft prone to engine failures. It was his personal aircraft, "Yellow 14."

The Luftwaffe aces who survived World War II have often speculated that if he had lived through the war, Marseille might have become the leading ace of all time, a title eventually claimed by his Luftwaffe contemporary, Erich Hartmann.

Saburo Sakai flew the formidable Japanese Navy Zero (Mitsubishi A-5 and A-6) in combat from 1938-1945, having enlisted at age 16. He is credited with at least 64 kills (mostly American), while some historians believe his total victories could be as high as 100. The Japanese did not keep official kill records.

After the war, he ran a successful printing business. As often happens with fighter pilots, he became friends with former enemy aces from the U.S., including Joe Foss. In the post-war years, Sakai strongly condemned the Japanese decision-makers who sent him and his fellow citizens to war. His personal credo was "Never give up."

Pursuing a family research project that spanned two generations of warriors, a retired Army Colonel and West Point graduate (Class of '57), Francis R. Stevens, Jr., was searching for information on his father's death in World War II. I fully understand Colonel Stevens' motivation for this research, because I experienced the same determination to learn the details of my own father's death in that war.

His father, Lt. Col. Francis R. Stevens, had been sent to the Pacific theater in 1942 to review the Allied resources on behalf of General George Marshall. While flying as an observer in a B-26 on a bombing raid on the Japanese base at Lae, New Guinea, Lt. Col. Stevens' aircraft was shot down by a Japanese Zero. From information supplied by an author-researcher in 1964, the younger Stevens learned that the pilot of that Zero was Saburo Sakai. A future President, Lyndon Johnson, would have also been an observer on the fatal flight, but his aircraft had a mechanical problem that scrubbed him from the mission.

In 1987, following his retirement, Colonel Stevens had a chance meeting in Yakima, Washington, with Saburo Sakai. The famous ace was in the U.S. as a VIP guest at an air show. Through translators, the two confirmed that Sakai indeed had shot down the elder Stevens' B-26, which carried the logo "Wabash Cannonball." Sakai apologized profusely, but the two men knew each combatant was doing his duty for his country at the time. Colonel Stevens had now met and spoken with the man who had killed his father.

During their discussion, Stevens told Sakai that his daughter was training to be a pilot in the U.S. Air Force. Sakai was delighted. He brought out his old flying scarf, which he actually wore throughout his years in combat, including the shoot-down of Stevens' father. Stevens described the scene in his article, *My Father and I and Saburo Sakai,* which he completed July 10, 1998:

> With that, he took the tattered scarf and tore from it a piece, which he handed to me. I was instructed to give it to my daughter and tell her to carry it with her whenever she flew—that, if she did so, whatever gods there be would surely protect her from any possible danger in the air. With this, the poor interpreter was once again reduced to uncontrollable tears—but at that point, I don't think that there was a dry eye in the room.
>
> My daughter still carries this most powerful of talismans; and, while I am still not much of a believer in things supernatural, I rest much easier when she is flying, knowing that she has that simple scrap of silk with her.

*Col. Francis R. Stevens, Jr. and Saburo Sakai.*

Colonel Stevens closed his family's chapter of historic coincidence with this moving quote: *"Rest quietly now, most honorable warrior. You did your duty, in war and in peace."* It is not clear whether Colonel Stevens intended this tribute for his father, or Saburo Sakai—or both of them.

In 2000, Saburo Sakai died of a sudden heart attack at a dinner in Atsugi, Japan, two years after the Stevens article was written. At that moment, he was shaking hands with an American pilot.

I started to realize that my own fighter pilot days were coming to a close. In October, 1972, the first F-14 Tomcats began to arrive at Miramar, replacing some F-8 and F-4 squadrons. By the spring of 1974, I had been flying Navy aircraft for nearly ten years. The Reserves were notified that the Miramar squadrons would be transitioned from the F-8 to the F-4 Phantom.

My job with Continental was going well at the time, and I foolishly did not see the need to continue with the Reserves, which was a big mistake. I have since learned one of life's important lessons—when you have something of special value, you should not give it up easily. In May of 1974, I resigned from the  Reserves and returned irreversibly to civilian life. Within the short span of the next 13 years, I would become a labor negotiator with the pilot union; see Continental go into bankruptcy; go to law school at UCLA; and become a litigator of multi-million dollar cases. My life's trajectory continued in the fast lane. However, I later regretted my decision to sever my ties with Naval Aviation. If I learned a lesson by my hasty decision, it is this: When you make big decisions, keep focused on the "forest" and ignore the "trees."

My relationship with my family continued to deteriorate. My half-sister, nine years younger than I, was even more neurotic than my mother. She was an obnoxious, temperamental child and not pleasant to be around. She took after Stepfather Ted, and I felt no bond between us. As the years went by, she sent me a series of hateful letters, accusing me of "abandoning the family" and other perceived shortcomings as a brother and son. Sometimes, wars tend to get in the way of such things.

Finally realizing that Stepfather Ted and his family were on a different track, I stopped communicating with all of them, including my mother. Mom had made her choice, and now she had to live with it. I wished them well, and told them never to contact me again.

Although I could no longer fly the F-8, I found the next best place to pick a fight—a *courtroom*. A court battle is no different from a dogfight, and sometimes it is even more violent. During my career as a lawyer, some old fighter pilot rules also applied by analogy in the courtroom arena:

--Don't run out of gas [or evidence];
--Don't land gear up [Do your checklist!];
--Check your six frequently [Be aware of what your opponent is doing!];
--Maintain situational awareness at all times [Watch the judge and jury!];
--Strike the enemy when and where they least expect it; and
--The first guy to land a well-aimed shot usually wins.

Now is the time to look back and reflect. My family's legacy had now gone full-circle. In later life, a time inevitably arrives in which you must evaluate your successes and failures, and decide what should be inscribed on your headstone. Have you lived your life in a manner that shall cause you to be missed? Or will your passing be a relief to those who knew you?

~ ~ ~

*The United States of America*
*honors the memory of*

WENDEL J. A. NELSON

*This certificate is awarded by a grateful nation in recognition of devoted and selfless consecration to the service of our country in the Armed Forces of the United States.*

*Lyndon B. Johnson*
*President of the United States*

# Chapter 25: *American Fratricide—Why Does the Eagle Eat Her Young?*

For any living species, one of the most barbaric and disgusting acts is cannibalism. Close behind in the ranking of despicable conduct is the vicious killing of one's own kind, without justification. This is even truer when the human species is involved. Instinctively, all rational people know this. For those directly involved in the mortal combat of a war, their religious beliefs and moral systems are often stressed to the breaking point, as they must sometimes do the unthinkable. Killing, for most people, is neither a normal nor a desirable activity, and it usually leaves deep, emotional scars on those who must do it.

Sometimes the most cold-blooded and hideous acts are committed by those in positions of authority, who should know better. In the background of normal military operations, one often finds that government and military organizations may pursue strange objectives under the rubric of "national security." From time to time, the senior members of the U.S. military and civilian government have shown a tendency to experiment with the lives and health of our citizens, without their knowledge or permission. Three horrendous examples, out of many, prove my point.

## *Tuskegee, Alabama—a place of national pride and shame*

Between 1932 and 1972, the U.S. Public Health Service ("PHS") conducted a secret medical study on about 400 African-American civilians in Alabama, which came to be known as "The Tuskegee Syphilis Experiment." In a completely unrelated activity, another branch of our government—the Army Air Force—was concurrently conducting its own strange experiment in the Tuskegee area. It was similarly entitled "The Tuskegee Experiment," and its objective was to determine *whether Blacks could fly airplanes*. Sometimes the truth *is* stranger than fiction.

The stated purpose of the Tuskegee medical experiment was to track the progress of syphilis in human subjects, and to document and study the effects of this ultimately fatal disease. It specifically called for *denying* the infected subjects the life-saving antibiotics that could have cured the disease, giving them placebos instead, and not informing them of the devastating symptoms and prognosis. The government sacrificed these human "guinea pigs" without their knowledge or voluntary consent to such a suicidal program. This is one of the most outrageous breaches of medical and governmental ethics in American history. Even if such a horrific experiment could somehow be justified, which is doubtful, it is noteworthy that only Blacks were targeted.

While unaware that PHS doctors were conducting secret medical experiments on local Blacks in the nearby Tuskegee area, the black graduates of the Tuskegee air base overcame racial prejudice and showed the world they could fly and fight as well as anyone. They went on to perform brilliantly in combat as members of the all-black 332nd Fighter Group, establishing a remarkable record of bravery and aviation excellence. Several became senior officers in the USAF after World War II, clearing a path for Blacks into top military positions.

The juxtaposition of these independent, racist government activities, in precisely the same place and time, aptly demonstrates the racial bias of our nation leading up to World War II. In spite of such obstacles, the "Tuskegee Airmen" became heroic pioneers who—by their example—inspired public support for a more open society. As for the victims of the syphilis medical experiment, the survivors were finally given free medical benefits and an official apology from President Bill Clinton in 1997, which was unfortunately too late for many of the original test group.

*Poison gas, psychedelic drugs, and radiation experiments*

The second program spanned the period from World War II through at least the 1970's, and involved drug and radiation experiments on unknowing Servicemen and women. In 1994, the U.S. Senate Committee on Veterans Affairs conducted hearings and produced a staff report, entitled "Is Military Research Hazardous to Veterans' Health?—Lessons spanning Half a Century." (103rd Congress, 2nd Session; S. Prt. 103-97, December 8, 1994). Some of the excerpts are shocking:

**Working with the CIA, the Department of Defense gave hallucinogenic drugs to thousands of "volunteer" soldiers in the 1950's and 1960's. In addition to LSD, the Army also tested quinuclidinyl benzilate, a hallucinogen code-named BZ. Many of these tests were conducted under the so-called MK-ULTRA program, established to counter perceived Soviet and Chinese advances in brainwashing techniques. Between 1953 and 1964, the program consisted of 149 projects involving drug testing and other studies on unwitting human subjects.**

**One test subject was Lloyd B. Gamble, who enlisted in the U.S. Air Force in 1950. In 1957, he volunteered for a special program to test new military protective clothing. He was offered various incentives to participate in the program, including a liberal leave policy, family visitations, and superior living and recreational facilities. However, the greatest incentive to Mr. Gamble was the official recognition he would receive as a career-oriented noncommissioned officer, through letters of commendation and certification of participation in the program. During the 3 weeks of testing new clothing, he was given two or three water-size glasses of a liquid containing LSD to drink. Thereafter, Mr. Gamble developed erratic behavior and even attempted suicide. He did not learn that he had received LSD as a human subject until 18 years later, as a result of congressional hearings in 1975. Even then, the Department of the Army initially denied that he had participated in the experiments, although an official DOD publicity photograph showed him as one of the valiant servicemen volunteering for "a program that was in the highest national security interest."**

>According to Sidney Gottlieb, a medical doctor and former CIA agent, MK-ULTRA was established to investigate whether and how an individual's behavior could be modified by covert means. According to Dr. Gottlieb, the CIA believed that both the Soviet Union and Communist China might be using techniques of altering human behavior which were not understood by the United States. Dr. Gottlieb testified that "it was felt to be mandatory and of the utmost urgency for our intelligence organization to establish what was possible in this field on a high priority basis." Although many human subjects were not informed or protected, Dr. Gottlieb defended those actions by stating, "...*harsh as it may seem in retrospect, it was felt that in an issue where national survival might be concerned, such a procedure and such a risk was a reasonable one to take.*"

However, this was not the only covert activity using Service personnel and other citizens, without their knowledge and consent. From the same Senate report, we learn that even more illegal government conduct of this type has occurred:

## WORLD WAR II VETERANS

>As recently as 1993, the Institute of Medicine of the National Academy of Sciences reported that an atmosphere of secrecy still existed regarding World War II testing of mustard gas and lewisite. Although many documents pertaining to the World War II testing programs were declassified shortly after World War II ended, others remain "restricted" even today. In addition to the classified or restricted documents, World War II veterans who participated in the research were sworn to secrecy. These classified documents and promises of secrecy have impeded medical care for thousands of veterans during half of the last century.
>
>For example, Rudolph R. Mills participated in gas chamber experiments as an 18-year old in 1945, one year after he joined the U.S. Navy. He was sworn to secrecy and did not learn until 46 years later that approximately 4,000 servicemen were human subjects in mustard gas experiments conducted from 1942 through 1945 by the Chemical Warfare Service. Although his health began to deteriorate even before his discharge from the Navy in 1946, he did not learn that mustard gas might be responsible for his physical problems until more than 40 years later.
>
>At a May 6, 1994, hearing of the Senate Committee on Veterans' Affairs, entitled "Is Military Research Hazardous to Veterans' Health? Lessons from World War II, the Persian Gulf War, and Today," Mr. Mills testified, "I had on an experimental mask and the Navy was trying to determine if people wearing these masks could communicate with each other. I was enticed to sing over the intercom....No one ever told me that the mask became less effective against the gas with each use....We were sworn to secrecy....At the age of 43 I underwent a long series of radiation treatments and later surgery to remove part of my voice box and larynx....It didn't occur to me that my exposure to mustard gas was responsible for my physical problems until June 1991, when I read an article in my hometown newspaper."

John T. Harrison participated in Navy chemical tests in 1943 to get an extra week pass. He was also sworn to secrecy. According to written testimony submitted to the Senate Committee on Veterans' Affairs by Mr. Harrison, "[I] was never warned or told anything about the dangers of what [I] volunteered for....told never to reveal what [I] did or where [I] was; if anyone asked [I] was to say [I] was on rowing maneuvers." At the time of his discharge from the military, he could not even describe his exposures to a Navy doctor who was trying to determine the cause of his severe respiratory illnesses. Although Mr. Harrison has suffered from recurrent breathing problems and has greatly diminished pulmonary function, he has never received any compensation for his illness. According to the VA and DOD, his medical and service records have been lost, making it difficult to prove that his disability is service-connected.

## COLD WAR VETERANS

During the years immediately following World War II, military personnel were intentionally exposed to radiation during the testing of atomic bombs and during radioactive releases. While it is unclear how many of these service members were intentionally exposed to what were known to be harmful levels of radiation, there is clear evidence that in some cases military personnel were ordered to locate themselves in areas of high radioactive fallout. *They were given no choice in the matter, and they were not told of the potential risks of those exposures.* (italics added)

Similarly, military personnel were intentionally given hallucinogenic drugs to determine the effects of those drugs on humans. The service members were not told that they would be given experimental drugs, they had no choice of whether or not to take them, and even after the unusual effects of the drugs were obvious to researchers, the unwitting human subjects were given no information about the known effects of the drugs. Even if the DOD did not know about the potential long-term effects of the drugs, that would not justify their failure to provide information to thousands of service members about the known short-term effects of the drugs.

The U.S. military deliberately exposed our military personnel to massive doses of radiation and radioactive contamination in the 1946 nuclear weapon tests of "Operation Crossroads" at Bikini atoll. The high level of radioactivity of the island resulted in the U.S. declaring it uninhabitable and relocating the original native residents. Nevertheless, immediately after the blasts, our military ordered our Service personnel to go aboard and survey the test ships, which were highly contaminated with radioactive particles. This has resulted in higher than normal death rates from various cancers for the people involved.

## The "rainbow" chemicals

My third example of the government sacrificing its citizens involves the use of "Agent Orange" and "Agent Purple," sprayed as defoliants in Vietnam. The government again showed its propensity to jeopardize the health and safety of its Service personnel. Those who served in Vietnam did not know it at the time, but senior officials within the military and the civilian government deliberately exposed them to these chemicals, having full knowledge of their toxic effects.

**C-123s spraying Agent Orange in Vietnam.**

Agents Orange and Purple, manufactured by several U.S. chemical companies, were powerful substances that contained dioxin, a known carcinogen. Nevertheless, these deadly substances were used freely—even near our own personnel—in a ridiculous effort to defoliate the jungles of Vietnam and Laos to expose enemy troop movements. This was somewhat like attempting to "boil the ocean" or "catch the stars," equally futile efforts.

Agent Orange was dispensed primarily by Air Force C-123 aircraft in Operation Ranch Hand, from 1962 through 1971. Somewhere between 12 and 18 million gallons of this hideous poison fell from the sky on hundreds of thousands of American personnel and Vietnamese.

The Navy's F-8 squadrons were frequently assigned to provide fighter protection for the Ranch Hand aircraft, especially when the spraying was conducted near the border of North Vietnam. Apparently, senior military commanders in Saigon believed that MIGs might try to shoot down the C-123 aircraft. It probably would have been better for our troops on the ground if they had done so. Although we normally flew well above the sprayers, our F-8 pilots, including myself, could easily have been exposed to droplets of the spray, carried up by the wind currents or aircraft turbulence from the C-123s.

Several of my Academy classmates who served in Vietnam have contracted diseases clinically associated with Agent Orange exposure. The number of illnesses is growing in number as the victims are identified and studies are completed. The Department of Veterans Affairs has connected Agent Orange to the following diseases, with more listed as "probable" or "possible":

**Acute peripheral neuropathy, AL amyloidosis, B-cell leukemia, chloracne, chronic lymphcytic leukemia, type 2 diabetes, Hodgkin's disease, ischemic heart disease, multiple myeloma, non-Hodgkin's lymphoma, Parkinson's disease, porphyria cutanea tarda, prostate cancer, respiratory cancer, and soft tissue sarcoma.**

Severe birth defects have also been documented among the children of exposed Vietnamese and American veterans. For these victims, the war is not over, and is now affecting even their children and grandchildren. (*See* Dept. of Veterans Affairs, Office of Public Health and Environmental Hazards, at *http://www.publichealth.va.gov/exposures/agentorange/diseases.asp,* January 8, 2010.)

My good friend and Academy classmate, John Sande, was forced to divert into air bases in South Vietnam several times during his two combat tours. On one occasion, the catastrophic fire on the carrier *Oriskany* prevented him from landing aboard, and the carrier sent him to one of the air bases in South Vietnam. While waiting on the ground for orders to fly back to the carrier, he noticed clouds of white dust swirling around his aircraft on the ramp. When he asked an Air Force sergeant what this was, the man said, "Oh, that's just Agent Orange, Lieutenant. It's harmless."

Forty years later, John developed two of the diseases from the list above: multiple myeloma (bone cancer) and chronic lymphcytic leukemia, which killed him. John survived many dangerous encounters, including the *Oriskany* fire and two tours in combat, but he was ultimately killed by the gross negligence of his own government and its haphazard use of Agent Orange.

Another close friend and West Point graduate, Bob Strauss, was an Air Force officer during the war, and was stationed in Saigon for several years. I worked with him at Continental and in the Air Line Pilots Association during the late Seventies. A few years later, in his early forties, he died of cancer. I strongly suspect that Agent Orange exposure was the cause.

In a cruel irony, Admiral Elmo Zumwalt's son was stricken by cancer and health problems related to Agent Orange. The young Zumwalt had served as a Naval officer in South Vietnam, in areas where Agent Orange was aggressively used. Sadly, the young man died at age 42, leaving a grieving family. His father, Admiral Zumwalt, was actually the senior commander who had authorized the spraying of Agent Orange during his son's service in Vietnam. Perhaps God expresses his disapproval to us in subtle but unmistakable ways.

Approximately 2.9 million Americans served in Vietnam, and most of us were exposed to Agent Orange to some degree, whether we knew it or not. The clock is ticking for all who served there.

### *The ultimate hypocrisy*

Following World War II, the United States prosecuted and hanged people responsible for conducting medical experimentation on prisoners without their knowledge or consent. See *United States of America vs. Karl Brandt, et al.* ("the Nazi Doctors' Trials") Dr. Joseph Mengele, called the "Angel of Death" because of his medical atrocities in the death camp at Auschwitz, was hunted relentlessly during his life, although he escaped to South America and died in secrecy.

The questions for our government and the American public to answer are these: *How are the three examples given above different from the atrocities of the Nazi doctors? Should our responsible leaders—military or civilian—who ordered these secret experiments and deliberate toxic exposures on innocent, unknowing Americans also be prosecuted as war criminals? If not, <u>why</u> not?*

~ ~ ~

# Chapter 26: *Epilogue and Requiem for Warriors*

All things—good or bad—eventually come to an end. War, like other human endeavors, is no different. The Vietnam War ended with America's cowardly abandonment of the South Vietnamese, and our chaotic stampede to escape the invading North Vietnamese. Domestic politics and lack of national will, not military realities, had decided the conflict in favor of the North Vietnamese Communists. In the end, Ho Chi Minh knew America and its weaknesses better than we knew ourselves. However, three of our West Point brothers, each a historical icon of his own era, understood the inherent folly of ill-conceived wars, and warned us:

*I have never advocated war except as a means of peace. ~Ulysses S. Grant*
*We are going to have peace even if we have to fight for it. ~Dwight D. Eisenhower*
*The military don't start wars. Politicians start wars. ~William Westmoreland*

For those many of us who participated in the Vietnam War or have learned its history, unfiltered by political bias, we can see the best and worst of America. Four presidents—Eisenhower, Kennedy, Johnson, and Nixon—demonstrated varying degrees of incompetence, false assumptions, dishonesty, and fatal machismo about Vietnam. *All* of them underestimated the determination of the North Vietnamese to unify the country, and they failed to understand how to apply military power effectively to achieve U.S. foreign policy objectives. Johnson and Nixon, in particular, showed a willingness to sacrifice American lives, but a reluctance to inflict reciprocal damage on the North Vietnamese enemy.

Richard Nixon showed a brief glimmer of understanding the application of power, when he finally removed bombing restrictions on Hanoi in late 1972 in the "Linebacker II" air assault on Hanoi. However, like the other three involved presidents, he worried that domestic opposition to the war would result in congressional de-funding, which did, in fact, occur after 1973. This caused him, like our other leaders, to place "peace" in front of "victory" as his priority—always a doomed strategy in warfare.

Although Nixon might have been able to lead our nation out of Vietnam in an orderly fashion, he was ultimately consumed by his own political paranoia in the debacle of Watergate. From that moment on, the South Vietnamese were cast adrift in a sinking lifeboat, encircled by Communist sharks. The symbolic image of defeat and abandonment, which our country's leaders brought upon us, will forever be the helicopter evacuation of the last Americans in Saigon.

This type of geo-political bumbling is impossible for the fighter pilot mentality to understand. Regardless of the flag for which they flew, fighter pilots carry a unique spirit that is a common denominator among them. This is why they can forget the pain and agony of their own conflicts of years past, and even embrace their former enemies as members of the same special fraternity of arms. As a 19th century French novelist wrote, "The more things change, the more they stay the same." As I think back on my Naval Aviation career, the words of great fighter pilots resonate through the decades of aviation history. In their own style, they have described what it takes to succeed and survive in the brutal air warfare environment:

**"Only the spirit of attack, born in a brave heart, will bring success to any fighter aircraft, no matter how highly developed it may be. . . . Their function is to attack, to track, to hunt, and to destroy the enemy. Only in this way can the eager and skillful fighter pilot display his ability. Tie him to a narrow and confined task, rob him of his initiative, and you take away from him the best and most valuable qualities he has: aggressive spirit, joy of action, and the passion of the hunter."**—Gen. Adolf Galland, Luftwaffe (104 Allied kills)

Some readers may have been surprised, shocked, or perhaps even appalled at my descriptions of the fighter pilot lifestyle of the Vietnam era. However, as Baron Manfred von Richtofen, the famous German ace (80+ kills), stated in WWI: **"The duty of the fighter pilot is to patrol his area of the sky, and shoot down any enemy fighters in that area. Anything else is rubbish. . . . The aggressive spirit, the offensive, is the chief thing everywhere in war, and the air is no exception."**

For the young fighter pilot, this unique but vital attitude dominates his life. This is an obsession with "big game" hunting in its ultimate form. Everything revolves around his squadron and flying his aircraft. With age, rank, and maturity, he may mellow—but not without risk to himself and his mission. Most of the world was and still is a truly nasty place, populated by murderers, thugs, and thieves. We need special people who can deal with this dangerous level of humanity without being concerned about protocol and wringing their hands over what needs to be done. Only those who sit safely *behind* the lines of combat have the luxury of dissecting events and second-guessing the deeds of those who step forward and engage the enemy.

America willingly recruits, trains, and uses this type of special warrior, but when the shooting stops, it often becomes uncomfortable with what it has created. In the minds of many, Marine Major Gregory "Pappy" Boyington and his famous

VMF-214 "Black Sheep" Squadron epitomized this "point of the spear" warrior species. "Pappy" was a six-kill ace with the Flying Tigers *before* joining the Marine Corps and adding another 22 Japanese aircraft to his list of kills. He was shot down in a dogfight and taken prisoner by the Japanese.

Upon his return at war's end, he received the Medal of Honor and the Navy Cross, among other decorations, and a promotion to full Colonel. However, like many returning war heroes, he was plagued by alcoholism, financial problems, and sequential divorces. After leaving the Marine Corps, he worked at several civilian jobs, and even refereed wrestling matches. A successful publication of his memoirs, *Baa baa Black Sheep,* culminated in a popular TV series for which he was the technical advisor. "Pappy" died of cancer in 1988, but his legend lives on as another recalcitrant warrior who could not find peace in peacetime.

The leading ace of all time, Erich "Bubi" Hartmann, was another fiercely independent warrior of that era. His boyish good looks disguised the intensity of an expert killer. He achieved an incredible *352 kills by age 23* as an ME-109 pilot with the World War II Luftwaffe. Most of his kills were on the Eastern Front against the Soviet Air Force, but included some Americans in the Eastern European campaigns.

**Hartmann by his Me-109, with the distinctive "black tulip petals" nose marking.**

In addition to his impressive number of kills, Hartmann was never wounded or shot down by an enemy aircraft, although he made a total of 14 forced landings during his combat tours. On one occasion, he was captured by the Russians and escaped. By the end of the war, he had received Germany's highest military decoration, The Knight's Cross with Oak Leaves, Swords, and Diamonds. In an artistic touch, he had his engine cowling painted with distinctive black tulip petals. Soviet

pilots nicknamed him "the Black Devil," while the German press dubbed him "the Blond Knight."

Hartmann's tactics were those of a clever hunter: detect the enemy first; evaluate the situation to determine the moment of attack; make a single, devastating pass; and pick your time to disengage. Predators of many species have similar instincts. Like Saburo Sakai, Hartmann prided himself on the fact that he never lost a wingman.

When Germany's forces were overwhelmed, he was taken prisoner by the Soviets and endured ten years of hard labor in Siberia before his release. The Soviets offered to release him early, if he would agree to become a pilot for Communist East Germany. He refused.

After his release in 1955, he became a Colonel in the West German Air Force. He strongly opposed the adoption of the American F-104G, which killed over 100 West German pilots in operational accidents. His refusal to support this dangerous aircraft forced his early retirement. His superiors described him as a "good pilot, but a poor officer." In his own words, from *Aces of WWII*:

> The American F-104 Starfighter was a great plane, but it had problems, and I did not feel that Germany needed, or that our pilots could even handle this machine without a lot more experience. Many higher up felt that I was out of line, but I stated what I thought was accurate, and I was proven correct, but this made me enemies. I also did other things that were considered criminal, such as having the unit's F-86s painted with my old tulip pattern, and I created the squadron bars [fuselage markings], like in the old days, and this raised eyebrows. I felt that morale was important and camaraderie through a unique and distinguishing emblem was needed. The bars were [removed] under superior directives, although today all squadrons have them. I did have supporters, such as General Kammhuber, but he was a rare breed from the old days.

Hartmann's independent spirit made him an undefeated champion in combat, but a political liability to his superiors in peacetime. Many warriors of many nations have been the victim of this recurring and paradoxical theme. Warriors simply have little value in times of peace, where politicians dominate. Erich Hartmann died in 1993, at the age of 70. It is unlikely his kill record will ever be equaled or surpassed. Although he was on the "wrong" side of the war, his accomplishments as a fighter pilot deserve great respect.

During World War II, the intensive air war in the skies over Britain resulted in many RAF aces. The top-scoring RAF ace (38 kills) was the legendary Johnnie Johnson. This Spitfire maestro was both an expert tactician and an outstanding leader. He often flew with Group Captain Douglas Bader, the famous amputee ace who flew with artificial legs. Johnson retired as a Vice Air Marshal and died in 2001.

Also worthy of note is Adolph "Sailor" Malan (35 kills), an RAF pilot from South Africa, who commanded 74 Squadron, known as "The Tiger Squadron." Its motto was "I fear no man," remarkably similar to the F-8 pilot motto, seeking to be the "meanest mutha' in the valley." During those few months of the 1940 Battle of Britain, although vastly outnumbered, Malan and his squadron shot down over 80 German aircraft. "Sailor" was an excellent shot and brilliant tactician, as evidenced by his rules for success in combat:

## "SAILOR" MALAN'S TEN RULES OF AIR COMBAT

1. Wait until you see the whites of his eyes. Fire short bursts of one to two seconds only when your sights are definitely "ON".

2. Whilst shooting, think of nothing else, brace the whole of your body: have both hands on the stick: concentrate on your ring sight.

3. Always keep a sharp lookout. "Keep your finger out".

4. Height gives you the initiative.

5. Always turn and face the attack.

6. Make your decisions promptly. It is better to act quickly even though your tactics are not the best.

7. Never fly straight and level for more than 30 seconds in the combat area.

8. When diving to attack always leave a proportion of your formation above to act as a top guard.

9. INITIATIVE, AGGRESSION, AIR DISCIPLINE, and TEAM WORK are words that MEAN something in Air Fighting.

10. Go in quickly - Punch hard - Get out!

These rules are essentially identical to the tactics used by other aces, including the Luftwaffe's Erich Hartmann and Japan's Saburo Sakai. In navigating the unforgiving crucible of combat, all of the top aces appeared to discover the same set of principles for success in the air. Combining them yields this list:
- Detect the enemy before he detects you
- Do not fly straight and level in the combat area
- Do not stay in the combat area by yourself
- Position yourself with an altitude advantage and the sun behind you, if possible
- Be tactically flexible, and protect your leader/wingman
- Evaluate whether you are properly positioned to attack
- If attacked, turn hard into the attackers
- If the attacker is overly aggressive, use that against him to cause an overshoot
- Try to start with a speed advantage and avoid slowing down in the fight, if possible
- Once you decide to attack, do so aggressively and press for the kill
- Attack the last enemy aircraft in their formation, and work your way forward
- Maneuver to minimum range for a shot, and do not waste precious ammo
- Stay vigilant for that "unseen" enemy who tries to get you while you are attacking
- Plan your exit and regrouping strategy and do not abandon your stragglers

The successful fighter pilots of all nations also had closely similar, if not identical personal characteristics:
- Excellent eye sight
- Fast reflexes
- Superior marksmanship/weapons delivery
- An independent, aggressive, unstructured personality

Even today, in the era of advanced radars and missiles, these rules still apply. The pilot that chooses to ignore them is flirting with disaster for himself or his wingman. As we learned in Vietnam, the long-range, head-on missile (e.g., the Sparrow) is of limited value in most air-to-air engagements. It is still necessary in almost all situations to identify the bogey visually, in order to avoid a "friendly fire" accidental kill of your own pilots. That reduces the fight to a tail-shot scenario, where either the Sidewinder-type missile or guns will be the weapons of choice. In essence, nothing much has changed since WWI except speed and altitude, once the engagement begins.

As a ghostly reminder to those decision-makers who are tempted to dabble in armed conflict without knowing what they are doing, our nation erected the Vietnam Wall Memorial, which displays the names of those 58,000 heroes who were needlessly sacrificed. Our leaders forgot the simple lesson that little boys usually learn early in life on their school playground: *Do not engage in a fight unless you are committed to win.* For many of our nation's leaders, victory often seems more frightening than defeat. They rush to cut negotiated diplomatic settlements instead of pressing on to crush our enemies and eliminate the threat. The fighter pilot cannot understand this thinking, because success in *his* world is defined by a simple rule: *Hunt down the enemy and kill him before he kills you!*

The F-8 Crusader pilots who etched their indelible statements of skill, courage, and individual achievements in American fighter pilot history are now either old men or dead. With a few exceptions, I will always treasure my association with them and remember how they flew the F-8 Crusader—that beautiful, unforgiving aircraft—into combat from a ship at sea, over the most dangerous environment imaginable. As Admiral Tarrant (Fredric March) said in *Bridges at Toko-Ri,* "Where do we *get* such men?"

To all of my fellow Americans who served their country during the Vietnam War in a branch of our military or intelligence services, regardless of your specialty, rank, or branch of service—I give you my respectful salute and dedicate *The Contrail Chronicles* to each of you. Even if you did not want to be there, you were *there*, you *sacrificed*, and you *stepped up* for your country during an unpopular war. You deserved better than the treatment you received from your country.

For those eternal heroes whose names are found on that forbidding black granite wall in Washington—like Mike Estocin, Mike Newell, Smokey Tolbert, and Bob McMahan—and those who were wounded, poisoned by Agent Orange, or who suffered as prisoners of the North Vietnamese, there are no words to express my feelings of respect and awe for what *you* gave up for our country. While our political and military leaders lacked the courage to stay the course, *you* gave it all. Our nation's debt to you can *never* be repaid.

Some of these sacrificed warriors finally returned in 1973 from the terrible misery of imprisonment by the North Vietnamese. Others met a different fate, and died a hero's death in their aircraft, doing what their nation's leaders had ordered them to do. Their remains are scattered throughout Southeast Asia or in cemeteries around the U.S. Many more Vietnam veterans continue to struggle with the diseases and wounds—psychological and physical—that they incurred while serving their country. America has largely neglected these wounded warriors and has sometimes even dishonored them and their service.

As with all wars, Vietnam is becoming a distant memory for many of our citizens. For others, the pain of that experience is still felt through the death of loved ones, the pain of terrible wounds, or lasting bitterness at the humiliating outcome. There are many heroes to remember, but here are a few of mine:

Frank Harrington's body was escorted back to his family in Vermont in 1967, after he died in that runway ejection at Naha Air Base. Bill Kiper, a former Red Lightning, was the escort officer. This somber task is difficult for anyone, but it was especially painful for Bill, since he had actually known Frank before his death. Frank's death was difficult for all of the Red Lightnings to accept, because we knew it was unnecessary. That damaged aircraft should not have flown.

Gator was furloughed by TWA and moved to the Lake Tahoe area. He and his wife are now divorced. I have only seen him once since we left the Navy. Sometimes lives go in different directions. I will always be grateful for the privilege to have known and flown with him.

Rick Millson, my SAM-hunting partner, became a Blue Angel for two tours, and then left active duty. He is still actively involved with aviation as a jet flight instructor and test pilot. Rick was and is "a pilot's pilot." If you want to learn how to fly like a pro, contact Rick. He lives in the Seattle area.

Skipper Conklin retired from the Navy and cruised the East Coast and Florida waters in a sailboat with his wonderful wife Buzzy, who has now passed away. He is a Coast Guard-certified captain and has written several books on marine subjects. He lives in Florida, and still looks like he could fly an F-8 into combat. The Navy needed more senior officers like him. Perhaps cloning is the answer.

Teddy Fox, my high school buddy who gave me the Arkansas Toothpick knife, my good luck charm for over 200 combat missions, became an Army dentist. He married my high school girlfriend and had two kids. Now divorced, he lives in rural North Carolina.

The remains of two of the Red Lightnings' lost brothers, Mike Newell and Bob McMahan, were finally located where they died in North Vietnam. Bob's remains were found in 1990, near the wreckage of his F-8E. He was returned to his family.

Mike's crash site was found by the joint recovery team in North Vietnam in 2004, and his remains were identified in 2006. He received a military burial with full honors at Arlington National Cemetery in 2007, as shown in this photo.

Devil retired from the Navy as a captain after a distinguished Navy career. After leaving the F-8 RAG, he joined VF-51 as a lieutenant commander and transitioned to F-4s. In May of 1972, Devil gained his own place in history when he shot down a MIG-17 with a Sidewinder missile. He currently lives with his lovely wife Shirley in Texas, and is probably gloating over the fact that *he* got a MIG while the rest of the Red Lightnings are "MIG-less."

Our POW heroes were finally released by the North Vietnamese and repatriated in 1973. Among the returnees were Commander Mel Moore, Lieutenant Commander Dick Stratton, and Lieutenant Commander "Moon" Mullen, all from my air wing, and five of my Academy classmates—Dave Carey, Aubrey Nichols, Ted Triebel, Read Mecleary, and Charlie Plumb.

Some of the POWs had been imprisoned since 1965, and lost a large part of their adult lives that can never be restored to them. In some cases, their marriages disintegrated, or their children met them for the first time, as strangers. For others, they found out that close friends or family members had passed away or had

become ill during their imprisonment. After a six or seven-year absence, it obviously takes a lot of effort to get your life restarted. America had changed for the worse in their absence. It must have been a great culture shock for them to learn of these changes.

Many medals have been awarded and numerous books have been written about the suffering endured by these men, and the great courage and

integrity that they displayed in the face of terrible adversity. These are men who were left by our nation to be abused by sadistic captors and exploited by anti-war radicals, including Jane Fonda and Ramsey Clark. What *is* sufficient compensation for this kind of sacrifice? How *do* we repay these patriots? They, together with the hundreds of Servicemen still missing and unaccounted for, put themselves on the line while politicians played their cowardly games, avoiding the hard decisions in order to gain reelection.

Although most of the POWs made it back, how does our government explain its failure to make their sacrifices worthwhile? Speaking only for myself, I will always feel guilty that I did not become involved in some meaningful way to help some of our brave POWs make the difficult transition back into their lives, or offer some direct help at that time to families of our deceased air warriors. Selfishly, I concerned myself with my own comfortable life. I did nothing more than sit and watch the happy TV images as the POWs returned, thinking, *I'm glad that didn't happen to me.* Like many Americans at that point in time, I suppose I wanted to put Vietnam far from my thoughts. Like many combat pilots, I had learned to cope with my own bad memories by desensitizing myself to the suffering of others. This self-centered attitude kept me from doing the right thing. I am ashamed and deeply regret this moral failure on my part. In either this or my next life, I must atone for that.

Frank Prendergast, the courageous navigator who made the miraculous escape from the North Vietnamese after ejecting from his RA-5C, went to flight training and received his pilot wings. He left the Navy as a Commander, and died in 1998 at age 55.

Skippers Chew and Ostrand are now deceased, as are nearly all of the XOs and all of the CAGs and carrier captains mentioned in the *Chronicles*. Gator and I kept our commitment and got Skipper Ostrand safely through his combat cruise. I wonder if he ever knew we were looking out for him. Sadly, he died of cancer a few years later. He truly was a good and courageous man. His family should be very proud of him.

Maggot retired from the airlines and the Naval Reserve and continued to work with special test versions of the F-8 under government contract. We still share a few laughs about some of our F-8 adventures and stories about The Buzzard. He lives in California.

Porky has dropped out of touch, but I heard that he retired from the airlines and was living on a boat with his wife somewhere in Florida. Like The Buzzard, he was a real fighter pilot. The things he taught me about the F-8 kept me alive in many bad situations. I will always be grateful to him.

Snake had a very successful Navy career, and retired as a Rear Admiral. He lives in Virginia. As far as I know, he still holds the scoring record for aerial gunnery. Like Conklin and a few others, he had the special qualities needed in a combat leader.

Spanky retired from the Navy and went to work for San Diego Gas & Electric as an engineer. A few years later, he died in a freak accident when he fell from the roof of his house while cleaning leaves from the gutters. After all of the dangerous situations that he survived, this was indeed a strange and tragic way for him to lose his life. We will all miss his shy smile, excellent piloting skills, and subtle humor.

Captain Bill Kiper, my last Reserve Skipper, retired from the Naval Reserve and United Airlines and lives in California. He was an active member of the group that established and maintained the *USS Hornet* Museum at Alameda, California.

Marine Major John R. Love, the officer who caught me in the Bancroft Hall elevator, retired as a full Colonel after an outstanding career, including combat duty in Vietnam. If he had not overlooked my elevator infraction, I would not have graduated from the Naval Academy. He passed away on March 5, 2010, and is missed by all of us who knew him as a wonderful example of what a Marine officer should aspire to be.

"Duke" Cunningham, the Navy's only Vietnam ace, instructed in Top Gun and then ran successfully for Congress, where he served for years. In 2005, he pled guilty to tax evasion, conspiracy to commit bribery, mail fraud and wire fraud. He was sentenced to eight years in prison, and as of this writing, is serving his time in the Federal prison in Tucson, Arizona. Sadly, Duke has wasted his legacy and diminished his own historic achievements. Sometimes the worst wounds are those that we inflict upon ourselves.

Smokey Tolbert ('62), who acted as airborne referee for my Dallas Reserves dogfight contest with the Marines, went back for another combat cruise. He was killed in action in an A-7 over North Vietnam in November of 1972, shortly after I last saw him. His aircraft was hit by flak in what turned out to be the very last phase of the air war. In just two months from his death, there would be a total cessation of air operations. He flew one mission too many.

Previously, Smokey had been the first Academy graduate to become a member of the Blue Angels, where he flew with my old SAM-killer Iron Hand teammate, Rick Millson. In the 1968 Blue Angel photo above, Smokey is second from the left; Rick is fourth from the right.

Smokey's remains were returned by the Vietnamese in 1989. He is buried in Troy, Oklahoma, near his hometown. The last F-11 Tiger that he flew as a Blue Angel sits in forlorn solitude on a pole in front of Murray State College, Oklahoma. Her big jet engine is quiet now, and her cockpit is empty. A brass plaque describing Smokey's life is nearby.

In another tragic combat loss, Commander Harley Hall, another former Blue Angel, was shot down by ground fire in his F-4J and allegedly killed, just *twelve hours* before the final cease fire in January 1973. His RIO was captured and later released along with the other POWs in March of that same year. Hall was XO of Fighter Squadron 143 on *USS Enterprise* at the time.

Considerable controversy remains as to whether he died at that time, or was captured and died later. Rumors of intelligence reports suggest he may have been taken to the Laotian border, paraded through North Vietnam as a propaganda prize, and that he was interrogated by Soviet military personnel.

His remains, consisting only of bone fragments and three teeth, were returned to his wife in 1995, and he was declared "legally dead" by the Navy. She challenged the official version of his death and demanded more information. The mystery of his fate will not go away.

George "Jäger" Talken was one of our favorite F-8 RAG instructors, who inspired us and taught Gator and me how to fly the F-8. Jäger eventually transitioned to the A-7 attack aircraft and deployed to the Tonkin Gulf aboard USS Kitty Hawk for his second combat tour. In August of 1969, he was returning from a night mission and apparently flew into the water during a night carrier approach. His remains were not recovered, but his memory lives on with all of those who had the honor to know and serve with him. His daughter, Michelle, was four years old when he was lost. Having been through this same personal tragedy, I know how she must feel.

The nation's retired aircraft carriers have been variously sold for scrap (*Ticonderoga, Bon Homme Richard, Hancock, Coral Sea, FDR*), decommissioned (*Kitty Hawk, JFK*), turned into floating museums (*Intrepid, Hornet, Midway*), scuttled or scheduled to be scuttled (*Forrestal, America, Independence, Constellation*), mothballed (*Ranger, Saratoga*) or sunk as an artificial reef (*Oriskany*). Others are in bureaucratic limbo, waiting to learn of their fate. Each of these old warships served their country courageously and many veterans share their legacy. Indeed, each of these great ships had a history and a soul of her own. They shall be remembered and revered by all who served on them.

As I did research for this book, I made a shocking discovery on a Web site that is produced by a British aviation archaeology organization, the East Anglian Aircraft Recovery Group. They have been most gracious in providing research information about my dad. Members of this organization have been locating and excavating World War II crash sites, and then correlating them with official military records. The following excerpt describes my father's 1945 crash site, where he died in a P-51:

> **Mustang—Bridge Farm, Grundisburgh, Suffolk: P51D-15NA, serial No 44-15305, PI-N; the 360th Fighter Squadron, 356th Fighter Group, based at Martlesham Heath: Saturday, 13th January 1945 was a day that saw typical British winter weather, the sort that is particularly poor for flying, [with] bad icing, thick clouds and snow storms. The fighter groups of the 8th Air Force were nonetheless tasked with escorting the heavy bombers that were to attack German bridges and rail marshalling yards. This resulted in the deaths of six fighter pilots, as their Mustangs crashed within the space of about one hour in East Anglia that morning. Very probably, all the crashes**

were the result of the pilots suffering from vertigo—severe disorientation while relying on instruments, something that was difficult to train for in the clear skies of the American mid-west.

Lt Wendel J.A. Nelson, of Fremont, Nebraska had volunteered to fly with the RCAF whilst America was still neutral. He flew with the RAF in the desert at the time of the battle of El Alamein, later transferring to the USAAF after America had joined the war. His aircraft crashed shortly after take off from Martlesham Heath, and Lt Nelson was killed. With the 360th Fighter Sqdn since November 1944, he had flown 10 missions with them by the time of his death.

This crash site was originally investigated in the 1970's when the engine was recovered. It was re-dug about twenty years later, when it was discovered that many finds on the original dig had been discarded. The complete instrument panel, control column, pilot's goggles, engine cowlings and many small items, discarded on the first dig, were re-discovered.

*The 356th Fighter Group had a magenta and blue diamond nose marking. Each of the Group's three squadrons had distinctive rudder colors, with solid red for the 360th FS, my dad's squadron.*

 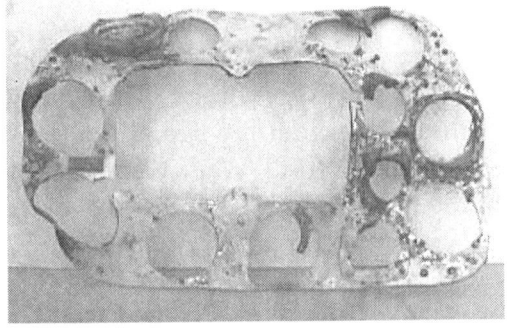

*Actual P-51 cockpit shown at left. Note the instrument panel template is identical to the crash artifact shown above, right.*

A "Fairburn-Sykes" fighting knife of the type commonly known as a commando dagger had been found on the first dig, at the time this was believed to belong to Lt Nelson. However research has shown that the 356th FG had a policy of having a knife taped to the control column on most of their aircraft, this was to aid the pilot if he became entangled while trying to exit the aircraft in an emergency. When the control column was recovered and cleaned, remnants of tape could still be seen on the shaft.

[Above left], the control column after a wash in the nearby stream. Above right, the complete instrument panel, which had been discarded on the first dig. [At right] the pilot's "Polaroid" goggles. The plastic lens has turned orange with age.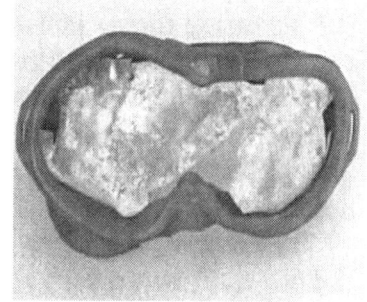

Reading this narrative the first time was a very difficult experience for me. I felt emotionally drained for the rest of that day. The control stick in the photo was probably gripped by my dad's hand at the moment he crashed, and he was wearing *those* charred goggles when he died. It was like meeting a ghost from the distant past, face to face. I cannot help but wonder what his last thoughts were as he prepared to die. In my own mind, I have imagined the helpless terror he must have felt, realizing that he had lost control of the aircraft and would die in a matter of seconds.

All pilots, especially the good ones, know such a fate is always lurking just over the horizon or behind the next cloud. The Angel of Death can come in many ways—from mechanical failure, direct enemy action, fuel starvation, mid-air collision, pilot fatigue or an unlucky confluence of minor events that are unrelated, but combine to cause a catastrophic accident. When the Dark Angel finally taps you on the shoulder, there is no escape.

From a pilot's perspective, I doubt the researcher's contention that my dad and the other five Mustang pilots all crashed because of "vertigo." That was the "official" cause given by the Air Force for all six crashes, with no supporting evidence. He was certainly not a novice pilot, having flown in military aircraft since 1940. With nearly 2,000 hours of flight time, he had trained in Canada and the UK (not the Midwest), where the weather is notoriously bad. In addition, he had the most flight hours of all pilots in his squadron. This was no "rookie." My dad obviously knew how to fly in instrument conditions.

In the type of winter weather described, it is more likely *icing* was the primary cause, because fighter aircraft of that period lacked effective de-icing systems for the airframe, engine and instruments. One expert commented on the P-51: "The Mustang is normally certified in the 'limited' category. . . .If properly equipped the aircraft can be flown IFR and at night. <u>Due to the lack of de-icing equipment (other than pitot heat), most P-51's fly very limited IFR [instrument flying]</u>."

World War II Mustang pilots also complained about problems with carburetor icing, which frequently would cause engine failure if the conditions were right.

These six crashes, all of which occurred *within one hour* in the same geographical area, are more likely the result of desk-bound generals launching sorties in dangerous winter weather conditions, without considering the aircraft's cold-weather limitations. To blame all of the dead pilots for getting "vertigo" is outrageous. If the combination of the weather and the P-51's instrument limitations induced this problem, then this mission should not have launched. This is a recurring theme that still occurs in modern combat operations. In combat, knowledgeable leadership is everything. For example, the British Fighter Command won the Battle of Britain because *their* senior leadership had the fortitude and the analytical ability to formulate a winning strategy with very limited resources. They never risked their pilots unless it was operationally necessary.

By contrast, American generals willingly incurred horrific losses in aircraft and crews. They waged a statistical war of numbers, where they launched suicidal waves of aircraft into occupied Europe, with terrible weather conditions and overwhelming German air defenses. They were not sufficiently knowledgeable about their own weapons systems, and they did not understand the threats faced by their pilots. Safely removed from the deadly conditions of aerial combat operations, they frequently ordered nonsensical missions, disregarding target defenses, weather, and adequate fighter escort. These were classic "arm-chair" generals, dealing with maps and status boards instead of faces. I will always believe their incompetence caused my father's death.

When I made the decision to include my dad's three letters to my mother in this book, I was tormented by strong emotions, unanswered questions, and personal self-doubts. These letters contained very personal information. Would he approve of me making these letters public? Was he thinking of me when his life was snuffed out? What would I have done differently with my own life, if he had lived? What kind of father would he have been? Would he have been disappointed in me? Is he looking down on me now, shaking his head in disbelief? I will always be haunted by his loss and the gaping, jagged hole that his death ripped in my life.

The photograph (above) of my dad was taken in late 1944, seated in his P-51. The goggles he is wearing are probably the ones found buried in the crash site and recovered. At the precise moment of this photograph, he had only a few weeks to live, and I was 2½ years old. Twenty years later, I was following in his footsteps, also flying military aircraft. I have often wondered if I measured up to his expectations. In the end, one must live his or her life in the context of the times. No two lives can ever be perfectly congruent, especially when they are separated by 25 years. One thing is for certain—I would love to have flown with my dad and shared the unique experience of flying.

Although I am not a church-going person, I once had a powerful, spiritual experience, while flying a pre-dawn mission in the Tonkin Gulf. My wingman and I were just east of Haiphong as the sun came up, presenting us with a spectacular picture of fragmented sun rays, shining through towering clouds. In my years of flying, I had never seen a cloud formation as dramatic as this. The iridescent clouds gave a dazzling light display as the sun struggled to shine through and reach the water below.

A feeling of overwhelming emotion suddenly gripped me as I stared at the sight. I realized this was much more than another beautiful sunrise. There was no doubt that someone or something was communicating with me through these powerful images. At the same time, I felt a paralyzing, ghostly chill that overcame me and brought a flood of tears, blurring my vision for several minutes. Returning to the carrier, I was shaken—more so than I had ever been while in actual combat. I felt that I had just been touched by my dad, who was reminding me to keep the faith and to "check my six." I hope he would have enjoyed my story of our lives, as contained in this book.

Perhaps Gary Claude Stoker explained the enigma of the pilot culture most eloquently with his timeless poem, describing how a pilot's love of flight overcomes his fear of death:

*Flight is freedom in its purest form,*
*To dance with the clouds which follow a storm;*

*To roll and glide, to wheel and spin,*
*To feel the joy that swells within;*

*To leave the earth with its troubles and fly,*
*And know the warmth of a clear spring sky;*

*Then back to earth at the end of a day,*
*Released from the tensions which melted away.*

*Should my end come while I am in flight,*
*Whether brightest day or darkest night;*

*Spare me your pity and shrug off the pain,*
*Secure in the knowledge that I'd do it again;*

*For each of us is created to die,*
*And within me I know,*
*I was born to fly.*

In World War II, my dad's war, approximately 400,000 U.S. Service personnel died in action, with another 700,000 wounded. In the Vietnam War, over 58,000 Americans died, with another 1,700 still missing and nearly 200,000 receiving combat wounds. Sadly, the latent health effects of the Agent Orange chemical continue to increase that number by causing cancer and other diseases for the veterans involved.

It is certainly appropriate to ask: *How and why* did we lose those people, torn from their lives, families, and futures? Was it *worth it* to those warriors who died, and to those they left behind? Would they feel they had traded their lives for a worthy cause? From each of our nation's wars, the voices of our dead heroes whisper to us from their graves and battlefields around the world, echoing that plaintive, ghostly verse, found carved below a cross in the hallowed British war cemetery at Kohima, India, near the border with Myanmar (Burma):

**"WHEN YOU GO HOME, TELL THEM OF US AND SAY, FOR <u>THEIR</u> TOMORROW, WE GAVE <u>OUR</u> TODAY."**

*---John M. Edmonds, "The Kohima Epitaph"*

May God grant us the wisdom to remember and understand the meaning of our warriors' sacrifices, and to ensure by *our* patriotism and actions that *their* lives, however short, made a difference and were not wasted. God bless America.

# The End

*Dad, I'll be seeing you soon. Save me a seat at Saint Peter's bar. And don't hang out with The Buzzard up there—he'll get you in a lot of trouble!*